LOCAL AREA NETWORKS

DAVID A. STAMPER

The Benjamin/Cummings Publishing Company, Inc.

Redwood City, California • Menlo Park, California
Reading, Massachusetts • New York • Don Mills, Ontario
Wokingham, U.K. • Amsterdam • Bonn • Sydney
Singapore • Tokyo • Madrid • San Juan

To Kay, Tae, and Shawn

Sponsoring Editor:	Michelle Baxter
Developmental Editor:	Kathy Galinac
Production Editor:	Cathy Lewis
Text Design:	Irene Imfield
Cover Design:	Ark Stein, Studio Silicon
Ilustrations:	Abigail Rudner
Copy Editor:	Barbara Conway
Proofreader:	Eleanor Renner Brown
Composition:	Interactive Composition Corporation

Many of the names used by manufacturers and sellers to distinguish their products are claimed as trademarks. Where those names appear in this book, and Benjamin/ Cummings was aware of a trademark claim, the symbol for trademark (^{TM}) or registered trademark ($^{®}$) appears after the name.

Library of Congress Cataloging-in-Publication Data

Stamper, David A.
    Local area networks / David A. Stamper.
        p.   cm.
    Includes index.
    ISBN 0-8053-7724-7
    1. Local area networks (Computer networks)   I. Title.
TK5105.7.S784   1993   93-14331
004.6'8—dc20   CIP

1 2 3 4 5 6 7 8 9 10 -DO- 97 96 95 94 93

The Benjamin/Cummings Publishing Company, Inc.
390 Bridge Parkway
Redwood City, CA 94065

Over the past decade, local area networks (LANs) have made an increasingly significant impact on the way companies conduct business. With the assistance of LAN technology, both large and small companies can take advantage of the ability to share valuable hardware and software resources among multiple users. Because LANs are becoming such an integral part of today's business community, students in management information systems and computer information systems programs need to have fundamental LAN knowledge and experience. This experience can strategically position today's students for the growing opportunities in LAN management.

This textbook provides a good foundation in the theory and practical application of LAN use and administration. Since most LANs do not exist in isolation, this text also discusses how LANs can be connected to other LANs, wide area networks (WANs), and larger mainframe computers. Finally, this text provides readers with insight into emerging LAN technologies and their potential impact on the future of LANs.

Key Themes and Features

Focus on LAN Management   This text is written primarily from the perspective of LAN management. The focus is on administrative responsibilities and strategies, which range from selecting and installing LAN hardware and software to designing backup and recovery options. However, a LAN administrator must frequently consider the issues important to other segments of the LAN community, such as users, so we provide appropriate coverage of these perspectives as well.

Complete, Up-to-Date Coverage   This text discusses a variety of the most popular LAN hardware and software to help prepare students for any LAN environment. To provide consistency, most of the examples are based on Novell Netware, the leading LAN operating system which the majority of students will encounter as LAN administrators. Despite the rapid rate at which new LAN technology is being introduced, *Local Area Networks* provides up-to-date coverage and anticipates emerging technology. The following is a sample of the topics covered in this text:

- Novell NetWare, IBM LAN Server, and Banyan Vines (throughout the text)

- Basic data communications principles, including the OSI reference model (Chapter 2)

- LAN selection criteria (Chapter 2)

- Data link and MAC protocols (Chapter 3)

- Token passing versus CSMA/CD (Chapter 3)

- Security options and virus protection (Chapter 8)

- Creating and maintaining the printing environment (Chapter 9)

- Backup, recovery and disaster planning (Chapter 10)

- SNMP and CMIP network management protocols (Chapter 11)

- Packet Distribution Networks (PDNs) (Chapter 12)

- Bridges, routers, and TCP/IP routing protocol (Chapter 13)

- Client-server, peer-to-peer, and multimedia on LANs (Chapter 14)

In-Text Learning Aides

Pedagogical features, such as boldfaced key terms, end-of-chapter summaries, review questions, problems and exercises, and bibliographic references are included to fully support a learning environment. In addition, examples are used throughout the text to illustrate practical applications of LAN management.

Chapter Preview   Each chapter begins with a brief overview that outlines the goals of the material to be covered in the chapter.

Key Terms   Key words are boldfaced when they first occur in the chapter for easy identification.

End-of-Chapter Material   The end-of-chapter material begins with a **Summary** of the key concepts. **Key Terms** are listed for review, and **Review Questions** are provided to assist the student in recalling important ideas and concepts. These Review Questions along with **Problems and Exercises** encourage students to apply their understanding of the concepts in the chapter. A list of **References** is provided for further exploration and serves as a valuable resource for individual or group projects.

Glossary   The extensive glossary includes acronyms for a comprehensive, easy-to-use reference guide.

Organization

The text is divided into five parts:

Part 1: Introduction to Microcomputers, LANs, and Data Communications Part 1 introduces LAN technology and explores how LANs are used to extend the power of the stand-alone microcomputer.

Part 2: Hardware   Part 2 outlines criteria for evaluating network layouts and choosing hardware components that can be integrated to form a system.

Part 3: Software   Part 3 explores the role of network software in the successful interaction of application software, workstation systems software, and server systems software.

Part 4: Installation and Management   Part 4 explores the LAN administrator's core responsibilities, including creating and managing the user environment, security, backup and recovery, and strategies for managing both planned and unplanned network changes.

Part 5: Connecting to Other Systems and Networks   Part 5 covers Wide Area Networks (WANs) and interconnection between LANs and WANs. This part concludes with an overview of several important, but less commonly used technologies and a look forward to emerging LAN technologies. nologies.

Supplements

Instructor's Disk   The Instructor's Disk includes additional exercises, solutions to end-of-chapter review questions, case studies, lab exercises, and advice for setting up a networked lab. Available for the IBM PC and compatible machines on one $3\frac{1}{2}$ inch disk (37725-5).

Of Related Interest

Also in the Benjamin/Cummings series on Information Systems: *Business Data Communications*, 3rd Edition, also by David A. Stamper (37720-4); *Information Systems: A Management Perspective*, by Steven Alter (51030-8); and *Database Management*, 4th Edition, by Fred R. McFadden and Jeffrey A. Hoffer (36047-6).

Acknowledgments

Many thanks to the following reviewers for their feedback and suggestions:

Lynda Armbruster
Rancho Santiago College

Frank Paiano
Southwestern Community College

Harvey Blessing
Essex Community College

William Rodgers
Morehead State University

Kip Canfield
University of Maryland, UMBC

Sachi Sakthivel
Bowling Green State University

Nancy Groneman
Emporia State University

Norman Schneidewind
Naval Postgraduate School

Patricia Harris
Mesa Community College

Robert Schultheis
Southern Illinois University at Edwardsville

Dennis Milbrandt
Northeast Metro Technical College

First, I want to thank my wife, Kay, for all her support and encouragement. A special thanks to the key people at Benjamin/Cummings who contributed to the success of this project: Developmental Editor Kathy Galinac ensured superior consistency and quality; Production Editor Cathy Lewis directed the timely efforts of numerous people; and Sr. Acquisitions Editor Michelle Baxter helped guide this book on its path to success.

David A. Stamper

BRIEF TABLE OF CONTENTS

PART 1   INTRODUCTION TO MICROCOMPUTERS, LANS, AND DATA COMMUNICATIONS   1

Chapter 1   Introduction to Microcomputers and Local Area Networks   3

Chapter 2   Introduction to Data Communications   27

PART 2   HARDWARE   55

Chapter 3   Topologies and Media Access Control   57

Chapter 4   LAN Hardware   91

PART 3   SOFTWARE   115

Chapter 5   LAN Systems Software   117

Chapter 6   Application Software   147

PART 4   INSTALLATION AND MANAGEMENT   171

Chapter 7   LAN Installation   173

Chapter 8   LAN Administration: Users, Groups, and Security   201

Chapter 9   LAN Administration: The Printing Environment   229

Chapter 10   LAN Administration: Backup and Recovery   253

Chapter 11   LAN Administration: Reactive and Proactive Management   277

PART 5   CONNECTION TO OTHER SYSTEMS AND NETWORKS   307

Chapter 12   Wide Area Networks   309

Chapter 13   Making Network Connections   335

Chapter 14   Emerging Technologies   367

Glossary   389

Index   396

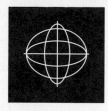

CONTENTS

PART 1
INTRODUCTION TO MICROCOMPUTERS, LANs, AND DATA COMMUNICATIONS 1

CHAPTER 1   Introduction to Microcomputers and Local Area Networks 3

Chapter Preview 3
Stand-alone Microcomputers 3
    Early Stand-alone Hardware 4
    Early Stand-alone Software 4
    Evolution of the
        Microcomputer 6
Why Use LANs? 9
    Resource Sharing 9
    Communication 12
    Management Control 13
    Cost Effectiveness 14
    Downsizing 15
    New Application Software 15
Application Software 16
    Personal Productivity
        Applications 16
    Workgroup Applications 17
Characteristics of Local Area
    Networks 19
    Transparent Use 19
    Mixed Hardware and
        Software 20
    Limited Geographical Area 20
    High Speed 20
    Resource Sharing 21
    LAN Media 21
    Media Access Control
        Protocols 21

    Local Ownership 22
Additional LAN Responsibilities 22
Summary 23
Key Terms 24
Review Questions 25
Problems and Exercises 25
References 26

CHAPTER 2   Introduction to Data Communications 27

Chapter Preview 27
Essential Elements of
    Communication 27
    The Message 27
    The Sender 28
    The Receiver 28
    The Medium 28
    Understanding the Message 29
    Error Detection 29
Network Definition 29
The OSI Reference Model 32
    Functions of OSI Layers 34
    The OSI Model at Work 36
    Functional Layer Standards 40
LAN Selection Criteria 40
    Cost 41
    Number of Workstations 43
    Type of Workstations 43
    Number of Concurrent
        Users 44
    Type of Use 44
    Number and Type of
        Printers 45
    Distance and Medium 45
    Speed 46
    Applications 46
    Expandability 46
    Device Connectivity 46
    Connectivity to Other
        Networks 47

LAN Software and
    Hardware   47
Adherence to Established
    Standards   47
Vendor and Support   47
Manageability   48
Security   48
Summary   49
Key Terms   50
Review Questions   51
Problems and Exercises   52
References   53

PART 2
HARDWARE   55

**CHAPTER 3   Topologies and
Media Access Control   57**

Chapter Preview   57
The LAN System   57
LAN Media   58
**Broadband and Baseband
    Technologies   60**
Broadband Transmission   61
Broadband Strandards and
    Use   63
Baseband Transmission   63
**LAN Topologies and the Physical
    Layer   64**
Ring Topology   64
Bus Topology   69
Star Topology   69
**Data Link and Media Access Control
    Protocols   73**
Data Link Protocols   73
MAC Protocols   76
Making the Decisions   80
Token Passing and CSMA/CD
    Compared   81
Medium Tradeoffs   81
Topology and Protocol
    Tradeoffs   82
Summary   85
Key Terms   85
Review Questions   87
Problems and Exercises   87
References   88

**CHAPTER 4   LAN Hardware
91**

Chapter Preview   91
Server Platforms   91
File Services   91
Server Disk Drives   95

Server Memory   97
Processor Speed   99
Expansion and Power   99
Compatibility   99
Backup Devices   99
Floppy Diskette Drives   100
Hard Disk Drives   101
Optical Disk Drives   101
Magnetic Tape Drives   101
Workstations   102
Diskless Workstations   103
Workstation Memory and
    Speed   103
LAN Adapters   104
Printers   104
Other Hardware   105
Making Connections   105
Summary   110
Key Terms   110
Review Questions   111
Problems and Exercises   112
References   113

PART 3
SOFTWARE   115

**CHAPTER 5   LAN System
Software   117**

Chapter Preview   117
**Generic Functions of LAN System
    Software   117**
A Workstation
    Environment   118
System Software Functions   119
LAN Workstation Software   121
Workstation Software
    Interface   121
Workstation System
    Software   123
Specifics of Server Software   123
Server Operating Systems   124
LAN Operating System
    Functions   125
Novell Operating Systems   129
Novell Network Interface and
    Utilities Software   129
IBM's LAN Server and OS/2
    Operating System   130
BanyanVines   131
Interoperability of Server
    Software   131
Print Spooler   132
Backup Software   135
Utility and Administrative
    Software   135

Software Requirements for Shared
Usage 135
Hardware Configuration 136
Application Settings 136
Contention 137
Access Security 140
Summary 140
Key Terms 141
Review Questions 142
Problems and Exercises 143
References 144

CHAPTER 6   Application
Software 147

Chapter Preview 147
Database Software 147
Workgroup Software 151
Electronic Mail Systems 152
Other E-mail Features 153
Electronic Calendaring
and Conferencing
Applications 154
Work-flow Automation
Software 155
Document Coauthoring
and Management
Applications 157
Group Decision Support 158
Primary Business Software 158
Software Standards 158
Software Protection 161
Software License
Agreements 163
Owner's Rights 166
Summary 166
Key Terms 167
Review Questions 168
Problems and Exercises 169
References 170

PART 4
INSTALLATION AND
MANAGEMENT 171

CHAPTER 7   LAN
Installation 173

Chapter Preview 173
Administrative Details 173
Purchase Contract 174
Support and Maintenance
Agreements 177
Installation Tasks 178
Documentation 179
Site Planning 180

Medium Installation 181
Hardware Installation 182
Software Installation 186
Conversion and Data
Preparation 190
Creating the Operating
Environment 190
Testing and Acceptance 190
Cutover 192
Training 192
User Training 192
Group Manager Training 194
Operator Training 194
LAN Administrator
Training 194
Summary 195
Key Terms 196
Review Questions 197
Problems and Exercises 198
References 198

CHAPTER 8   LAN
Administration: Users,
Groups, and Security 201

Chapter Preview 201
Users and Groups 201
Users 202
Groups 203
Systems Programming 203
Security 203
Password Administration 205
Logon Restrictions 207
Encryption 209
Novell NetWare 386 Data Access
Security 209
Determining File Access
Security 211
Establishing Trustee Rights 214
File and Directory
Attributes 214
Security Utilities 216
Viruses 218
Protecting Against Viruses 219
Summary 222
Key Terms 223
Review Questions 224
Problems and Exercises 225
References 226

CHAPTER 9   LAN
Administration: The Printing
Environment 229

Chapter Preview 229
Introduction to Printing 229
Creating a Printing
Environment 230

A Generic Spooler 231
Hardware-Oriented
Functions 231
Application-Oriented
Functions 233
Administration-Oriented
Functions 235
User-Oriented Functions 238
Novell Spooler Configuration 239
The CAPTURE Program 239
The Print Server Spooler
System 242
Novell Print Queues 242
Special Printing Needs 245
Print Servers 245
Summary 248
Key Terms 248
Review Questions 249
Problems and Exercises 250
References 250

CHAPTER 10   LAN
Administration: Backup and
Recovery 253

Chapter Preview 253
Data Backup 253
The Need for Backups 254
Backups for Static and Dynamic
Data 255
Backup Hardware, Software, and
Procedures 256
Making Backups 257
Backup Procedures 258
Other Data Reliability
Options 264
Recovery 268
Low-Level Recovery 270
Diagnostic Tools 270
Dealing with Errors 271
Disaster Planning 271
Summary 273
Key Terms 274
Review Questions 274
Problems and Exercises 275
References 276

CHAPTER 11   LAN
Administration: Reactive and
Proactive Management 277

Chapter Preview 277
Reactive Network Management 277
Problem Identification and
Correction 279
Information Gathering 279
Diagnosis and Analysis 281

Identification and
Resolution 286
Documentation 286
Proactive Network
Management 286
System Tuning and Capacity
Planning 287
Tuning a System 288
Capacity Planning 290
Planning System Expansion 292
Configuration of Hardware and
Software Upgrades 293
Upgrade Configuration
Steps 293
Planning Software
Upgrades 294
Network Management Systems 295
Network Management
Protocols 299
Simple Network Management
Protocol (SNMP) 299
Common Management
Information Protocol
(CMIP) 302
Summary 302
Key Terms 303
Review Questions 304
Problems and Exercises 304
References 305

PART 5
CONNECTING TO
OTHER SYSTEMS AND
NETWORKS 307

CHAPTER 12   Wide Area
Networks 309

Chapter Preview 309
WAN Network Terminology 310
WAN Network Topologies 311
Hierarchical Network 311
Interconnected (Plex)
Network 313
Combination Networks 313
WAN Data Link Control
Protocols 314
Bit Synchronous Protocols 314
WAN Network Layer Functions 316
Message Routing in a WAN 317
IBM's Systems Network
Architecture 321
Hardware Components 322
Logical Units and Sessions 322

Packet Distribution Networks 325
   PDN Terminology 325
   PDN Advantages and
      Disadvantages 325
Comparing WANs with LANs 327
   Topology, Protocols, and
      Routing 327
   Media 327
   Ownership 328
   Transmission Speed 328
LAN-WAN Interconnections 328
Summary 329
Key Terms 330
Review Questions 331
Problems and Exercises 332
References 333

CHAPTER 13   Making
Network Connections   335

Chapter Preview 335
The OSI Reference Model
   Revisited 335
LAN-to-LAN Connections 340
   Repeaters 342
   Bridges 343
   Other Bridge Capabilities 347
   Routers 349
   TCP/IP Routing Protocol 349
   Choosing the Right
      Interface 352
   Gateways 352
LAN-to-HOST Connections 353
   The Host as a LAN Mode 356
   Asynchronous Connections 356
   Other Types of Host
      Connections 359
   IBM System Connections 359
Interconnection Utilities 359
Summary 361

Key Terms 362
Review Questions 363
Problems and Exercises 363
References 365

CHAPTER 14   Emerging
Technologies   367

Chapter Preview 367
Client/Server Computing 367
   C/S Computing Examples 370
   Advantages of C/S
      Computing 370
   C/S Technology 373
Nondedicated Servers and
   Peer-to-Peer LANs 375
Wireless Media 376
Diskless Workstations 377
Global Naming and Distributed
   Systems 378
ISDN 378
High-Speed Local Area
   Networks 378
Multimedia on LANs 381
Servers 383
Uninterruptable Power
   Supplies 385
Pocket LAN Adapters 386
Technology and Network
   Management 386
Summary 386
Key Terms 387
References 387

GLOSSARY   389

INDEX   396

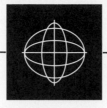

I
INTRODUCTION TO MICROCOMPUTERS, LANS, AND DATA COMMUNICATIONS

Beginning with the evolution of microcomputers, their software, and their place in business and personal computing, we will explore how LANs are used to extend the power of stand-alone microcomputers. Before introducing LANs, we will review the basics of data communication principles, including the OSI reference model, as a foundation for the discussion of LAN technology in following chapters. We will conclude with LAN selection criteria.

Chapter 1
Introduction to Microcomputers and Local Area Networks

Chapter 2
Introduction to Data Communications

INTRODUCTION TO MICROCOMPUTERS AND LOCAL AREA NETWORKS

CHAPTER PREVIEW

Technologies such as telecommunications, typewriters, copy machines, and computers have significantly changed the ways companies conduct business, and this evolution of the modern office is continuing. Two computer technologies that flourished in the 1980s are microcomputers and data communications. It is only natural that these two technologies should combine to provide a computing environment with a greater impact than either technology alone could provide. This chapter begins with a discussion of stand-alone microcomputers, their software, and their place in business and personal computing. Following that you will see how **local area networks (LANs)** are used to extend the power of the stand-alone microcomputer.

Specific topics you will read about in this chapter include

characteristics of stand-alone microcomputing

reasons organizations use networks

popular network applications

distinguishing features of LANs

situations in which a LAN can be useful

added responsibilities of using a LAN

At the end of this chapter, you should have an understanding of some of the capabilities and some of the limitations of stand-alone microcomputers, how LANs can be used to remove some of these limitations, and some of the implications of networking microcomputers.

STAND-ALONE MICROCOMPUTERS

The first microcomputer, the Altair 8800, was introduced in 1975. But it was the introduction of the Apple microcomputer in 1977 and the IBM microcomputer in 1981 that really launched the microcomputer age. IBM has been the dominant computer company almost since computers became commercially available. Because of its commanding position in business, IBM's introduction of its microcomputer, dubbed the **Personal Computer (PC),** provided the impetus for corporate as well as private microcomputer use. Although only IBM's system was officially dubbed the PC, that abbreviation has been generically extended to include other brands of microcomputers. Henceforth we will use the term *PC* to mean any microcomputer, not just IBM's.

IBM's first entry into the microcomputer world was aptly named. It *was* a personal computer. It operated in a stand-alone manner, which means the microcomputer was an entirely self-contained processing platform and did not rely on any external resources for data or processing. The PC was designed to provide its user with all the necessary hardware and software— disks, printers, operating system, applications, and data—making it a tool that helped individuals become more productive in the workplace and at home.

Early Stand-alone Hardware

The first PCs were primitive by today's standards. They had limited main and secondary memory capacities and slow processors compared to CPUs used today. A typical system had 256 or 384 kilobytes (KB) of memory (very early systems had only 64 or 128 KB) and two floppy disk drives, each with a capacity of 360 KB. Serial and parallel ports, which are standard equipment on most of today's systems, were purchased as options. A mouse was uncommon, and graphics capabilities, if they existed, were at very low resolutions.

Most early systems also had a dedicated printer, usually a dot matrix printer or a character printer using a daisy wheel, type thimble, type ball, or similar character-printing mechanism. By today's standards printing speeds were slow—frequently under 150 characters per second.

Early Stand-alone Software

Early microcomputer software was designed for the individual user. The stand-alone design for limited hardware architectures was characteristic of most early software. The software had to fit on one or two floppy diskettes and did not have much available main memory with which to work. Early microcomputer software was thus limited by the available hardware. The major advantages of the early software were ease of use coupled with basic personal productivity applications.

Nowhere is the stand-alone orientation of early microcomputing more clear than in the operating systems. Early operating systems, such as CPM, DOS, and Apple DOS, allowed one user to run one application. Multiple users could run multiple applications in minicomputer and mainframe operating systems but not in microcomputing operating systems. A multiprocessing operating system is more complex, requires more memory and disk storage, and often is more difficult to use than a single-user system. Operating systems and application software could take advantage of the single-user environment. Designing and building software were simplified because pro-

grammers did not have to deal with the issues of security, contention for resources, and tailoring an application to several hardware configuration and
several user preferences (user profiles). We will explore these issues later in
Chapter 8, but a few comments are in order now concerning why ignoring
these issues made program development easier.

Security   Data is a valuable resource and, like all valuable resources, should
be protected. **Security** means preventing disclosure of data to anyone who
does not need it and safeguarding it from accidental or intentional loss or
misuse. Security can be physical or logical. **Physical security** denies unauthorized users physical access to data, hardware, and software. For instance,
locking data in a safe and placing locks on computer room doors are physical protection measures. **Logical security** protects data to which a user might
have physical access. For example, you might set up file and user attributes
that allow a user to read data in a file but keep that user from changing data.
Another user might have both read and write privileges for that data, and
another user may be denied any access. Consider a company's payroll data:
A payroll clerk can use the data in preparing reports but cannot change an
employee's salary; a payroll supervisor can read payroll data and make
salary adjustments; and a marketing analyst, who has no need to use payroll
data at all, is denied access to that data. A common type of logical security is
identification and authentication, which is usually accomplished by user IDs
and passwords.

Stand-alone microcomputers mainly use physical security. Access to the
computer gives access to all data and programs stored on its disks. This is
not always a good security practice when several people can use the same
computer. If you have sensitive data stored on a stand-alone microcomputer, you can protect the data by storing it on removable disks and removing the disks when the data is not needed. Alternatively your security application can use a technique to hide, or encrypt, sensitive data from
unauthorized users. **Encryption** is a method of scrambling the data using a
confidential encryption key. The encryption key is simply some combination
of characters or bits. When data is encrypted, only people who know the encryption key can decipher the data. Someone who has physical access to
that data cannot easily make sense of it. Table 1-1 is an example of encrypted data: The text "data communications" was changed using the encryption key LAN. The details of encryption are beyond the scope of this
text; see Stamper (1991) for more details.

In networks you often share data; that is, you store it on a computer to
which many users have access. Each user has different data needs for his or
her job; therefore, physical security must be supplemented by logical security. Chapter 8 discusses how this is done.

Table 1-1   An Example of Encrypted Data

Plain Text	DATA COMMUNICATIONS
Encrypted Text	QVPMRCAJDXGPFXECFOL

Contention   **Contention** occurs when two or more users try to share the same resource, such as a printer, disk, application, or data. A word processing example can clarify this concept. Suppose that you and a partner are jointly writing a paper. You decide to make a change to one section of the paper, while at the same time your partner decides to make a change to a different section. Thus you are both editing the same document at the same time. You finish making your changes and save the document. Sometime later your partner finishes changing the document and saves it. What has happened? Your partner's changes have been saved, and your changes have been erased because your partner's document replaced your version of the file. At best two copies of the document exist, and neither reflects the complete set of changes. This situation is illustrated in Figure 1-1. Similar problems can exist when two or more users share data in a database or try to share devices like a printer. Stand-alone software does not have to concern itself with the problem of contention.

User Profiles   When an application supports **user profiles,** it can be tailored to individual needs. Suppose that an organization has different hardware configurations. Some users have color monitors, others have monochrome monitors. Moreover there may be differences in each workstation's graphics capabilities. The application ought to allow each user to take full advantage of his or her configuration. For example, users with high-resolution color monitors can select their own foreground and background colors and display graphic images at the resolution supported by their microcomputer. Users with monochrome monitors without graphics capabilities should also be able to use the same software as effectively as their machines allow. Many stand-alone applications support only one user's startup parameters and one hardware configuration. This is limiting in a network environment. An application that does not support user profiles probably is configured to accommodate the lowest common set of user capabilities. Table 1-2 shows examples of settings that might be found in a user profile.

In the early days of microcomputers, designing software for single-user, stand-alone microcomputers was a good decision: Applications were much simpler to design and implement and could be brought to market more quickly. Few microcomputer software designers anticipated the rapidity of microcomputer hardware growth—a growth that has made microcomputers more than just personal computers. Today new terms, such as **workstation, desktop computer,** and **network server,** describe these systems. Moreover today's microcomputers can run multiple, concurrent tasks or support multiple, concurrent users.

Evolution of the Microcomputer

Almost overnight, microcomputer hardware made great advances. The pace was so rapid that the hardware quickly left the software behind. Memory and disk capacities grew, enhanced graphics capabilities became available, printers increased in speed and capability, and price per performance plummeted. These changes occurred in the space of a few years, and because of

Figure 1-1   An Example of a Contention Problem

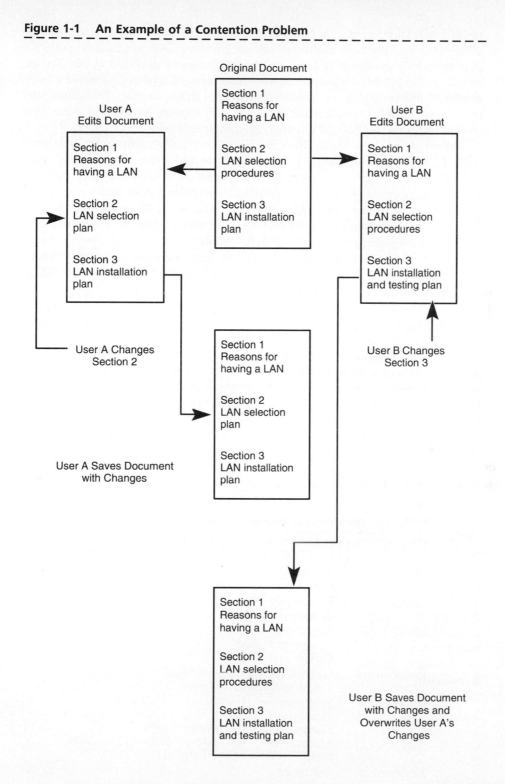

Original Document

Section 1
Reasons for
having a LAN

Section 2
LAN selection
procedures

Section 3
LAN installation
plan

User A
Edits Document

Section 1
Reasons for
having a LAN

Section 2
LAN selection
plan

Section 3
LAN installation
plan

User B
Edits Document

Section 1
Reasons for
having a LAN

Section 2
LAN selection
procedures

Section 3
LAN installation
and testing plan

User A Changes
Section 2

User B Changes
Section 3

Section 1
Reasons for
having a LAN

Section 2
LAN selection
plan

Section 3
LAN installation
plan

User A Saves Document
with Changes

Section 1
Reasons for
having a LAN

Section 2
LAN selection
procedures

Section 3
LAN installation
and testing plan

User B Saves Document
with Changes and
Overwrites User A's
Changes

them applications could be enhanced to take advantage of the expanded environment and provide multiuser enhancements. Soon application software demanded the existence of large amounts of memory and disk space. For example, most of today's **graphical user interfaces (GUIs)** recommend a *minimum* of 2 million bytes, or megabytes (MB), of main memory for satisfactory operation. A GUI (pronounced "gooey") uses menus, icons, and a pointing device like a mouse to make using the computer easier.

Most of the new hardware capabilities originally came with high price tags. Hard disk drives added about $1000 to the price of a system, even though the disk capacities were 10 MB or less. Although the price per byte quickly dropped, disk capacities almost immediately began increasing. Users could thus spend the same amount and receive about 30 times more storage or pay approximately one third less and still receive four to eight times the storage. Laser printers provided letter-quality printing at speeds much greater than that available with the low-speed, character-oriented printers. High speed and high quality also came at a relatively high cost—over $2000. Equipping a stand-alone microcomputer with top-of-the line peripherals like a large hard disk and a laser printer drove the price of systems higher or kept the prices at the same level even though the cost of microcomputer technology was steadily declining.

For many offices it is impractical to equip each user's system with large hard disk drives and laser printers; however, most users need (or want) access to the added speed and capabilities these devices offer. If you observe a user working at a microcomputer, you notice that person probably uses the printer infrequently. Rather than dedicating an expensive printer to each user, a natural solution is to allow several users to share one printer. Likewise, rather than providing each user with a large hard disk, it is more practical to allow several users to share one. For example, consider an office with 20 stand-alone microcomputers, where each user must use a word process-

Table 1-2   Possible User Profile Settings

Monitor	Color monitor
	Super VGA graphics
Mouse	3-Button
	COM1 Port
Colors	Foreground—Green
	Background—Black
Menu	Display menu—Yes
	Foreground—Red
	Background—White
Environment	Original file backup enabled
	Timed backup enabled every 30 minutes
File Location	Spell checker C:\WP
	Thesaurus C:\WP
	Document files C:\USERS\JSMITH
	Macro files C:\USERS\JSMITH\WPMACROS
	Style sheets C:\USERS\JSMITH\WPSTYLES
Keyboard	Enhanced

ing program. Some current word processing programs require 6 MB of disk storage for the programs and supporting files. Each user storing an individual copy of the word processor files on a local hard disk drive requires 120 MB of storage. If the users share one copy, only 6 MB on one disk drive is needed. One of several ways in which sharing is possible is to use a LAN.

WHY USE LANs?

We use networks for a variety of reasons. Most early microcomputer LANs were implemented for resource sharing. Since then additional advantages—communication, management control, cost effectiveness, downsizing (sometimes referred to as rightsizing) and new application software—have materialized. Let us now look briefly at each of these purposes.

Resource Sharing

The need to share resources is still one of the primary reasons for using a network. A network consists of a variety of resources, such as disk drives, tape drives, printers, data, application programs, modems, scanners, and **facsimile (FAX) machines.** Dedicating resources of this type to each user is expensive. In a network some or all of these resources may be shared. For example, the stand-alone microcomputer workstations in Figure 1-2 illustrate three basic ways that a user can print a document: Each workstation can have its own dedicated printer, as illustrated in Figure 1-2(a). Alternatively several workstations can share one printer, either by using a data switch, as illustrated in Figure 1-2(b), or by the user of one workstation placing the data to be printed on a floppy diskette and carrying it to another workstation with an attached printer (a technique sometimes called sneaker-net), as illustrated in Figure 1-2(c). A **data switch** is a hardware device to which two or more computers and one printer may be attached. The data switch allows one computer to connect to the printer and use it exclusively. When that computer finishes printing, another computer can connect to the printer and print its output.

With a data switch a user needing access to the printer must activate the switch to connect his or her workstation to the printer. The switch may be a manual switch, as illustrated in Figure 1-3, a software switch activated through a software utility, or a switch that senses when an attached microcomputer wants to send printer data. In the latter case the switch continually rotates through connections with each microcomputer. If a microcomputer wants to print, the switch recognizes it and locks onto that channel until the entire job is printed. The switch then resumes sampling each available connection for other print jobs.

With simple switches only one user can use the printer at a time. More sophisticated switches have memory that allows several users to write "logically" to an attached printer at the same time. This is accomplished by holding one job in the memory buffer while another job is being printed, as illustrated in Figure 1-4.

A third alternative is to connect the workstations and printers on a network, as illustrated in Figure 1-5. Each workstation has access to the printer as though it were locally attached. Naturally several users may request to use the printer at the same time. A software application called a **spooler,** located within the network server, handles contention for the printer. The spooler accepts print jobs and saves them in a disk file. When the printer is available, the spooler selects a completed print job in the disk file and prints that job. When that job is done printing, the spooler selects another job for printing.

Resources other than printers, such as disks, files, FAX machines, and so on, can be shared among LAN users. A variety of techniques are used to

Figure 1-2   Stand-Alone Microcomputers and Printer Sharing

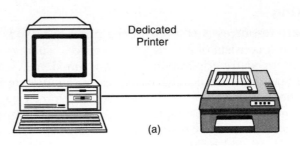

Dedicated
Printer

(a)

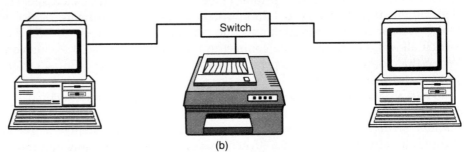

Printer Shared by
Two Computers

Switch

(b)

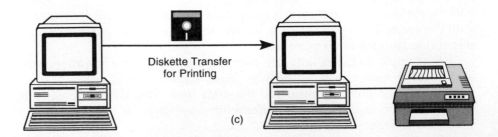

Diskette Transfer
for Printing

(c)

Figure 1-3   Manual Data Switch

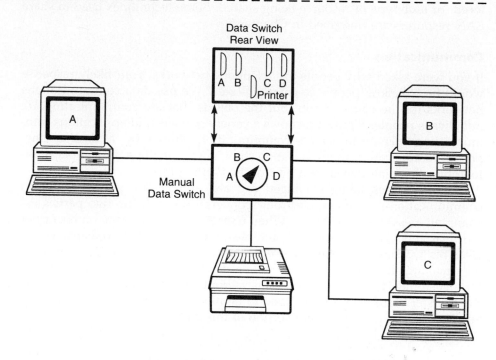

Figure 1-4   Switch Using Memory to Hold One Job While Printing Another

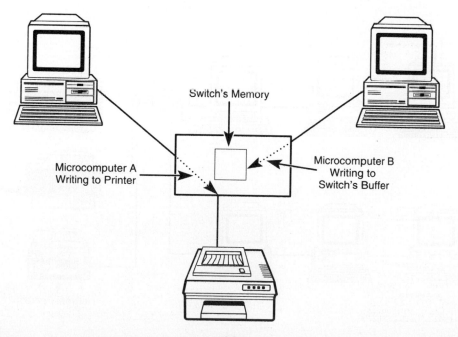

accomplish sharing; individual techniques, like a spooler for printers, are tailored for each type of resource being shared. Some techniques used to share LAN resources are described in Chapter 5.

Communication

If you were asked why people use telephone networks, your likely response would be "to allow people to communicate." We use data communications networks for the same reason, but the objects that are communicating are not always people. Figure 1-6 shows a variety of users and applications communicating: person-to-person communication shown by a dashed line, person-to-application communication shown by a solid line, and application-to-application dialogue shown by a dashed/dotted line.

The messages being exhanged can also differ. The person-to-person communication may be an electronic conversation with the two parties exchanging messages in real time: When User A types a message on his or her terminal and hits the enter key, the message is immediately displayed on User B's workstation. The person-to-application communication may be a user making an inquiry into a corporate database, checking on a shipment for a customer, for example. The application-to-application dialogue may be the transfer of a file from one node to another. Examples of other network applications are cited in a later section of this chapter.

Figure 1-5   Workstations and Printers Connected on a LAN

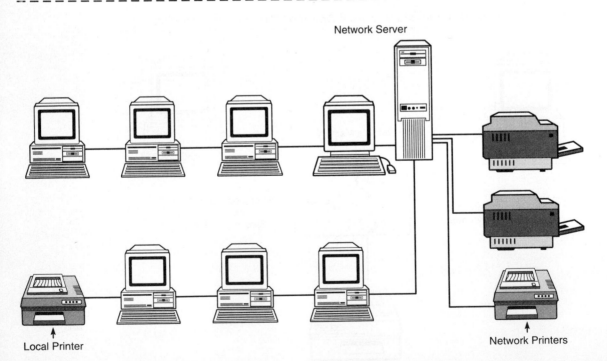

Network Server

Local Printer

Network Printers

Management Control

A third reason for using a network is management control. A LAN can help standardize the microcomputer environment. At the outset of the microcomputer age, some companies left the choice of software and hardware to individuals or to departments. As a result they found a variety of software being used on hardware platforms that were not homogeneous. That is, there were two or three different word processors, two or three spreadsheets, two or more database managers, and so on running on IBM-compatible, Apple-compatible, and other types of microcomputers. Having such a variety of software and hardware creates two immediate problems, portability and education. **Portability** means the ability to transfer an application or application data from one system to another. Files maintained on one word processor must be converted before being used by another user with different hardware or different word processing software. Alternatively users must learn to use several different software packages to perform the same function—a time-consuming and expensive proposition.

Furthermore imagine a work environment in which each user maintains his or her own copy of data. Changes in the data are not reflected in all copies of the data at the same time. Thus if User A makes a change to an employee's address and telephone number in her database, that change is not immediately reflected in User B's database. Coordinating changes of

Figure 1-6   Objects Using a Network to Communicate

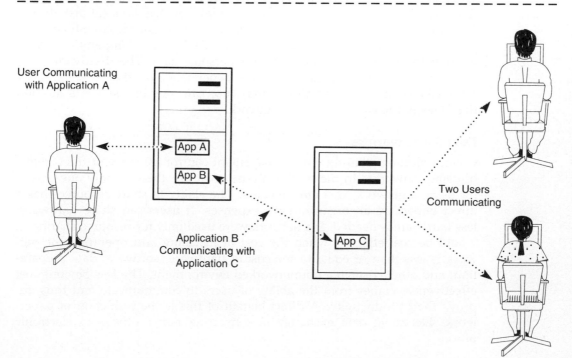

User Communicating
with Application A

App A

App B

Application B
Communicating with
Application C

App C

Two Users
Communicating

data in several databases is usually not a simple task. The result is inconsistent data—the data equivalent of anarchy. With a network, users can share data and avoid data inconsistencies. Data consistency and integrity can be further enhanced through management control of data and file backups. In the stand-alone computing environment, each user is responsible for maintaining backups, and the frequency and completeness of backups is usually poor. With a LAN, management can carry out a comprehensive backup policy for shared data. This provides for better data and file protection against intentional or accidental data destruction.

Application standards can be set up more easily in a network, because most application programs—for example, word processors and spreadsheet programs—can be installed on one or more network nodes called servers. Users can then access these applications over the network. For example, in a small network all users may run the same word processing program located on a specific network node. When all users use the same version of the same word processor, document interchange is a simple matter. Contrast this with two or more users having different versions of the same word processor, or worse yet, completely different word processing software. In this case documents created under one system would need to be converted and possibly reformatted before being used by the other word processing system.

LANs can also help control one of the most unsettling problems facing computer users today, **computer viruses.** With **diskless workstations** and **virus detection software,** management can reduce the risk of viral infections. A diskless workstation, as the name implies, has no local disk drives. This reduces the ways in which a virus can be introduced. An added security benefit of diskless workstations is the inability of a company's workers to copy software or corporate data for personal gain. The disadvantage of diskless workstations is their complete dependence on the network. They cannot be used in a stand-alone mode, nor can they be used in a location that does not have access to the network.

Cost Effectiveness

Communicating, sharing, and management control are three of the benefits of using networks. In the final analysis, however, there is only one reason for using a network, cost effectiveness. The ability to share resources has a direct impact on an organization's expenses. If users can share hardware, less hardware is needed. If a network were used only for resource sharing, it would be cost effective when the cost of installing and operating the network is less than or equal to the cost of hardware, software, data preparation, and other costs in a nonnetworked environment. The less obvious cost effectiveness comes from the ability of users to communicate and thus improve their productivity. A direct benefit of this is the reduction of paperwork. Electronic data exchange is converting paper offices to electronic offices.

Downsizing

In some companies LANs have been used to downsize the data processing hardware, software, and personnel requirements. **Downsizing** refers to using smaller computer platforms in place of large computers. Some companies have replaced their mainframe computers by one or more microcomputer LANs. These companies found they could provide better data processing services at much lower hardware, software, and personnel costs. For details on two companies' experiences with downsizing, refer to Chivvis (1991) and Watt (1991). The first article reports that "While the size of FGIC's [Financial Guaranty Insurance Company's] portfolio grew by 40 percent, downsizing cut the company's annual systems budget from $10 million to $2 million and reduced its information services staff from 70 programmers to 20." This represented an 80 percent cost savings. A diagram of that company's computer configuration before and after downsizing are shown in Figures 1-7 and 1-8, respectively.

New Application Software

Personal productivity applications are designed to help individual users do their job better and easier. One of the newer application technologies associated with networks is called **groupware**—applications oriented toward improving the productivity of a group of people working together. Groupware

Figure 1-7   Data Processing Configuration Before Downsizing

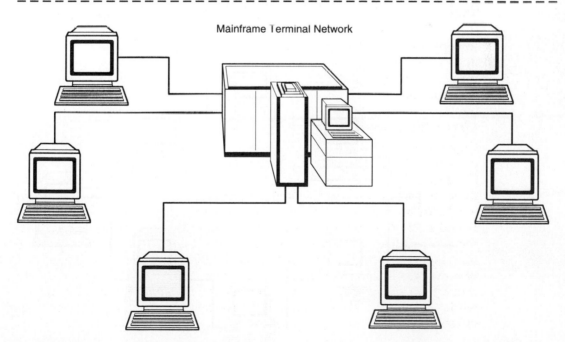

Mainframe Terminal Network

automates work functions that require the communcation and collaboration of two or more individuals. These tools raise office productivity and make LANs even more cost effective.

The main reason we use computers is to solve problems, and it is the applications software that actually goes about solving problems. Let us now look at both personal and workgroup productivity software and their relationship to LANs.

APPLICATION SOFTWARE

The scope of network applications software is so varied that it would be a monumental task to describe each of them. Let us look just at applications that allow users to make more effective use of their microcomputers on a LAN.

Personal Productivity Applications

Personal productivity software is single-user oriented. It helps improve the productivity of individual users. Personal productivity software is often found on LANs to provide hardware and software sharing. In contrast, groupware provides idea sharing.

Word Processing and Desktop Publishing Microcomputer word processing and desktop publishing applications continue to expand in scope. Many

Figure 1-8   Data Processing Configuration After Downsizing

Local Area Network

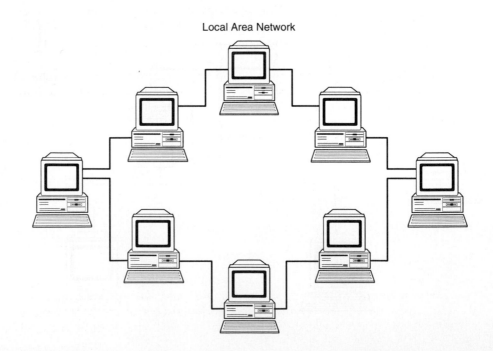

of them are still single-user oriented, but document-processing competition is intense, and software vendors must improve their products to keep competitive. It is therefore reasonable to assume that future versions will allow several users to pull out sections of a single document, at the same time, allow one user to update a document and let others concurrently view but not change it, and allow users to work concurrently on the same document and view or edit the document in concert. Each of these capabilities helps improve workgroup productivity.

Spreadsheets Spreadsheet applications are used extensively on LANs, primarily for applications that require the manipulation of numbers. Examples of specific uses include budgeting, cost analysis, preparation of financial statements, and performing "what-if" analyses. **"What-if" analysis** is a form of modeling that allows a user to see the effects of changing parameters in a specific situation. For example, a marketing analyst can see the effects of price and interest rate changes on profits. Using spreadsheets on a LAN, users can easily share templates, and multiple users can access, modify, and print completed spreadsheets. However, most spreadsheets in use today do not allow several users to work simultaneously on the same spreadsheet.

Today's spreadsheet software is expanding to encompass multiple files. For example, one spreadsheet file might be linked to another, so changes in one are automatically reflected in the other. A LAN can provide the setting for widespread sharing. At the same time, the LAN can also provide protection against unauthorized changes to spreadsheets and against update contention.

Database Management A **database management system (DBMS)** gives you the ability to define, use, and manage data. Not only can you create, retrieve, modify, and delete data, but also most modern DBMSs have high-level data languages, report generators, and application generators. With these facilities nontechnical people can direct the DBMS to produce tailored reports and respond to adhoc enquiries. With LAN-oriented databases users share the database. This reduces the amount of redundant data storage that occurs when individuals maintain their own databases on stand-alone systems. Reduction in data redundancy also helps eliminate data inconsistencies. When a DBMS allows data sharing, it must also reconcile the problems arising from data contention mentioned earlier.

Presentation Services **Presentation services** refers to the generation and use of graphics. Graphics hardware and software can be rather expensive. A LAN allows these expensive resources to be shared, providing a cost-effective way of distributing graphics capabilities.

Workgroup Applications

One motive for having a LAN is communication. For years workers have been communicating in person, via telephones, and with printed material. The first two methods require the correspondents to be at the proper place at the proper time and also to be available for the dialogue. Written material does not require this coordination but often lacks the timeliness and spontaneity of oral communication. An ideal communication system provides the timeliness, spontaneity, and interaction of oral communication with the scheduling independence and recording of written communication. One part of workgroup applications, or groupware, addresses this issue. Although we have not yet attained the ideal, we are constantly getting closer.

One of the most explicit communication applications is electronic messaging. The most publicized of the electronic messaging applications is electronic mail, but other types, such as voice mail, time-staged message delivery systems, and electronic conferencing, are also in use. These applications are written explicitly for networks and may eventually surpass resource sharing as the primary motive for a LAN.

Electronic Mail   An **electronic mail (E-mail)** application allows users to exchange messages via an electronic postal system. Like conventional mail systems, the electronic postal system is responsible for accepting and delivering correspondence. Most E-mail systems also provide a word processing capability for message composition and editing. These capabilities are discussed more completely in Chapter 6.

Electronic Conferencing   Another communication capability used on LANs is **electronic conferencing.** Two or more employees can use this facility to carry on a dialogue interactively. This feature is used less frequently on LANs, where most users are near each other, than it is on **wide area networks (WANs),** where the users may be geographically dispersed; however, it is also gaining use on LANs.

Electronic Meeting Systems   One of the newer LAN applications is the **electronic meeting system (EMS).** An EMS incorporates decision-support software with electronic messaging to coordinate communication and decision making. For example, suppose that the managers of a corporation need to brainstorm a new idea or set up a budget. The traditional method of doing this is to hold a meeting or a series of meetings. Frequently during such meetings a few participants tend to dominate. With an EMS system the participants communicate via their workstations and the LAN. Ideas proposed by one user can be displayed for all users to see, but the display remains anonymous so participants are unaware of the source of the suggestions. Anonymous comments from other users can be added and displayed. The entire electronic meeting is thus conducted in an egoless and unintimidating setting. The application software helps lead the group toward its goals. Users of these systems have experienced better and quicker decision making.

Electronic Calendaring   Have you ever been required to organize a meeting involving several people? Often one of the most difficult problems in doing this is finding a time convenient for all members. **Electronic calendaring** or scheduling performs this task automatically. With electronic calendaring each user has an electronic calendar available on the network. If a manager needs to schedule a meeting of department heads, she or he can do this by invoking the calendaring application and providing it with the names of the participants and an approximate meeting date. The calendaring application checks the on-line calendars of the participants, determines the best meeting time, blocks out the time on their calendars, and perhaps sends each an E-mail message showing that they have been scheduled to attend.

These groupware applications are only a few of those being used today. The future holds even greater promise. For example, in April 1992 the *Austin American Statesman* newspaper printed an article about the possibilities of **virtual reality.** The article described a future work scenario in which two car designers in different locations work together on the design of a new car model. Each designer can see immediately the work done by the other. Moreover the designers can change the contours of the automobile body by molding it with an electronic glove, much like a sculptor molds a clay figure. The difference is that the car model designers form a graphics image, and that image can be changed by two or more designers working together but in different rooms or locations.

CHARACTERISTICS OF LOCAL AREA NETWORKS

Let us look now at the general characteristics of LANs, which are listed in Table 1-3. In later chapters we will go into detail about LAN hardware and software. In this section we will compare LAN technology with wide area network (WAN) technology when appropriate. These comparisons will help you understand the place of each technology.

Table 1-3   LAN Characteristics

Transparent Use
Mixed Hardware and Software
Limited Geographical Area
High Speed
Resource Sharing
Media Access Control Protocols
Local Ownership

Transparent Use

One of the objectives of most LANs is to achieve **transparent use;** that is, users connected to a LAN should detect few differences between using a stand-alone microcomputer and using one connected to a LAN. Access to the file server's disk should be carried out as though it were a locally attached disk drive. Printing to a network printer ought to be done in the same manner as directing output to a local printer. The only major difference between stand-alone and LAN microcomputers should be security. The network user usually must log onto a server by providing a user ID and a password. Even this requirement can be made transparent to the user by using a logon script. A logon script or batch file is a set of network commands that set up the user's environment. Thus a logon script can be used to set a user's DOS search path, default disk drive and directory, default network printer configuration, startup menu, and so on.

Mixed Hardware and Software

Most LANs in operation today are microcomputer based; that is, most nodes on LANs are microcomputers. However, LANs also connect large computing systems, and it is not uncommon for large systems to be nodes on a LAN with microcomputers, in which case the large computer often functions as a server. A server is a computer (usually) dedicated to providing one or more services to the other nodes. For example, a file server provides file and disk access services, and a printer server provides printing services. Thus a node may access data on a file server and route its printed output to a printer server. In contrast, most of today's WANs have only minicomputers, mainframes, or supercomputers for nodes. Moreover, LANs may include a variety of microcomputers. With these mixed hardware LANs, it is also common to find a variety of operating systems being used. Having mixed hardware and software allows users to use the right equipment for the right job and to make good use of existing equipment. Mixed hardware and software also complicates the job of LAN administration.

Limited Geographical Area

A LAN is designed to operate in a limited geographical area. The limits depend on the type of network. Appletalk, a network for Apple Macintosh computers, spans 300 meters. In an Ethernet network, the maximum network distance is 2500 meters. A third network, the fiber distributed data interface (FDDI), spans distances up to 200 kilometers. As you can see there are considerable variances in the limited area LANs can serve. In contrast a WAN can be either geographically distributed or confined to a local area; that is, there are no restrictions on the media distances for WANs.

High Speed

The speed of a LAN, like the distance spanned, depends on the specific implementation. In general the speeds exceed 1 megabyte per second (Mbps), with speeds of 1, 2.5, 4, 10, 16, and 20 Mbps common for microcomputer LANs. The transmission speeds have been constantly increasing, and speeds of 100 Mbps will become common. The FDDI LAN cited in the previous paragraph operates at 100 Mbps, and fiber optic LANs in the laboratory have reached speeds of 2 billion bytes per second (Gbps). To put this speed into perspective, an average textbook contains about one million characters or eight million bits of text. Thus a speed of 2 Gbps is roughly equivalent to transmitting all the characters from 250 texts each second! In contrast a common WAN speed is 9600 bps. Higher WAN speeds of 56 Kbps and just over 1 Mbps are available, but are less common. WAN speeds are also increasing, and WANs may soon operate at LAN speeds. When this occurs, you can expect to see many of the differences between LANs and WANs disappear.

Resource Sharing

As discussed earlier, one of the basic goals of networks is resource sharing. Data, programs, and hardware (for example, printers and disks), are all resources that can be shared.

LAN Media

Attaining high LAN transmission speeds requires a high-capacity communications medium. Most of the early LANs used coaxial cable as the transmission medium. Today the popularity of coaxial cable is giving way to twisted-pair wires for low-speed LANs (20 Mbps or lower) and fiber optic cables for both low- and high-speed LANs. At the end of the 1980s, wireless LAN media, such as **infrared light,** broadcast radio, and microwave radio, were also introduced. Wireless LANs operate at speeds up to 15 Mbps, and one vendor has said it will be providing wireless speeds up to 100 Mbps. A LAN configuration using a conducting medium like twisted-pair wires, coaxial cable, or fiber optics is shown in Figure 1-9. Use of a radiated medium such as infrared light and a LAN using radio waves is illustrated in Figure 1-10. WANs use each of the media used by LANs. In addition a WAN might use satellite transmission. Often a WAN's transmission medium is obtained from a common communications carrier, such as a telephone company.

Media Access Control Protocols

Each network has specific ways in which it gains access to the **communications medium,** transmits data over the medium, and routes messages. LANs

Figure 1-9   A LAN Using Conducted Media

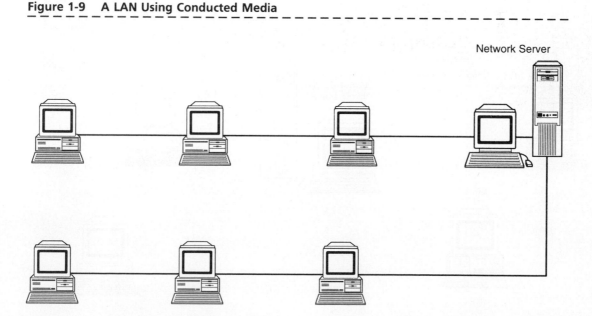

Network Server

generally differ from other networks in their methods for doing this. The technical details of **media access control (MAC) protocols** are covered in Chapter 3.

Local Ownership

Usually, a LAN is completely owned and managed by the using organization. That is, the organization is responsible for all of the equipment and software, including installing and controlling the communications medium. In contrast most WANs use media supplied by a common carrier such as a telephone company.

ADDITIONAL LAN RESPONSIBILITIES

Thus far we have mentioned several problems that a LAN can help solve and benefits that can result from implementing a LAN. A LAN also comes with added responsibilities. Earlier we mentioned that in stand-alone computer systems, each user is also the computer operator. As such, users are principally responsible for making backups, keeping the system running, reporting problems, replacing paper in the printer, and so on. With a LAN

Figure 1-10   A Wireless LAN

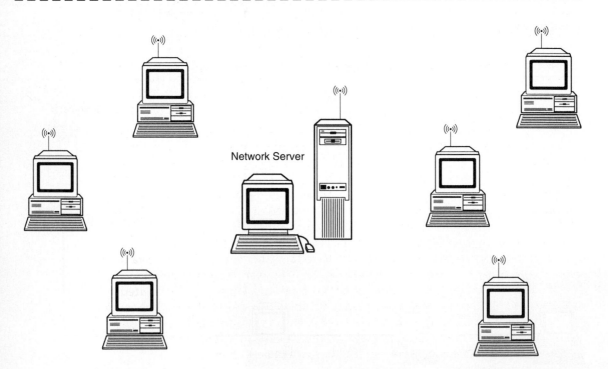

Network Server

many resources can be shared, but one thing that should not be shared is the responsibility for managing the LAN. When management is everyone's responsibility it is also no one's responsibility. Thus a LAN must be managed, and there must be someone given that responsibility and authority. We devote several chapters to this important topic. For now suffice it to say that a well-managed LAN requires additional skills than those usually required by individual microcomputer users.

SUMMARY

Microcomputers and data communications combined in the 1980s to add a new dimension to corporate computing. The expanded power of microcomputer hardware provided the ability for microcomputers to do more than could be done with early microcomputer systems. Taking advantage of expanded hardware and software capabilities on stand-alone microcomputers not only is expensive but also can lead to data inconsistencies and less-efficient use of resources. LANs help overcome these problems by providing a way to share hardware, data, and programs and to provide additional management controls over microcomputing. In some companies LANs have even replaced large computer systems and reduced the data processing budget. Replacing large computers with small computers is called downsizing.

The use of LANs has required changes in the way early microcomputer software worked. Specifically provisions had to be made to provide security, control contention for resources, and allow applications to be tailored to individual workstations and user preferences.

Many network applications are available today. For microcomputer networks, applications can be separated into personal productivity applications and workgroup applications. Personal productivity software is available on stand-alone microcomputers. Workgroup productivity applications require the use of a network. The principal personal productivity applications are word processing, desktop publishing, spreadsheets, database management, and presentation services. Workgroup applications, also referred to as groupware, include electronic mail, data interchange, conferencing, meeting systems, and scheduling. The main reason for using LANs today is resource sharing. The ability to increase workgroup productivity may eventually be a more important reason for using a LAN than resource sharing.

There are two general classes of networks, local area networks and wide area networks. Each has characteristics that make them suitable for certain networking situations. Implementing a LAN creates a new layer of responsibility—LAN management. Stand-alone computing relies on distributed management: Each user of a stand-alone system is responsible for managing the resources of that computer. LANs require that an individual or group be responsible for operating and maintaining the shared LAN resources as well as providing for assistance at the individual workstation level.

KEY TERMS

communications medium

computer virus

contention

database management system (DBMS)

desktop computer

diskless workstation

downsizing

electronic calendaring

electronic conferencing

electronic mail (E-mail)

electronic meeting systems (EMS)

encryption

facsimile (FAX) machine

graphical user interface (GUI)

groupware

infrared light

local area network (LAN)

logical security

media access control (MAC) protocol

network server

personal computer (PC)

personal productivity software

physical security

portability

presentation services

security

spooler

switch, data

transparent use

user profile

virtual reality

virus detection software

"what-if" analysis

wide area network (WAN)

workgroup productivity software

workstation

REVIEW QUESTIONS

1. Describe the characteristics of early microcomputer hardware and software.

2. What changes need to be made to transform stand-alone microcomputer software to a shared LAN environment?

3. Explain how a local area network can help people communicate.

4. Explain how a network is used to share resources. What resources are commonly shared?

5. What are personal productivity applications? List four examples of personal productivity applications.

6. What is groupware, or workgroup productivity applications? Identify four workgroup applications.

7. Why is the security needed for microcomputers on a LAN different from the security required for stand-alone microcomputers?

8. What are the differences between managing a stand-alone microcomputer and a LAN?

9. What are the general characteristics of a LAN?

10. Describe some differences between LAN and WAN characteristics.

PROBLEMS AND EXERCISES

1. Research a database management system, word processor, or spreadsheet application that was originally designed to operate in a stand-alone manner and has been enhanced to run on a local area network. What changes were needed to make the application network compatible?

2. If you have access to a LAN, describe what users must do differently when using the LAN (compared to using a stand-alone microcomputer).

3. Identify three responsibilities of a LAN manager.

4. Diskless workstations provide an extra dimension of management control. At a college, diskless systems can help prevent the introduction of computer viruses and the piracy of software. What are the disadvantages of having diskless workstations in an academic LAN environment? Do these disadvantages also apply to corporations? Why or why not?

5. Describe a networking situation in which a WAN might be used in preference to a LAN.

REFERENCES

Becker, Pat. "Down or Out?" *LAN*, Volume 7, Number 10, October 1992.

Chivvis, Andrei M. "Downsizing: The Business Decision." *LAN Times*, Volume 8, Issue 10, May 20, 1991.

Chivvis, Andrei M. "FGIC: A Case Study in Success." *LAN Times*, Volume 8, Issue 10, May 20, 1991.

Stamper, David A. *Business Data Communications.* Redwood City, CA: The Benjamin/Cummings Publishing Company, Inc., 1991.

Watt, Peggy, Soper, Bill, and Berry, Dave. "Deciding on Downsizing." *DBMS*, Volume 4, Number 13, December 1991.

CHAPTER 2

INTRODUCTION TO DATA COMMUNICATIONS

CHAPTER PREVIEW

A detailed knowledge of data communications and networks is not essential to understanding local area networks (LANs) and their connection to other networks. To fully understand LAN technology, however, you should have a basic data communications background. This chapter gives you an overview of data communcations terminology, concepts, and networks, which will help you understand the technical material in later chapters.

In this chapter you will learn about the following:

requirements for communication

what constitutes a network

the OSI reference model

LAN selection criteria

At the conclusion of this chapter you should have a general understanding of the essential elements of communication, network types, how data flows from one network node to another, and the items to consider when selecting LAN hardware and software.

ESSENTIAL ELEMENTS OF COMMUNICATION

For communication of any type to occur, there must be four basic elements: a message, a sender, a receiver, and a medium. Figure 2-1 shows the sender, receiver, medium, and message in a telephone connection. In addition to these four elements, the message should be understandable and there should be some method for error detection. Let us look at each of these components.

The Message

For two entities to communicate, there must be a message. A **message** can have several forms and be of varying length. Data communications message types include files, requests for services, responses to requests, device or

27

network status messages, device or network control messages, and correspondence, such as electronic mail.

The Sender

The **sender** is the transmitter of the message—either a person, an application, or a machine with enough intelligence to originate a message or response without human intervention. The sender can also be a system user,
sensor, badge reader, or other input device.

The Receiver

Receivers include computers, terminals, remote printers, people, and
devices such as drill presses, furnaces, and air conditioners. There can be a
message and a sender without a receiver; however, without a receiver there
is no communication. For instance, signals have been beamed into space in
an attempt to contact intelligent life forms; until something receives these
signals, no communication has taken place. In a LAN a message can be sent
to all nodes saying that a new system feature is available; if all nodes happen to be turned off at that time, no communication occurs.

The Medium

Messages are carried from sender to receiver through some communications
medium. For instance, in oral communication, sound waves are transmitted

Figure 2-1   Essential Elements of Communication

through air (the medium). LANs use several media to transmit data, including wires, coaxial cable, fiber optic cable, radio waves, and infrared light.

Understanding the Message

Even if each of the four components just discussed are present, if the message is not understood correctly, then accurate communication has not taken place. In human communication the most obvious obstacles to understanding are language differences, for which translators or interpreters may be necessary. Computer systems have similar obstacles to overcome. For instance, data can be represented by any of several different codes, the two most common being the **American Standard Code for Information Interchange (ASCII)** and the **Extended Binary Coded Decimal Interchange Code (EBCDIC).** Sometimes you must translate from one code to another to be sure that data is interpreted correctly.

Error Detection

In human communication **error detection** is a frequent and basically simple task because humans can reason and interpret. A human receiver can usually correct grammatical errors, misspellings, and even some misstatements. But computer networks generally don't reason. Even when a human computer operator realizes that a received message is erroneous, that operator may be unable to correct the error. When the receiver is a piece of hardware, incapable of reasoning and unable to detect or correct errors, the user must employ special schemes for determining if an original message has been distorted during transmission. All such schemes involve transmitting additional information along with the data to increase the chances of detecting errors; however, no error-detection schemes can detect every possible combination of errors.

NETWORK DEFINITION

This book is primarily about one type of data communications network, a local area network. There are several types of networks, and therefore the term *network* has a variety of connotations. As a prelude to discussing why people use networks and network applications, you should have an understanding of the term *network* as used in this text.

In electronic communications, there are two basic types of networks. One type of network is a **terminal network.** Figure 2-2 shows that this network consists of a single host computer with attached terminals. In today's networks these terminals may be microcomputers with software and hardware that allow them to emulate a standard terminal. In a terminal network the **host computer** does all or most of the processing, and the terminals simply act as devices through which a person gains access to the host's applications. When the terminal is a microcomputer, the microcomputer may download data from the host for local processing or upload new data to the host for incorporation into other application systems or for distribution to

Figure 2-2   A Terminal Network

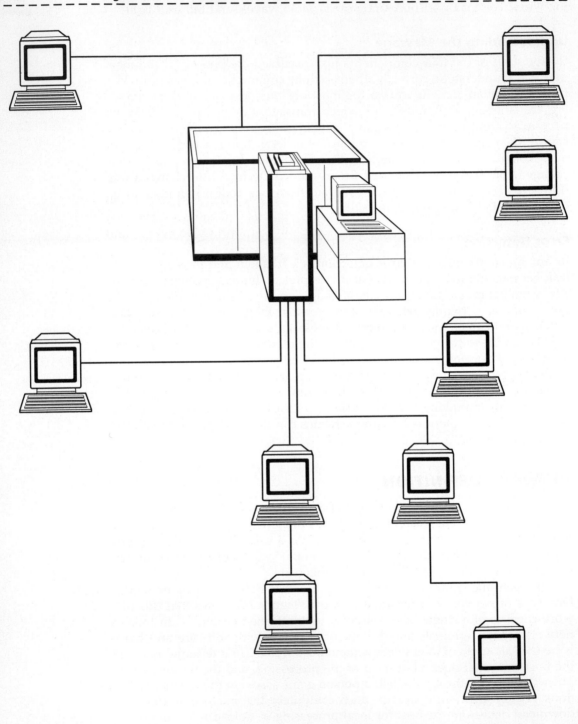

other terminal users. Except for the chapter on connecting a LAN to a host computer or wide area network, this type of network is not addressed in this text.

The second type of network is a **network of computers,** as shown in Figure 2-3. This network consists of two or more computers connected by a data communications medium. The computers are called **nodes,** and individual nodes may have terminals attached to them. Thus a single node on this network can look just like the terminal network described in the previous paragraph. In a network of computers, communication can be from a terminal to its host (the computer to which the terminal is directly attached), a terminal to another node on the network, or among network nodes themselves. Henceforth, unless otherwise stated, the term *network* will refer to this type of network.

There are two general network subtypes, a local area network (LAN) and a wide area **network (WAN).** The fundamental differences between these two network subtypes are distance covered, transmission speed, and

Figure 2-3   A Network of Computers

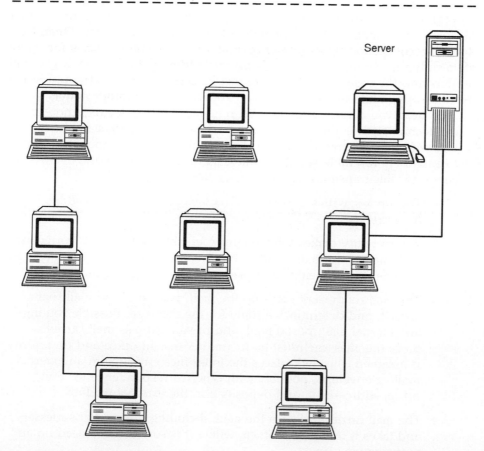

types of nodes. WANs can cover a broader area and use slower-speed communications links than LANs, and generally WANs use mainframes or minicomputers as network nodes. A network may also consist of interconnected LANs and WANs, as illustrated in Figure 2-4.

THE OSI REFERENCE MODEL

The basic objective of a network is for an application in one node to communicate with an application or device on another node. While this may sound simple, some complexities are involved. Many different WAN and LAN implementations are possible, and consequently, so are many different types of interfaces. That is, you need one type of hardware and software to connect to one type of LAN, say a token ring, a different set of hardware and software to connect to a contention bus LAN, and still another type of hardware and software to connect to a particular WAN. Because of the variety of network types available and the frequent need to interconnect them, a thriving business has been created for establishing connections among networks. Moreover the problem of network interconnection is so important that the **International Standards Organization (ISO),** an international agency for the development of a wide range of standards, created a reference model that describes the functions a generic network needs to provide. The **Open System Interconnection (OSI) reference model** has become the basis for many data communications standards. By understanding the OSI model, you will understand the basic functions that must be carried out to move a message from an application on one node to an application on another node.

To help you understand the OSI reference model, let us ignore computer technology for the moment and look at how a worker might send a message from his or her office to a colleague in another location. This simple act can closely resemble sending a message in an OSI network. A possible scenario for this transmission might be as follows:

1. The worker writes a message on a tablet and delivers it to her or his secretary.

2. The secretary makes the memo presentable by typing it, correcting grammatical mistakes, and so on. The secretary places the memo in an interoffice envelope and places it in the outgoing mailbox.

3. The mail room clerk picks up the mail, takes it to the mail room, sorts it, and determines a route for the message. Possible routings are internal mail, postal mail, and private express mail carriers. Since this message must go to another distant office and no priority is assigned, the clerk places the interoffice envelope in an external mailing envelope, possibly with other correspondence for that office, addresses it, and deposits it in the external mailbox.

4. The mail carrier picks up the mail, including the worker's message, and takes it to the post office, where it is sorted and placed on an outgoing mail truck.

Figure 2-4   WAN and LAN Networks Interconnected

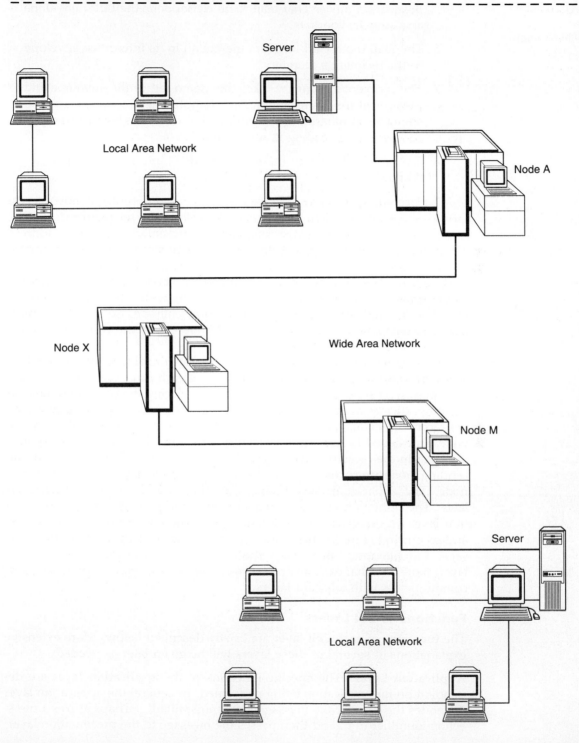

5. The post office physically delivers the mail to the mail room of the destination office. That mail room clerk opens the outer envelope and sorts its contents.

6. The mail room clerk delivers the memo in its interoffice envelope to the recipient's secretary.

7. The recipient's secretary takes the memo out of the envelope and prepares it for the recipient. For example, the secretary may time stamp it, summarize the memo, make comments, set a priority for the recipient's reading it, and so on.

8. The recipient receives the memo, reads it, and reacts to the worker's message.

The preceding scenario described a variety of different functions necessary to move a message from the sender's desk to the recipient's desk. The functions consisted of message composition, presentation services, address determination, enveloping, selecting transmission routes, physical transmission, and so on. In general these same functions must be performed when transmitting a message between computers in a network. The OSI reference model explicitly identifies seven layers of functions that must be performed in network interconnections: application, presentation, session, transport, network, data link, and physical. Figure 2-5 represents the OSI layers in two network nodes.

In the letter-routing example above, each functional layer on the sending side performed a specific set of functions, and each function was performed for a peer layer on the receiving side. That is, placing the correspondence in the interoffice envelope was done by the sending secretary and undone by the receiving secretary. In the OSI model each layer in the sending network node is designed to perform a particular set of functions for its corresponding layer in the receiving network node. That is, the application layer in the sending node prepares the data for the application layer in the receiving node. The application layer then passes the message to the presentation layer. The presentation layer formats the message properly for the presentation layer on the receiving node and passes the data to the session layer, and so on. In Figure 2-5 the solid line shows the physical route of the message, and the dotted lines show the logical route, from peer layer to peer layer. Note also that each layer has a well-defined interface through which it communicates with adjacent layers.

Functions of OSI Layers

The functions of each OSI layer are briefly described below. More extensive explanations of several of these layers will be given later as needed.

Application Layer The specific functions of the **application layer** are dependent on the application being performed. In general the application layer generates the data for the message to be transmitted, perhaps affixes a transaction identifier to it, and then passes the message to the presentation layer.

Figure 2-5   Peer Layers in the OSI Reference Model

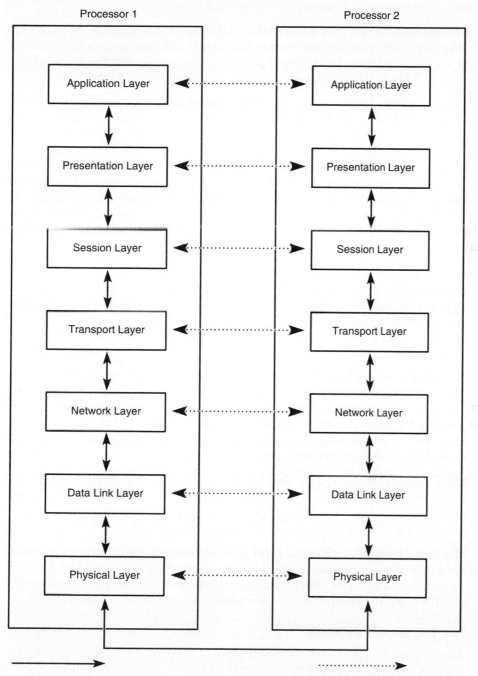

An example of an application layer standard is the X.400 standard for electronic mail systems. This standard describes the application requirements for interconnecting different electronic mail systems.

Presentation Layer   The **presentation layer** accepts a message from the application layer, provides formatting functions, and then passes the message to the session layer. The types of presentation services that might be accomplished include data compression, encryption, and code conversion.

Session Layer   Whenever one application communicates with another, a **session** is said to exist between the two. When you telephone someone you begin a session with that person. However, several events can occur when you call someone: The other party may not be there, they may already be using the telephone, or they may refuse to communicate with you. Each of these events may occur when applications try to communicate. The general functions of the **session layer** are to set up the dialogue between two applications, set up the dialogue rules, and control the dialogue. Specific functions include controlling the data flow and providing recovery if a failure occurs.

Transport Layer   The **transport layer** ensures that all messages are delivered, that no messages are lost or duplicated, and that messages are free of errors. One mechanism the transport layer may use to account for messages is a message sequence number. The transport layer in the receiving node tells the transport layer in the sending node which messages have been successfully received. If a message is not acknowledged, it is sent again.

Network Layer   The **network layer** is responsible for determining the address of the recipient and routing the message accordingly. A variety of paths may exist along which the message can be sent. The network layer chooses the path(s) most appropriate for the message. For example, a short, time-critical message may be transmitted via a leased communication line while a long file transfer may use a satellite link.

Data Link Layer   The **data link layer** is responsible for preparing the message for physical transmission to the next node. Specific functions it performs are low-level error detection, delineation of data, and establishing the protocol by which a node can send and receive data.

Physical Layer   The **physical layer** is responsible for physically transmitting data over the communications medium. It specifies how the data is represented on the medium, the physical connections that must exist between the medium and the computer, and the speed at which transmission occurs.

The OSI Model at Work

An example of the changes a message goes through as it passes from layer to layer of the OSI model is illustrated in Figure 2-6. The example shows a message being transmitted from node A to node M in the network shown in Figure 2-4. Typically each OSI layer adds some control information to the message, a process sometimes called **enveloping.** The steps shown in Figure 2-6 are explained in the following sections.

Application Layer   The application on node A builds a record with a transaction identifier, the number of the account to be updated, the date and time of the transaction, and the amount to be deducted. The transaction identifier tells the message recipient what to do with the record, inserts it, updates it, and so on. The message is illustrated in Figure 2-6(a). The application then invokes a procedure call to send the message to the recipient.

Presentation Layer   The application layer formatted each field in the record being transmitted according to its own format rules. The receiving application may have a different set of format conventions. For example, the sending application may view a date in one format, while the receiving application uses a different date format. The presentation layer is responsible for translating from one format to another. It can do this by changing to a standard transmission format that is converted by its peer layer or by converting it directly to the format expected by the receiving application. The message after such translation has taken place appears in Figure 2-6(b). The presentation layer then sends the message down to the session layer by requesting the establishment of a session.

Figure 2-6   OSI Reference Model Formatting

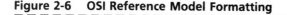

Trans-Id Data Date = dd/mm/yy

(a) Application Layer

Trans-Id Data Date = mm-dd-yyyy

(b) Presentation Layer

| ID | Length | Trans-Id Data Date = mm-dd-yyyy |

(c) Session Layer

| TSAP | ChkSum | ID | Length | Trans-Id Data Date = mm-dd-yyyy |

(d) Transport Layer

| Address | Seq Nbr | TSAP | ChkSum | ID | Length Trans-Id Data Date = mm-dd-yyyy |

(e) Network Layer

| Header | Address | Seq Nbr | TSAP | ChkSum | ID | Length | Trans-ID Data Date = mm-dd-yyyy | Chksum |

(f) Data Link Layer

Session Layer The session layer's major functions are to set up and perhaps monitor a set of dialogue rules by which the two applications can communicate and to bring a session to an orderly conclusion. A session dialogue can be one way (simplex) or bidirectional. In **simplex transmission** one application sends messages to another but receives no messages in return. In bidirectional sessions messages flow in both directions simultaneously (**full-duplex mode**) or in both directions but in only one direction at a time (**half-duplex mode**). **Flow control** refers to setting up message transmission. Once the connection has been made, data transfer can occur. The session layer appends an identifier and length indicator at the beginning of the data block, as illustrated in Figure 2-6(c). These two fields identify the function of the message (which contains user data as opposed to control functions like session establishment or termination).

Transport Layer The transport layer is the first of the OSI layers responsible for actually transmitting the data. The higher layers are oriented toward the data and application interfaces, not to data transmission. The transport layer uses an address called a **transport services access point (TSAP)** to uniquely identify session entities. TSAPs of the source and destination session entities, together with a checksum to detect errors and message sequence numbers, are appended to the message received from the session layer, as shown in Figure 2-6(d). The message sequence numbers ensure that all parts of the message are received and place the parts in the proper order if they were received in a different order than the original sending order. Parts of a message may be received out of order because they have been sent over different paths.

Network Layer The network layer provides accounting, addressing, and routing functions. Upon receiving a message from the transport layer, the network layer logs the event to the accounting system and then prepares the message for transmission to the next node on the path to the destination, node M in our example. It does this by looking up the destination address in its network routing table to find the next address along that path. A routing table for a node in a small network is shown in Figure 2-7. The address and a sequence number are appended to the message, as illustrated in Figure 2-6(e).

Data Link Layer The data link layer is responsible for data delineation, error detection, and logical control of the link. The media access control defined earlier for LANs operates at the data link level. Logical link control consists of determining how and when a station can transmit, connection and disconnection of nodes on the link, and flow control between data link entities. In Figure 2-4 node X is between nodes A and M. The data link layer facilitates flow control between nodes A and X and nodes X and M. Note that data link flow control is for one computer to another, while transport layer flow control is end-to-end, that is, between source and destination applications. To fulfill its function, the data link layer appends a header and trailer to the message, as illustrated in Figure 2-6(f). The header contains a

Figure 2-7   Example of a Network Routing Table

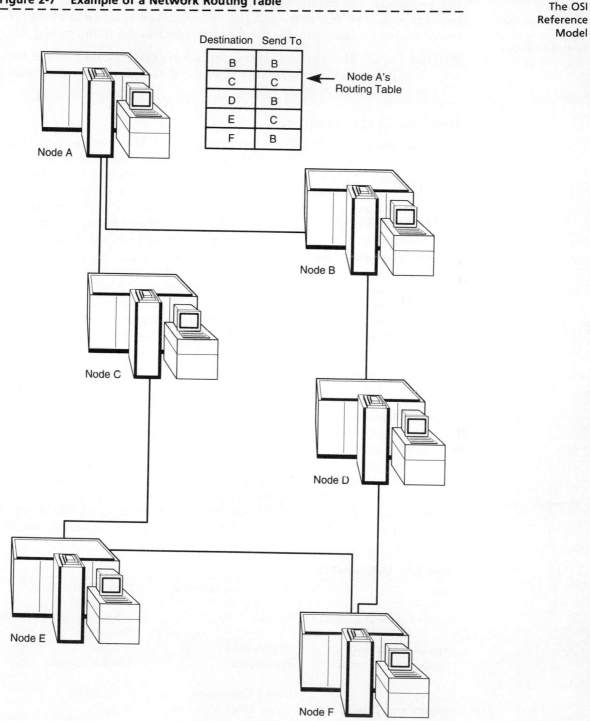

Destination	Send To
B	B
C	C
D	B
E	C
F	B

Node A's
Routing Table

Node A

Node B

Node C

Node D

Node E

Node F

flag to indicate the beginning of the message, the address of the recipient, message sequence numbers, and the message type (data or control). The trailer contains a checksum for the data link block and a frame-ending flag.

Physical Layer   The physical layer does not append anything to the message. It simply accepts the message from the data link layer and translates the bits into signals on the medium.

Functional Layer Standards

You may realize by now that even though the OSI reference model cites seven functional layers, different strategies may be used at each layer. For example, there are many different data link layer protocols in use today. The OSI model will gain power as standards are developed at each layer. With such standards in place, it will be easier to build networks that can be connected to other networks. Even if two networks choose to implement different standards at a given layer, having both networks based on established standards will make their interconnection easier.

Now that you know why we use LANs, the general characteristics of LANs, and the OSI reference model's description of how messages travel from one node in a network to another, let us look at some of the factors we must consider when choosing LAN hardware and software. With this information, we can begin to look at the details of LAN systems.

LAN SELECTION CRITERIA

Table 2-1 lists the major factors to consider when selecting a LAN. You need to provide prospective vendors with sufficient information to size the system. This is best done by analyzing the problems you are trying to solve and any factors that may constrain your selection. Some of these constraints need to be communicated to the potential vendors, while others (for example, your budget) should not be given to vendors. (If you tell vendors how much money you intend to spend or are able to spend, you will be surprised at how many configurations will cost this amount of money.) The effects of the criteria given in Table 2-1 on the selection process are described below.

Table 2.1   LAN Selection Criteria

Cost	Distance and Medium	LAN Software and Hardware
Number of Workstations	Speed	Adherence to Established Standards
Type of Workstations	Applications	Vendor
Number of Concurrent Users	Expandability	Vendor Support
Type of Use	Device Connectivity	Manageability
Number and Type of Printers	Connectivity with Other Networks	Security

Cost

If cost were not a consideration, LAN selection would be easier. You could buy the fastest, biggest workstations and **servers** available and use the most comprehensive LAN software available. Deciding which hardware and software modules fit this description would not be simple, but lack of price constraints would make selection much easier. For most of us, however, cost is an overriding constraint, and you must choose the best solution within your budget. Usually cost is the most inflexible constraint under which you must operate, and in the final analysis the LAN must be a cost-effective solution to your problem.

In general, as the speed of a LAN increases, so does the cost. For instance, the **LAN adapters** that provide computer-to-LAN medium connection for a high-speed LAN are more expensive than those for a low-speed one. Also, as the number of users and workstations increases, so does the cost of the LAN. Each workstation needs a LAN adapter, each of which may cost $300 or more (LAN adapter prices start under $100), and each workstation must have LAN software, (often paid for on a per-station basis). As the number of concurrent users increases, so does the amount of work required of the server. Increased demands on the server require you either to obtain a more powerful computer as a server (sometimes called a platform) or to buy several servers. Moreover installing cabling can be an expensive proposition, particularly in an existing building. An existing building has barriers such as ceilings and walls that restrict your ability to install new cabling. You must pull cables through ceilings and walls rather than simply stringing it in the exposed areas of a new building.

Hardware and software are not the only costs you will incur. Other costs you must plan to incur include the **immediate** and **recurring costs** shown in Table 2-2.

The following sections briefly describe immediate and recurring costs.

Table 2.2   Immediate and Recurring Costs of a LAN

Immediate Costs

Equipment upgrades	Training of users, operators, administrators
Documentation	
Installation of cabling	Site preparation
System software installation	Hardware installation
Creating user environments	Installing applications
Space required for new equipment	Testing
	Supplies and spares

Recurring Costs

LAN management—personnel costs	Hardware and software maintenance

Immediate Costs You may already have some equipment—workstations, printers, and so on—that can be integrated into the LAN. This equipment may need upgrading to function on the LAN. Workstations may need extra memory because the LAN software uses some of each workstation's memory. Workstations will need to have a LAN adapter card installed, or an additional serial or parallel port may be needed if you use a zero-slot LAN. All those involved in working with the LAN must be educated. Even if your company assumes the responsibility for doing this, it will incur an expense in people, time, and materials. You must provide users, operators, and administrators with the proper documentation to allow them to do their jobs effectively. Some of this documentation may come with the system. Additional copies of vendor-supplied documentation may need to be purchased. An organization might also need to write and distribute user procedures for using the LAN.

Installing a LAN usually requires some site preparation. You may need to dedicate work space for the server nodes, which ideally are located in a room with restricted access to protect it from unauthorized use. If you use a conducted medium, you must arrange for a safe way to string the cables between the workstations. Cables should be placed in floor channels, dropped from the ceiling, or otherwise distributed to prevent people tripping over or accidently pulling on cables and breaking the connections. You must install LAN hardware—at a minimum this means cabling and LAN adapters. You may also need to install additional memory.

Another installation task is to load or install the application and system software on the server and the network software on the workstations. To make the LAN easier to use, each user ought to have a LAN **environment.** A user's LAN environment consists of a wide variety of specifications that control the user's access to LAN resources as well as his or her workstation settings. The environment assists in the login process, maps the user to a home directory, and sets search paths for application software. For example, if a user needs to use word processor, spreadsheet, and database applications, the environment is set up to make running those applications easy. Some of the items that might be specified in a user's environment are listed in Table 2-3.

Table 2.3   Some Items Specified in an Environment

Default disk drive	Default disk directory
Disk drive mappings	Disk drive/directory search paths
Printer mappings	Initial program/menu

The LAN must be tested after being installed, and each user environment must be tested to ensure that it meets the user's specific needs. Work space must be allocated to store the new equipment, supplies, and spare parts.

Recurring Costs Some of the costs you incur in setting up a LAN are ongoing. A LAN must be managed. For small LANs this may be a part-time duty for an existing employee. For large LANs it is a full-time responsibility. In either case LAN management represents a recurring expense. The hardware and software you use must be kept up-to-date, and you need to use preventive maintenance on the hardware to keep it running correctly. This can be accomplished by paying for the services when needed or by subscribing to hardware and software maintenance services.

To keep your network operational and to reduce downtime, you may want to stock spares of parts that have a short life or are consumable. For instance, you need to stock toner cartridges for laser printers, printer paper, and so on. These supplies are required for stand-alone systems, so this expense may not vary significantly from your stand-alone needs. Typically an organization will also stock extra LAN adapters and cables. Finally you will probably need a continuing education program. Again, training is required for stand-alone systems; however, on a LAN the users must learn some additional material to be effective LAN users.

Number of Workstations

The effect the number of workstations has on the immediate costs of attaching a LAN has already been discussed. The number of workstations is also a key factor in network configuration. Each LAN is physically capable of supporting some maximum number of workstations. If you exceed that maximum number, you must make some provision for extending the maximum number. A variety of techniques exist for doing this, and each increases the cost of the LAN.

Other workstation costs can be incurred as well. If you intend to use existing microcomputers on the LAN, they may need to be upgraded. For example, for IBM-compatible workstations, you should use DOS version 3.*nn* or later. Because LAN software will be resident in each workstation, the amount of memory available to applications will be reduced. You may therefore need to add memory to some workstations.

Type of Workstations

The type of workstations you use will be a significant influence in your LAN alternatives. If your LAN will consist of Apple Macintoshes, a number of DOS-oriented LAN systems will be eliminated. Similarly, if your workstations are IBM-compatible systems, Apple LANs will be eliminated. The same logic applies if your LAN consists of any of the other possible workstation platforms, for example, those of Sun Microsystems. The LAN hardware and software must be compatible with the workstations used. If you need to mix the types of workstations on the LAN, for example, allowing both Apple and IBM-compatible workstations, you will again eliminate a number of LAN options and, perhaps, increase the cost somewhat.

Number of Concurrent Users

The number of concurrent users may differ from the number of workstations. Some networks have restrictions regarding the number of active users. For example, one network operating system allows four concurrent users, but more than four workstations can be attached. As the number of concurrent users goes up, so does the LAN workload. As the LAN workload increases, you have two basic choices: You can allow system responsiveness to decrease, or you can increase the work potential of the system to maintain or improve the responsiveness. Naturally the second option involves higher costs. Some ways to improve LAN responsiveness are to select a faster LAN (one with higher transmission speeds), use additional or more powerful servers (which means more expensive computers), or use more efficient (and typically more costly) LAN software. The number of concurrent users of an application also has an impact on the cost of the application. Software vendors vary in their user license provisions; in general, however, application costs are directly proportional to the number of concurrent users. That is, as the number of concurrent users goes up, so do software costs.

Type of Use

The impression you may have gained from the preceding paragraph is that having more concurrent users increases the LAN workload. However, you need to understand more about the effect of concurrent users of LAN performance. To do so, let us look at two very different LAN usage profiles.

Suppose the primary LAN application is word processing, and the operating mode is as follows: LAN users access the word processing software on the file server at the beginning of their work shift, they save their documents on a local disk drive, and they periodically print a document. What demands are there on the LAN? The demand is heavy when a user starts the word processing program. It must be **downloaded,** that is, transferred from the server to the workstation. The user does not need LAN services again until he or she prints a document or, in some cases, requires an overlay module for the word processor. An example of an overlay is a spelling checker module. Today's microcomputer software is so rich in capabilities that all the functions cannot always be included in one memory-resident module. An overlay module overcomes this constraint by sharing memory with other overlay modules. LAN requests are therefore infrequent, but the amount of data transferred is large. Adding users may not significantly increase the LAN workload if there is a considerable amount of idle time. If you have used a LAN in a classroom situation, you probably have experienced this type of usage. At the beginning of the class, LAN response is slow because many students are starting an application at nearly the same time, and the demand for LAN resources is high. After that, however, LAN responsiveness improves because the LAN usage becomes intermittent.

Suppose instead that the primary LAN activity is database access. That is, users are continually accessing and updating a database. In this case the

LAN is constantly busy transferring large and small amounts of data. Adding new users in this instance can have a noticeable impact on LAN performance.

Number and Type of Printers

The number and distribution of printers can affect your LAN decision as well. Some LAN operating systems require that network printers be attached to file servers, and each file server can support only so many printers. With such systems, if you have a need for a large number of printers, you may need to add server hardware and software simply to provide printing services. Also, you must be sure that the LAN you select is capable of supporting the types of printers you will be using. Each printer requires printer driver software to direct its operation. The driver software knows how to activate the special printer features needed to print special typefaces, underlining, graphics, and so on. Recall that spooler software is responsible for writing printed output to shared printers. If follows that there must be an interface between the spooler and the printer drivers. Often the drivers are included as part of the server software. When selecting a LAN you must ensure that the printers you plan to use are supported. Also, you must ensure that they are supported in the manner in which you plan to use them. For example, a certain printer may be supported for printing text but not for printing graphics.

Distance and Medium

LANs serve a limited geographical area at high speeds. Distance and speed are related. Attaining high speed over long distances can be very expensive. Thus each LAN has a maximum distance it can cover. Moreover different types of LANs have different distance limitations. The distance is measured in wiring length. If you snake a cable back and forth through an office complex, you may not cover a wide geographical area, but the cable distance can be quite long. In general, as the distance your LAN needs to cover increases, your LAN options decrease. Distances for popular microcomputer LANs range from a few hundred meters to several thousand meters.

The type of medium also influences the selection process. If your facility already has wiring installed, you may select a LAN that can use that type of wiring. Each medium has speed and error characteristics. Earlier you read that **twisted-pair wires** support lower speeds and are more susceptible to errors than either **coaxial cable** or **fiber optic cable.** If your LAN wiring needs to pass through areas that can induce transmission errors (for example, areas that produce electrical or magnetic interference) you may need to select a LAN that can use a more noise-resistant medium, such as coaxial cable or fiber optic cable. One company came to this realization the hard way. In wiring the building with unshielded twisted-pair wires, the company ran the wiring through the shaft of a freight elevator. The freight elevator was seldom used; however, every time it was operated, the motor interfered with the data being transmitted on the LAN, causing numerous failures. Replacing the cabling in the elevator shaft with more error-resistant wiring eliminated the periodic failures.

Speed

LAN speeds can be somewhat deceptive. A LAN speed quoted by the vendor is the speed at which data are transmitted over the medium. You cannot expect the LAN to sustain this speed at all times. Time is required to place data onto the medium and to clear data from the medium. This is done in a variety of ways, and you will learn more about them in Chapter 3. It is important, however, that you select a LAN capable of meeting your performance goals. For example, suppose that you expect access to data on your LAN's file server to have a transfer rate comparable to that of a hard disk, say 5 Mbps. This requirement eliminates a number of low-speed LANs. Common LAN speeds available for microcomputers are 1, 2.5, 4, 10, 16, 20, and 100 Mbps, and the trend is for increasing speeds.

Applications

Most major application software packages are now available in LAN-compatible versions. This does not mean, however, that all applications can run on all LANs. Applications communicate with the network through interfaces called **application program interfaces (APIs),** and a variety of APIs are in use. If the application uses an interface not supported by a particular LAN, then the application probably will not work on that network. Moreover some software is not LAN compatible. Either it cannot run on a LAN at all or it does not support sharing on a LAN but can be used by one user at a time. If you have custom-written applications, they may not be LAN compatible. It is important to determine if software you need to use will work on the LAN you are considering.

Expandability

After installing a LAN you probably will need to add workstations to it or more workstations from one location to another. The ease of doing this varies among implementations. In some instances the ease depends on the medium used and on the way in which the medium was installed. For example, adding new nodes to some systems using twisted-pair wires or coaxial cable is relatively easy. Adding a new node to a fiber optic cable may require cable splicing, which means that you must cut the cable, add the connectors, and rejoin the cable so the light pulses can continue along the cable. Fiber optic cable splicing technology has improved and is not difficult; however, the ease of adding a new node is still more difficult than for twisted-pair wires or coaxial cable.

Device Connectivity

Some organizations need to attach special devices to the LAN, for example, an optical disk. LAN interfaces for such devices may not be available on some LANs or on some LAN file servers. This, of course, reduces your options to the LANs and servers that support the interface.

Connectivity to Other Networks

A LAN is often only one part of an organization's computing resources. Other facets may be a WAN, a large stand-alone computer, or other LANs. If there are other LANs, they may be of different types. When a variety of computing resources are available, it is frequently desirable to connect them. Thus a node on the LAN can communicate with a node on a WAN or can access data on a central mainframe system. A variety of connection capabilities exist, but a given LAN may not support all of them. If you have immediate connectivity needs or anticipate them in the future, you need to select a LAN that will support the connection protocols you expect to use.

LAN Software and Hardware

If you already have microcomputers and associated software and hardware, you probably want to preserve your investment in them. That means that you need to select LAN software and hardware that will be compatible with your existing equipment. Furthermore there are notable differences in the capabilities of LAN software and hardware. These differences may be important in making your LAN selection.

Adherence to Established Standards

There are several standards for LAN implementation. Some LANs conform to these standards while others do not. Several nonstandard LANs have been adopted by many users and have thus become de facto standards. Other LANs are neither covered by standards nor so widely adopted that they have become de facto standards. A LAN's adherence to a standard does not necessarily mean that it is superior to nonstandard LANs. However, there are benefits to choosing a LAN that conforms to a standard. Because standards are published, any company is able to design components that work on the LAN. This creates competition, gives users alternative sources of equipment, and usually drives down the cost of components. Because adopting a standardized LAN is often regarded as a "safe" decision, the community of users is frequently large. This in turn generates a body of expertise that new users can tap for either information or personnel. On the other hand, a nonstandard LAN may provide innovative features that are not yet covered by standards. Adopting such a LAN can place an organization ahead of competition that is using a more conventional system. You can read about LAN standards in Chapter 3.

Vendor and Support

When you select a LAN, you are selecting much more than hardware and software. You are selecting a vendor or vendors with whom you expect to have a long-term relationship. Your vendors ought to be available to help you in times of problems, provide you with maintenance and support, and supply you with spare parts, hardware and software upgrades, and new equipment. You can be more successful with a good vendor and a less capable LAN than with a poor vendor and a superior LAN, especially if your vendor can quickly resolve problems, obtain needed equipment, and so on. Thus you should evaluate prospective vendors and their support policies as carefully as you evaluate the equipment itself.

Manageability

Do not understimate the time and effort required to operate and manage a LAN. Even a small, static LAN requires some management once installed and set up. Occasionally a new user might be added or deleted, new applications added or existing ones updated, and so on. The major on-going activity will be making backups of files, taking care of printer problems, and solving occasional user problems. In a large LAN, however, management can be a full-time job—perhaps for more than one person. In Part 4 you will learn the details of LAN management. During the selection process you must ensure that your LAN will have the necessary management tools or that third-party tools are available. Third-party tools are those written by someone other than the LAN vendor. The tools you need depend on the size of the LAN and complexity of the users and applications involved. As a minimum you should be able to easily accomplish the tasks listed in Table 2-4.

Table 2-4   Basic LAN Management Tasks

User/Group Oriented

Add/delete users and groups	Set user/group security
Set user environment	Solve user problems

Printer Oriented

Install/remove printers	Set up user/printer environment
Maintain printers	

Hardware/Software Oriented

Add/change/delete software	Add/change/delete hardware
Diagnose problems	Establish connections with
Plan and implement changes	other networks

General

Make backups	Maintain operating procedures
Carry out recovery as necessary	Educate users
Plan capacity needs	Monitor the network
Serve as liaison with other network administrators	

Security

With stand-alone microcomputers security generally is not an issue, because stand-alone microcomputer systems are usually single-user systems, and thus, no security provisions were built into the operating systems or application software. As a result, access to the system is tantamount to access to all data stored on that system. By contrast, data in a LAN is shared. Sharing should not, however, imply that all users have unlimited access to all data. The LAN software must have the ability to control access to data. For each user you should at least be able to establish read, write, create, and purge rights for each file. Chapter 8 gives a more comprehensive coverage of LAN security.

SUMMARY

Data communications is a subset of communications in general. All forms of communication—oral, written, electronic, and so on—have common requirements. The four basic components of communication are a sender, a receiver, a medium, and a message. In addition the message must be understood and errors must be detected and corrected. Data communications networks must meet these basic requirements.

There are two major classes of networks, local area networks and wide area networks. A variety of different implementations exists for each of these types. Generally a WAN operates at lower speeds, uses different types of media, and spans a greater distance than a LAN. The main reasons for using networks are communicating, sharing resources, control, security, and cost effectiveness.

Standards organizations have recognized that there are different types of networks and different ways to implement a particular type of network. For example, there are several different types of LANs. One of the major standards efforts is based on the International Standards Organization's Open System Interconnection (OSI) reference model. The OSI reference model defines seven functional layers: application, presentation, session, transport, network, data link, and physical. Each layer carries out well-defined functions. The OSI layer in the sending computer performs its functions for its peer layer in the receiving computer. Messages are passed between adjacent layers through well-defined layer interfaces.

When selecting a LAN you must understand your application and how LAN technology can be applied to meet your application needs. Many general and technical considerations will influence your decision. The general considerations include the following:

cost

number of workstations

type of workstations

number of concurrent users

type of use

number and type of printers

medium and distance

speed

applications

expandability

device connectivity

connectivity to other networks and nodes

LAN sofware and hardware

adherence to established standards

vendor and support

manageability

security

– –

KEY TERMS

American Standard Code for Information Interchange (ASCII)

application layer

application program interface (API)

coaxial cable

data link layer

downloaded

environment

error detection

Extended Binary Coded Decimal Interchange Code (EBCDIC)

fiber optic cable

flow control

full-duplex mode

half-duplex mode

host computer

immediate costs

International Standards Organization (ISO)

LAN adapter

message

network of computers

network layer

node

Open Systems Interconnection (OSI) reference model

physical layer

presentation layer

receiver

recurring costs

sender

server

session

session layer

simplex transmission

terminal network

transport layer

transport services access point (TSAP)

twisted-pair wire

REVIEW QUESTIONS

1. What are the four basic requirements for communication?

2. What does an error-detection scheme for data transmission do?

3. Distinguish between a terminal network and a network of computers.

4. What are the seven layers of the OSI reference model?

5. List two functions performed by each layer of the OSI reference model.

6. Distinguish between immediate and recurring costs. Give two examples of each.

7. Explain how each of the following influences the selection of a LAN:

   a. cost

   b. number of workstations

   c. type of workstations

d. number of concurrent users

e. type of use

8. Explain how each of the following influences the selection of a LAN:

   a. number and type of printers

   b. distance and medium

   c. speed

   d. applications

   e. expandability

9. Explain how each of the following influences the selection of a LAN:

   a. device connectivity

   b. connectivity to other networks and nodes

   c. LAN software and hardware

   d. adherence to established standards

   e. vendor and support

   f. manageability

   g. security

PROBLEMS AND EXERCISES

1. The objective of the OSI reference model is to define and organize the functions required to move a message from an application on one node to a destination on another node. There are some parallels between the way the reference model sends messages and the way in which we send objects from one place to another. Compare the ways in which we prepare and transmit letters, large heavy packages, and new automobiles.

2. Identify the sender, receiver, medium and error detection methods for the following forms of communication:

   a. people speaking in a room

   b. people speaking on a telephone

   c. television and radio

   d. CB radio

   e. telegraphy

3. Security was not listed as an essential element of communication. Do you think that security is an essential element of communication? Justify your decision.

REFERENCES

Stamper, David A. *Business Data Communications.* Redwood City, CA: The Benjamin/Cummings Publishing Company, Inc., 1991.

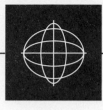

II
HARDWARE

A LAN administrator is often confronted with the task of evaluating different LAN systems and choosing from a variety of vendors. In Chapter 3 we explore the network layouts most frequently proposed by vendors, and you learn to evaluate the capabilities, strengths, and weaknesses of each layout. The key to successful LAN hardware selection is choosing components that can be integrated to form a system. In Chapter 4 you learn the role each component plays in a LAN and some of the considerations to be made in selecting this equipment.

Chapter 3
Topologies and Media Access Control

Chapter 4
LAN System Hardware

TOPOLOGIES AND MEDIA ACCESS CONTROL

CHAPTER PREVIEW

When you select LAN hardware and software, you will probably investigate the capabilities provided by a variety of vendors. You will discover a variety of ways in which you can build a LAN, and you might also hear conflicting statements about the relative merits of these ways. In this chapter you will learn about the network layouts that vendors most commonly propose. The objective of learning about this technology is not only to understand the different available capabilities but also to understand their strengths and weaknesses.

In this chapter you will read about:

baseband and broadband LANs

LAN topologies

media access control protocols

common ways in which topologies and media access control protocols are combined

strengths and weaknesses of different LAN configuration

The LAN components covered in this chapter exist at the OSI physical and data link layers.

THE LAN SYSTEM

As you begin to evaluate vendor responses, you may first read statements intended to give you a general idea of the type of solution proposed. Here are some examples:

"We are happy to propose a Novell IEEE 802.3 network for your consideration."

"We believe a Banyan Vines token ring network will best suit your purposes."

"Our solution uses Microsoft's LAN Manager software and Ethernet."

These statements encapsulate three major LAN components: the LAN software, the **topology,** and the media access control (MAC) protocol. A network topology is the model used to lay out the LAN medium and connecting computers to the medium. A MAC protocol describes the way in which a network node gains access to the medium for transmitting data. The combination of these three components provides much of the uniqueness of a LAN. In general, you will be considering three basic topologies—ring, bus, and star—and two basic media access control protocols—contention and token passing. The major distinctions between one token ring or contention bus or token bus and another are in the network operating system, the hardware, and the medium. A number of vendors, for example, IBM, Microsoft, Banyan, and Novell, provide networking software.

When selecting a LAN you must keep one idea paramount: You are selecting a *system.* The system has many components, and the overall success of the LAN is how well these components can be integrated to form a system. Interoperability is the key, not the efficiency of a single component. For example, you must be able to attach workstations to the LAN and support each workstation's operating systems. The LAN might have IBM or IBM-compatible workstations together with Apple Macintosh or compatible systems, with a variety of operating systems and printers. In this case the system you choose must support all of these components; some networks cannot do this.

LAN MEDIA

The LAN medium conducts the signals from a sending node to a receiving node. The primary LAN media are separated into two general categories: those that use wires or cables to conduct the signals and those that are wireless. Wires and cables are the most common LAN media. **Wireless LANs** are newer and less frequently used. Wireless LAN signals are transferred through the air as light pulses or radio waves rather than through a conductive cable or wire.

Originally most LANs used coaxial cables as their media because they provide high speeds and low error rates and allow for easy expansion. Coaxial cable is still one of the most common LAN media. A coaxial cable consists of one or two conducting wires surrounded by several layers of insulation and shielding, as illustrated in Figure 3-1(a). The shielding protects against external signal interference. The disadvantage of coaxial cable is its cost relative to twisted-pair wires. Two media, twisted-pair wires (telephone wires) and fiber optic cable, have begun to erode the dominance of coaxial cable as the medium of choice. On the low-speed end, twisted-pair wires are frequently used, and fiber optic cable is becoming the medium of choice for high-speed LANs.

Twisted-pair wires are cheaper than coaxial cable, can sustain the speeds common to most microcomputer networks (100 Mbps or lower), and are easy to install. Two standards, Fast Ethernet and **Copper Data Distributed Interface (CDDI),** have been defined for 100-Mbps high-speed LAN transmission. Twisted-pair wires come in two configurations, unshielded and shielded. **Unshielded twisted-pair wires** are more susceptible to signal interference than shielded ones. As the name implies, **shielded twisted-pair wires** have a cladding that protects the wires from external signal interference. Twisted-pair wires are illustrated in Figure 3-1(b).

Fiber optic cable is the medium of choice for high-speed LANs—those operating at 100 Mbps or higher. A fiber optic cable uses light pulses to represent data. The light source is usually either a laser or a light-emitting diode (LED). Fiber optic cables also provide excellent error characteristics. The light signals are not distorted by electrical or magnetic fields. The main disadvantages of fiber optic cable are its expense and the ability to add or remove stations. A fiber optic cable is illustrated in Figure 3-1(c).

A few LANs use wireless connections. The media for these LANs are usually infrared light or radio waves. At least one implementation uses **microwave** radio signals to carry LAN signals. Wireless LANs are relatively new technologies and will probably see increased use. A wireless medium transfers signals from one node to another via a sending and receiving unit similar to the technologies used for satellite or microwave transmission. Wireless media are sometimes used to link LANs in two different locations.

Table 3-1 summarizes the characteristics of common LAN media.

As an alternative to installing its own wiring for a LAN, a company can acquire the transmission circuits from a common carrier, such as a telephone company. One likely technology for this is the **integrated services digital**

Figure 3-1 LAN Conducted Media

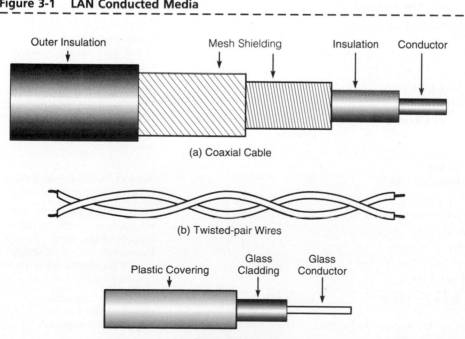

(a) Coaxial Cable

(b) Twisted-pair Wires

(c) Fiber Optic Cable

network (ISDN). ISDN is designed to carry a variety of data types to include voice, text, graphics, and video. It provides a wide range of speed options and may be suitable as the delivery mechanism for some LANs. The advantage of ISDN is that you avoid the cost of installing wires by using your telephone company's wires instead. The disadvantages are that you must make monthly payments for the wiring, and security risks increase because LAN data is routed off premises to your telephone company's switching office and then back to your company's premises, as illustrated in Figure 3-2.

BROADBAND AND BASEBAND TECHNOLOGIES

Broadband transmission and **baseband transmission** are different ways in which you can use a medium. Broadband transmission divides the medium into several channels, thus allowing the medium to be used for distinct transmission needs. Baseband transmission dedicates the entire data-carrying capacity of the medium to the LAN. Most of today's microcomputer LANs use baseband transmission. In the future broadband LANs may become more common, and therefore you should understand both technologies and the advantages and disadvantages of each.

Table 3-1   Media Characteristics

Medium Type	Common Speeds (Mbps)	Error Characteristics
Conducted		
Unshielded Twisted-pair Wires	1, 2.5, 4, 10, 16, 20	Poor relative to other conducted media.
Shielded Twisted-pair Wires	1, 2.5, 4, 10, 16, 20, 100	Better than unshielded twisted-pair wires, but lower than other conducted media.
Coaxial Cable	10, 16, 20, 50, 100	Good, but less than fiber optic cable.
Fiber Optic Cable	10, 16, 20, 50, 100 (2000 possible)	Best of all media. Immune to electromagnetic interference.
Radiated		
Broadcast Radio	2	Subject to interference from other radio transmissions.
Microwave Radio	15 (100 possible)	Directed radio signals. Can be interfered with by other signals of the same frequency (low probability) or can be interfered with by obstructions.
Infrared Light	1, 10	Essentially the same characteristics as for microwave radio.

Broadband Transmission

In a broadband system one communications cable can carry multiple signals simultaneously. For broadband transmission to be practical for a LAN, the medium must have sufficient carrying capacity to allow at least one channel to be fast enough for LAN communication. For small LANs this might be 250 Kbps or faster; for bigger LANs, speeds of 1 Mbps or more are needed to provide proper performance levels. Recall from the previous chapter that the speed you needs depends on how the LAN is being used.

The technique that allows one medium to carry multiple signal channels is similar to a technique used by telephone companies to carry several different telephone conversations over one telephone line. With this technique, called **frequency division multiplexing,** the total bandwidth of the medium is divided into separate subchannels, or frequency bands. The **bandwidth** of a medium is the range of frequencies that the medium can carry without incurring signal disruption. Also described as the carrying capacity of a medium, the bandwidth is measured in hertz, a measure for electrical fre-

Figure 3-2 ISDN LAN Implementation

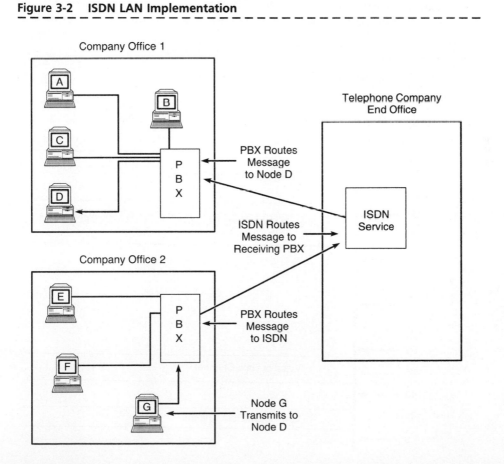

quency that represents one cycle per second, or megahertz (MHz), which represents one million cycles per second. The bigger the bandwidth, the greater the data-carrying capacity of the cable. Coaxial cable is the primary medium used for broadband transmission. Because twisted-pair wires do not have the bandwidth to support a wide range of broadband channels, they are seldom used as a medium for broadband systems.

A proposal for broadband channel allocations, shown in Figure 3-3, is suggested by Harris et al. (1983). Notice that the channels include voice, video, low-speed data, and high-speed data bands.

The voice channel shown in Figure 3-3 can be used for telephones, and the video channel can carry a closed-circuit television channel used for training. The low-speed data channel can have several low-speed subchannels, which can be used to connect terminals to a host system. The high-speed data channel may operate at speeds of 10 Mbps or higher and can be used as the LAN channel. Thus one cable system can meet many of the communications needs of an organization.

Devices are connected to a broadband system through a radio-frequency modem. Suppose that a terminal is set up to use the low-speed data band to communicate with a host computer. The terminal's modem places data on the cable at the frequencies designated for that terminal's subchannel. A

Figure 3-3   Suggested Broadband Frequency Allocations

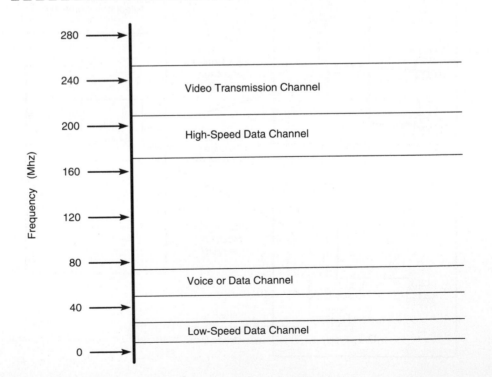

workstation using the high-speed LAN band places its data signal on the cable at the frequencies designated for the high-speed data band, and so on.

Broadband Standards and Use

Several organizations are responsible for formulating data communications standards. Foremost among these are

CCITT (Consultative Committee on International Telegraph and Telephony)

ISO (International Standards Organization)

ANSI (American National Standards Institute)

IEEE (Institute of Electrical and Electronics Engineers)

EIA (Electronic Industries Association)

One object for standardization is the LAN. The two standards organizations most active in this effort are the **IEEE** and the **ANSI.** The IEEE has a committee, called the 802 committee, that has been charged with setting LAN standards. These standards cover the specifics of several LANs as well as define key LAN facets, for example, the use of fiber optic cables. The reports of the committee are referred to by the name of the subcommittee setting the standards. Thus the 802.3 subcommittee formulated the IEEE 802.3 standard that covers LANs based on Ethernet technology, the 802.4 committee formulated the IEEE 802.4 standard for token-passing bus LANs, and the 802.5 committee formulated the IEEE 802.5 standard for implementing token-passing rings.

The IEEE has also adopted several standards for implementing broadband LANs. Broadband standards are a part of the 802.3 and 802.4 specifications. Another broadband implementation is covered by the **manufacturing automation protocol (MAP)** LAN specifications proposed by General Motors Corporation. MAP conforms in some respects to the IEEE 802.4 standard.

Because a broadband system can provide a wide range of communications capabilities, it would seem preferable to a baseband system, which can carry only one data signal. Broadband transmission does, however, have disadvantages. The equipment required for a broadband system is more expensive than that required for most baseband systems. Moreover broadband systems, being more complex than baseband systems, are more difficult to install and manage. For example, frequency allocations need to be designated for each subchannel, and cable disruptions can impair an organization's entire communications system.

Let's take a closer look at baseband transmission.

Baseband Transmission

Baseband transmission allows only one signal to be transmitted on the medium at one time. Most microcomputer LANs use this technology because it is easier and cheaper to implement than a broadband system. Baseband systems are implemented on all three primary media types—twisted-pair wires, coaxial cable, and fiber optic cable—as well as on wireless media. A wide variety of speeds are supported, ranging between several hundred thousand bits per second at the low end to over 100 Mbps on the high end. Speeds of over 2 Gbps have been attained in the laboratory using a fiber optic medium.

Broadband and baseband technologies address how we use the medium. Another issue that must be decided is how we arrange the nodes on the medium—the LAN topology. We introduced topologies in the preceding chapter. We will explore the workings of LAN topologies in more detail in the following sections.

LAN TOPOLOGIES AND THE PHYSICAL LAYER

What do we mean when we talk about a LAN topology? First, the term *topology* derives from a mathematics field that deals with points and surfaces in space—that is, with the layout of objects in space. Thus LAN topology is the physical layout of the network. Another way you can look at a topology is as a model for the way in which you configure the medium and attach the nodes to that medium. In general, LAN topologies correspond to the OSI physical layer described in Chapter 2.

LANs have three basic topologies: ring, bus, and star. Each of these configurations is illustrated in Figure 3-4. Let's take a closer look at each topology.

Ring Topology

In a **ring topology,** illustrated in Figure 3-4(a), the medium forms a closed loop, and all stations are connected to the loop or ring. Let us first look at the basics of a ring and then at some specifics of two implementations.

On a ring data is transmitted from node to node in one direction. Thus if node A in Figure 3-4(a) wants to send a message to node E, the message is sent from A to B, from B to C, and so on, until it reaches node E. Usually node E then sends an acknowledgment that the message was successfully received back to node A, the originator of the message. The acknowledgment is sent from node E to F, and then from F back to A, completing one journey around the loop.

Nodes attached to the ring may be active or inactive. An active node is capable of sending or receiving network messages. An inactive node is incapable of sending or receiving network messages; for example, an inactive node may be powered down. Naturally nodes may go from the inactive state to the active state and from active to inactive. For example, when a worker leaves at night, she might turn her workstation off, placing the workstation in an inactive state. In the morning she powers up her system and brings it into the active state. A failed or inactive network node must not cause the network to fail; an overview of how this happens is covered later in this chapter.

Figure 3-4   LAN Topologies

65
LAN Topologies
and the Physical
Layer

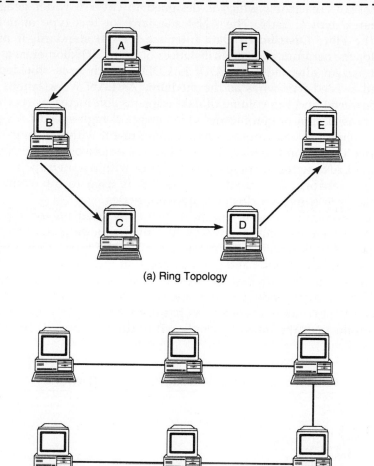

(a) Ring Topology

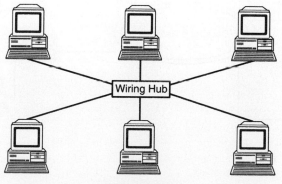

(b) Bus Topology

(c) Star Topology

One type of network that uses a ring topology is a high-speed metropolitan area LAN, which is designed to cover a wider geographical area than a typical LAN. The ANSI standard for this type of network is called the **Fiber Distributed Data Interface (FDDI)** standard. It uses fiber optics for the medium and spans distances of up to 200 kilometers at a speed 100 Mbps. An alternative to FDDI is CDDI, which uses shielded or unshielded twisted-pair wires as the medium. As LAN workstations become more powerful and the volume of data transmission increases (perhaps due to the transmission of graphic and video images), high-speed LANs may be used to connect microcomputers in one department within a company. Currently one use for an FDDI LAN is as a backbone network connecting microcomputer LANs within a company complex or within a metropolitan area. A **backbone network,** illustrated in Figure 3-5, is used to interconnect other networks or to connect a cluster of network nodes.

A **token-passing ring** is the most frequently used microcomputer ring network. **Token passing** is the way in which a node gains access to the medium and passes messages. A token is a unique type of message that is passed from node to node and gives a node that receives the token the right to transmit data. A node that receives the token can send a message to another node, or if the node does not have a message to send, it must pass the token to the next node. Once a node has used the token to send a message, it must relinquish the token by sending it to the next node. Thus one node

Figure 3-5   Backbone Network Connecting Local Area Networks

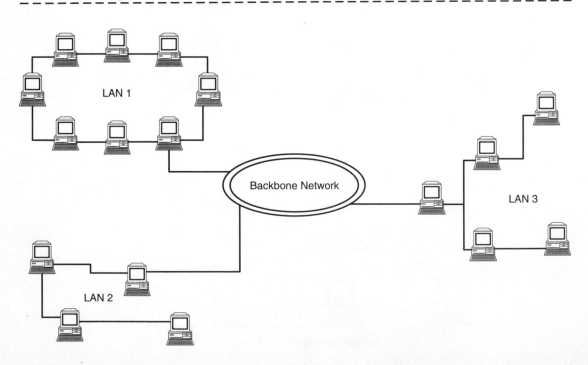

cannot monopolize the medium by keeping the token indefinitely. Token passing is a type of media access control protocol and is discussed in a subsequent section of this chapter.

IBM chose the token ring as its principal LAN topology and media access control protocol. IBM's LAN approach has been widely adopted and conforms to the **IEEE 802.5 standard,** so we will describe it here. Realize, however, that we are only discussing the topology and media access control. The token-passing ring we are describing can be implemented using a variety of different network operating systems to include Novell Netware, Banyan Vines, and IBM's LAN Server.

In IBM's Token Ring network, stations (nodes) are connected to a **multistation access unit (MAU or MSAU),** as shown in Figure 3-6. You can see that this configuration looks somewhat like the star configuration of Figure 3-4(c): The MAU forms the ring internally. Figure 3-7 shows the connection of two MAUs. IBM Token Ring speeds are 4 and 16 Mbps using twisted-pair wires or fiber optic cable as the medium. The 16 Mbps speed originally required fiber optic cable or shielded twisted-pair wires, and these two media are the best to use at that speed. Unshielded twisted-pair wires have been used at 16 Mbps, but this medium is subject to signal disruption at high speeds. With technology improvements, unshielded twisted-pair wires may become better-suited to high data transfer rates. Both speeds are supported within the same LAN; that is, transmission between two stations can be at 4

Figure 3-6   Ring Connections Established by a MAU

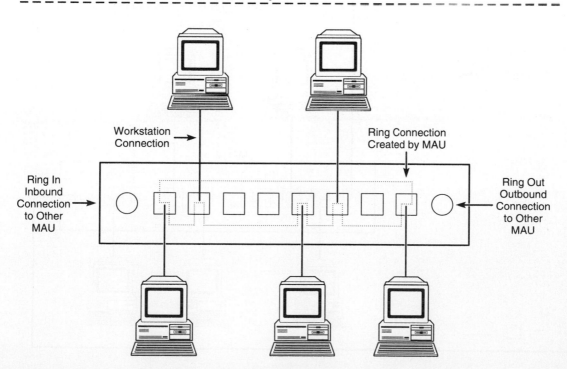

Workstation
Connection

Ring Connection
Created by MAU

Ring In
Inbound
Connection
to Other
MAU

Ring Out
Outbound
Connection
to Other
MAU

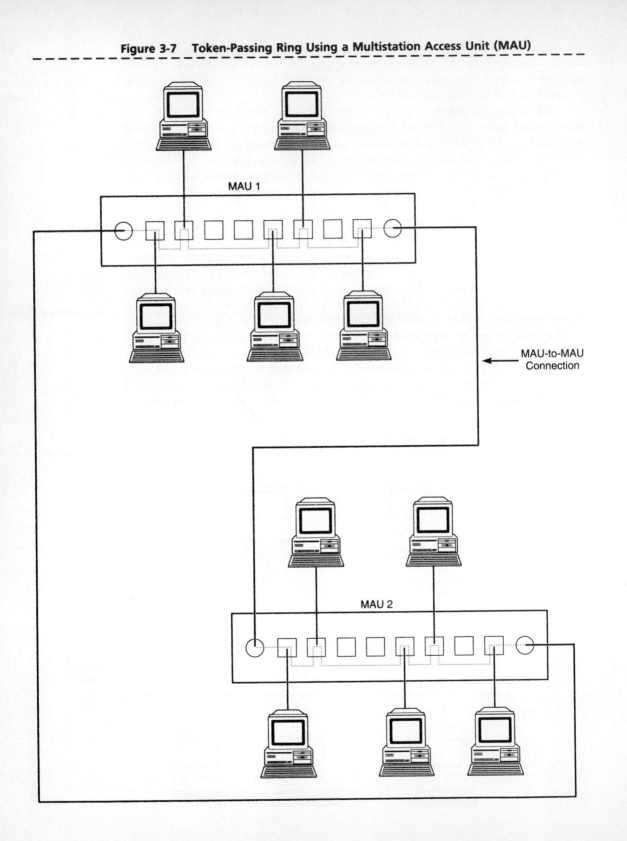

Figure 3-7   Token-Passing Ring Using a Multistation Access Unit (MAU)

Mbps while two other stations communicate at 16 Mbps. IEEE 802.5 speeds are 1 and 4 Mbps, but you can expect these speeds to increase.

Bus Topology

In a **bus topology,** illustrated in Figure 3-8(a), the medium consists of a single wire or cable to which nodes are attached. Unlike a ring, the ends of the bus are not connected. Instead the ends are terminated by a hardware device aptly called a **terminator.** The purpose of the terminator is to eliminate signal feedback or signal loss at the endpoints. A variation of a bus topology, illustrated in Figure 3-8(b) has spurs to the primary bus formed by interconnected minibuses. This variation of the bus topology is quite common.

As with ring topologies, there are several standards that describe a bus implementation. The most common of these is an implementation originally known as **Ethernet.** Ethernet LAN specifications were originally proposed by Xerox Corporation in 1972. Soon thereafter Xerox was joined in establishing the Ethernet standard by Digital Equipment Corporation (DEC) and Intel Corporation. The IEEE 802 committee then developed the **IEEE 802.3 standard,** which encompasses most of the premises of the original Ethernet specification. Thus the IEEE 802.3 standard is sometimes referred to as an Ethernet implementation. The **IEEE 802.4 standard** also proposes a bus technology. The primary difference between the two is the media access control protocol. The IEEE 802.3 standard specifies a contention protocol, and the 802.4 standard uses a token-passing protocol. Again, these protocols are covered later in this chapter.

The common speeds of bus LANs are 1, 2.5, 5, and 10 Mbps. Versions of the IEEE 802.3 and 802.4 standards specify each of these speeds. Speeds of 50, 80, and 100 Mbps exist and are found in LANs with high demands for data transfer. IEEE 802.3 and 802.4 media are either twisted-pair wires or coaxial cables. Very high-speed bus architectures use coaxial cables or fiber optic cables as media. Fiber optic cables are also used for 802.3 LANs. However, the IEEE 802.3 and 802.4 standards have not included specifications for fiber optic interface as of this writing. You can expect these standards to eventually encompass fiber optic cables. Ethernet technology has also been implemented using microwave radio as the medium.

Star Topology

Figure 3-9 shows true **star topology,** which consists of a central computing node to which all other nodes are directly connected. This type of topology, however, is rather rare in microcomputer networks. A variation called a **star-wired LAN** has gained wide acceptance. In a star-wired LAN, a wiring hub is used to form the connection between network nodes. An example of this configuration is shown in Figure 3-4(c). Two common star-wired LANs are known as ARCnet and StarLAN.

ARCnet technology was developed in the 1970s by Datapoint Corporation to form networks of their minicomputers. The technology was well de-

Figure 3-8a   Bus LAN with Spurs

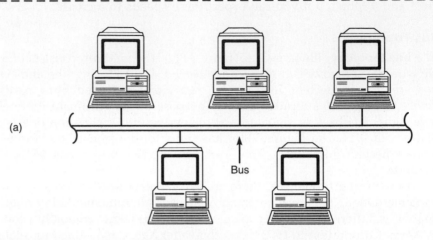

(a)

Bus

Figure 3-8b   Bus LAN with Spurs

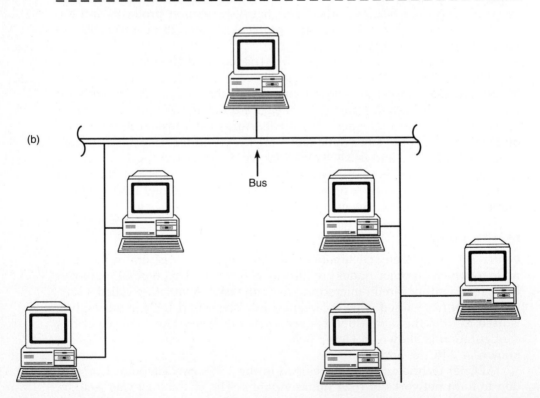

(b)

Bus

veloped when microcomputer LANs were evolving, and the technology was readily adopted for microcomputer LANs. Because it has been so widely used, ARCnet has become a de facto microcomputer LAN standard and also has been submitted to ANSI for formal standardization. An ARCnet configuration, illustrated in Figure 3-10, uses both active and passive hubs to connect network nodes. An **active hub** allows cable runs of up to 2000 feet between the hub and a workstation. A **passive hub** allows cable runs between a workstation and a passive hub of 100 feet. The reason for this difference is that the active hub regenerates the signal before transmitting to a node, while a passive hub does not. ARCnet speeds are 2.5 Mbps and 20 Mbps, and both speeds can be used in the same network. ARCnet media are usually either twisted-pair wires or coaxial cables. Fiber optic cables are also used for ARCnet LANs, primarily in high-speed implementations.

StarLAN technology was developed by American Telephone and Telegraph (AT&T) Corporation. The topology was also adopted and marketed by several other companies and has been included as a low-cost, low-speed option in the IEEE 802.3 standard. Originally the StarLAN speed was 1 Mbps, but today 10 Mbps implementations are also available. A StarLAN configuration is similar to the LAN illustrated in Figure 3-4(c). Note that the configuration is also similar to that of the ARCnet configuration shown in

Figure 3-9   Star Topology

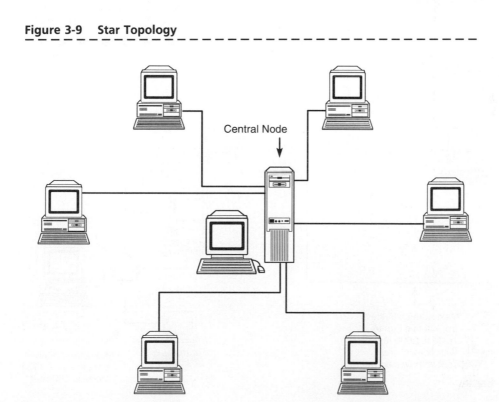

Figure 3-10   ARCnet with Active and Passive Hubs

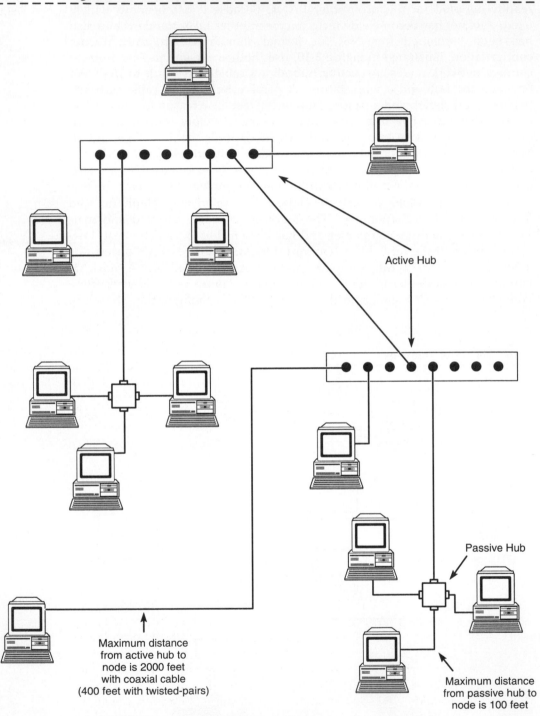

Active Hub

Passive Hub

Maximum distance
from active hub to
node is 2000 feet
with coaxial cable
(400 feet with twisted-pairs)

Maximum distance
from passive hub to
node is 100 feet

Figure 3-10. The primary medium used for StarLAN implementations is twisted-pair wires.

LAN topology forms half of the LAN's circulatory system—its veins and arteries. The second half of the LAN circulatory system relates to the functions of the heart, pumping data through the system's medium. These functions are known as media access control (MAC). Referring back to the OSI reference model discussed in Chapter 2, MAC functions are found in the data link layer. Let us now look at these important functions.

DATA LINK AND MEDIA ACCESS CONTROL PROTOCOLS

The physical layer of the OSI reference model describes the medium, the connectors required to attach workstations and servers to the medium, and the representation of signals using the medium—for example, voltage levels for baseband transmission or frequencies for broadband transmission.

Once connected to the medium, a network node must have the ability to send and receive network messages. This function is described by the data link layer of the OSI reference mode. A convention, or protocol, must exist to define how this function is accomplished. The method by which a LAN workstation is able to gain control of the medium and transmit a message is called a media access control (MAC) protocol. The MAC protocol is implemented in LANs as one of two sublayers of the OSI reference model's data link layer.

Data Link Protocols

In general, a **data link protocol** establishes the rules of gaining access to the medium and for exchanging messages. To do this, the protocol describes several aspects of the message-exchange process, of which five of the most important are

delineation of data

error control

addressing

transparency

code independence

Delineation of Data A data link protocol must define or delineate where the data portion of the transmitted message begins and ends. You may recall from the discussion of the OSI reference model in Chapter 2 that each layer may add data to the message it receives from the layers above it. The data link layer is no exception to this. Some of the characters or bits it adds to the message may include line control information, error detection data, and so on. When these fields are added, a data link protocol must provide a way to distinguish between the various pieces of data. This can be accomplished in two basic ways: by framing the data with certain control characters or by using a standard message format wherein data is identified by its position within the message.

The framing technique is used in two types of data link protocols, asynchronous transmission and binary synchronous transmission. Asynchronous transmission sends one character at a time. Each character is framed by a start bit and a stop bit, as illustrated in Figure 3-11(a). In binary synchronous transmission multiple characters are transmitted in a single block. Special characters are reserved to indicate where fields begin and end within the message. For example, in Figure 3-11(b) the STX characters indicate the beginning of the data, and the ETX characters indicate the end of the data to the receiving node.

Many of today's LANs use a standard message format for sending data. For example, an Ethernet message has several distinct parts, as illustrated in Figure 3-12. The message frame begins with a 64-bit synchronization pattern. The synchronization bits give the receiving node an opportunity to sense the incoming message and establish time or synchronization with the sending node. The message is a stream of continuous bits, so it is important that the receiving node is able to clock the bits in as they arrive. The IEEE 802.3 standard uses a 64-bit synchronization pattern; however, the standard

Figure 3-11a Character Framing in Asynchronous Transmission

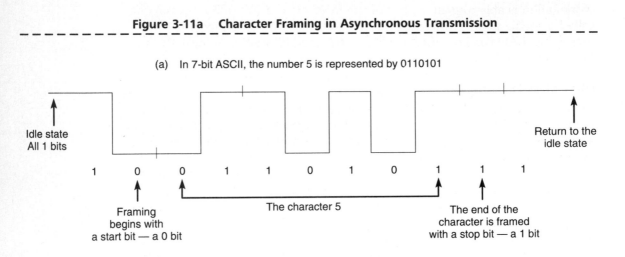

(a) In 7-bit ASCII, the number 5 is represented by 0110101

Idle state
All 1 bits

Return to the
idle state

1   0   0   1   1   0   1   0   1   1   1

Framing
begins with
a start bit — a 0 bit

The character 5

The end of the
character is framed
with a stop bit — a 1 bit

Figure 3-11b Binary Synchronous Data Link Control Characters—STX and ETX

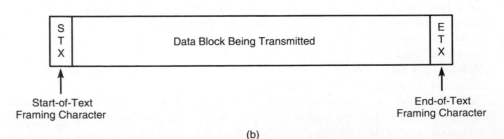

| S T X | Data Block Being Transmitted | E T X |

Start-of-Text
Framing Character

End-of-Text
Framing Character

(b)

divides this into a 56-bit group and an 8-bit group. The first 56 bits are for synchronization, and the 8 bits that follow signal the start of the frame and thus indicate where the first bit of the remaining frame can be found. The next two fields are the addresses of the destination node and the sending node. Each address is 48 bits long.

The 16-bit field type is a control field. In the IEEE 802.3 standard, this represents the length of the data field that follows. The length is expressed as the number of octets of data. An **octet** is a group of 8 bits. If the message is short, extra bits may be added to make the entire message sufficiently long to allow it to clear the length of the network before the sending node stops transmitting. This is essential to ensure correct transmission. The frame check sequence is a 32-bit **cycle redundancy check (CRC)** field. This is used for error detection.

Error Control   Error control is used to determine if data is corrupted during the transmission. This might happen if lightning strikes a wire carrying the data or if there is a loose connection at the wiring interface. To detect errors, additional data is attached to the message, for example, the 32-bit CRC field in the Ethernet message of Figure 3-12. The additional data allows the recipient to make a check to see if errors have occurred. You may be familiar with an error-detection scheme called parity. This is quite a primitive error-detection technique. Today most state-of-the-art data link protocols use the more complex and efficient cyclic redundancy check error-detection scheme.

Addressing   Communication between two network nodes is accomplished through an addressing scheme. Network addressing is similar to addressing we use for postal mail. A postal address is a hierarchical addressing scheme, with the hierarchy being individual recipient, street address, city, state, country, and zip code. Networks also use a hierarchical addressing scheme, with the hierarchy being application, network node, and network. Like postal addresses, network addresses must be unique; otherwise ambiguity arises as to which node is the recipient. At this point we are concerned only with network node addressing, not network or application addressing.

Each network has a specific way in which it forms station addresses. In Ethernet and the IBM token-passing ring, each address is 48 bits long. Each Ethernet or IBM token-ring LAN adapter card has its address set by the manufacturer. This ensures that all nodes, regardless of location, have a unique address. In ARCnet a node address is an 8-bit entity, and the LAN administrator typically sets the node address through switches on the LAN adapter. On a LAN, node source and destination addresses typically are included in the headers of messages being transmitted.

Figure 3-12   An Ethernet Message Format

Synchronization 56 Bits	Start frame 8 Bits	Destination Address 48 Bits	Source Address 48 Bits	Message Length 16 Bits	Data - Number of Bits Is Variable	Cyclic Redundancy Check - 32 Bits

Transparency   **Transparency** refers to the ability of the data link to transmit any bit combination. In the binary synchronous data link protocol (shown in Figure 3-11(b), the start-of-text and end-of-text framing characters have special meaning. These characters can be sent as part of the data only when special considerations are made. Without these special considerations, the protocol is not transparent. We like protocols to be transparent because they can be used to transfer binary data like object programs as well as text data. The Ethernet message illustrated in Figure 3-12 does provide transparency: No bit patterns in the data field can cause confusion in the message.

Code Independence   **Code independence** means that any data code, for example, ASCII or EBCDIC, can be transmitted. These codes use different bit patterns to represent many of the characters. Code independence is important because often you must communicate with or through a computer having a different data code than your computer. In the Ethernet protocol this is accomplished by sending data in groups of 8 bits, called octets. The 8 bits are not tied to any particular code, thus any code can be used. If your computer uses a 7-bit code, like one of the two ASCII codes, the only requirement is that the total number of bits transmitted be divisible by 8. Thus, if you are sending 100 7-bit characters, the total number of bits in the data portion must be 704. The last four bits are added to pad out to an integral number of octets. (700 / 8 = 87.5, and an integral number of octets must be transmitted; thus 704 bits are necessary since 704 is a multiple of 8.)

MAC Protocols

LAN technology adheres to two primary data link protocols, token passing and contention. In the IEEE 802 standards efforts, the committee divided the data link layer into two sublayers, **logical link control (LLC)** and MAC, as illustrated in Figure 3-13. The LLC provides the functions of flow control, message sequencing, message acknowledgment, and error checking. The MAC layer describes token passing and contention.

Contention   In a pure contention MAC protocol, each network node has equal access to the medium. While variations of this protocol exist, essentially it works like this; Each node monitors the medium to see if a message is being transmitted. If no message is detected, any node can begin a transmission. The act of listening to the medium for a message is called carrier sensing, because when a message is being transmitted, a carrier signal is present. Several nodes can have messages to send. Each of them may detect a quiet medium, and each may begin to transmit at one time. The ability for several nodes to access a medium that is not carrying a message is called multiple access.

If two or more nodes begin to transmit at the same time, a **collision** is said to occur. Multiple simultaneous transmissions cause the messages to interfere with each other and become garbled. It is imperative that collisions be detected and that recovery be effected. When a collision occurs, the messages will not be transmitted successfully. On detecting a collision, the sending nodes need to resend their messages. If both nodes immediately attempt to retransmit their messages, another collision might occur. Therefore, each node waits a small, randomly selected interval before attempting to retransmit. This reduces the probability of another collision.

There is only a small time interval during which a collision can occur. For example, suppose that two nodes at the extremities of a 1000-meter bus network have a message to send and that the medium is not being used. The collision interval is the time it takes for a signal to travel the length of the cable. Since the signal travels at the speed of light, the collision window is the time it takes for the signal to travel 1000 meters, the signal's propagation delay. The propagation delay is approximately 5 nanoseconds per meter. For a 1000-meter segment, the maximum propagation delay is therefore approximately 5 microseconds (5 millionths of a second). Although this interval is small, collisions can still occur.

The media access control technique just described is known as **carrier sense with multiple access and collision detection (CSMA/CD).** It is the most common of the access strategies for bus architectures. The CSMA/CD media access control protocol, sometimes referred to as listen-before-talk, is summarized in Table 3-2. You should note that the CSMA/CD protocol is a broadcast protocol. All workstations on the network listen to the medium and accept the message. Each message has a destination address. Only a

Figure 3-13 Two Bottom Layers of IEEE Standard—LLC and MAC Sublayers

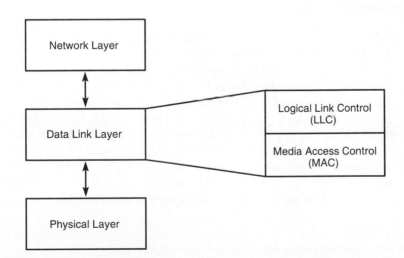

Table 3-2 CSMA/CD Media Access Protocol

1. Listen to the medium to see if a message is being transmitted.
2. If the medium is quiet, transmit message. If the medium is busy, wait for the signal to clear and then transmit.
3. If a collision occurs, wait for the signal to clear, wait a random interval, and then retransmit.

workstation having an address equal to the destination address can use the message. Using a broadcast technique makes it easy for new workstations to be added and taken off the network.

CSMA/CD is known as a fair protocol, meaning that each node has equal access to the medium. In a pure CSMA/CD scheme, no one node has priority over another. Variations of this protocol exist that give one workstation priority over another and minimize the likelihood of collisions. One of these protocol variations divides time into transmission slots. The length of a slot is the time it takes a message to travel the length of the medium. Nodes on the network are synchronized and can begin a transmission only at the beginning of its allocated time slot. This protocol has been proven to be more efficient for networks with lots of message traffic.

A variation of CSMA/CD is **carrier sense with multiple access and collision avoidance (CSMA/CA).** This protocol attempts to avoid collisions that are possible with the CSMA/CD protocol. Collisions are avoided because each node is given a wait time before it can begin transmitting. For example, suppose that there are 100 nodes on the network and the propagation delay time for the network is one millisecond. Node 1 can transmit after the medium has been idle for one millisecond. Node 2 must wait two milliseconds before attempting to transmit, node 3 must wait three milliseconds, and so on. Each node, therefore, has a specific time slot during which it can transmit and no collisions will occur. However, the node with the lowest time slot may experience long delays in getting access to the medium.

Token Passing   The second major media access control protocol is token passing. It is used on both bus and ring topologies. Token passing is a round-robin protocol in which each node gets an equal opportunity to transmit. The token-passing protocol is summarized in Table 3-3. With token passing, the right to transmit is granted by a token that is passed from one node to another. Remember that a token is a predefined bit pattern that is recognized by each node. In a ring topology, the token is passed from one node to its adjacent node, as illustrated in Figure 3-4(b). On a token-passing bus, the order of token passing is determined by the address of each node. The token is passed in either ascending or descending address order. If it is passed in descending order, the lowest address station passes the token to the node with the highest address. The routing of a token from high to low addresses in a token-passing bus is illustrated in Figure 3-14.

Table 3-3   Token-Passing Media Access Control Protocol

1. Wait for transmit token.
2. If transmit token is received and there is no message to send, send the token to the next node.
3. If transmit token is received and there is a message to send then
   a) transmit message
   b) wait for acknowledgment
   c) when acknowledgment is received, pass token to next node

When a node obtains the token, it has two options: it can transmit a message or, if it has no message to send, it can pass the token to its neighbor node. If the node has a message to transmit, it keeps the token by changing the format of the message header from "token" to "transmit" and sends the message. The message recipient keeps the message and then transmits it back onto the network. The message eventually arrives back at the sending node. When a node receives the message it sent, it accepts the message as an acknowledgment that the message was received successfully. The transmitting node then activates the token by sending it to the next node. The token-passing protocol does not allow a node to monopolize the token and hog the network. Note that, unlike the CSMA/CD protocol, the token-passing protocol does not allow collisions.

Token-Passing Ring   In token passing, the token can become lost if a node holding the token fails or if transmission errors occur. To allow recovery from this, one node is designated as the active monitor. Other nodes are designated as standby monitors. The active monitor periodically issues a message indicating that it is active. The standby monitors accept this status

Figure 3-14   Token-Passing Bus

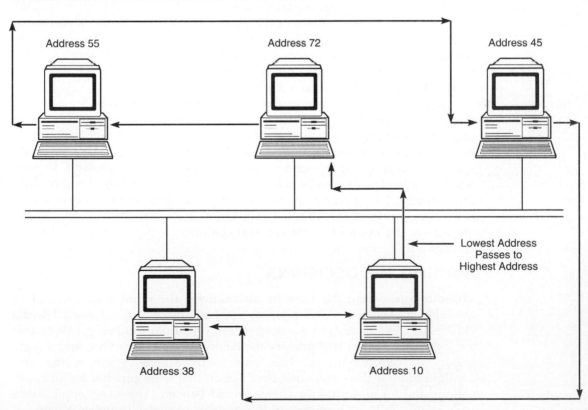

Path of the Token Based on Descending Station Address

and remain in standby mode. If the active monitor message fails to appear on time, a standby monitor assumes the active monitor role. A major function of the active monitor is to ensure that the token is circulating. If the token does not arrive within a certain amount of time, the active monitor generates a new token. This technique is guaranteed to work, as the token transmit time is very predictable.

Token-Passing Bus   Token passing is a bit different on a token-passing bus. On a bus the token is passed from one workstation to another based on station addresses. As mentioned earlier, the token can be passed in ascending or descending address order. Let us assume that the token is passed in descending address order, so the station with the lowest address forwards the token to the station with the highest address. This token-passing scheme is outlined in Table 3-3. Such a protocol must allow for new workstations to be inserted and active ones deactivated.

Suppose a station attempts to send the token to its next station, and that station has been shut down. Recovery must be possible when a station goes from active to inactive status. For example, when a sending station does not receive the token back in a prescribed interval, the sending station transmits the token to its neighbor again. If a second failure occurs, the sending station assumes that the neighboring station is inactive and issues a "who is next" message, asking for the address of the next station. The "who is next" message contains the address of the unresponsive station. The successor of the failed station recognizes the address in the "who is next" message as its predecessor station and responds. If that node has also failed, another "who is next" message is then sent out with the entire address range of the LAN. If any other stations are active, they respond.

Allowance also is made in the token-passing bus protocol for new stations to enter the LAN. Periodically stations issue a "solicit successor" message. This message contains the sending station's address and the address of that station's current successor node. Stations receiving this message inspect the addresses of the sender and the successor in the message. If a station has an address that falls in between these two addresses, it responds to the message. Two stations can respond at the same time. In this case a collision occurs, as in CSMA/CD, and collision resolution is effected. This allows an orderly process for insertion of new stations.

MAKING THE DECISIONS

Without considering the software alternatives, the number of alternatives available in choosing a LAN is large. You have three basic conducted media choices or three choices in the new wireless medium technology, three major topology choices, two primary media access control choices, and a wide variety of vendor choices. The issue then becomes which is the best configuration. If there were one clear option that were superior for all applications and for all users, the choice would be easy. However, applications vary significantly with respect to the number of nodes, number of concurrent users, data access needs, distance spanned, and budget. To help you make the right decision, we can offer only tradeoffs that you can consider.

Token Passing and CSMA/CD Compared

The pros and cons of each MAC protocol are summarized in Table 3-4. Note that each protocol has its advantages and disadvantages. In practice both have been noted to have good performance.

Medium Tradeoffs

In selecting a LAN medium, you have four basic options—twisted-pair wires, coaxial cable, fiber optic cable, and wireless media. Each has advan-disadvantages relative to cost, speed, availability, and expandability. The first two criteria are self-explanatory, but a few words about availability and expandability are appropriate. One meaning of *availability* is the ability of the medium to be used by the hardware. This addresses the issue of interfaces. Wireless media are quite new on the LAN scene, and interfaces still need to be created for some workstations. This will happen over time. Fiber optic cables are not readily available for some network types. For example, the IEEE 802.3 standard for CSMA/CD LANs does not yet cover a fiber optic interface; despite this, fiber optic cables are being used on some CSMA/CD bus systems. The availability of fiber optic LAN adapters for this type of LAN is

Table 3-4   Comparison of Token-Passing and CSMA/CD Media Access Control Protocols

Token-Passing	CSMA/CD
Equal access for all nodes	Equal access for all nodes
Predictable access window	Access window can be unpredictable
Maximum wait time to transmit is token circulation time	Maximum wait time to transmit is unpredictable and depends on collisions
Average wait time to transmit is predictable—half the maximum circulation time	Average wait time to transmit is unpredictable
Network congestion does not adversely affect network efficiency	Network congestion may result in collisions and reduce network efficiency
A node needs to wait for the token before being able to transmit	A node may be able to transmit immediately
One node cannot monopolize the network	One node may be able to monopolize the network
Large rings can result in long delays before a node obtains a ring	A node can transmit when network is quiet
Consistent performance for large, busy networks	Unpredictable performance for large, busy networks due to possibility of collisions

more limited than for twisted-pair wires or coaxial cable. Availability also refers to ease of installation. Wireless media are easier to install in a finished building than wire media.

Expandability refers to how easy it is to add new stations. Adding a station to wireless media ought to be quite easy. Adding a new station to a fiber optic cable is more of a problem because the cable must be cut and new connectors installed. The relative capabilities of these media are outlined in Table 3-5.

Topology and Protocol Tradeoffs

We will consider the three primary combinations of topology and protocol: CSMA/CD bus, token bus, and token ring. The StarLAN model LAN is covered under the IEEE 802.3 standard, and its characteristics are similar to that of the CSMA/CD bus. As of this writing, wireless LANs are so new that tradeoff data regarding their use is not readily available. When specifics are required, we will use popular implementations as examples: Ethernet or an IEEE 802.3 implementation for CSMA/CD buses, ARCnet for token buses, and IBM's Token Ring. Table 3-6 is a summary of the topologies and protocols, which are described in the following sections.

CSMA/CD Buses Most CSMA/CD bus implementations use either twisted-pair wires or coaxial cable. Less frequently, fiber optic cable and microwave radio are used. As previously stated, the IEEE 802.3 standard has not yet set the standard for using fiber optic cable. Common speeds for

Table 3-5 Medium Comparisons

Medium	Cost	Speed	Error	Security
Unshielded Twisted-Pair Wires	Low	to 10 Mbps	Poor	Fair
Shielded Twisted-Pair Wires	Low	to 20 Mbps	Good	Fair
Coaxial Cable	Moderate	to 100 Mbps	Excellent	Fair
Fiber Optic Cable	High	to 2.2 Gbps	Excellent	Good
Microwave Radio	High (new technology)	to 15 Mbps (100 Mbps possible in future)	Poor. Can suffer from interference. Weather or objects may affect signals.	Poor. Signal can be intercepted.
Broadcast Radio	High (new technology)	230 Kbps but 10 Mbps possible)	Poor. Can suffer from interference from other radio broadcasts.	Poor. Signal can be intercepted.
Infrared Light	High (new technology)	to 10 Mbps	Poor. Can suffer from interference from objects or weather.	Poor. Signal can be intercepted.

these LANs are 1 and 10 Mbps, with 10 Mbps being the more common. Speeds of 100 Mbps are also available. The distances spanned by these networks vary, but IEEE 802.3 standard, which covers several implementations, specifies 925, 2500, and 3600 meters. The number of supported nodes also varies. In the IEEE standard one implementation allows 150 nodes, and another allows 500. The number of nodes allowed is a hardware-based limit and addresses the issue of connectivity. The network operating system and performance needs may also limit the number of network nodes. Some network operating systems restrict the number of network nodes. We discuss network operating systems in Chapter 5.

One of the things you will want to know about a network is its performance. Performance depends on both the hardware and the software. The number of combinations of hardware and software is large, so let us look at the general outlook for CSMA/CD bus systems. The major concern people have voiced regarding CSMA/CD bus performance is its capacity under load. As the number of users and the number of messages being sent in-

Table 3-6 LAN Topology and Protocol Summary

	IEEE 802.3 or Ethernet	IBM's Token Ring	ARCnet	StarLAN
Speed	10Mbps	4 or 16 Mbps	2.5 or 20 Mbps	1 Mbps
Medium	Twisted-pair wires, Coaxial cable, or fiber optic cable	Twisted-pair wires	Twisted-pair wires or coaxial cable	Twisted-pair wires
Distance	500 meters for thick cable, 185 meters for thinnet cable segments; five segments can be connected with repeaters to give maximum lengths of 2500 and 925 meters	366 meters for the main ring; can be extended to 750 meters with repeaters and to 4000 meters with fiber optic cable	6110 meters maximum distance between active hub is 62 meters and between passive hub 31 meters	500 meters
Number of stations	802.3-100 per thick cable segment, 30 per thinnet segment Ethernet-1024	255	255	Not stated by 1Base5 standard (early StarLANs set limit at 50)
Standards	IEEE 802.3	Based on IEEE 802.5 but does not adhere strictly to that standard	De facto	IEEE 802.3 1Base5
Cost for NIC and connectors only	High (approx. $250 per station)	High (approx. $600 per station)	Medium (approx. $150 per station)	High (approx. $400 per station)

crease, so does the probability of collisions. If the collision rate is high, the effectiveness of the LAN decreases. That is, when the LAN is busy, the efficiency may drop, and you might lose effectiveness just when you need it most. LAN vendors and researchers have run numerous tests to gauge the effect of high collision rates. Under these tests the performance characteristics did not drop appreciably. The true test of performance comes from actual use. Under light load conditions, access to the medium and the ability to transmit is good; there is little waiting time to transmit. Performance under heavy loads can be unpredictable.

Token Buses and Token Rings   We discuss these two implementations together because their media access control characteristics are similar. ARCnet can be implemented in a bus or a star-wired topology. ARCnet operates at speeds of 2.5 Mbps on twisted-pair wires, coaxial cable, or fiber optic cable. At this writing a 20 Mbps capability has been introduced, but availability is limited. Both speeds can be used in the same LAN, because the 20 Mbps cards can work at either speed. The maximum distance that can be spanned by ARCnet is 20,000 feet (6110 meters). An example of an ARCnet configuration is shown in Figure 3-10.

IBM's Token Ring operates at 4 or 16 Mbps using twisted-pair wires or fiber optic cable as the medium. Transmission at 16 Mbps requires the use of shielded twisted-pair wires of fiber optic cable. Shielded twisted-pair wires are less-error prone than unshielded twisted-pair wires and are needed to support the higher speed. Stations on the LAN connect to a multistation access unit (MAU), as illustrated in Figure 3-6. A typical MAU contains ports for eight workstations plus an input and output connector to another MAU. One MAU can be linked to another MAU as illustrated in Figure 3-7. The ring is established by interconnections within the MAU as illustrated in Figure 3-7. The distance spanned by a ring is 770 meters. The maximum number of nodes allowed per ring is 255. Multiple rings can be connected with bridges.

Predictability is the key word in a description of token LAN performance. Since access to the medium is through the possession of a token, and since each station is assured of receiving the token, you can predict the maximum and average times needed for a station with a message to be able to transmit it. The problem of collision, inherent in contention LANs, does not exist. Thus, when network traffic is light, a station may need to wait longer than a station on a contention bus; however, when network traffic is heavy, the token-passing station may wait less time. Regardless of the wait time, a station is assured that it can transmit in a predictable time. The maximum time a station must wait is the number of stations, less 1, times the message transit time. That is, a station that has just passed the token to its neighbor may become ready to send a message. That station must wait until the token comes around. The worst case is that every other station has a message to transmit. Thus the station must wait on every other station to transmit and pass the token. On average the station must wait for half the other stations.

Of the common microcomputer LAN implementations, token-passing solutions provide the lowest and highest cost solutions. In general, ARCnet LANs have a lower per-station cost than Ethernet LANs, and Ethernet LANs have a lower per-station cost than token rings. This statement is based on the cost of the hardware—LAN adapters, MAUs, wiring hubs, cables, connectors, wiring, and so on. Since prices fluctuate over time and from one vendor to another, you should verify these costs.

SUMMARY

There are two basic ways in which LANs use a transmission medium. In broadband transmission the carrying capacity of the medium is divided into separate transmission bands. Each transmission band is able to support a data transmission type. One band may be used for video transmission, one for voice, one for high-speed data (a LAN band), and some bands may be available for low-speed data transmission. Thus one transmission medium, usually coaxial cable, can become the delivery mechanism for a corporation's various communications capabilities. In baseband transmission only one signal is allowed on the medium at one time. A baseband system is simpler to implement and manage and costs less than a broadband system.

A LAN topology is the pattern used to lay out the LAN. The main LAN topologies are a bus, a ring, and a star. Coupled with the topology is the way in which a station interfaces with the medium, known as its media access control protocol. The main media access control protocols for LANs are carrier sense with multiple access and collision detection (CSMA/CD) and token passing. CSMA/CD is used on bus topologies and star topologies. Token passing is used on bus and ring topologies.

The primary media used for implementing LANs are unshielded twisted-pair wires, shielded twisted-pair wires, coaxial cable, and fiber optic cable. Newer LAN technology features wireless LANs. Wireless LANs use broadcast radio, infrared light, and microwave radio waves to communicate between workstations and servers.

KEY TERMS

active hub

American National Standards Institute (ANSI)

backbone network

backup device

bandwidth

baseband transmission

bit rate

broadband transmission

carrier sense with multiple access and collision avoidance (CSMA/CA)

carrier sense with multiple access and collision detection (CSMA/CD)

code independence

collision

Copper Data Distributed Interface (CDDI)

cyclic redundancy check (CRC)

data link protocol

Ethernet

Fiber Distributed Data Interface (FDDI)

frequency-division multiplexing

IEEE 802.3 standard

IEEE 802.4 standard

IEEE 802.5 standard

infrared light

integrated services digital network (ISDN)

Institute of Electrical and Electronics Engineers (IEEE)

logical line control

manufacturing automation protocol (MAP)

microwave

modulate

multistation access unit (MAU or MSAU)

octet

passive hub

ring topology

shielded twisted-pair wires

StarLAN

token passing

token-passing bus

token-passing ring

transparency

unshielded twisted-pair wires

wireless LANs

REVIEW QUESTIONS

1. Explain the statement "Our solution for you is a Novell Ethernet LAN." That is, what is implied in the statement?

2. Compare baseband and broadband transmission.

3. What are the advantages and disadvantages of broadband transmission? of baseband transmission?

4. What is a topology?

5. What are the primary LAN topologies?

6. What is a media access control method?

7. What are the primary LAN media access control methods?

8. What types of wire or conducted media are commonly used in LANs? List an advantage and a disadvantage of each.

9. What is a wireless LAN? What types of transmission are used in wireless LANs?

10. What are the IEEE 802.3, 802.4, and 802.5 standards?

11. What is the ANSI fiber distributed data interface (FDDI)?

PROBLEMS AND EXERCISES

1. Frequency division multiplexing is just one type of multiplexing. Two other types are time division multiplexing and statistical time division multiplexing. From a data communications text, research how these other multiplexing techniques work.

2. The Hyperchannel is a high-speed (50 Mbps) LAN used to connect large computing systems. From a data communications text, determine what topology and media access control protocol the Hyperchannel uses. Which of the three technologies—token ring, token bus and contention bus—is closest to the Hyperchannel architecture?

3. The ALOHANet, an early example of a local area network, was developed by the University of Hawaii. Research the literature to find the details of this network's architecture.

4. What are some of the uses of a metropolitan area network like the Fiber Distributed Data Interface?

5. What are the advantages and disadvantages of LAN standards?

6. Suppose you had a LAN application in which guaranteed access to the medium within a specified time was essential. Which media access control protocol would you choose? Justify your choice.

7. Suppose you wanted to install a LAN in a small office. The LAN will have ten workstations. Which medium would you choose? Justify your choice.

8. Describe a situation in which a wireless LAN would be a good medium choice.

REFERENCES

Anderson, Rick and Woods, Kevin. "10Base-T Ethernet: The Second Wave." *Data Communications*, Volume 19, Number 15, November 21, 1990.

Berline, Gary and Perratore, Ed. "Portable, Affordable, Secure: Wireless LANs." *PC Magazine*, Volume 11, Number 3, February 11, 1992.

Clegg, Peter. "LAN TIMES Lab Tests Wireless LANs." *LAN Times*, Volume 8, Issue 13, July 8, 1991.

Coden, Michael H. "Why Fiber Will Fly." *LAN Technology*, Volume 8, Number 11, October 1992.

Derfler Jr., Frank J. "The Next Wave: LANs Without Wires." *PC Magazine*, May 29, 1990.

Derfler Jr., Frank J. "Building Network Solutions: Is ISDN Tomorrow's Interoffice Network?" *PC Magazine*, February 13, 1990.

"Ethernet Performance of Remote DECwindows Applications." *Digital Technical Journal*, Summer 1990.

Frank, Alan. "Networking Without Wires." *LAN Technology*, Volume 8, Number 3, March 1992.

Harris, Fred H., Sweeney, Jr., Frederick L., and Vonderohe, Robert H. "New Niches for Switches." *Datamation*, March 29, 1983.

Hayes, Victor. "Standardization Efforts for Wireless LANs." *IEEE Network*, Volume 5, Number 6, November 1991.

Head, Joe. "Fiber Optics in the '90s: Fact and Fiction." *Data Communications*, Volume 19, Number 12, September 21, 1990.

Head, Joe. "Token Ring LANs and UTP: Perfect Together." *Data Communications*, Volume 19, Number 12, September 21, 1990.

Keiffer, Tom, Richey, Leslie, and Christian, Tim. "Charting Network Topologies." *LAN Technology*, Volume 5, Number 3, March 1989.

Klein, Mike. "Cabling Do's and Don'ts." *LAN Technology*, Volume 6, Number 2, February 1990.

Leeds, Frank and Chorey, Jim. "Cutting Cable Confusion: The Facts About Coax." *LAN Technology*, Volume 7, Number 3, March 1991.

Leeds, Frank and Chorey, Jim. "Round Up Your Cable Woes." *LAN Technology*, Volume 7, Number 10, October 1991.

Love, R. D. and Toher, T. "Do the Right Thing: Choosing Tomorrow's LAN Cabling Today." *Data Communications*, Volume 19, Number 13, October 1990.

Mathias, Craig J. "Wireless LANs: The Next Wave." *Data Communications*, Volume 21, Number 5, March 1992.

McQuillan, John M. "Broadband Networks: The End of Distance?" *Data Communications*, Volume 19, Number 7, June 1990.

Thurber, Kenneth J. "Getting a Handle on FDDI." *Data Communications*, Volume 18, Number 8, June 1989.

CHAPTER 4

LAN HARDWARE

CHAPTER PREVIEW

Physical and data link layer conventions and topology are important aspects of your LAN decisions. Choosing the right hardware and software is also critical. In this chapter we look at the principal hardware components of a LAN. A wide variety of components are available—servers, workstations, adapters, and so on—but the key to success is choosing components that can be integrated to form an effective system.

In this chapter you will read about:

servers

backup devices

workstation hardware

LAN adapters

printers

miscellaneous hardware

At the conclusion of this chapter you should have an understanding of the role each component plays in a LAN and some of the considerations to be made in selecting this equipment.

SERVER PLATFORMS

In an ideal world your decisions regarding medium, topology, and media access would ensure the success of a network. But you can negate even the best decisions in each of those areas by making a poor choice of server hardware. To make an informed decision regarding server hardware, you must understand what the server does. Services provided by a server include file, print, terminal, modem, and facsimile services. File services are the most common and are the focus of our attention here.

File Services

File services is one of the primary jobs of a server. The objective of file services is to allow users access to data, programs, and other files stored on the server's disk drives. From the user's perspective it ought to be transparent that the data or files he or she is using are located on the server's disk drives. Over time several technologies have been used to provide file services, including disk, file, and database servers. File and database services are the most commonly used today, but let's look first at the more basic functions of the disk server.

Disk Servers   A **disk server** has one or more hard disks that can be used by someone at a workstation. Each user is given a dedicated portion of the disk server's disks. Essentially the disk drive is divided among the user base, as illustrated in Figure 4-1. Suppose you are a user of a disk server, and you need to use word processing, spreadsheet, and database applications. A

Figure 4-1   Disk Server Technology

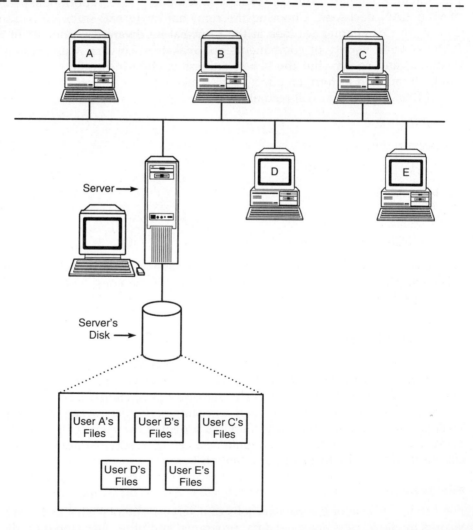

portion of the disk server's disk is dedicated to your needs, and each application you need is placed in your dedicated area. Thus the *disk* is shared, not the files. If ten users need to use word processing applications, then ten copies of the word processing software must reside on the disk server's disk, one copy per user.

Disk servers do not make efficient use of disk space, but they do have some advantages. Early software was single-user oriented. Giving each user a personal copy of single-user software means several users can use it concurrently. Some software still requires disk server technology for application sharing on a network.

File Servers   Disk servers soon gave way to **file servers.** A file server allows users to share files. Given the scenario of the preceding paragraphs, only one copy of the word processing, spreadsheet, and database software must reside on a file server. Individual users share these applications. When a user enters a command to start an application, that application is downloaded into the user's workstation, as it is with the disk server, but the file server gives each user a copy of the same file. File server technology is illustrated in Figure 4-2.

When a user needs data from the file server, that data is transferred to the user's workstation. This is suitable for small files, but consider the impact of such technology when accessing a large database. If a user enters a request that requires looking at thousands of records, each record must be transferred over the LAN to the user's workstation. This can place a heavy load on the file server and the LAN medium.

For example, suppose you want to determine the average grade point average (GPA) for all students in your school. Suppose further that there are 40,000 records in the student file. With file server technology the database application runs on your workstation. It is downloaded to your workstation when you start the application. When you make your request to find the average GPA, each student record is transferred over the network to your workstation, where the grade point average data is extracted and computations are made. Transferring all 40,000 database records over the network can place a heavy load on the medium and reduce its performance. In a case like this it is more efficient to have the server do the calculations and pass only the response over the network. A database server operates in this way.

Database Servers   The **database server** was developed to solve the problem of passing an entire file over the medium. The most common example of a database server is the **SQL server. Structured query language** (SQL) is a standard database definition, access, and update language for relational databases. An SQL server accepts a database request, accesses all necessary records locally, and then sends only the results back to the requester. In the GPA example all 40,000 student records still must be read, but the computation is done by the SQL server. Only one record containing the average GPA is sent back over the network to the requester. This reduces the load on the network medium, but it does place an extra load on the server. In addition

to accessing the records, the server also must perform some database processing. This can impact other users who are also requesting SQL services.
The SQL server must be powerful enough to provide effective services and
avoid becoming a performance bottleneck.

Also an interface must exist between the application software making
the database request and the SQL server. The interface must be capable of
translating an application's data needs into an SQL statement. Thus an SQL
server cannot work unless the application or an application interface exists
that can generate the SQL syntax. SQL server technology is illustrated in
Figure 4-3.

Figure 4-2 File Server Technology

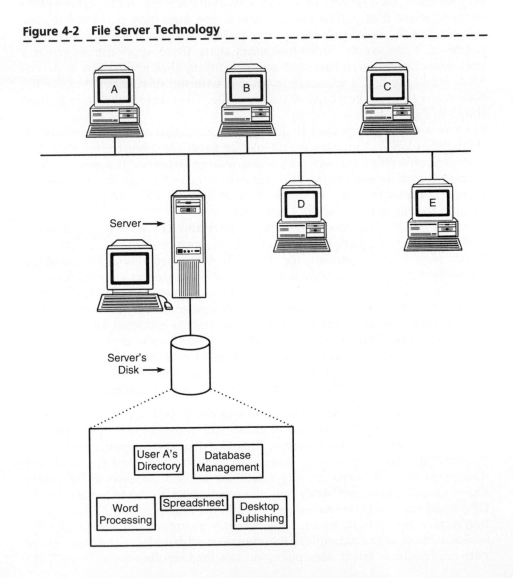

Server Disk Drives

Disk, file, and database servers all share a common need—to efficiently access data. Thus, when choosing a server, you should carefully select the server's disk subsystem. Two factors are critical when choosing a disk drive: storage capacity and average access time.

Disk drives on servers typically are high-capacity units; that is, they can store large amounts of data and have fast access times. The capacity to store large amounts of data is important because the server must store many data and program files. A file server, for example, is on each user's hard disk. Individual data storage, together with shared storage needed for application software, databases, several versions of operating system software, utility

Figure 4-3 SQL Server Technology

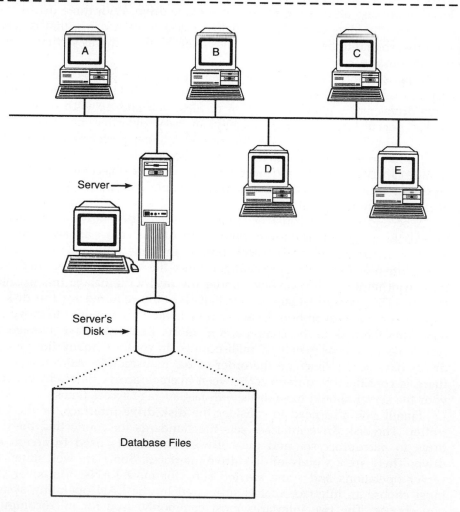

programs, and electronic mail messages, can easily require several hundred megabytes of storage. For example, the space required for one microcomputer database management system, dBASE IV, is 3.5 MB, exclusive of the data files. Some operating systems require over 5 MB of disk storage. An SQL server holds database files as well as the SQL server software. Organizations adopting this technology will likely have large databases and high-volume storage needs.

The need for large amounts of data storage might be satisfied with one high-capacity drive or with several low-capacity ones; both alternatives offer benefits. Having few disk drives provides a configuration that is easier to manage. However, having several smaller drives is beneficial because several disks can be working simultaneously to satisfy user requests. For example, suppose you need 300 MB of storage. You could select one 300-MB drive or three 100-MB drives. With one drive it is simple to determine file allocation because all files are placed on the one drive. With three drives you must place the data carefully to equalize access to each drive; that is, your objective should to be to spread the files over the three drives so that each is equally busy.

Suppose your application calls for 45 disk accesses per second. A single fast disk drive may have difficulty keeping up with this load. However, with three drives and a good distribution of files, you end up with only 15 requests per disk per second, usually an easy objective to attain. This configuration is more expensive but provides better performance. Remember, for file or SQL server disk drives, you should select those with sufficient storage capacity and speed to meet your performance objectives. A powerful processor with a slow disk subsystem can cripple your network. We cannot overemphasize this point.

A second factor to consider when choosing a disk drive is the **access time** of the disk itself. The three components of disk access are seek time, latency, and transfer time. The **seek time** is the time required to move the read/write heads to the proper cylinder. Once the heads are positioned, you must wait until the data revolves under the read/write heads; this is called **latency.** The average latency is one-half the time required for the disk to make a complete revolution. **Transfer time** is the time required to move the data from the disk to the computer's memory. Fast disks have average access times of approximately 15 milliseconds. In contrast, many floppy disk drives have access times on the order of 200 milliseconds. As you can see, there is considerable difference between average access times. In general, your file server should have disks with fast average access times.

Finally you also need to consider the **disk drive interface,** or the **controller.** The disk drive interface sets the standards for connecting the disk drive to microprocessor and the software commands used to access the drive. There are a variety of disk drive interfaces. Some are well suited for server operations and some are too slow for most LANs. Moreover you must choose an interface that is supported by the LAN operating system you choose. The two interfaces most commonly used for microcomputer based servers are the small computer system interface (SCSI, pronounced "scuzzy") and the enhanced small device interface (ESDI, pronounced "es-dee"). Both interfaces provide high-speed data transfers and large-capacity disk drives. The SCSI interface has been upgraded to provide more efficiency and is currently the interface of choice.

Server Memory

A server is a combination of hardware and software. The software should be designed to take full advantage of the hardware, and in the next chapter you will read about some techniques for ensuring this compatibility. Memory is often a good hardware investment, because many software systems can take advantage of available memory to provide better performance. Some LAN software systems do this by using memory as an extension of the disk drives, a technique called **disk caching.** Disk caching is similar in function to cache memory that is used on high-performance processors. **Cache memory** is a high-speed buffer for slower main memory. Main memory can, in turn, serve as a high-speed buffer for slower disk drives. Assuming that you choose a LAN operating system that does this, you need to configure the server with sufficient memory to make caching effective.

The fundamental premise of disk caching is that memory accesses are faster than disk accesses. A disk cache therefore attempts to keep highly accessed data in memory. Essentially caching works as follows: If a user's request is received for data, cache memory is searched prior to physically reading the data from the disk. If the data is found in cache memory—a process known as a logical read—then the data is made available almost instantly. If the data is not found in cache memory, then it is read from disk, which is called a physical access. As data is read from disk, it is also placed into cache memory so that any subsequent read for that data might be a logical read.

Disk caching, taken to the fullest extent, results in all data residing in memory and all reads being logical reads. This, of course, is rarely the case. However, it should be clear that effective use of cache memory can improve performance. Since disk caching requires memory, sufficient memory must be available to provide a large percentage of cache hits. A cache hit occurs when the data being read is found in cache memory. Consider the following example, which illustrates the effects of having too little memory.

Suppose that LAN data requests cycle through four records, A, B, C, and D. Furthermore you only have enough cache memory for three records. When additional space is needed, the cache-management scheme typically replaces the record that has been dormant the longest with a new record. Suppose that records A, B, and C have been read in that order and are in cache memory, as illustrated in Figure 4-4(a). A request is issued for record D, but it is not in cache memory, so a physical read is required. Record D is read and must be inserted into cache memory. Since record A is the least recently used, record D replaces record A, as illustrated in Figure 4-4(b). Next a request is received for record A. Since it is not in cache memory, a physical read is issued, and record A replaces the least recently used record, record B. Cache memory now looks like Figure 4-4(c). A request is made for record B, which is also not in cache memory. Record B is read and replaces record C. Unfortunately, record C is the next record to be read and again requires a physical read. It is read into cache memory, replacing record D. Then the cycle repeats again. In this simple, contrived example, the cache is one record too small and is totally ineffective. In fact, it is counterproductive, as it only incurs extra overhead for searching cache memory for records that are not cache resident.

The problem of insufficient cache memory can be corrected by expanding it. In the example just one more record slot results in 100 percent cache hits after the four initial reads. Again, this example is contrived, and 100 percent cache-hit rates are rarely attainable. However, you should learn from the example that there is a critical threshold for cache memory. If the available memory is under this threshold, cache can be ineffective. When the available cache memory is over this threshold, cache can be very effective. Some users have experienced cache hits on the order of 80 to 90 percent. The hit rate depends on the access patterns, so do not expect this figure to hold true for all systems.

Figure 4-4   Example of Disk Caching

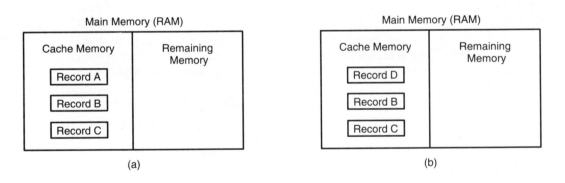

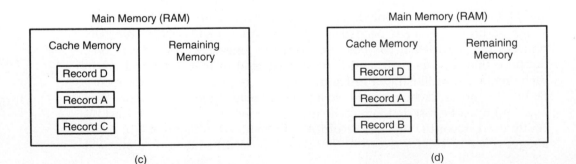

An ample amount of memory is important for reasons other than disk caching. You should also have sufficient memory available to avoid **disk swapping.** Most of today's memory management schemes are based on **virtual memory** management, which uses the disk as an extension of memory so each program has virtually all the memory it needs. Virtual memory management allows the real memory of a system to be less than the aggregate memory required by all the applications. To do this, application code and data are swapped back and forth between the disk and memory. If the available memory is too small, the swap rate goes up. When the swap rate increases, the operating system is spending extra time managing memory, and less time is available for doing application work. Thus the amount of application work done per unit of time decreases as the swap rate increases.

Processor Speed

The processing power of the server is also a critical factor. It seldom makes sense to select a server that has fast disks and plenty of memory but a slow CPU. In general, the server ought to be one of the fastest (if not the fastest) computer on the network. There are a few exceptions to this generalization, such as a server providing small amounts of data to graphics workstations. Most graphics applications require high-speed processors to create and print graphic images. In these networks the workstation computing power may equal or exceed that of the server.

Expansion and Power

A server should have sufficient expansion capability and the power to effectively use the expansion slots. Network server capacity can be expanded by adding hardware to the existing server or by adding additional servers. Expanding the capabilities of an existing server is less expensive than adding a new server, so the server you choose should be able to support expansion. For example, you may eventually want to add more memory, disks, printers, or other hardware devices that users can share, such as modems, facsimile machines, tape drives, and compact disc drives.

Compatibility

The server platform(s) you choose must be compatible with the topology, medium access control protocol, applications, and system software on the network. These components form an integrated package. It is conceivable that each component you choose is optimum and yet you still have a poor LAN system because the individual components do not fit together well.

BACKUP DEVICES

No LAN is complete without a backup device. One of the LAN administrator's most important duties is to make periodic file backups. A **backup** is a copy of files at a specific time and is used to restore the system to a workable state following a system failure or an event that damages the data, or to restore data that needs to be available only on a periodic basis. For example, research data that is needed only once or twice a month and year-end payroll data that is needed temporarily to file worker's tax notices can be backed up and then replaced on disk on an as-needed basis.

The principle backup device is a magnetic tape drive, a variety of which is available. Removable disk drives and optical disk drives are alternatives. The primary backup technologies are described below and are listed in Table 4-1.

Floppy Diskette Drives

You may use floppy diskettes as the backup medium. The diskette drives may be server or workstation drives. The major disadvantage of this backup method is the low capacity and speed of the backup media. Typical diskette capacities of IBM-compatible systems are 360 KB, 720 KB, 1.2 MB, and 1.44 MB. Diskettes with capacities of up to 20 MB are also available. Often the capacity of server drives is 100 MB or more. A large LAN may have several hundred million or even several billion bytes of disk storage. Backing up this amount of data to 1 MB (or even 20 MB) diskettes is cumbersome. The advantages of diskette backup are high availability on workstations and servers and low cost. Diskette backup for LANs with small disk requirements can be practical, but for large-disk systems, the number of diskettes needed to store

Table 4-1   Primary Backup Technologies

Diskette Backup
    360 KB
    720 KB
    1.2 MB
    1.44 MB
    20 MB

Hard Drive, Fixed
    Multiple capacities

Hard Drive, Removable Cartridge
    40 MB to over 250 MB

Tape Backup
    4 mm or 1/4 inch
      to 2.2 GB
      60 MB, 150 MB, 160 MB, 500 MB, 1.2 GB, 2.2 GB are common
    8 mm or VCR
      to 2.2 GB
    9-Track
      to 100 MB

Optical Drives
    WORM (write once, read many)
      to 4 GB
    Rewritable
      to 4 GB

all the data is high. This process is slow, subject to errors, and requires handling many diskettes.

Hard Disk Drives

A hard disk drive on either a server or a workstation may also be used for backup. The arguments for and against this alternative are much the same as those for diskettes. The major difference is the capacity of hard disk drives is greater than that of diskettes. If the hard disk is not removable, it is difficult to keep multiple generations of backups, a procedure that is important for a comprehensive backup plan. For example, you should have at least three generations or more of backups, which means that if you take a backup weekly, three weeks worth of backups are always available. Some hard drives have removable disk cartridges, which are an excellent backup alternative because they provide high capacity (90 MB or more per cartridge) and rapid access.

Optical Disk Drives

Optical disk drives are gaining popularity as backup devices. The reasons for this are their decreasing costs and large storage capacity, and the recently introduced ability to erase and write to optical disks. There are two classes of optical disk drives, WORM (write once, read many) and erasable drives. As the name implies, WORM technology allows you to write to the medium only once. You cannot erase a WORM disk. This can make the cost of backups expensive because the cost of cartridges for many such drives on microcomputers is over $150. An advantage of WORM technology is that the data cannot be changed, so the backup cannot be accidentally destroyed. Currently, erasable drives and optical disks are more expensive than WORM drives, but you can expect these prices to come down. The cost of erasable cartridges now starts at about $250. The capacities of both types of drives range from 300 MB to 1 GB or more.

Magnetic Tape Drives

As mentioned earlier, a magnetic tape drive is the usual choice for a backup device. Magnetic tapes are inexpensive relative to the other options. They hold large volumes of data, are easy to use and store, and generally provide good performance. A variety of tape backup devices are available. The drives themselves are less expensive than disk or optical drives with comparable storage characteristics, and a wide range of data capacities are available. Tape drives vary in the size of the tape and recording method. If more than one tape drive is to be used in one organization, it is best to establish a standard tape configuration so the tapes can be exchanged among the different drives. The main magnetic tape options are summarized in Table 4-2.

As with other hardware discussed in this chapter, the tape drive must be compatible with the server or workstation on which it is installed. A drive usually has a controller that must be installed in the computer, so you must select a drive that has a controller compatible with your equipment. Also you need backup software and procedures to take your backups. Backup software is covered in the next chapter, and backup procedures are discussed in Chapter 10.

WORKSTATIONS

Some LANs are homogeneous; that is, all the workstations are of the same basic type, all are running the same level of the same operating system, and all use essentially the same applications. It is easier to configure this type of network than a heterogenous one, but homogeneous networks are less common. Often a network is assembled from workstations acquired over time. These workstations usually represent different levels of technology and perhaps use different versions of operating systems. For example, consider a network with the following workstations:

IBM or compatible with an industry standard architecture (ISA) bus

IBM or compatible with an extended industry standard architecture (EISA) bus

IBM or compatible with a microchannel architecture (MCA) bus

Apple Macintosh or compatible

Sun workstation

When selecting components for a heterogenous network, your hardware and software options are more limited than for a homogeneous one. For example, you may be more limited in your choice of network operating systems (see Chapter 5) or LAN adapters. The limitations arise from the inabil-

Table 4-2   Magnetic Tape Backup Functions
- -

Back up all files
Back up all files modified since a particular date
Back up by directory
Back up by list of files
Back up all but a list of files to be excluded
Back up by index
Back up by interface to a database
Back up using wildcard characters in file names
Create new index on tape and disk
Maintain cross reference of tape serial numbers and backup
Back up manually
Back up automatically by time or calendar
Start backup from workstation or server
Compress data
Back up many volumes
Generate reports

ity of some LAN software to support different workstations or from the unavailability of required hardware, such as a LAN adapter. You will find many options for LAN with only IBM-compatible workstations and several for LANs with only Apple workstations, but few options can support both types of microcomputers.

Diskless Workstations

When configuring your LAN, you may want to consider **diskless worksta-tions.** As the name implies, a diskless workstation does not have any local disk drives. Instead a diskless workstation has its boot logic in a read-only memory (ROM) chip. This chip contains the logic to connect to the network and download the operating system from the server. Thus a diskless work-station cannot be used in a stand-alone mode; it is fully dependent on the server for all of its software, and it cannot function if the network or server is not operating. This is the disadvantage of a diskless system. Its advan-tages are cost, security, and control.

Since diskless workstations have no disk drives, they are inherently less expensive than those with disks. Moreover, the maintenance costs for disk-less systems are less than for systems with disk drives. Diskless systems provide extra security because users are unable to copy the organization's data onto local hard or floppy disk drives. This is important because an or-ganization's primary security risk is its employees. Diskless systems also provide a greater measure of control because employees cannot introduce their own software into the system. This not only ensures that standard soft-ware and data are used but also reduces the chances of computer viruses be-ing introduced into the network.

Workstation Memory and Speed

Like servers, workstation memory configurations are important. If you have stand-alone microcomputer systems, each with the minimum application memory configuration, you may need to add more memory to those systems to run the same applications on a network, because LAN software must also run in the workstations. Moreover LAN software stays memory resident. Suppose you have a microcomputer with 512 KB of memory and that this is just sufficient to load the operating system and your database management system. Placing that same microcomputer on a network requires that some of the memory be allocated to the LAN interface; thus, you may be unable to run your database management system because of insufficient memory. The solution, of course, is to expand the computer's memory. The amount of memory required for LAN software varies from one LAN to another. Some require less than 20 KB, and some require over 70 KB of resident memory.

The speed of the workstation's processor needs to be compatible with the type of work for which it is being used. If you use the workstation for word processing, a low-speed processor probably is satisfactory. However, a workstation used for graphics work requires a high-speed processor. Basi-cally it is the application and not the LAN that determines the power of the workstations.

LAN ADAPTERS

If you have chosen an architecture, medium, and media access control protocol, you have narrowed the options for LAN adapters. LAN adapters provide the connection between the medium and the bus of the workstation or server. LAN adapters are designed to support a specific protocol using a specific medium, although a few can support two different medium types. For example, there is one type of Ethernet card for twisted-pair wires and another Ethernet card for coaxial cable. After matching medium and protocol, there are additional alternatives regarding vendor and architecture.

The choice of a LAN adapter vendor determines the support, quality, and price of the LAN adapter. Just as you should be careful when selecting a LAN vendor, you should also be careful regarding the vendor of individual components, like a LAN adapter. The LAN adapter that is initially the least expensive may prove to be more costly in the long term if it is of inferior quality, it does not have a good vendor-support policy, or replacement LAN adapters are difficult to obtain should the vendor go out of business.

LAN adapters are installed in each workstation and server. Naturally the LAN adapter must be compatible with the hardware architecture of the computer into which it is installed. Moreover you need to ensure that a LAN adapter is available for each type of network node you anticipate having. Certain combinations of equipment may not be supported. For example, you may have difficulty finding ARCnet cards for each node in a network consisting of a Digital Equipment Corporation VAX server and Apple Macintosh, Sun, and IBM workstations. You also need to ensure that LAN adapters are compatible with the bus of the host computer. Thus, for IBM-microcomputer-based LANs, you may need ISA-, EISA-, and MCA-compatible cards.

LAN adapters also have an architecture. For example, LAN adapters for IBM or compatible systems often come in 8-bit and 16-bit architectures. The 16-bit cards are almost always more expensive and faster than the corresponding 8-bit cards. By faster we mean that a 16-bit card can transfer data between the computer and the medium faster than an 8-bit card; it does not affect the speed at which data is transferred over the network medium. A 16-bit card is faster than an 8-bit card because it transfers data 16 bits at a time, whereas the 8-bit card transfers data in 8-bit groups.

PRINTERS

One major factor that affects the success of a LAN is printer support. Some LANs have restrictions regarding the distribution of printers and the number of printers that can be supported by one server. For example, suppose that network printers must be attached to a server, and each server can support a maximum of five printers. An organization that needs 20 printers, therefore, must have at least four servers.

You must be concerned not only with the number of printers but also with the type of printers supported and the way in which they are supported. A **printer driver** is a software module that determines how to format data for proper printing on a specific type of printer. The printers you intend to use must be supported by the software drivers provided by the vendor. For example, you may find that a laser printer you attach to the LAN can operate in text mode but is restricted in its graphic mode operation or in its ability to download soft fonts. Again, you need to consider interoperability of hardware and software components to ensure that your needs are realized. Some LAN systems provide a utility program that allows you to tailor a generic printer driver to meet the needs of a specific printer you want to use. This utility allows you to define printer functions and the command sequences essential to invoking those functions. Because new printer technologies are constantly appearing, this utility is quite useful.

OTHER HARDWARE

Some of the other hardware components you may find in a LAN are

Terminal servers, which allows terminals to access the network; however, a terminal attached to a LAN will not have the same functionality as a microcomputer attached to a LAN.

Modem servers, which allow users to share one or more modems. A modem is used to transmit digital data over analog communications lines (like telephone lines).

Facsimile (FAX) machines, which may be attached to a server and shared by network users.

These services are important but are less common than either file or print services. As such, we shall not devote more coverage to them at this time. You may read more about these servers in Chapter 14.

Earlier we discussed the principal of disk caching. Most efficient network operating systems use this to enhance performance. A disadvantage to using disk caching is that several disk updates can be lost if the server experiences a power failure. To reduce the risk of this happening, many companies protect their servers with an **uninterruptible power supply (UPS).** A UPS uses batteries to provide power to a connected computer in the event of blackout or brownout conditions. Moreover many UPSs provide protection against power spikes and momentary power loss. For many business applications a UPS that costs several hundred dollars is a good investment.

MAKING CONNECTIONS

Thus far we have discussed the medium, the network nodes, the LAN adapter, and the printer. All that remains is to connect the nodes to the medium. Connections can be made in a variety of ways. You have already learned that you must pick a LAN adapter that is compatible with the medium you choose. Therefore it is the medium that primarily influences the way in which physical connections are made. Let us look at the problem from a generic perspective.

The objective of network connection—that is, connecting a computer to the LAN medium—is to provide a data path between the medium and the computer's memory. To accomplish this there must be a connection to the medium and a connection to the computer's bus or channel. The interface or connection to the medium is referred to as the **communications interface unit (CIU),** and the interface or connection to the computer's bus is referred to as the **bus interface unit (BIU).** These functions are illustrated in Figure 4-5 and are provided by the LAN adapter.

A key component of the network connection is a **transceiver,** which establishes the connection to the medium and implements the transmit and receive portions of the protocol. In a few Ethernet LANs, the transceiver is connected directly to the medium. In most of today's Ethernet implementations, the transceiver is located on the LAN adapter, as illustrated in Figure 4-6.

Figure 4-5   Details of Node-to-Medium Connection

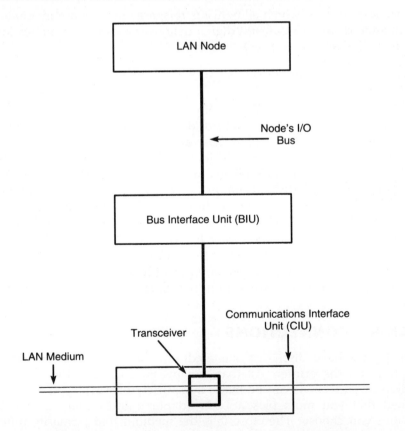

The physical connection between the computer and the medium is established through **connectors.** There are many different types of connectors that are used, but the principal ones are

BNC, TNC, or N-Type connectors for coaxial cable

RJ-11, RJ-45, or DB-nn (DB-25 or DB-15) connectors for wires

SMA connectors for fiber optic cable

The type of connector you need is determined by your LAN adapter. A wide variety of connector adapters allow you to change connector types. For example, one adapter can change a BNC connector to a TNC connector. **Baluns** are adapters that change coaxial cable connectors to twisted-pair wire connectors. These adapters allow you to transfer from one medium to another or from a connector for one medium to a different medium.

In some networks, connecting a computer to the medium is sufficient for making that computer active on the network. Some LAN implementations use wiring hubs to provide node-to-node connection. Several kinds of connection hubs are commonly used. For example, in an IBM Token Ring, individual stations are connected to a wiring hub called a multistation access unit (MAU). Externally this wiring scheme looks like a star-wired architecture. The ring is established via internal connections within the MAU, as illustrated in Figure 4-7.

An ARCnet LAN may use active and passive hubs for node connections, as illustrated in Figure 4-8. An active hub provides signal regeneration and allows nodes to be located at distances of up to 2000 feet from the hub. A passive hub does not provide signal regeneration, so nodes can be located no more than 100 feet from the hub.

A variety of other hardware components are sometimes needed to make the network function. For example, on bus networks or networks using wiring hubs, terminators are often needed to prevent signal loss. A terminator is used at the ends of a bus to prevent echo, and terminators are required on unused passive hub ports in an ARCnet network for the same reason. The location of terminators in a LAN configuration are shown in Figure 4-9.

Sometimes LAN connections go further than simply connecting a node to the medium. You may also need to connect one LAN to another or connect a LAN to a WAN. We discuss this subject in detail in Chapter 13.

Figure 4-6 Transceiver Located on LAN Adapter

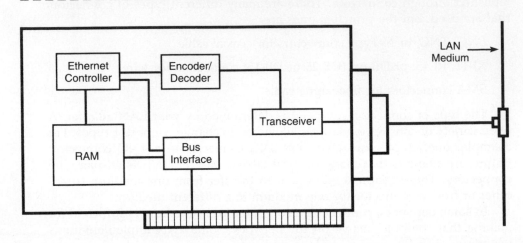

Figure 4-7 Implementation of a Ring Using a Multistation Access Unit

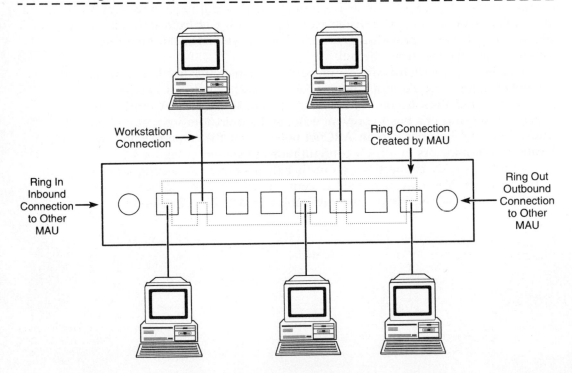

Figure 4-8 ARCnet Active and Passive Hubs

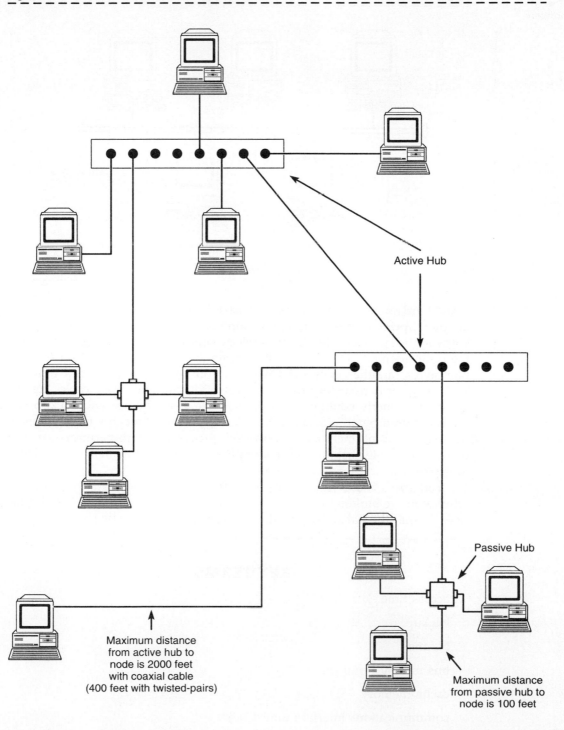

Active Hub

Passive Hub

Maximum distance
from active hub to
node is 2000 feet
with coaxial cable
(400 feet with twisted-pairs)

Maximum distance
from passive hub to
node is 100 feet

Figure 4-9   Terminators on a Bus Network

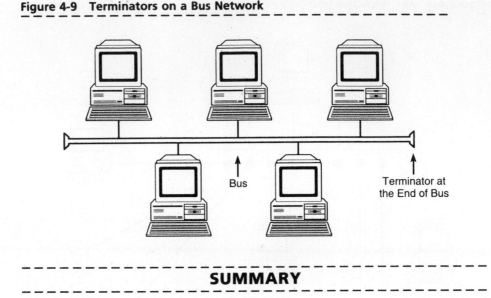

SUMMARY

LAN hardware mainly consists of server platforms, workstations, LAN adapters, printers, a medium, and connectors. The hardware combines with software to provide the LAN services. LAN adapters are protocol and medium oriented. Thus one LAN adapter supports CSMA/CD on twisted-pair wires, another supports CSMA/CD on coaxial cable, and a different LAN adapter is necessary for token passing using fiber optic cable. Servers must be properly configured to provide the performance and backup services required by an efficient LAN. The key to meeting this requirement is having sufficient memory, a powerful processor, high-performance disk drives, and a file backup unit. Naturally the software must also be available to exploit the hardware configuration.

You can choose from many combinations of hardware and software when you are building a LAN. The key to success is combining the alternatives so that the hardware and the software form an effective team.

KEY TERMS

access time

backup

baluns

bus interface unit (BIU)

cache memory

communications interface unit (CIU)

connectors

controller

database server

disk caching

disk drive interface

diskless workstation

disk server

disk swapping

file server

latency

printer driver

seek time

SQL server

structured query language (SQL)

transceiver

transfer time

uninterruptible power supply (UPS)

virtual memory

REVIEW QUESTIONS

1. What are the generic functions of a server?

2. Distinguish between file and SQL server technology.

3. What must you take into consideration when you select a server disk drive?

4. How do servers use memory to improve performance?

5. Explain how disk caching works. What is its benefit?

6. Why should servers have high processor speeds?

7. How do diskless systems work? What advantages do they have over disk systems? What are the disadvantages of a diskless system?

8. What is data backup? What devices are used to effect backup?

9. Why is a diskette usually ineffective as a backup device?

10. What options need to be considered when selecting a LAN adapter?

11. What does an uninterruptible power supply (UPS) do?

PROBLEMS AND EXERCISES

1. Suppose you need to establish a small network having one server and 15 workstations. Draw up a configuration for the server and for the workstations. Make all workstation configurations the same. Choose a network topology and medium access control protocol. Consult one or more recent magazines to help you determine the hardware costs for your LAN. Include the server, workstations, LAN adapters, a backup tape device, three laser printers, and three dot-matrix printers in your cost estimates. Configure the server with at least 600 MB of disk storage and 8 MB of memory.

2. Suppose you have a file server with 600 MB of data. If you use 1.4-MB diskettes to back up this data, how many diskettes are necessary? Suppose your backup utility provides data compression and you get 1.8 : 1 compression for your files. A 1.8 : 1 compression ratio means that on the average, 1.8 bytes can be compressed into 1 byte. How many diskettes are required?

3. Examine the literature and give an example of how each of the following is used:

   a. a terminal server

   b. a modem server

   c. a FAX server

   d. an uninterruptible power supply

4. Suppose a company has an IBM or IBM-compatible microcomputer with an 80386 processor, 2 MB of memory, and an 80-MB disk drive. The company wants to know if this computer will work as a file server for a 25-node network. The primary applications are word processing, spreadsheets, and desktop publishing. What would your response be to this inquiry? Justify your response.

5. Assuming that you decided the microcomputer in problem 4 could handle the job if it is upgraded, what upgrades to the microcomputer would you recommend?

REFERENCES

Allinger, Doug. "A Look at Low-End LANs." *LAN Technology*, Volume 5, Number 12, December 1989.

Axner, David H. "Wiring Hubs: Keys to the Network Infrastructure." *Networking Management*, Volume 10, Number 12, November 1992.

Barrett, Ed. "The Critical Steps to Hub Selection." *LAN Technology*, Volume 8, Number 11, October 1992.

Catchings, Bill and Van Name, Mark L. "Growing Pains." *Byte*, June 1990.

Derfler Jr., Frank J. "The LAN Survival Guide." *PC Magazine*, May 29, 1990.

Greenfield, David. "Super Servers Energize Networks." *Data Communications*, Volume 19, Number 3, March 1990.

Hirsh, Don. "Terminal Servers: Here to Stay." *Data Communications*, Volume 19, Number 5, April 1990.

Kent, Les. "Backup to the Rescue." *InfoWorld*, Volume 14, Issue 45, November 9, 1992.

Krivda, Cheryl. "Enterprising Hubs." *LAN Interoperability*, Volume 3, Number 2, Fall 1992.

Krivda, Cheryl. "The Hub of the Matter." *LAN*, Volume 7, Number 12, December 1992.

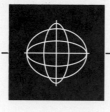

III
SOFTWARE

The success of a LAN in establishing communications capability depends on the interaction of application software, workstations system software, and server system software. In Chapter 5 you learn about the software system that drives the LAN hardware. Chapter 6 examines how application software allows us to solve business problems and the role LANs play as the tool that allows its users to access application software.

Chapter 5
LAN System Software

Chapter 6
Application Software

LAN SYSTEM SOFTWARE

CHAPTER PREVIEW

In Chapter 4 you examined the details of the LAN hardware system. In this chapter you will learn about the software system that drives the hardware. We will separate LAN software into three classes: application software, workstation system software, and server system software. The success of the LAN depends on how these three classes interact in setting up the communications capability. In the next chapter you will read about LAN application software and how application and system software interact.

Specific topics you will read about in this chapter include:

generic LAN system software functions

workstation system software

server system software

how LAN software differs from software on stand-alone systems

GENERIC FUNCTIONS OF LAN SYSTEM SOFTWARE

Application software is designed to solve business problems. It is assisted in this goal by supporting system software like the **operating system (OS)**, database management systems (DBMSs), and data communications systems. Like all system software, LAN system software is essentially an extension of the operating system. It carries out hardware-oriented LAN tasks, like interfacing to the medium, and **input/output (I/O)** oriented tasks, like directing print jobs and disk read and write requests to a server. A few operating systems are designed for LAN work and have these functions integrated. Other LAN system software implementations operate in partnership with a general-purpose operating system like UNIX or OS/2.

The purpose of system software is to insulate applications from hardware details like I/O and memory management. System software provides an interface through which the applications can request hardware services without needing to know the details of how the services are carried out. That is, the applications make requests for services, and system software contains the logic to carry out those requests for a specific type of hardware.

For example, there are several types of disk drives. An application makes disk access requests independent of the type of disk drive being used. A disk driver is a component of the operating system that fulfills the request for a specific type of disk drive.

LAN system software resides in both the application's workstation and in the server(s), as illustrated in Figure 5-1. The workstation's LAN system software includes the redirector and the medium interface software. Let us look at a specific example of a workstation's environment and use that example to examine the interaction between workstation and server software components.

A Workstation Environment

Consider a workstation in which the server provides file and printer services. The workstation has local disk drives A, B, and C. The file server's disk drives are known to the workstation as drives F and G. The workstation's local printer ports are LPT1 and LPT2. There is a local dot-matrix printer attached to LPT1. Output to LPT2 is directed to a network laser printer. The key to making this environment work is transparent access to all devices. From the user's perspective, printing to a network printer and accessing a network disk drive is transparent. That is, the workstation's user accesses remote drives F and G in exactly the same way as he or she accesses the local drives A, B, and C, and the user prints to the laser printer as though it were locally attached. This transparency is carried out by the LAN

Figure 5-1   LAN Software in Server and Workstation

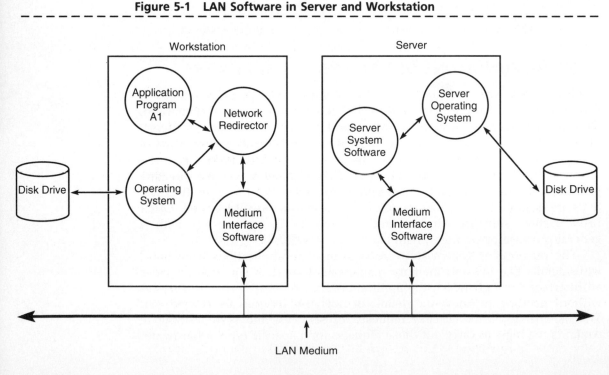

LAN Medium

system software. Let us now see how it is accomplished by considering an application that issues a read for a record that is located on the file server.

System Software Functions

You read in Chapter 3 and 4 that the hardware provides the physical connection between a workstation and a server. The software forms the logical connection; that is, the software uses the hardware to carry on sessions between applications on a workstation and the server. The first function of the LAN software is to set up these logical connections. A variety of protocols are used to do this, and you will learn some details of these later. For now let us assume that this is done by the user issuing a server logon request. If the logon is successful, the user can use the server in accordance with his or her security controls.

The operating system (OS) running in the workstation is aware only of the devices physically attached to that workstation. In our example it is capable of handling requests to drives A, B, and C and to LPT1 on its own. However, it cannot handle I/O requests to drives F and G or direct output to the network printer, LPT2. Ordinarily, when the application issues any file or print request, the request is accepted by the OS, and the OS carries out the request. If a request is made to access a device not attached to the workstation, the OS returns a "device not found" error message. In the LAN situation, to prevent the error message being returned, the requests for drives F and G must be intercepted before they get to the OS. The software that does this is generically called a **redirector.**

The redirector is a software module that intercepts all application I/O requests before they get to the workstation's OS. The redirector passes requests for access to locally attached devices to the OS. Local device access requests are carried out as usual. If the redirector gets a request for a remote access to a LAN server, it sends the request over the network to the server. This is illustrated in Figure 5-2.

The server receives a request for file or print service. Assume for now that the request is for a database record; we will look at printer services later. Many workstations are attached to the network, and any of them can make server requests at any time. Thus the server may receive several requests at nearly the same time. Efficiency requires that the server be able to work on multiple requests at once. This capability is know as **multithreading,** because the server can have multiple transactions in progress at the same time. The server software must keep track of the progress of each transaction.

Suppose, for example, that the server simultaneously receives two requests for a database record, three requests to write to a network printer, and one request to download an application program. These requests arrive in single file, as illustrated in Figure 5-3. The server accepts the first request, a database record read, and searches disk cache memory. If the record is not in cache memory, the server issues a disk read to satisfy it. It also remembers the address of the workstation that requested the read. While the disk is working to find the requested record, the server takes the next request, a

Figure 5-2   LAN Redirector Functions

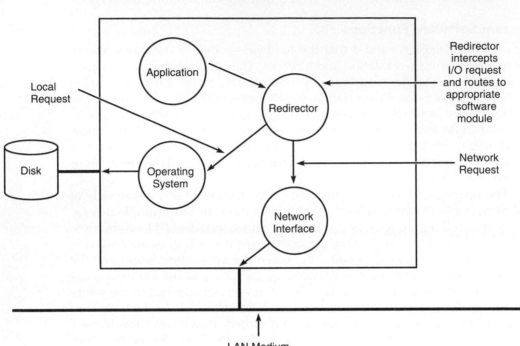

Application

Redirector

Redirector intercepts I/O request and routes to appropriate software module

Local Request

Disk

Operating System

Network Request

Network Interface

LAN Medium

Figure 5-3   LAN Server Request Queue

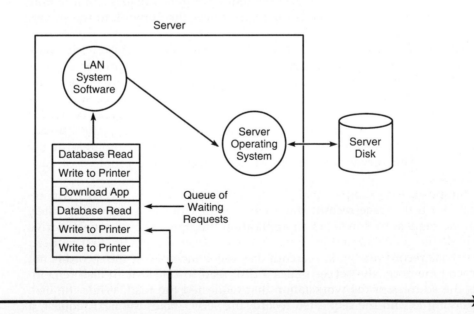

Server

LAN System Software

Server Operating System

Server Disk

Database Read
Write to Printer
Download App
Database Read
Write to Printer
Write to Printer

Queue of Waiting Requests

printer write request, and issues a write to the print file. The server then accepts the next request, one for downloading the application program, and issues a read request for the first segment of the program.

At this point the server is notified that its read for the first database record has been completed. The server recalls the address of the workstation making the request and sends the record back to that workstation. Following that the server takes the next request, a database read, and issues the read that satisfies the request. Thus the server software spends most of its time changing between accepting requests, issuing reads or writes to satisfy them, reacting to completions of those reads and writes, and sending the results back to the requester.

The application/server protocol just described is called a **client/server** or **requester/server protocol.** You should realize the importance of the multithreading capability of the server. A real-world example of single-threading versus multithreading will show why. Suppose you went to a restaurant and your waiter could wait on you only when all tables ahead of you were done. You would end up waiting a long time before getting service, but the service would be great when you finally got it. However, the waiter would have large amounts of idle time waiting for the food to be cooked and so on. In a small restaurant, such as a quick-order restaurant, you may be willing to wait for the person ahead of you in line to be served before placing your order. Likewise in a small LAN such a service protocol might work well. However, the larger the LAN, the more likely there will be multiple, concurrent requests and the more important multithreading becomes.

Let us now look at the LAN system software in more detail. As the software components are discussed, we will discuss how the component becomes involved in handling a server request.

LAN WORKSTATION SOFTWARE

LAN workstation software can also be divided into three classes: application software, workstation system software, and LAN system software. LAN workstation software is simple when compared to server software, but do not expect this to continue. The simplicity of today's environment follows from workstations being primarily single-application, single-user systems; that is, the workstation is doing only one thing at a time. This means that the LAN workstation software can be single-threaded. As workstations become more powerful, you can expect the associated software also to be more powerful to fully exploit the hardware. However, we will consider the current workstation environment.

Workstation Software Interface

We use computers as tools to solve problems. Application software has the logic necessary for solving specific problems, but it does not do all the work essential to the problem solution. With today's systems, applications make requests to system software, which assists applications in carrying out their work. One type of support provided by system software is low-level interfacing with the hardware, such as writing to disks and printers. System software support may come from workstation system software or from LAN system software, depending on the application's needs. Workstation system software assists with local requests, and LAN system software assists with requests needing LAN services.

If you have experience with a programming language, you are likely familiar with procedures, which contain the logic to perform a certain kind of processing. You pass input to a procedure, and it carries out the necessary processing on the input and returns output. For example, you may have a procedure called FIND_MAXIMUM that accepts a list of numbers as input and returns the largest value in the list. When you invoke the procedure, you are making a request. The procedure acts on your request and returns the results. It is not important that you know how the procedure arrived at its conclusion, only that it is done correctly. Similarly, when you make a read or write request to a disk drive, you do not write directly to the disk. Instead you actually pass data to the operating system that carries out this activity on your behalf.

When an application requests a service from the operating system, it does so by issuing a signal called an **interrupt.** A computer's operating system recognizes many interrupts, some generated by application software and some generated by the hardware, for example, to signal an I/O completion. Each interrupt reflects a different class of service. The LAN system software reacts to the interrupt and decides if it is a LAN request or a local request. Thus there must be a match between the interrupt generated by the application and those that are expected by the LAN software.

Today most widely used software packages can run on a LAN; however, some applications operate correctly on one LAN implementation but not on a different one. This can happen because some application software is written specifically for one type of LAN and generates the proper interrupts only for that LAN's software. Therefore, when selecting software that is compatible with your hardware and LAN software, you need to go beyond asking if the application runs on a LAN. You must determine if the software will run on the LAN you will be using and if the software will support concurrent users.

An application communicates with the network through an application program interface (API). Some of the several APIs available are listed in Table 5-1. The basic function of an API is to accept a request from an application, format the request in an API standard format, and send the request over the network to the server. When an API protocol is set up, both the server and the workstation use that protocol to transfer data. If the protocol is not followed, communication is disrupted. When selecting your LAN software you must be careful to ensure that the server and workstations have a common API through which they can communicate. Some LANs support several different APIs. The wider the vareity of APIs supported, the greater the likelihood that an application can run on the LAN.

Table 5-1   Some Application Program Interfaces (APIs)

NETBIOS
Named Pipes
Xerox Network System (XNS)
Advanced Program to Program Communications (APPC)
Novell's Internetwork Packet Exchange and Sequenced Packet Exchange (IPX/SPX)

Workstation System Software

From the previous section you learned that an application uses an API to communicate with the LAN and the operating system. The LAN system software basically consists of two parts: one part that interfaces with the applications and the operating system, and one part that interfaces to the network hardware. These interfaces are illustrated in Figure 5-2.

The portion of the software that interfaces with the applications, the redirector, is responsible for handling the application's interrupts. In general, the application is not aware that the device it is reading from or writing to is a LAN device. Thus each potential LAN service interrupt must be acted on. The LAN redirector therefore accepts all such interrupts, whether they are for local or remote requests. Local requests are sent on to the operating system. Network requests are passed on to the medium-oriented portion of the LAN system software.

Workstations connected to the LAN may use different versions of operating systems. For example, in one LAN system some workstations may use various DOS versions from 2 through 6, some may use OS/2, some may use Apple DOS, and still others may use a version of UNIX. The API for a heterogeneous system must be able to accommodate each of these versions and the interrupts they expect. Inability to do so limits the operating systems that can be used and, as an extension, limits which workstations can be used.

The medium interface portion of the LAN workstation software has two basic functions: placing the data onto the network and receiving the data from the network. This portion of the software is responsible for formatting a message block for transmission over the network. It is closely tied to the LAN server software because it must format message blocks so they are compatible with what is expected by the server, and the workstation software must be able to recognize the format of messages received from the server. The data communications software also interfaces directly to the LAN adapter card.

SPECIFICS OF SERVER SOFTWARE

As previously stated, server software is more complex than workstation software, because server software usually is multithreaded and because the software must work well with the hardware to provide efficient service. We have already discussed the benefits and general strategy of multithreading.

Let us now look at several other functions that might be found in LAN server system software.

Server Operating Systems

Two basic approaches are taken in creating server software. One approach is to integrate the server and operating system functions into one complete software package. The other approach is to write LAN functions that run under an existing operating system, such as UNIX or OS/2. There are advantages and disadvantages to each approach. Table 5-2 lists several of the leading LAN network operating systems.

Novell's **NetWare** is the leading example of the integrated software approach. The primary advantage of this approach is that the designers can optimize the software for LAN operation. That is, the system is designed specifically to provide server functions and can be custom-tailored for that one purpose. The disadvantage of this approach is it requires writing complex software that may already be provided by an existing operating system. This makes the development effort longer and the maintenance becomes more complex.

Table 5-2 Some LAN Software Systems

LAN Name	Vendor Name	Topology	Protocol
Novell	Novell, Inc.	Ring or Bus (Supporting Ethernet, IBM Token Ring, ARCnet)	CSMA/CD or Token Passing
LAN Server	IBM Corporation	Ring	Token Passing
LAN Manager	Microsoft, Inc.	Bus or Ring	CSMA/CD or Token Passing
Apple Talk	Apple Computers, Inc.	Bus	CSMA/CA
PC Network	IBM Corporation	Bus	CSMA/CD
LANtastic	Artisoft, Inc.	Bus	CSMA/CD
TOPS	Sun Microsystems, Inc.	Bus, Star	CSMA/CD
ViaNet	Western Digital Corporation	Bus, Star	CSMA/CD
StarLAN	AT&T Corporation	Star	CSMA/CD
Nexos	DSC Communications Corporation	Bus, Ring	CSMA/CD or Token Passing
VMS	Digital Equipment Corp.	Bus	CSMA/CD
PC/NOS	Corvus Systems, Inc.	Bus (Supporting Ethernet, IBM Token Ring, and ARCnet)	CSMA/CD
Vines	Banyan Systems, Inc.	LAN OS (supporting Ethernet, IBM Token Ring, and ARCnet)	

Creating LAN software that runs under an existing operating system overcomes the disadvantages cited for the integrated approach. Examples of LAN software that run under an existing OS are Banyan Vines, which runs under UNIX, and Microsoft's **LAN Manager** and IBM's **LAN Server,** both of which run under OS/2. The disadvantages are that a general-purpose operating system may be less efficient than one designed to carry out only the special functions required for LAN services.

Some operating systems, such as MS-DOS, are not well suited for hosting a LAN, primarily because of their inherent memory limitations, single-user orientation, and lack of security provisions. Despite these limitations, some LAN software run under DOS and are successful in supporting LANs with few workstations or with limited server requirements. The operating systems that most frequently host LAN software are UNIX and OS/2.

First let us look at some of the functions you might find in a LAN OS. Then we will look briefly at specific LAN operating systems by Novell, IBM, and Banyan. The other OS options listed in Table 5-2 are competitive with those systems, although we do not discuss them in detail here.

LAN Operating System Functions

A LAN OS provides a variety of special capabilities. Among these are I/O optimization and fault tolerance.

Optimized I/O   One of the main services provided by a server is file access. Optimizing this task, or **I/O optimization,** increases the performance of the server. This can be done in a variety of ways. Some methods are hardware oriented, and some are software oriented. One technique that is frequently used is called disk caching, which you can read about in Chapter 4.

Another I/O optimization technique is **disk seek enhancement.** A disk read requires that the read/write heads be positioned to the proper disk location. The act of moving the read/write heads is called a seek. The place to which the heads are moved is called a cylinder or track. Disk requests typically arrive in random order. Disk seek enhancement arranges the requests in order so the read/write heads move methodically over the disk, reading data from the nearest location. This is illustrated in Table 5-3. In Table 5-3(a) you can see the order in which several disk requests are received. Shown in Table 5-3(b) is the optimum way to access those records and the savings in number of cylinders when processing the requests in the optimum order. Reducing the seeks improves performance.

Fault Tolerance   Some network operating systems provide increased reliability through a feature called **fault tolerance.** If you have only one server and it fails, the network is down. A LAN with fault tolerance allows the server to survive some failures that would ordinarily be disabling. Fault tolerance usually is provided by a combination of backup hardware components and software that is capable of using the backup hardware.

The lowest level of fault tolerance is the ability to recover quickly from a failure. That is, a failure that shuts the server down may occur, but the system can quickly be recovered to an operational state. One technique that makes this possible involves writing backup copies of critical disk information—for example, disk directories, file allocation tables, and so on—to an alternate disk drive. Another helpful technique is called **read-after-write.** After writing data to a disk, the system reads the data again to ensure that no disk write errors occurred. If the data cannot be read again, the area of the disk containing that data is removed from future use and the data is written to a good area.

Fault tolerance also can be proved by **mirrored disks,** which are two disks that contain the same data. Whenever a disk write occurs, the data is written to both disk drives. If one of the disks fails, the other is available and processing continues. Mirrored disks have an additional benefit: Two disk drives are available for reads, so both disks can work simultaneously on behalf of two different requests. For added support some LAN servers also allow duplexed disk controllers. In such a configuration a controller can fail and another is available to continue working. Thus you can survive a controller failure and a disk failure.

Mirrored disk reliability can be extended using **redundant arrays of independent disks (RAID).** (Sometimes the letter I in RAID stands for inexpensive not independent.) RAID technology spreads data over three or more disk drives. The stored data consists of the actual data plus **parity data**—additional data that provides the ability to reconstruct data that has been corrupted. Thus, if one drive fails, the data stored on that drive can be reconstructed from data stored on the remaining drives. Parity data can be reconstructed because the remaining parts of the file are still available. If a section of the file is lost, it can be reconstructed from the parity data and the remaining parts of the file. The advantage of RAID over mirroring is that fewer disk drives are required for redundancy. For example, with mirroring, two drives of data require four disk drives; with RAID, the same information can be stored on three drives with the same level of reliability. Disk mirroring and RAID technology, illustrated in Figure 5-4, can provide more

Table 5-3   Disk Seek Enhancement Example

(a)

Disk Read Requests (Cylinder or Track) in order of arrival	Number of Cylinders Moved (assume a starting position of cylinder 0)	
50, 250, 25, 300, 250, 50, 300	50 + 200 + 225 + 275 + 50 + 200 + 250 = 1250	

(b)

Disk Read Requests (Cylinder or Track) in optimal order		
25, 50, 50, 250, 250, 300, 300	25 + 25 + 0 + 200 + 0 + 50 + 0 = 300	Savings = 950 Cylinders

efficient data access because they make available multiple disk drives for reading and writing.

The best fault tolerance is provided by **duplexed servers.** With this configuration one server can fail and another is available to continue working. Even though it appears that this fault tolerance capability is primarily hardware oriented, software must exist that takes advantage of the duplexed hardware. A fault-tolerant duplexed server is illustrated in Figure 5-5. Fault tolerance has been provided commercially by large systems since 1977. Today fault tolerance features are available in most of the leading network operating systems, which we will examine now.

Figure 5-4   Disk Mirroring and RAID Technology

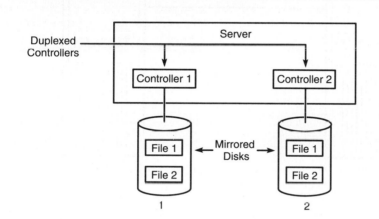

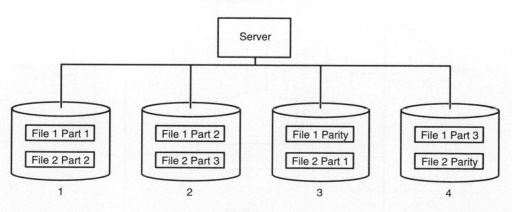

RAID Disks

Figure 5-5   A Fault-Tolerant Duplexed Server

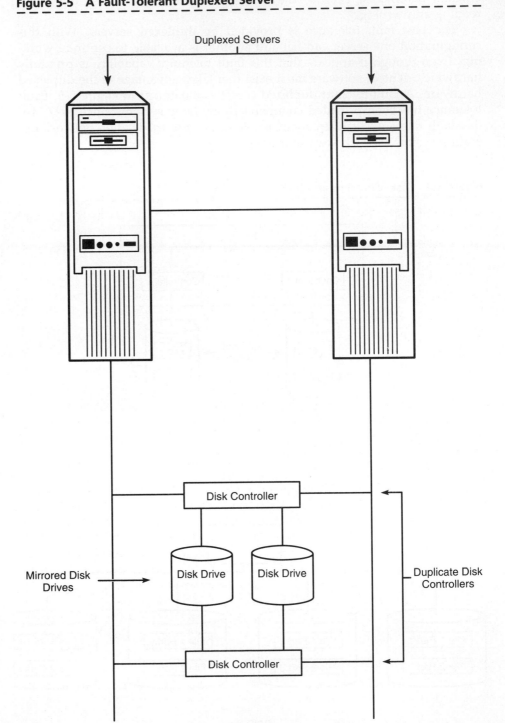

Duplexed Servers

Disk Controller

Mirrored Disk
Drives

Disk Drive   Disk Drive

Duplicate Disk
Controllers

Disk Controller

Novell Operating Systems

Over time Novell has offered several versions of network operating systems. Today Novell offers three basic systems with a variety of configuration options for two of the versions. For very small networks using peer-to-peer workstations, Novell offers Netware Lite. A **peer-to-peer network** is one that has no dedicated servers, and the network administrator can make the resources of each network node accessible to other network nodes. This technique is most suitable for networks with few nodes.

For high-end networks Novell offers NetWare 286, NetWare 386, and NetWare 4.0. Fault tolerance capabilities are available with each version. NetWare 4.0 is Novell's newest network operating system. Its market is companies with very large networks and those having several networks. NetWare 4.0 supports up to 1000 nodes per LAN, simultaneous connection to multiple servers, and a network naming directory that helps users locate local and remote network resources. NetWare 386 is designed to run on server hardware based on the 80386, 80486, and later model processors only. Netware 286 runs on 80286 server platforms as well as on the more advanced processors. These network operating systems are available for networks with a wide range of users. For example, Netware 386 can be purchased for networks ranging from five to several hundred users, and Netware 4.0 fills the need for larger networks. The cost of the system is scaled according to the maximum number of supported users. Thus small networks can realize the same operating system technology as that used on very large LANs but at a much lower cost (that is, the cost per user for the LAN software remains somewhat constant).

One significant feature available from Novell is **System Fault Tolerance (SFT),** which provides an environment in which certain hardware failures do not cause network failures. For example, SFT supports mirrored disk drives. Thus if one of the mirrored disk drives fails, the other is available to provide continuous service.

All Novell OS versions are designed to optimize LAN performance. An efficient file server must be able to quickly retrieve data from its disks. Novell provides optimized disk directory support and disk caching to maximize performance. With disk caching, data is held in memory buffers after being read from the disk. Thus, if the data is needed by two users or must be reused by one user, physical disk accesses can be eliminated. For example, suppose that two LAN users start a word processing program at nearly the same instant. Rather than reading the program file from disk for each user, it is read only once, improving the response time to the requests. Naturally sufficient memory must be available to take advantage of disk caching.

Novell Network Interface and Utilities Software

Novell also provides a variety of network interface products and utilities, including

LAN to SNA gateway

LAN to IBM minicomputers, for example, System 38 systems

X.25 gateway

LAN-to-LAN interconnection products using X.25 or T1 lines

structured query language (SQL) server

Btrieve, a file management system

network management services

Transmission Control Protocol/Internet Protocol (TCP/IP) protocol suite

The breadth of their interface products makes it clear that Novell does not view its LAN systems as isolated islands of computing. Instead Novell is active in building bridges and gateways to other networks and systems.

IBM's LAN Server and OS/2 Operating System

OS/2 is the second generation of operating systems for IBM and IBM-compatible microcomputers. It incorporates several data communications capabilities, including both LAN interfaces and terminal emulation features. Although this chapter is oriented to LANs, both the LAN and data communications facilities are presented in this section.

There are two versions of OS/2, standard and extended. The standard OS/2 version provides multitasking, presentation services, and data communications capabilities similar to those of the original IBM PC operating system, DOS. IBM's extended OS/2 version provides several enhanced data communications capabilities via their LAN Server and a communications manager and a database manager.

Several vendors are providing different extended versions of OS/2. Each provides different combinations of the LAN server and communications manager capabilities. For instance, IBM's LAN Server supports only IBM Token Ring LANs (although support for other MAC protocols may be added by the time you read this). Microsoft's version supports both token rings and IEEE 802.3 LANs. Additional vendors that have announced extended OS/2 versions include AST Research Inc., Rapid Software, and Digital Communications Associates, Inc. It is likely that other companies will also release extended OS/2 versions either to compete with existing products or to augment existing capabilities.

The following sections give you an overview of the major capabilities of the IBM LAN Server and communications manager.

LAN Server IBM's LAN Server supports IBM's Token Ring LAN only. Other vendors also support IEEE 802.3 networks. Some LAN managers provide components that allow a microcomputer to function as a server or as a workstation. A variety of LAN hardware components from multiple vendors can also be accommodated by some vendor offerings.

Communications Manager The communications manager provides terminal and gateway support. Most vendors provide a variety of asynchronous terminal emulation, IBM 3270 terminal emulation, X.25 services, and a program-to-program gateway to an IBM host system. Other capabilities include a variety of interfaces to IBM's Systems Network Architecture (SNA), which is discussed in Chapter 12. Some of these communications manager functions also exist under DOS; however, OS/2 provides these functions in one comprehensive package rather than as a variety of individual packages from various vendors. Moreover OS/2's multitasking capabilities allow more terminal sessions to be active than in the DOS environment. Connections to multiple hosts as well as to a LAN can be supported concurrently.

Banyan Vines

Banyan Vines is recognized for its support for large networks and network interconnections. Banyan Vines runs on UNIX-based servers. Being UNIX based gives Banyan a distinct advantage, because many WANs contain nodes running the UNIX operating system. This makes it easier for Vines systems to connect to those nodes. Moreover a server based on UNIX can be effectively used as an application system in addition to providing LAN services; that is, the server platform can function not only as a server but also as a platform for running application programs. OS/2 operating systems allow multitasking but not multiuser capabilities and thus cannot match UNIX-based machines, which allow several users to run applications.

One of the major strengths of Vines is a global naming strategy called **StreetTalk.** StreetTalk is a database that identifies network resources—users, files, hardware, and so on. This database is replicated on each server in the network, thus providing a measure of fault tolerance as well as making resource lookup more efficient. Applications use StreetTalk to locate needed resources; for example, a mail application can use it to find the location of mail recipients. LAN managers use StreetTalk to assist in controlling the network and network users; for example, the access rights of each user can be placed in the StreetTalk database. A rather unique feature of StreetTalk, particularly for international networks, is the ability to store certain information like status and error messages in several languages. Although other LAN vendors, such as Novell, have announced or released such a product, none has yet to match StreetTalk's capabilities.

Interoperability of Server Software

If you have a large LAN, you may need more than one file server. (The point at which a second server is needed varies according to the number of active, concurrent users and their server access profiles.) If two or more servers are required, you must ensure that they operate correctly. Often, if all servers are using the same hardware and software platforms, they can operate correctly in concert. It is not always true, however, that two different server software packages can interoperate correctly. As an example, there has been a reasonable amount of press coverage regarding the compatibility of IBM's LAN Server with Microsoft's LAN Manager system, even though both are based on the OS/2 operating system and have common roots.

What do we mean by interoperability? Basically **interoperability** means the ability of all network components to connect to the network and to communicate with shared network resources. With a global view this means the ability to interconnect different networks and to have nodes on one network able to communicate with nodes on the same network or another network (provided they have the appropriate security). On a single network it means that any node can access resources to which it has appropriate security. Interoperability is usually easy in a homogeneous network—one in which only one network operating system version is used and where the workstations are all of the same type and use the same operating system. Networks using a mixture of network operating systems and workstation platforms make interoperability more complex.

Banyan Vines with its StreetTalk network directory services and internetwork protocol support makes interoperability easier. Networks that support internetworking protocols like TCP/IP also facilitate internetwork operations. We will discuss internetwork operations in Chapter 14. Let us now look at interoperability in a single network.

Consider a network that has two servers with different network operating systems, say Novell and Banyan. If users were to use only one or the other server, it would probably be easier to divide the network into a Novell network and a Banyan Vines network. If both servers are available on one network, then we may assume that some users must have access to both servers. In doing this some of the complications given in Table 5-4 may exist. How well the server operating systems can handle these issues affects the interoperability of the network.

Print Spooler

LAN users share LAN printers. It ought to be obvious that only one user can be physically printing to a printer at one time and yet several users will need to logically write to one printer at the same time. Logically writing to a printer means that the user has opened a printer and has written to that printer; however, the printed output may not be physically written to the printer at that time. The output is first written to a disk file and is printed after the complete output has been collected. The software subsystem that

Table 5-4 Possible Complications of Having Two Network Operating Systems in One Network

Compatibility of user identifiers and passwords
Synchronization of user identifiers and passwords across servers
Ability to simultaneously access data on two servers
Ability to access data on one server and print to spooler on another
Applications that can run from both servers
Support for common application program interfaces (APIs)
Support for common protocols at the OSI network and transport layers
Ability to use/have two redirector processes

allows several users to logically write to one printer at the same time is called a spooler. The operation of a spooler is graphically shown in Figure 5-6. Let us trace the activity of a print job through the spooler.

The user at one workstation is using a word processing program to create a report, and the user at another workstation is using a spreadsheet program to prepare a budget. At nearly the same time, each user prints the document he or she is working on. The output is directed to LPT2 on each system. On each system LPT2 is mapped by the network software to the laser printer attached to the server. Before writing to the printer, each application first opens the printer. The redirector at each system directs the open request to the server. When the server receives the printer open request, it is passed to the spooler software. The spooler software prepares to receive each workstation's printed output into a disk file. When each application receives an acknowledgment that the "printer" has been successfully opened, it begins to send output to the printer.

The spooler receives the output from each workstation and stores it in that workstation's print file on disk. This process continues until each workstation is done. When the application closes the printer file, the print job is ready to be physically written to the printer.

Be aware that some applications, for example, some versions of Lotus 1-2-3, do not close the print file until the user explicitly chooses a close printer option or until the application terminates. If this occurs, a user may not get a printout when expected. For example, suppose that Maria is working on a spreadsheet and prints a portion of it. If the printing had been sent to a locally attached printer, it would print immediately. With a spooler, however, the spreadsheet program does not close the printer, and the job is left open. This allows for another portion of the spreadsheet to be printed directly after the first print range. The spreadsheet program continues to hold the file open until Maria exits from the spreadsheet. Her job then is scheduled for printing. In this case printing on a LAN differs from printing to a local printer and may not be what Maria wants. She may want the range to be printed immediately so she can use that information for her further work. For such instances some spoolers also allow the print job to be closed if a certain time elapses before receiving additional print data. This feature allows the user to obtain the printed results without having to exit from the application.

When a print job has been closed, the spooler schedules it for printing. Spoolers have a priority scheme by which they decide which job prints next. Some spoolers print the jobs in the order in which they became ready to print (first in, first out); some print the smallest available job; others print jobs according to user-assigned priorities. When the job has been printed, it may be removed from the disk to make room for other print jobs. Alternatively the job may be held on disk for printing at a later time, for printing to a different device, or for perusal from a workstation. Spooler systems provide a variety of options regarding the association of logical print devices with physical printers and the treatment of jobs captured in the spooler files. Some of these options are listed in Table 5-5.

Figure 5-6 Spooler Operating Environment

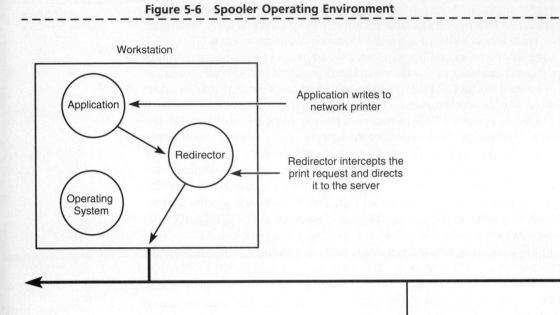

Workstation

Application

Redirector

Operating System

Application writes to network printer

Redirector intercepts the print request and directs it to the server

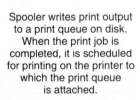

Spooler writes print output to a print queue on disk. When the print job is completed, it is scheduled for printing on the printer to which the print queue is attached.

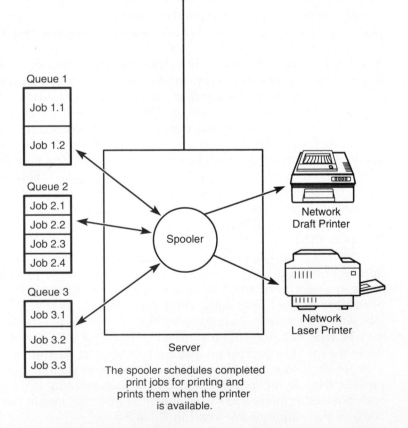

Queue 1

Job 1.1

Job 1.2

Queue 2

Job 2.1

Job 2.2

Job 2.3

Job 2.4

Queue 3

Job 3.1

Job 3.2

Job 3.3

Spooler

Server

Network Draft Printer

Network Laser Printer

The spooler schedules completed print jobs for printing and prints them when the printer is available.

Backup Software

The previous chapter discussed backup hardware. The software used to perform the backups is as important as the hardware. **Backup software** is responsible for reading the files being backed up and writing them to the backup device. During recovery a restoration module reads the backup medium and writes the data back to disk. There are several backup software options available. They all provide the basic functions of backing up and restoring data. They differ with respect to how they do this, the options they provide, the devices they support, and their ease of use. Frequently backup devices come with a backup/restore program (both capabilities are contained on one program) and most LAN system software includes a backup/restore module. For example, Novell's backup/restore program for one version of their network software is NBACKUP. Some LAN administrators, however, choose to purchase a separate, more functional backup system than the LAN or backup device versions. In Chapter 4 Table 4-2 lists some of the features supported by backup software.

Utility and Administrative Software

A LAN administrator must have utility and administrative software to assist in fulfilling the administrative tasks. These software modules are discussed in the next chapter.

SOFTWARE REQUIREMENTS FOR SHARED USAGE

Most early microcomputer applications were written for single-user systems, which means that the software developers could make certain simplifying design decisions. To use these applications in a shared LAN system, accom-

Table 5-5   Some Spooler Options

Collect printed output
Direct print jobs to designated printers
Hold jobs in disk queue after printing
Hold jobs in disk queue before printing
View jobs on hold in print queue
Set number of print copies
Setting print job priorities
Delete jobs from print queue
Attach/detach printers from print queue
Set/change job priorities
Add/delete printers
Start/stop printers
Start/stop spooler process
Print banners
Close print jobs based on time-out interval
Print statistical reports

modations must be made by the LAN administrators, by the LAN system software, or by the application itself. Let us now look at the required changes.

Hardware Configuration

Software written for a single user need not be concerned with problems of computer configuration. You are probably aware that microcomputers may be configured with a variety of options. The primary variations are in memory, disk configurations, printer configuration, and monitor support. In a stand-alone system the application software is set up to match the configuration of that system. However, a LAN might have many different workstation configurations, and application software ought to support each configuration as much as possible. This can be done in several ways.

Some applications support only one configuration. The hardware settings of such applications are stored in a single file. One way to use this type of application is to configure the application for the lowest common denominator of hardware and have each user get essentially the same configuration. Users with high-resolution color graphics monitors might have images displayed in monochrome at low resolution, or a user with a hard disk drive might have to use a flexible disk drive rather than the hard disk for some files. Usually LAN administrators can avoid this type of configuration by storing multiple versions of the application in different disk directories. Users can then use the configuration that most closely matches their computer's profile.

Some applications allow several configuration files and decide which to use by a run-time parameter or by making a default choice if the startup parameter is not specified. LAN administrators can provide each user with a tailored environment by virtue of a batch startup file.

Applications that are designed for LAN use usually have a user-oriented configuration file. Each LAN user has his or her personal configuration that is custom-tailored for a specific user and his or her specific hardware. This provides users with the most flexibility and requires little or no customization by the LAN administrator. These options are illustrated in Table 5-6.

Table 5-6   Multiple Application Configurations
— — — — — — — — — — — — — — — — — —·

Default disk drive
Default disk directory
Disk drive mappings
Disk drive/directory search paths
Printer mappings
Initial program/menu

Application Settings

The software equivalent to hardware configurations are application settings. Ideally users tailor application settings to meet personal preferences. For example, one word processor user might prefer green characters on a black background with tab stops every five character positions. Another user might prefer white characters on a blue background with tab stops every four character positions. Each user ought to receive these settings as the default. Application settings can be defined in a way similar to setting hardware options.

Contention

You already learned a little about contention in Chapters 1 and 3. Remember that whenever two users are capable of accessing the same resource at the same time, contention for that resource can occur. Earlier you read how the spooler resolved contention for a printer: First the print outputs are captured on disk, and then the spooler schedules each job to be printed when the printer is available to accept new print jobs. You experience similar problems when accessing files.

One of the classic examples of a contention problem is illustrated by two users working on one document at the same time. Refer to Chapter 1, Figure 1-1, to review this problem. The same type of problem can occur when two users access and update the same database record.

A primitive way to handle contention is simply to avoid it by scheduling user activities so they do not interfere with each other. On small LANs this may be possible, but as the number of concurrent users increases, this method becomes clumsy. Rather than avoiding contention, an application or LAN software should prevent contention problems. Contention is prevented by exerting controls over files or records.

One contention prevention mechanism is activated when an application opens a file. There are three basic file **open modes:** exclusive, protected, and shared. In **exclusive open mode,** an open request is granted only if no other user has the file already open. Moreover file open requests from other users are denied until the application having an exclusive open closes the file.

Exclusive opens may be too restrictive for some applications. Suppose, for example, that two users, Alice and Tom, are both working on the same word processing document. Alice needs to update the document, and Tom only needs to read it. In this case Tom will not interfere with the work being accomplished by Alice. A **protected open mode** can satisfy both user's needs. Protected open mode is granted only if no other user already has been granted exclusive or protected mode. Once open in protected mode, only the application with protected open can update the document. **Shared open mode** allows several users to have the file open concurrently. In **shared update mode,** all users can update the file. In **shared read-only mode,** all users can read the file but cannot write to it. For example, if Alice opens the document in protected mode and Tom opens the document in shared read-only mode, Alice can read and update the document and Tom can read it. However, Tom cannot open the document in exclusive, protected, or shared update mode while a protected open exists.

Sometimes, a read-only application must be protected against file updates. For example, an application that is doing a trial balance of an accounting file must prohibit updates during the reading and calculations. If another application makes changes while the file is being read, the figures may not balance. The trial balance application can protect against this by opening the accounts file in protected read-only mode. This disallows other processes from opening the file in update mode while allowing processes to open the file in shared read-only mode. Table 5-7 shows the combinations of exclusive, protected, and shared open modes.

Table 5-7 Exclusive, Protected, and Shared Open Combinations

Open Mode Requested	Currently Opened As			
	Exclusive	Protected	Shared Update	Shared Read-Only
Exclusive	denied	denied	denied	denied
Protected	denied	denied	denied	granted
Shared, Update	denied	denied	granted	granted
Shared, Read-Only	denied	granted	granted	granted

Exclusive and protected open modes are sufficient for meeting some contention problems, like the word processing one described earlier. However, they are overly restrictive for other applications, such as database processing. One objective of database applications is for several users to share data. Exclusive opens allow only one user at a time to use the data. The problem with file open contention resolution is overcome by exerting controls at a lower level, the record level. Record level controls are called **locks.**

Suppose that our two users, Alice and Tom, want to update a database. So long as they are using different records, they will not interfere with each other. However, suppose that at some time both Alice and Tom need to update and access the same record. Contention problems like those experienced in updating the word processing document might occur. If, however, Alice locked the record when accessing it, Tom's read request would be denied until Alice unlocked the record. This is illustrated in Figure 5-7. Note that Tom waits until the record has been unlocked before being allowed to proceed.

Record locking can, however, cause another problem—**deadlock,** or **deadly embrace.** To illustrate this, suppose that Alice and Tom are accessing the database. Alice's application reads and locks record X, and at nearly the same time, Tom's application reads and locks record Y. After reading record X, Alice attempts to read record Y and, of course, waits because the record is locked. If Tom then attempts to read record X, deadlock occurs: Alice and Tom are waiting for each other, and neither can continue until the record they are waiting for is unlocked, which can never happen because there is a circular chain of users waiting on each other. Note that three or more users can also be involved in this circular chain of events. The deadlock problem is illustrated in Figure 5-8. Deadlock avoidance or resolution methods exist but are beyond the scope of this next. You can read about these methods in many database texts.

Some database systems take care of contention for users. They recognize when contention is occurring and prevent the problems associated with it. One convention used to do this is outlined as follows:

1. User A reads record X.

2. User B reads record X (and the read is allowed).

3. User A updates record X (and the update is allowed).

4. User B attempts to update record X.

5. The database management system recognizes that the record has been changed since User B read it.

Figure 5-7 Waiting for Lock Release

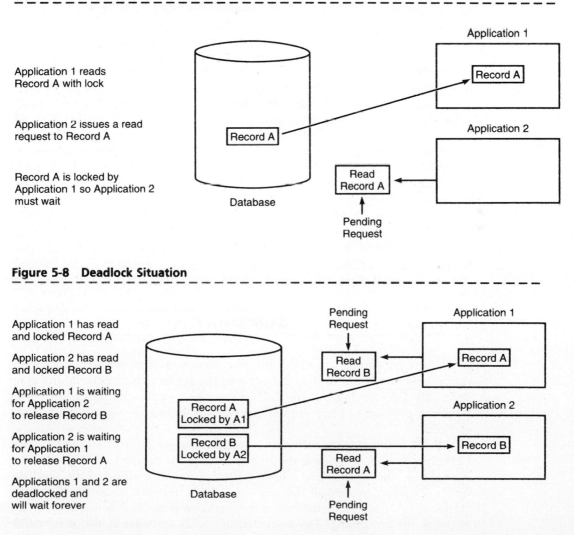

Figure 5-8 Deadlock Situation

6. The database management system sends the revised copy of record X to User B and notifies the user that the update was rejected because the record was changed by another user.

7. User B reissues the update or takes another course of action.

In selecting LAN software, it is critical that you understand the problems of configuration and contention. Without a resolution to these issues, the effectiveness of the system is reduced or, worse yet, the data becomes corrupted. Sharing data has another side effect that must be addressed—security.

Access Security

Early operating systems, and many current ones for stand-alone microcomputers, do not provide file security. Even though only one user can use a microcomputer at one time, several users might use one system. Without security these users not only have access to another user's sensitive data, but also might accidentally (or intentionally) remove another user's files. Access to the computer essentially provides access to all data stored on that computer. A user might store sensitive data on a stand-alone microcomputer's disks, but those users are limited with respect to their ability to protect that data from unauthorized reading, changes, or destruction. The user could store the data on a removable disk and store it in a secure place when not being used. Another alternative is buying an application that provides password security or allows hiding or encrypting data to protect it from misuse.

When you install a LAN, data that must be shared and was once stored as "private" data on one or more stand-alone systems will likely end up being placed in a database on a server. Without security all data on the servers can be accessed, updated, and deleted by any LAN user. For most applications this is not acceptable. Therefore, the LAN system software must provide protection through security. Other security concerns include protecting against software piracy and preventing the introduction of computer viruses. We will discuss security in more detail in Chapter 8.

SUMMARY

LAN software can be separated into two classes, system software and application software. LAN system software in the servers and workstations is responsible for carrying out the LAN functions. Application software solves business problems. LAN system software is found on servers and workstations.

Workstation system software is responsible for intercepting application I/O requests and deciding if the request is local or network. If the request is a local one, the workstation's LAN software passes it along to the workstation's operating system. If the request is for a network resource, the workstation's LAN software formats a network message and sends it over the network for processing. The workstation's LAN software is also responsible for accepting LAN messages and passing them along to the proper application. Because LAN workstation software must remain resident in the workstation's memory, a stand-alone workstation may need a memory upgrade to run some LAN applications.

LAN server software is more complex than workstation software. Some functions it may provide are

I/O optimization	fault tolerance
printer services	file backup and restoration
utility and administrative support	contention resolution
access security	

These functions help either to make performance better, to improve reliability, or to protect data from accidental or intentional damage.

When choosing LAN software, one consideration you need to make is how that software will interoperate with other software, other networks, and your hardware. Poor interoperability increases the complexity of using a LAN and decreases its usability.

KEY TERMS

backup software

client/server protocol

deadlock

deadly embrace

disk seek enhancement

duplexed servers

exclusive open mode

fault tolerance

input/output (I/O)

I/O optimization

interoperability

interrupt

LAN Manager, Microsoft

LAN Server, IBM

lock, record

mirrored disks

multithreading

NetWare, Novell

open modes, file

operating system (OS)

parity data

peer-to-peer network

protected open mode

read-after-write

redirector

redundant arrays of independent disks (RAID)

requester/server protocol

shared open mode

shared read-only mode

shared update mode

StreetTalk, Banyan

System Fault Tolerance (SFT), Novell

Vines, Banyan

REVIEW QUESTIONS

1. Explain the functions of the workstation redirector software.

2. Explain how an application's network request is processed by both the workstation and the server.

3. Why may a stand-alone workstation need a memory upgrade when added to a LAN?

4. Explain why multithreaded server operation is important.

5. What is a client-server or requester-server protocol? Give an example.

6. What is an application program interface (API)?

7. What is the purpose of I/O optimization? Give two examples.

8. What is the benefit of fault-tolerant servers?

9. Describe three fault tolerance capabilities.

10. Explain how a print spooler works.

11. Explain two ways in which application software can be tailored to individual users.

12. Describe two ways in which data contention can be avoided.

13. What is deadlock? Give an example.

PROBLEMS AND EXERCISES

1. Use the literature to identify and briefly describe five capabilities of fault tolerance systems, such as Novell's SFT system or Tandem's NonStop systems. The following magazine sources may prove helpful: *Network Management, LAN Times, LAN Technology, LAN,* and *Network Computing.* You may use CD-ROM sources, such as *Computer Select.*

2. Evaluate a LAN-compatible database management system to determine how it resolves contention. Is contention resolution the responsibility of the user of the database management system? Systems you may want to examine include Paradox and dBASE IV from Borland and FoxBase from Microsoft.

3. Research the literature for references to a LAN server that runs under the DOS operating system. How many users does the system support? Attempt to determine the expected level of performance.

4. Investigate one of the backup/restore software packages available. What functions does it provide?

5. You have been asked to configure the hardware for a local area network to provide office automation capabilities for a small office. The office manager wants you to provide a LAN that will make use of four IBM ATs with 1 MB of memory, two IBM XTs with 640 KB of memory, two IBM XTs with 512 KB of memory, one laser printer, and two dot-matrix printers that the office currently owns. Draw a network diagram of your proposed LAN using a bus topology. Label all hardware components in your diagram. Prepare a report to accompany your diagram that gives the following details:

   a. the equipment, software, and cabling that will be needed to connect each device to the LAN

   b. necessary upgrades to any of the existing hardware to make it LAN-usable

6. Consider the office LAN described in problem 5. Suppose that some employees want to access the LAN from their home to transfer files and do remote printing. Configure the hardware, software, and communications capabilities required at the LAN and user end of the connection.

7. Suppose the office described in problem 5 wants to add FAX capabilities to the network. The capabilities needed include the ability to send and receive FAX transmissions and to store FAX images on

disk. Images sent and received may be in either hard copy or disk image format. Describe the hardware, software, and communications equipment necessary to create this capability.

REFERENCES

Allinger, Doug. "Beyond Basic Backup." *LAN Technology*, Volume 6, Number 7, July 1990.

Allinger, Doug. "Fault Tolerance Comes to LAN Servers." *LAN Technology*, Volume 7, Number 1, January 1991.

Bolt, Robert C. "Battle of the Database Servers." *LAN Technology*, Volume 7, Number 1, January 1991.

Bigley, Tom. "Backup for Safe Keeping." *Infoworld*, October 15, 1990.

Cavanagh, James P., Guaraldi, Robert L., McKinney, Kathleen, and Cleary, Mary Anne. "Anatomy of a Network OS Selection." *LAN Technology*, Volume 6, Number 6, June 1990.

Cavanagh, James P., Guaraldi, Robert L., McKinney, Kathleen, and Cleary, Mary Anne. "Anatomy of a Network OS Selection." *LAN Technology*, Volume 6, Number 7, July 1990.

Cavanagh, James P., "Anatomy of a Network OS Selection." *LAN Technology*, Volume 6, Number 8, August 1990.

Cavanaugh, Jim. "Decision '92: The Network Choice." *LAN Technology*, Volume 8, Number 12, November 1992.

Day, Mike. "Network Printing: The Second Generation." *LAN Times*, Volume 9, Issue 15, August 10, 1992.

Derfler, Jr., Frank J. "Network Operating Systems Go Corporate." *PC Magazine*, Volume 11, Number 11, June 16, 1992.

Derfler, Jr., Frank J. and Thompson, Keith. "LAN Operating Systems: The Power Behind the Server." *PC Magazine*, Volume 9, Number 10, May 29, 1990.

Germann, Christopher. "High-Performance Network Operating Systems." *LAN Times*, Volume 7, Issue 4, April 1990.

Gilliland, Jim. "Surveying OS/2 2.0 Networking Options." *LAN Technology*, Volume 8, Number 10, October 1992.

Gillooly, Caryn. "Prepping Peer NOSes for the Enterprise." *Network World*, Volume 9, Number 33, August 17, 1992.

Janusaitis, Robert. "Meeting the NOS Selection Challenge." *Network World*, Volume 9, Number 41, October 12, 1992.

McCann, John T. "NetWare 386: A Breed with a Future." *LAN Technology*, Volume 6, Number 11, November 1990.

Mendelson, Edward. "Premium Insurance: Backup Software Gets Better." *PC Magazine*, Volume 10, Number 11, June 11, 1991.

Nance, Barry. "Interoperability Today." *Byte*, Volume 16, Number 12, November 1991.

Pritchett, Glenn. "Now Printing at a Network Near You." *LAN Technology*, Volume 8, Number 2, February 1992.

Seelbach, Geoffre. "Continuous Backup Systems." *Network World*, October 22, 1990.

CHAPTER 6

APPLICATION SOFTWARE

CHAPTER PREVIEW

In the preceding chapter you read about LAN system software. Realize, however, that a LAN is simply a tool that allows its users to do their work more effectively. We use LANs because they provide cost-effective solutions to business problems. It is the application software that allows us to solve these problems. We can easily lose sight of this when we get involved in LAN technology. In this chapter you will read about the general considerations for choosing application software. Several key application software systems are covered in some detail.

Specific topics you will read about include:

database software

workgroup software

primary business software

setting software standards

software protection

DATABASE SOFTWARE

Database management systems (DBMSs) have been mentioned earlier, so we will concentrate here on additional LAN-oriented functions you must look for when selecting a DBMS. For several reasons, DBMS software selection may be one of your most difficult tasks. A DBMS is not only a personal productivity tool but also a key subsystem for workgroup productivity and corporate computing applications.

Frequently you'll need to import and export database data, a task requiring interoperability between other application programs and other DBMSs. Also, database files tend to be highly shared and thus more prone to contention problems than word processing, spreadsheet, and similar files. In a word processing or spreadsheet application, users typically do not use one file at the same time; in a database management system, users frequently need to use the same file simultaneously. If errors occur when a user is updating the database, the data could unfortunately be left in an inconsistent state. Your DBMS choice should contain provisions to protect you and your users from such risks.

Some of the issues of multiple concurrent users, the ability to have individual user profiles, and so on, have already been covered. We do not intend to lessen the importance of these issues in other software packages; however, the likelihood of contention and inconsistency problems are less for these applications when used in the normal way. For example, the normal way to use a word processing application for personal productivity is for each user to be working on a different document, not on different parts of the same document. Word processor users often open a file exclusively to prevent other users from inadvertently editing a file being used by someone else, or they open the file in protected mode so only one user can update the document while others can access it for read-only purposes.

In Chapter 1 we introduced the concept of contention, and in Chapter 5 we showed how contention resolution can result in deadlock. You may wish to refer back to these chapters to refresh your understanding of contention and deadlock. In choosing a DBMS you should understand how the system resolves contention and how it deals with deadlock.

Another major concern when selecting a DBMS is how it supports **transaction processing.** Two fundamental methods are used to process data: batch and on-line transaction processing. In **batch processing**, you collect pieces of data over time and process them as a group. Often only one group of updates is processed at a time; that is, you have no concurrent updates to a file. In **on-line transaction processing,** you process events as they occur. In both cases you must be concerned with the integrity of data in the database. In batch processing you often make backups of files before beginning a batch update. If a fault occurs during the batch processing, the backup file allows you to return to a consistent state. Alternatively you can use periodic synchronization points in the processing. At synchronization points you are assured that the database is consistent. If a failure occurs during processing, you can return the database back to its state at the last synchronization point by writing **before** and **after images** of the records you are updating. The techniques for doing database recovery are beyond the scope of this book.

With on-line transaction processing, two or more users may be involved in making updates at the same time. Ideally each user's work does not affect the work of other database users. However, unless you carefully schedule the work, you cannot count on this. Thus the ability of a DBMS to support transaction definition and recovery is important for databases that may be updated concurrently.

A **transaction** is a database activity that moves the database from one consistent state to another consistent state. A **consistent state** is one in which the data is accurate and complete. A transaction is an atomic unit of work, which means that the transaction either is completed in its entirety or leaves the database in the state it was in before the transaction started. Some database transactions only read data in the database. For example, you may run a database query to find the average employee salary. This transaction does not update the database and thus does not affect its consistency. From a database consistency perspective, we are interested only in transactions that perform updates.

Now, let us consider an update transaction and its problem potential. A bank account transfer transaction is a simple illustration of the problem. Other transactions that update two or more records are similar to this example. This account transfer transaction moves funds from a savings account to a checking account. This transaction has two phases: In phase 1 the savings account record is read, the account balance reduced, and the record rewritten. In phase 2 the checking account record is read, the account balance increased by the amount of the savings account reduction, and the record rewritten. Clearly it is not appropriate to take the money out of the savings account while failing to put the money into the checking account. To do so leaves the database in an inconsistent state and the bank customer in an irate state. The database states for this transaction are illustrated in Figure 6-1. Your DBMS should prevent a user from leaving the transaction in a state of partial update and leaving the database inconsistent.

To provide transaction integrity, the DBMS should support the ability to define a transaction and ensure either that the transaction ends successfully or, if it is unsuccessful, that any uncompleted transaction updates are reversed, thus leaving the database in the state it was in prior to the start of

Figure 6-1   Account Transfer Database States

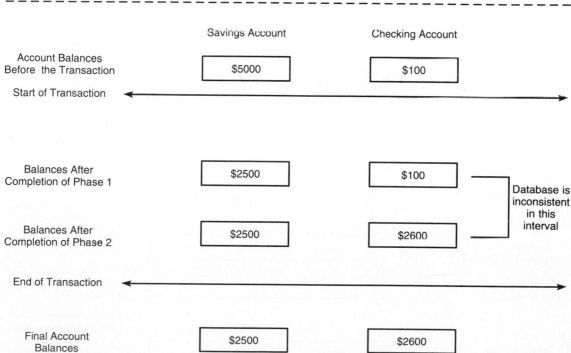

the transaction. Alternatively the DBMS could ensure that the partially com-pleted transaction is carried through to its successful conclusion, although this alternative is not frequently used.

The most common way to reverse an incomplete transaction is to have the application first declare the start of the transaction. Before a record is up-dated, its contents are saved in before images. If the transaction cannot com-plete, the before images replace the changes made by the transaction, thus returning the database to its state at the start of the transaction. When the transaction has completed, the application declares the end of the transac-tion and discards the before images. The account transfer transaction with its before images is illustrated in Figure 6-2. When a DBMS cancels a transac-tion and applies before images to return the database to a consistent state, it performs what is called a **transaction rollback.**

Another requirement of on-line transaction processing is that the records updated during one transaction must remain unavailable for update by other transactions until that transaction ends. Preventing records from being updated by other transactions is necessary in the event the transaction fails and must be rolled back. If another user has already made an update to a record being rolled back, the rollback reverses both updates. Again the data-base you choose should ensure transaction integrity by disallowing other transactions from updating a record being changed by another transaction.

Figure 6-2   Account Transfer Transaction with Before Images

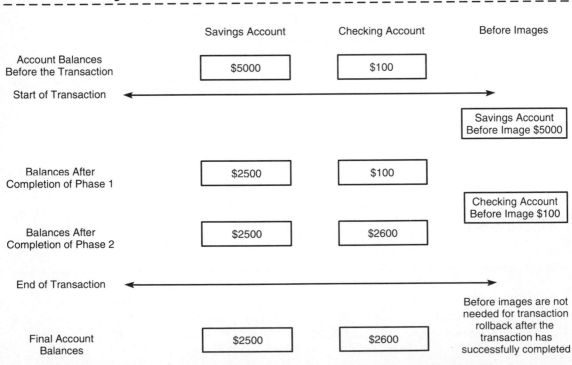

Exerting controls over records or files, generally referred to as contention resolution, was discussed in Chapter 5.

A multiuser DBMS should also provide **recovery facilities** to assist with data restoration following a failure. A variety of failures can occur that damage database data. Among these are program logic errors, disk head crashes, server failures, and disasters likes fires and floods. You are already aware of backup and restore operations. File restoration is one component of database recovery. A restore utility returns the database to a consistent state. However, many transactions might have been processed since the backup was taken. Hundreds or thousands of update transactions per day are not uncommon. Most large-system DBMSs and a growing number of microcomputer DBMSs provide facilities for reconstructing the work done by transactions processed after the last backup. Moreover, these DBMSs usually provide automatic transaction rollback to a consistent database state following events like a server failure. These recovery capabilities can help you avoid a considerable amount of manual work recovering from errors.

WORKGROUP SOFTWARE

Most LAN implementations have the potential for effectively using **workgroup software,** sometimes called **groupware.** In this section you will learn what a workgroup is and some of the workgroup software available to increase the group's productivity.

A workgroup consists of two or more workers. In doing their jobs these workers must share information, communicate with each other, and coordinate activities. Some specific tasks that are group activities are meetings, office correspondence, and group decision making. Groupware is designed to make arranging and carrying out these tasks easier and less time consuming.

The tasks performed by workgroup software are not new. For years they have been done manually or with a limited amount of computer support. Networked systems in general and LANs in particular provide the necessary communication link that was previously missing. The groupware applications that have been created thus far fall into the following broad categories:

electronic mail

electronic conferencing

work-flow automation

document coauthoring and management

decision support

Before we examine each type of workgroup software, we must emphasize that groupware is not intended to replace person-to-person interactions. Our future should not be one in which we get assignments from computers, are computer graded, or are fired or promoted by computers. Instead groupware complements person-to-person interactions. Groupware provides a tool for assigning and monitoring the group's tasks with the objective of making the group more productive.

Electronic Mail Systems

Like a conventional postal system, an **E-mail** system is responsible for collecting and distributing correspondence of various sizes and types and routing that correspondence to its recipients in a timely manner. And we have come to expect much more from an E-mail system than we ever did from a conventional postal system. But before we discuss the capabilities of E-mail, let us first see how an E-mail system operates on a LAN by tracing a piece of correspondence through a hypothetical system. Suppose that a LAN user, Maria, must create and send an E-mail message announcing a meeting to five other department heads—Alice, Mike, Tom, Shelly, and Chen—who then must read the message.

Creating the Message   In general, there are two ways to create an E-mail message: through the facilities of the E-mail system or through an external word processing, desktop publishing, or other text/graphics system. If an external message-creation facility is used, Maria can start that application, create the message, and save it on disk. Following that, she starts the E-mail application and imports the message into the system. Alternatively most of today's E-mail systems allow users to designate their message-creation software. Thus the message can be composed from within the E-mail system itself; that is, the word processor is invoked from the E-mail system and essentially becomes an E-mail application.

Sending the Message   Once she has created the message, Maria can schedule it for delivery, but to do so she needs the network addresses or identities of the recipients. The **mail administrator,** the person responsible for installation and management of Maria's E-mail application, will have identified all eligible E-mail users and their associated network addresses. To send her message, Maria gives the mail administrator either the name of each user, the name of a predefined **distribution list** that contains those names, or a combination of these two alternatives. A distribution list contains the names of individual users or the names of other distribution lists and thus provides a simple mechanism to send messages to workgroups. Maria may have defined a distribution list called DEPT_HEADS and can send the message to that destination. The E-mail system breaks down the distribution list into its individual components.

When the delivery system gets the message and a list of its recipients, it can route the message to the proper destinations. For each recipient, the message is delivered into a disk file called the user's **mailbox.** Almost immediately the message is available to each of the recipients.

Reading the Message   Once Maria delivers her message, it is available for the workgroup to read. Suppose that Chen has just logged on to the LAN. Because Maria's message is in his mailbox, he receives a message that he has mail. If an E-mail message arrives while he is working at his workstation, he also receives a mail-waiting message. When Chen wants to read his mail, he starts the E-mail application and receives a listing of his mail headlines. After viewing the available messages, usually identified with the sender's identification and a subject line, Chen has several available options. He can

ignore Maria's message

leave it in his mailbox for later viewing

delete the message without reading it

read the message and delete it

read the message and file it in an electronic folder

read the message and forward it to other mail users

do combinations of the above

Suppose that Chen decides to read Maria's message. His options now include responding to the message and sending Maria his comments, editing the message and forwarding it to another recipient or distribution list, or routing it to several users who will receive the message one after the other like an office routing memo. Each of the recipients of the routed message can add his or her comments before releasing the message to its next destination.

Other E-mail Features

Now let's look at the capabilities that an E-mail system offers you, other than simple message transmission.

Expiration Dates and Certified Mail   If the recipient of a message does not read it within a designated time limit, that message is automatically deleted from the recipient's mailbox. A sender, however, can send a message by **certified mail.** When a recipient reads a certified E-mail message, the sender receives a notice that the message has been read. A notice is also sent if the message expires without being read.

Mail Classes and Mail Agents   With E-mail you can classify your mail into, say; first, second, and third classes. First class could be used for individual correspondence and second class for business news, such as company stock quotes and product announcements. Third class could be used for junk mail, such as garage sales notices, want ads, and social group announcements. A **mail agent** is a software module that can automatically act on behalf of a user. For example, if a user goes on vacation, a mail agent can forward the user's mail to another user or file it in an electronic folder. The mail agent can also send each correspondent a message stating that the user is on vacation and nominating an alternative recipient.

Broadcast Messages and Message Attachment   A **broadcast message** is sent to all users (or all but a few) on the network. Broadcast capability is convenient for sending messages of general interest to all network users. Sometimes such correspondence is an assemblage of several discrete components that calls for E-mail's message-attachment capability. For example, a message may consist of text created by a word processor, graphic images created by a graphics or spreadsheet application, FAX images, and digitized voice all brought together to form one E-mail message.

Interfaces and Gateways A LAN that has connections to other LANs, WANs, or a host computer may need mail interfaces to these systems. A LAN user may need to send mail messages to users on other networks or to users attached to the host. Sometimes only a data communications interface is necessary to do this. When different mail systems are involved, the interface must also provide the ability to change messages from the originating mail system's format into a format compatible with the destination mail system. This type of interface can be a direct mail-system-to-mail-system interface. Alternatively the interface can be through a standard mail interchange system, such as that defined by the CCITT **X.400 standard.** As one example of the OSI application layer standards, the X.400 standard specifies the interfaces for a common mail interchange system. Another type of interface that may be required is a modem interface that allows remote users or mobile users to access the mail system.

Miscellaneous Capabilities E-mail systems seem to be constantly expanding in capabilities as software vendors strive to remain competitive. Some of the capabilities offered are

spelling checking	notification of mail arrival
searching messages for key words	message prioritizing
voice overlaying	carbon copying
security and message encryption	notification of failure to deliver a message
creating user profiles	
	interactive mail

Other groupware applications focus more directly on improving the productivity of smaller groups. Let us now look at some of their features.

Electronic Calendaring and Conferencing Applications

The capabilities of **electronic calendaring** and conferencing applications range from simply arranging meetings to actually conducting the meetings. Arranging a meeting or conference requires that the participants be notified and a mutually agreeable meeting date and time be set. Electronic calendaring applications (sometimes called schedulers) provide assistance with one or more of these tasks. If each attendee has an electronic calendar, this type of groupware can book the meeting at the best time. Given an interval during which the meeting must take place, the scheduler consults the calendars of the attendees. It notes the date and time that all attendees are available and schedules the meeting on their electronic calendars. If scheduling conflicts arise, the application can help resolve them. Some schedulers double-book participants and allow them to choose which appointment to keep; others report the conflicts and suggest alternative meeting times, allowing the person holding the meeting to find the best possible time. Once a meeting is scheduled, the electronic calendaring software can issue an RSVP notice to the participants. Like personal calendars, groupware calendars can issue reminders of forthcoming events. The reminder might be a mail message or an audio tone. Some groupware allows users to declare meetings to be recurring—weekly, monthly, biweekly, and so on. The scheduler automatically books these meetings for the attendees.

If the meeting is held with participants in different locations, **electronic conferencing** groupware can assist with communications among the attendees. Some conferencing applications allow images displayed on one computer's monitor to be displayed on remote monitors. Individuals at all locations can modify the screen's image and have the changes immediately reflected on the screens of the other participants. Thus conference attendees can both view and modify computer generated data and graphs. Viewing and modifying data coupled with audio transmission and freeze-frame or full-motion video allow geographically distributed conferences to be held, saving both travel costs and personnel time. Electronic conferencing applications also can create and distribute electronic minutes.

Work-flow Automation Software

At a meeting the attendees may accept action items they must complete. Alternatively a workgroup manager may assign tasks to workgroup members. One responsibility of a workgroup manager is monitoring the progress of such tasks. Progress monitoring is not a new concept. For many years, managers have used **program evaluation and review technique (PERT)** charts or similar methods to track a project's progress and determine its **critical path.** The critical path of a project is the sequence of events that takes the longest to complete. Often a project can be divided into several tasks. Some tasks can be done in parallel; other tasks cannot start until one or more tasks have been completed. For example, when building a house, the roof cannot be put on until the building is framed. Plumbing and electrical wiring can possibly be done concurrently. A project cannot complete until the path with the longest duration is completed. Thus project managers pay close attention to the project's critical path to avoid delays.

Some project-management work has been computerized for many years. However, much of the monitoring work was done manually. **Work-flow automation software** has extended the abilities of earlier systems by automating the tracking function.

A PERT chart for selecting a LAN vendor is shown in Figure 6-3. The critical path for the selection process is indicated by the heavier line. It is the critical path because it is the path between the start and the end with the longest elapsed time. A delay in any task along this path results in a delay of the project completion. So long as another path does not fall behind and become the critical path, a manager uses his or her resources to keep the critical path on plan. Work-flow automation software helps in monitoring the critical path and keeping the group working together in concert. Through this type of groupware application, group members can also keep aware of the status of other tasks that may affect their work.

With work-flow automation software, a manager can assign tasks to individuals or groups (through the group leader). The individual can either accept the task, negotiate a change, or refuse to accept the task. Once a task is accepted, a completion date is set. The worker uses the groupware application to record his or her progress and to signal the completion of the task. The manager can either agree that the task is complete and close it out or reach the decision that the task has not been satisfactorily completed and refuse to accept the work. If the manager determines that the task is not complete, the worker is notified and must rework the task until it is complete. The work-flow automation software tracks all tasks and evaluates progress. The group manager can interrogate the system and obtain reports of task status. If several tasks are in progress at once and other tasks are awaiting the outcome of those tasks, the groupware monitors the progress of the critical paths and helps the manager keep the project on schedule.

Other functions that may be simplified with work-flow automation software are

establishing and monitoring to-do lists

allowing task delegation

holding completed tasks until they are released by a manager

deleting tasks

preventing a worker from modifying an accepted task

Figure 6-3 PERT Chart for Selecting a LAN Vendor

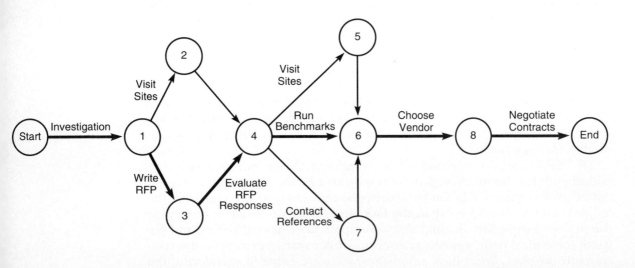

setting or resetting task start and stop times

adding, deleting or changing the people responsible for tasks

providing task and group reports

Document Coauthoring and Management Applications

Word processors, text editors, and document exchange software were among the early computer applications. Most of these systems, however, were designed to allow only one person to manipulate a document at one time. If you have ever worked on a team to write a program, a report, or manual, you are probably aware of the limitations inherent in these systems. If you and one of your team members wanted to work on the document at the same time, you either found it could not be done or that concurrent document updates created the contention problems described earlier. A workgroup often wants or needs to have several people actively working on one document simultaneously. Document coauthoring and management applications provide this capability.

Full-function **document coauthoring software** allows two or more people to work on one document concurrently. Concurrent processing presents some complex problems regarding posting of changes to the same pages. Some of today's coauthoring systems do not deal with such problems; however, they do provide the management and control necessary for a document to be shared without risk of contention problems.

Document management software helps control the flow of documents through the production cycle. Group users are identified as the principal document author, coauthors, or editors. The document management software controls access to the document by a checkout mechanism. Workers can check out all or part of a document. Once a document is checked out, update access to that document by other users is typically restricted because the worker checking it out may change it. If a worker changes the document, the document management software monitors the changes and records the identity of the person making the change. When the document is ready for review, the application can route the document to the proper reviewers and editors, allow them to make notations and suggestions (with or without changing the document itself), and keep track of the identity of the person making those remarks.

Other document management features include document organizing, archiving, locating, and full-file searching. Some law offices generate over 50,000 documents per year—wills, contracts, legal briefs, trial notes, and so on. Keeping track of such a volume of documents almost necessitates the use of a system that allows documents to be stored, archived to backup media, and found when needed. For such large systems, standard directory and file naming conventions are often severely limited. A document management system allows users to store a single document under a variety of different subjects. Like a library card catalog, the document can then be found by the name of the attorney, client, subject, date created, last date accessed, project, department, author, and a variety of other descriptive topics. Some systems allow users to specify combinations of these attributes as well. Full-file searches systematically scan files stored on disk or archival directories looking for user-defined text strings.

Group Decision-Support Software

Group decision-support software on LANs facilitates the communication of ideas among members of a group. Each person has a workstation from which to make comments and suggestions. These comments and suggestions are exchanged among the users in an anonymous way. Thus the lowest member in the hierarchy can feel free to criticize suggestions made by the person highest on the organizational ladder. The key to making this work is protecting the source of ideas and comments. The software includes tools to gather and manipulate data from a variety of sources, such as databases, spreadsheets, and graphics images. Companies that have used decision-support technology have found that better decisions are reached in a shorter time.

PRIMARY BUSINESS SOFTWARE

In some companies the LAN provides all computing resources. Some companies reached this level of LAN use through growth: They implemented a LAN as a small company, and the LAN grew with the company. Many companies reach this position from the opposite direction: Formerly users of minicomputers and mainframes, they **downsized** their data processing operations by substituting a microcomputer LAN for larger computers as the processing power of individual workstations and servers increased and the software available on LANs became more sophisticated. The reasons for downsizing vary, but three primary reasons are ease of use, lower cost, and the availability of primary business software.

Primary business software handles a variety of tasks, including personnel management, payroll, accounts receivable/payable, general ledger, inventory management, financial management, and manufacturing. LAN-compatible software packages for these applications are available, but some companies have developed their own primary business software using microcomputer software tools like DBMSs, graphical user interfaces, menuing systems, and so on. As the processing power of desktop systems continues to grow, LAN speeds increase, and new applications become available, the trend toward downsizing will likely continue.

SOFTWARE STANDARDS

Usually when we mention software standards we think of language standards, interface standards, and so on. However, many companies set up their computer systems with their own internal software standards. When you begin to acquire microcomputer systems, you should begin to think about setting up your internal software standards because they can reduce the costs of software, hardware, and training. One lesson some companies learned during the early days of microcomputer technology was that supporting several brands of the same software application soon became a management and control problem. To encourage the use of personal productivity tools and microcomputers in the early days of microcomputing, one company, let's call it Company X, originally took the approach that individuals could choose their own hardware platform and application software. Allowing individual hardware and software decisions resulted in a variety of hardware and software being used. Most of the hardware was based on either Apple or IBM technology, and variety of application packages were chosen. At one time six different word processing programs were in use! We will use word processing as the example in looking at the problems Company X experienced. On a smaller scale, the same problems existed with other software applications.

The mixture of hardware and software at Company X soon gave rise to several problems, the most critical of which was portability. The file formats of each word processing program were different, so transferring files among users was simple only if those users had chosen the same word processing application. For example, if Carlos used WordPerfect and Anita used Microsoft's Word, they could not work on each other's documents without first going through a conversion. The company soon found it necessary to purchase file-conversion programs for the word processing applications. Having conversion programs helped reduce the problem of portability, but it did not completely eliminate it. Some word processors supported features not found in others. The use of those features was limited when porting documents from one word processor's format to another's.

The amount of user training required in Company X's mixed software environment was much greater than for similar companies that had established one standardized word processing package. Company X found that as new employees were added, they needed to be trained to use one of the products. Because the training was distributed over more products, classes were smaller and the number of classes was greater than was necessary for comparable companies. Moreover users involved in document exchange had to learn the use of the conversion program, and extra time was required to do the conversion. Every time a new version of one of the word processing systems came out with new features, the conversion program also had to be upgraded. Sometimes the availability of new conversion software lagged behind the introduction of upgraded word processing software. After conversion, it was often necessary to do some manual formatting of the converted data.

The problems just described resulted in higher overall costs. The costs were seen in real dollars needed for conversion software and training and in intangible dollars for lost productivity resulting from workers doing conversions and manual formatting and from the reluctance of many users to get involved in document exchange.

To avoid some of the problems Company X experienced because they did not set software standards, look for the following when choosing a software application:

- Does the software run on a variety of hardware platforms? That is, are there versions that operate on IBM, Apple, minicomputer, and mainframe platforms?

- What are the license agreement provisions? (We discuss license agreements in the next section.)

- What is the average cost per user? Factor in costs like the need to buy 30 user licenses when there are only 25 concurrent users.

- What functions are provided relative to other applications? For example, does the desktop publishing software accept the formats of the word processing software?

- Is the application mature? That is, does it provide robust capabilities and is it relatively free of bugs?

- Does the software vendor provide good service? What kind of service is available (for example, do they offer on-site, telephone, or toll-free telephone service), and what is the cost?

- Does the software come with complete and useful documentation?

- Does the software vendor have a good record for enhancing the product?

- Is the software dependent on other software, for example, a windows environment or specific operating system? If so, which one(s)?

- Is the software LAN compatible? If so, on which LANs?

- Is training readily available? Where? At what cost?

- Is it likely that new employees will already be trained on this product?

- Does the application interface readily with other software applications? For example, can the word processing application import graphs from spreadsheet programs, or can the spreadsheet program import data easily from the database management system?

- What are the hardware requirements of the application? Memory? Disk? Mouse?

- What hardware capabilities are supported? Graphics? Color? Other?

- Are user profiles allowed? If so, how and to what degree?

- Does the application allow for shared use? That is, is there a provision for contention resolution?

- Is a system key disk or other enabling hardware device required?

SOFTWARE PROTECTION

One of the most important things to know about your software is its licensing agreement. Virtually all software you buy is covered by a **license agreement.** This is true for both systems and applications software. The license agreement covers the rules under which you are allowed to use the product. It is a way of protecting both the manufacturer and the user of the product. To better understand the need for license agreements, let us first look at an analogy.

Consider a book you purchased for school. It was probably rather expensive. Of course, the publisher does not pay nearly that much to print the book. Part of the cost of your book goes to profit, of course, but the publisher incurs other expenses: One or more authors wrote the material, editors worked with the authors to develop the format and content, designers laid out the style (graphics and pages formats), marketing analysts determined a marketing strategy and created advertising brochures, and the sales people were told about the book, its target markets, and key selling points. All of this activity required a considerable investment. Some books never become popular, and the publishing company loses money on them. Others become very popular and the publishing company makes a profit. Some of that profit is used to offset losses on other projects. Now suppose someone decides to illegally reprint and sell a successful book. With today's technology it does not cost much to print such copies. This person could sell the copies for much less than the publisher, because he or she has not had to make the investment of developing the work, paying the salaries of editors and production workers and royalties to the developers, and so on.

Patent and copyright laws protect the investment of designers, artists, film makers, authors, publishing companies, and so on. You may be asking, "How do these examples relate to software?" Software companies also make a sizable investment in creating each application or system software. Systems analysts designed the product, programmers wrote and debugged the code, marketing analysts created a marketing plan, advertising campaigns were developed and implemented, manuals were created, a support organization was staffed and trained, and the product was brought to market. Several years probably elapsed from the time the product was conceived to the point at which it was ready to sell and make a profit. Thousands of dollars were probably expended before there was any opportunity to sell the software. Moreover, once a software product is released, expenses continue. Support staff must be paid and new enhancements designed. Like the book publisher, the software company can see its profits from all this effort eroded by illegal copying. To give you an idea of the magnitude of this problem, at the end of the 1980s, several software piracy shops in Hong Kong were raided. Some estimate the annual loss of revenues to software companies resulting from software piracy being conducted in one building alone to be hundreds of millions of dollars.

Software vendors must therefore take steps to protect their investment. Software is protected in six basic ways:

1. The code is kept secret so other software houses cannot use special algorithms developed by the company to write a competing system.

2. The code is copyrighted to prevent another company from copying the code and writing a competing system.

3. Legislation penalizing those who do not adhere to the copyright and license restrictions is enforced.

4. The software is copy-protected to deter someone from making an illegal copy.

5. License agreements are used to establish the terms of ownership and use.

6. The software requires a special hardware device to run.

The first two measures protect the source code from being used by someone else. During software development companies commonly keep the source code of the software secret. However, after the product has been released, it is always possible to derive the source code, even if the software is released only in object code format. Deriving the source code from object code is done through reverse engineering. To protect itself from reverse engineering, software manufacturers usually copyright their software. **Copyright laws,** originally intended to cover books, films, and works of art, have been extended to include software. Moreover new legislation has been enacted to further define the restrictions and penalties for unauthorized software copying.

Software piracy has always been a problem, even before the introduction of microcomputers. Minicomputers and mainframe systems make software piracy easier to detect, so its incidence is negligible relative to its occurrence on microcomputers. Large-system software piracy is easier to detect for two reasons: First, large computers are used by large organizations with professional data processing departments. Software piracy is difficult to hide in such organizations, and anyone found using pirated software is subject to dismissal and the company subject to lawsuits. Second, large-computer sites typically work closely with the software vendor's personnel. The vendor's employees are aware of the software its customers are authorized to use, and it is easy to detect the presence of unauthorized software. Easy piracy detection is not the case with microcomputer software.

A few software companies protect their software by requiring the use of a special hardware device that attaches to a serial or parallel port. The device and an application work together to provide application security. When started the application attempts to read data encoded in the device. If the device is not attached, the application terminates. One disadvantage to this approach is that, if you have several applications, you need a different device for each one. Since the number of serial or parallel ports is limited, changing from one application to another may require changing the device.

Other companies have accomplished somewhat the same effect by requiring a **key disk.** The key disk usually is a flexible disk that must be in a disk drive when the application is run. The application uses the key disk only to verify its presence. This technique is seldom used today and, of course, cannot be used with diskless systems.

Originally many microcomputer software vendors used copy protection to deter software piracy. That is, the software diskette was encoded to prevent someone copying it using a standard operating system copy facility such as DOS's COPY or DISKCOPY command. In general, copy protection only gave rise to a new software indsutry—software that allows copying of copy-protected software. Of course, vendors of such software were careful to point out that the sole purpose of their software was to make a backup copy and not to make illegal duplicate copies. Today, many companies that once copy-protected their software have abandoned that practice because it proved relatively ineffective. Instead of, or in addition to, copy protection, software vendors now rely on copyright protection together with software license agreements.

Software License Agreements

When you buy software, both application software and LAN system software, the diskettes that hold the software often are sealed in an envelope. Written on or attached to the envelope is text regarding the license agreement and a message that when you open and use the software, you make a commitment to adhere to the stipulations of that license agreement. The license agreement states the conditions under which you are allowed to use the product.

In essence, when you buy software you do not get ownership of that product; you are simply given the right to use it. An attorney might quibble with this statement, but the basic premise is correct. Some license agreements explicitly state that you own the diskette but not the contents of the diskette. Thus you cannot make copies of the software to give to your friends, you cannot run it on several workstations at the same time, you cannot reverse-engineer it to produce source code for modification or resale, and so on. Your rights to the software are limited to using the software in the intended manner. You can, if you like, destroy it, cease to use it, sell it, or give it as a gift. In the latter two cases, you also transfer the license agreement to the recipient. Some software vendors go so far as to state that transferring ownership of the software must be approved by the software vendor. Moreover in some cases the software license covers the use of the accompanying documentation as well.

When selecting your application and system software, you must take care to understand fully all the conditions of the license agreements. You want each user to have the necessary software services available. Differences in license and pricing policies between competing products can result in substantial differences in availability to you or cost to your company.

One of the problems with license agreements is that no standards have been established. Thus if you buy two different applications, you are liable to find two different license agreements. To protect yourself and your organization from civil and criminal suits, you must understand the provisions of each agreement. Several companies, including a major state university, have been investigated for illegally copying software, found guilty of the offense, and forced to pay heavy fines. Therefore, it is important that a company and individuals respect the license agreements. In general, license agreements take one of the following forms:

single user, single workstation licenses

single user, multiple workstation licenses

restricted number of concurrent users licenses

server licenses

site licenses

corporate licenses

Single User, Single Workstation License   Single user, single workstation license agreements are the most restrictive. They specify that the software is to be used on one workstation only and by only one person at a time. For example, if you have a multiuser microcomputer, only one user can be running the software at any time. In most instances restricting the software to only one machine also implies a single user.

This license agreement also means that if an office has two or more computers, a separate copy of the software must be purchased for each machine on which it is to be used. Thus, if you have two employees, one on the day shift and one on the night shift using the same software but on different workstations, each needs an individual copy of the software. In this situation the software is never used concurrently, yet two copies are required. One of the ways in which software vendors enforce this policy is through the software installation procedure, which counts the number of installations. When you install the product the counter is decremented to zero and you are not able to install the programs on another system. To move the software to another system you must de-install the software, a process which removes the application from the computer's disks and increments the installation count. Another method used to enforce a single user, single workstation license is the requirement for a system disk described earlier.

Single User, Multiple Workstation Licenses   The constraints of the single user, single workstation agreement are relaxed by the **single user, multiple workstation license** agreement. It usually also relies on the honor system for enforcement. The software vendors that use this agreement recognize that different people may want to use the software and at different workstations, for example, in the office and on a portable computer. The purchase of a single copy of the software allows the owner to install it on several systems.

However, the license restricts the use of the software to one user at a time per software copy. For example, suppose an office with ten workstations must do word processing. At some time each employee can use the word processor, but at any time, only five employees can be using the product concurrently. With this license agreement, the company can buy five copies of the software and install them on ten different systems. So long as five or fewer employees use the word processing application at any one time, the company has lived up to the license agreement. Note also that it is possible for six users to inadvertently use the application at the same time in violation of the license agreement.

Restricted Number of Concurrent Users Licenses On a LAN commonly several users run an application concurrently. Three employees may be doing word processing, ten may be using the spreadsheet software, and 25 may be using the database software. With file or database server technology, only one copy of each application is on the server's disks. Most LAN-compatible software inherently is designed for multiple users; however, some software vendors limit the number of concurrent users with a **restricted number of concurrent users license** agreement. The main idea behind this strategy is to charge by the number of users.

Consider the database needs of the company just mentioned, where the maximum number of concurrent database users is 25. Suppose the database vendor has a license agreement that allows 10 concurrent users for a certain fee. The company also has an expansion policy that allows additional concurrent users to be added in groups of 10, with an additional fee for each such group. The company must purchase three modules, to satisfy its need of 25 concurrent users. This type of license typically is enforced by a meter program that controls the concurrent use of the application. When a user starts the application, the meter program increments a counter by 1. When a user exits from the application, the counter is decremented by 1. If the license agreement is for 30 users, a user can run the application so long as the counter is 29 or fewer. If the counter is 30, a user requesting the application receives an error message indicating that the file is not available.

Server Licenses A **server license** allows an application to be installed on one server. All users attached to that server may use the application. If a company has several servers, say three, and wants to use the application on each of them, then the company must purchase three licenses or three copies of the software.

Site Licenses A **site license** gives the user unlimited rights to use the software at a given site. The site may be a single LAN or multiple LANs at one location.

Corporate Licenses A **corporate license** gives the corporation unlimited use of the software at all locations. Some companies restrict a corporate license to all locations within one country. Sometimes, the right to reproduce documentation is also granted.

Owner's Rights

The license agreement is intended primarily to protect the rights of the manufacturer. However, the owner of a license agreement also has certain rights:

1. The owner can transfer or assign the license to another user.

2. The owner can get a refund if the product is defective or does not work as stated.

3. The owner has legal rights granted by certain states or countries regarding the exclusion of liability for losses or damage resulting from the use of the software.

4. The owner can terminate the license by destroying the software and documentation.

SUMMARY

LAN application software can be separated into three major classes, personal productivity software, groupware and primary business systems. Personal productivity software includes word processing, spreadsheets, graphics, database management systems, and so on. These are the systems that are used as effectively on stand-alone systems as on LANs. Groupware needs workstation communications to operate. Of the personal productivity software, database management systems (DBMSs) need the most additional LAN support, because databases are highly shared, and concurrent usage problems must be avoided. In addition to the needs cited in earlier chapters, database management software for LANs should also support transaction processing and recovery to ensure the integrity of the database.

The use of a LAN as a vehicle for primary business system software may result from downsizing from a large computing platform or from upsizing a smaller company. The applications that fall into this category include personnel management systems, payroll, accounts receivable/payable, general ledger, inventory control, and so on. This segment of LAN applications is increasing as LAN software and hardware expand.

A variety of groupware products are available, and new or improved applications are constantly being released. Some of the main groupware applications are electronic mail, electronic calendaring and conferencing, workflow automation, document coauthoring and management, and decision support. The features provided by individual application packages differ considerably, so care must be taken to choose the applications that are most consistent with your needs.

Selecting software can be a difficult job because there is such a variety of choices. Some companies delegated software choice to its employees; thus, each employee was free to choose the software he or she wanted. Individual selection resulted in a variety of word processing, spreadsheet, and database systems being used and the associated problems of training users and exchanging data. To avoid this dilemma, an organization should establish an organizational standard for widely used software. These standards define the brands and versions of application software that can be purchased and used. With a good set of standards in place, management can be assured that training and software costs can be better controlled and that the need for importing and exporting of data between products is minimized. Procedures for changing the application standard to add new applications or change existing ones should include testing to ensure that the application is LAN compatible.

Because software development, advertising, distribution, and support is a significant expense, software vendors attempt to protect their investment in a number of ways. The primary ways software can be protected is through copyright and license agreements. License agreements detail the conditions under which a purchaser can use the product. Details of licensing agreements differ between software vendors and even between products from one vendor. The general types of license agreements are: single user, single workstation licenses; single user, multiple workstations licenses; restricted number of concurrent users licenses; server licenses; site licenses; and corporate licenses. When you select your LAN system and application software, you must study each vendor's license agreements and abide by them. Failure to follow these agreements can result in civil or criminal proceedings. Software costs can vary considerably depending on the license agreements.

KEY TERMS

after image

batch processing

before image

certified mail

consistent state

copyright laws

corporate license

critical path

distribution list

document coauthoring software

document management software

electronic calendaring

electronic conferencing

electronic mail (E-mail)

group decision-support software

groupware

key disk

license agreement

mail administrator

mail agents

mailbox

on-line transaction processing

primary business software

program evaluation and review technique (PERT)

recovery facilities, database

restricted number of users license

server license

single user, multiple workstation license

single user, single workstation license

site license

transaction

transaction processing

transaction rollback

work-flow automation software

workgroup software

X.400 standard

REVIEW QUESTIONS

1. What is a transaction?

2. Describe a problem that can occur if transaction integrity is not provided?

3. What is a workgroup?

4. List five classes of workgroup software.

5. Describe five features that are likely to be found in E-mail systems.

6. What is work-flow automation? How does it help promote work-group productivity?

7. How does a document coauthoring and management system differ from a word processing application?

8. What is downsizing? Why does a company downsize?

9. List four ways a software vendor can protect its investment in software.

10. What are the advantages of having standard software products?

11. What is a software license agreement? Why are they needed?

12. Briefly describe each of the following general classes of license agreements.

   a. single user, single workstation license

   b. single user, multiple workstation license

   c. restricted number of concurrent users license

   d. server license

   e. site license

   f. corporate license

13. In a restricted number of concurrent user license agreement, how does an organization control the number of concurrent users?

PROBLEMS AND EXERCISES

1. Find a company that uses electronic mail (LAN or WAN based). Interview several mail users to determine how frequently they use the mail, their likes or dislikes of electronic mail, and the overall impact of the mail system on how they do business. How would their work be different if electronic mail were not available?

2. Some people feel that work-flow automation, electronic calendaring, and E-mail are intrusive systems because they automatically schedule people for a meeting, monitor their work progress, report back to the originator of a message that the message has been read, and so on. Discuss the merits of this position. What are your personal viewpoints on these groupware applications?

3. Compare the software license agreements from three different software vendors.

4. Your company is considering purchasing a software product that provides a layered pricing scheme for licensing. A five-user system costs $1000 and includes two copies of documentation. Additional user licenses may be added in increments of five users for $500. The incremental licenses do not include documentation. Additional documentation sets can be purchased for $35. Your company has 75 workstations, but it has been determined that the maximum

number of concurrent users for this software package is 53. What is the total cost of the software and documentation if 40 additional sets of documentation are required?

REFERENCES

Becker, Pat. "Down or Out?" *LAN*, Volume 7, Number 10, October 1992.

Black, David. "The Squeaky Wheel." *LAN*, Volume 8, Number 1, January 1993.

Bochenski, Barbara. "Workgroup Goals Push Groupware Boundaries." *Software Magazine*, November 1990.

Carr, Grace M. "Share and Share Alike." *LAN Technology*, Volume 9, Number 12, November 1992.

Derfler, Jr., Frank J. "Building WorkGroup Solutions: Voice E-Mail." *PC Magazine*, July 1990.

Dern, Daniel P. "Groupware Can Leverage the Most from Your LAN." *MIS Week*, June 25, 1990.

Harrison, Bradford T. "Workgroup Integration Strategies." *DEC Professional*, October 1990.

Nunamaker, Jr., Jay F. "Teamwork Tools Lead the Way to Creative Collaboration." *Corporate Computing*, Volume 1, Number 2, August 1992.

Rasmus, Daniel W. "Integrating Distributed Information." *Byte*, Volume 16, Number 12, November 1991.

Scheier, Robert L. "In the Eye of the Storm: Downsizing to PC-based LANs." *PC Week*, Volume 9, Number 41, October 12, 1992.

Spence, Chris. "Downsizing with NetWare." *InfoWorld*, Volume 14, Issue 41, October 12, 1992.

Van Name, Mark L. and Catching, Bill. "Syzygy: Groupware for Project Scheduling." *PC Week*, May 22, 1990.

Vaughan-Nichols, Steven J. "Transparent Data Exchange." *Byte,* Volume 16, Number 12, November 1991.

Williams, Bob, Iacobucci, Ed, and Bernath, Wendy. "Downsizing Thrust Gaining Momentum." *LAN Times*, Volume 8, Issue 20, October 21, 1991.

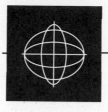

IV
INSTALLATION AND MANAGEMENT

After the LAN hardware and software have been selected, they must be installed, made operational, and then administered. In Chapter 7 you learn about installation, the most difficult phase in a LAN's life cycle. Chapter 8 examines the LAN administrator's responsibility for creating and managing the user environment, including key issues such as security and virus protection. In Chapter 9 you learn the LAN administrator's role in creating a printing environment which allows users to effectively share output resources. Chapter 10 explores the backup and recovery of a LAN, which prepares the LAN administrator for planned changes, such as adding new users, as well as unplanned changes, such as power failure or user error. In Chapter 11 you learn the roles both proactive and reactive management play in the administrator's responsibilities.

Chapter 7
LAN Installation

Chapter 8
LAN Administration: Users, Groups, and Security

Chapter 9
LAN Administration: The Printing Environment

Chapter 10
LAN Administration: Backup and Recovery

Chapter 11
LAN Administration: Reactive and Proactive Management

LAN INSTALLATION

CHAPTER PREVIEW

After you have selected the LAN hardware and software for your configuration, you must begin the process of installing it, bringing it to an operational status, and then administering it. Installation is thought by some people to be the most difficult phase of a LAN's life cycle. Planning the installation begins as soon as you select the hardware and software. It continues until the entire LAN is operational. What determines when a LAN that is operational varies. For our purposes it is when all hardware, system software, and application software have been installed, all user profiles have been created, security has been set up, and users are able to use the LAN in carrying out their tasks.

In this chapter you will read about:

administrative details such as contracts, support, and maintenance

hardware installation details such as site planning and cabling

testing and acceptance procedures

training for users, managers, and administrators

At the conclusion of this chapter, you should know some procedures to follow in setting up a new LAN. You should also realize that LAN installation can be quite complex, and installation details vary with the hardware, software, and LAN architecture you choose. This chapter contains general guidelines that are independent of particular implementations.

ADMINISTRATIVE DETAILS

LAN installation and testing can be a complex task that requires considerable planning and documentation. Plans provide the direction for equipment acquisition, installation, testing, and training. The LAN administrator should be aware of two key points during the installation process: First, plans may be incomplete or incorrect, so you must have a mechanism for changing the plans to meet the realities of the installation process. Second, people sometimes deviate from plans that you have set up, and these deviations can have unexpected and undesirable consequences. The rules for installation should be, if the plan is defective, change it; if the plan is correct, avoid deviations.

You have two choices when installing a LAN: You can be the primary contractor, acquiring yourself the essential hardware, software, documentation, and training you need from a variety of vendors; or you can select one or more vendors to handle the installation process for you. If you are the primary contractor, you may not need sophisticated contracts, and portions of this section may not apply to your situation. The reason the contracts may be less sophisticated is that you have assumed the responsibility for configuring the network and assuring it meets your needs. If a vendor has these responsibilities, the contract must include provisions for network acceptance and overcoming any deficiencies.

After selecting your hardware and software, the first thing you usually do is contract with the vendor who will supply your LAN components. If you elect to have one company provide all your LAN needs, you will have one contract; if you choose several vendors, for example, separate hardware and software vendors, you probably will have a contract with each; if you decided to be the primary contractor, you may need even more contracts. You must know when a contract is necessary and how to enter into a contract. The best source of information on this is an attorney, preferably one specializing in contract law. We can offer you a few guidelines in establishing a relationship with your vendors, but these guidelines are not a substitute for an attorney.

Purchase Contract

When you purchase a system from a single vendor, you must have an understanding with that vendor about what is being supplied, when it will be ready, and what constitutes being ready. Too often the goodwill and good intentions that both the vendor and the user express at selection time turns to bitterness during system installation. Usually this happens because the vendor and the user have different ideas about what the results should be. A well-defined **purchase contract** clearly states the responsibilities of both parties and eliminates the ambiguities of what is to be done.

LAN installation has both tangible and intangible elements. Disagreements between the vendor and the user can arise from either element, but the intangible elements are more apt to cause disagreements and thus require more explicit contract terms. The most tangible elements of LAN installation are hardware components. There is little room for disagreement regarding the delivery and installation of 50 LAN adapters. Either the adapters work or they don't; either they are the correct type or they aren't. Thus it is usually easy to write explicit contract provisions for hardware. Software is less tangible than hardware. You may receive software from your vendor that differs from your expectations in any of the following ways:

It does not provide the functions you expected.

It provides the functions you expected but is difficult to use.

It may be an older or newer version than you expected.

It may be produced by a software company other than what you expected.

It may not be functional because it does not match your hardware or software configurations.

It may not be functional because it has too many bugs.

It may not have the license provisions you expected.

Still less tangible than software are the conditions under which the vendor has satisfied his or her obligation to your company. That is, when are the terms of the contract met? A good contract can help make the intangibles more concrete. The more specific the contract is, the better. What specifics should you include in a purchase contract?

First, understand that when a vendor offers you a contract to sign, it probably has been drawn up by the vendor's attorneys and is designed to protect the interests of the vendor. This is not necessarily bad; however, the contract should also protect your interests. If you use a vendor's contract, you should definitely have it reviewed and approved by an attorney representing your interests. You can sign the vendor's standard contract, negotiate changes, or propose a contract drawn up by your attorney. Most contracts result from negotiation. Both parties agree that the terms are acceptable and they can abide by the terms.

Your contract should detail what, where, when, and how items are to be delivered. For hardware, the contract should specify the vendor, quantity, part numbers, and cost for each component or the aggregate cost for all components. For example, suppose the vendor is contracted to supply 50 LAN adapters. Simply specifying 50 of "Vendor X's Ethernet cards" is not sufficient. Vendors frequently have several models of Ethernet cards. You must include the vendor's part number or a more complete description. Making the correct choice of LAN adapter interface is another example of the importance of specification. One MCA bus card does not work in an EISA or ISA bus computer, and vice versa. ISA cards work in an EISA bus computer, but an EISA card does not work in an ISA bus computer. For example, the following LAN adapter options are available from one LAN adapter manufacturer:

8- or 16-bit ISA bus

8- or 16-bit EISA bus

16-bit MCA bus

The vendor may want to use alternate sources for LAN adapter cards. In this case again be specific about the alternatives. For example, specifying "Vendor X's Ethernet LAN adapter Model 123-456 or equivalent" is not specific enough; you must qualify what constitutes equivalency or specify who determines what is equivalent.

Your contract should also set up a **payment schedule.** LAN installation often occurs in stages: First site preparation is done, wires or cables are installed, hardware is delivered and installed, software is delivered and installed, testing is conducted, and finally the system is accepted. Several months may elapse between starting and completing the installation. Vendors invest their money and time on the installation project, and they reasonably expect to be compensated for work completed satisfactorily. A payment schedule is usually established that allows the vendor to receive reimbursement at the completion of well-defined stages. For example, when the wiring installation is complete, a payment covering that portion of the network can be made. The payment schedule therefore, represents **progress payments.** However, a substantial portion of the installation payment, say 15 to 25 percent, should be held until all conditions of the contract are fulfilled. The amount of the final payment should depend on the size of the contract and the number of progress payments in the payment schedule. The reason for holding the final payment is to ensure that the vendor completes final details. Sometimes a vendor that has been paid in full for an almost-finished project moves on to a new project, and the remaining installation tasks for your system become a low priority for that vendor.

A good contract identifies the conditions under which the network is complete. This is often an exacting condition to define. From both the user's and vendor's perspectives, a specific set of events should be well defined. For example, simply defining completion by when all hardware and software are installed is usually not adequate. The user should also ensure that the system meets some minimum performance standards, that training is completed or at least scheduled, that the documentation is complete, and so on. The details of what must occur vary according to the size of the LAN and an organization's specific needs. Again, your attorney must ensure that the conditions are legally acceptable.

A company can take all the proper steps in setting up the final acceptance criteria but then jeopardize their legal status by placing the system into production before actually accepting it. Once a company begins to use the system in production, that company becomes dependent on the system. In some sense, until the system is accepted, it is still the responsibility of the vendor. Placing a LAN into production before it is formally accepted reduces the vendor's ability to make changes and gives the vendor a good argument for showing that the system has really been accepted.

As a final consideration regarding a purchase contract, you must attempt to protect yourself from losses in the event the vendor is unable to live up to the conditions of the contract. Here are some things that can happen:

The vendor fails to meet completion schedules.

The system fails to meet performance objectives.

The vendor fails to complete delivery of all components.

The vendor fails to deliver software custom-tailored to your environment.

The software fails to meet functional requirements (that is, it has too many bugs).

You can protect yourself from such problems by inserting **protection** or **penalty clauses** in your contract. A penalty clause holds the vendor liable for damages if the terms of the contract are not met. For example, the vendor might agree to a penalty clause that requires it to pay $1000 per week for each week beyond the scheduled completion date that the LAN is not acceptable. Thus a vendor that is four weeks late in completing its obligations will have a $4000 penalty. For obvious reasons many vendors are uneasy about entering into contracts with penalty clauses; in fact, most vendors will not sign such contracts. Still, you should attempt to protect your company from losses resulting from the failure of the vendor to live up to the terms of the contract. Another possible penalty clause is to require the vendor to provide sufficient hardware to realize the performance or capacity goals. For example, suppose the contract specified a maximum time to download an application. If the hardware supplied is incapable of meeting that goal, the contract might require the vendor to add or substitute hardware to attain the stated performance level. Thus in this situation the vendor may have to substitute a faster disk drive, add more memory, or install a faster server CPU. The expenses of such upgrades are absorbed by the vendor.

Support and Maintenance Agreements

When you purchase an expensive item like a car or a house, you protect your investment through proper maintenance—both **preventive** and **restorative maintenance.** Just as you change the oil in your car periodically, paint your house every few years, and keep your lawn mowed, so must you protect your investment in LAN hardware and software, which is substantial. You will want to get software upgrades and bug fixes as they become available, repair or replace hardware components that fail, and carry out periodic preventive maintenance on the components. Your company may assume the responsibility for some of this. Some companies with large data processing organizations repair their own microcomputers. Some companies repair their equipment on an as-needed basis; thus, if a device fails, the company takes it to a repair facility and pays for the repairs. Other companies subscribe to hardware maintenance contracts that cover preventive and restorative maintenance.

Microcomputer hardware and software are rapidly becoming more sophisticated. The hardware is still at a level that allows someone with modest technical skills to replace a defective printed circuit board, add in new options, and so on. Moreover much of the software is updated by purchases of an entirely new product or new version of the existing product. Some microcomputer software companies now offer maintenance services. With these services you can receive periodic interim releases that contain bug fixes and minor enhancements. As the sophistication of system components increases, so will the problems associated with them. Corporate users, particularly those who have large systems, are used to receiving periodic bug fixes to their software and hardware. These fixes usually come automatically under hardware and software maintenance agreements. You must decide which components, if any, are so critical that they should be covered by maintenance agreements. Multiple maintenance agreements may be necessary to cover all system components. For example, you may have a hardware and LAN software maintenance agreement with your LAN vendor and individual software maintenance agreements for each application.

If you are installing a LAN for the first time, you may need quite a bit of support during the first months or year of operation. Over time you build a level of expertise that makes you less dependent on technical help from others. Thus, if you are a new LAN user, it is usually wise to arrange for technical support from your vendor or from another source, such as a consultant. Many companies just entering the world of LANs hire consultants to make the transition easier. You should also consider subscribing to a support service for critical software, especially for software products with which you are unfamiliar. For example, if LAN system software, network mail, and groupware are critical to your users, and your organization is unfamiliar with those products, a support agreement can help you solve problems quickly and allow you to use the software more efficiently.

You also must evaluate the costs of hardware and software maintenance agreements carefully. Any agreement must be cost effective. Occasionally a vendor has levels of maintenance and support: For example, at the highest level you may have permanent on-site vendor support personnel. At the next level you may find on-site support within a specified time, such as a four-hour response time during normal working hours and an eight-hour response time during nonbusiness hours. A lower support level may offer unlimited telephone support; below that you may get measured telephone support, for example, two free calls per week with added fees for additional calls; below that you would pay a fee for each call made to the support line. In general, a support and maintenance agreement compatible with your organization's technical expertise is a good investment, particularly during the first year of your LAN's operation.

Having negotiated your purchase, support, and maintenance contracts, you must prepare for the arrival and installation of the equipment. After an agreement is reached, planning and installation tasks begin in earnest.

INSTALLATION TASKS

Installing a LAN can be difficult because there are a multitude of details to attend to and a number of rules that must be followed. As the size of the LAN increases, so does the potential for problems and the chance to break rules about medium distances, number of nodes, distances between nodes, and so on. To illustrate what we mean by rules, Table 7-1 shows some of the restrictions outlined in the IEEE 802.3 standard for CSMA/CD bus LANs. In addition to these, you must know about technology, such as local codes for wiring, how to make connections between media and between a medium and nodes, and how to change from one medium to another, for example, from coaxial cable to twisted-pair wires or from one type of coaxial cable to another.

Table 7-1   IEEE 802.3 Distance Standards

Feature	Thick Coax	Thin Coax
Maximum Segment Length (meters)	500	185
Maximum Number of Segments	5	5
Maximum End-to-End Cable Length (meters)	2500	925
Minimum Distance Between Nodes (meters)	2.5	0.5
Maximum Nodes Per Segment	100	30

LAN installation has several well-defined stages. Some of these stages can be worked on in parallel, and some phases require the completion of one or more other phases before they can begin. The major installation phases are

1. Documentation
2. Site planning
3. Medium installation
4. Hardware installation
5. Software installation
6. Conversion and data preparation
7. Creation of the operating environment
8. Testing and acceptance
9. Cutover
10. Training

Figure 7-1 is a PERT chart showing the relationships among these events and the critical path. Let us now look at what is accomplished at each step.

Documentation

Documentation is a part of each phase of LAN selection and implementation. When selecting the LAN, you must document your problem and your objectives, the options considered, the reasons for selecting and rejecting certain approaches, and so on. Because documentation is so pervasive, we will cite key documents you must create during certain phases of the installation.

Site Planning

Site planning defines the layout of the LAN and identifies the building and environment modifications necessary to house the components. During this phase you identify and plan the following:

workstation placement	power requirements
power point locations	medium locations
ambient conditions	server locations
printer locations	building code conformance
safety code conformance	hardware relocation
telephone line placement	network and computer interconnections

Site planning essentially produces the blueprints for laying out the network. During this phase you draw floor plans showing the location of cable runs (or transmitters and receivers for a wireless LAN), workstations, servers, printers, and wiring hubs. You also must ensure that your configuration conforms to your local building codes. These vary from one location to another. Some require that wires be strung through conduits or that cables on

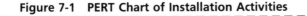

Figure 7-1 PERT Chart of Installation Activities

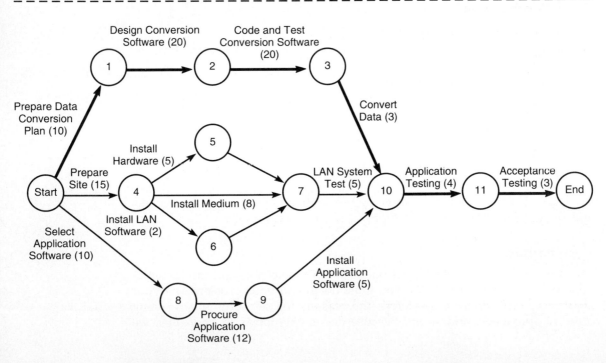

the floor be placed into recessed areas called **channels.** Also some building codes relate to power distribution.

When planning your LAN layout, you must consider where to install the servers. Workstations and printers are located where users can easily access them. On the other hand, servers are often located in secure areas to avoid accidental or intentional disruption of LAN operations. For example, you do not want some well-meaning employee powering down the server because no one is using it. Moreover, an employee intent on disrupting the organization's computing can cause problems by shutting down the server or destroying files located on the server. Therefore, it is usually a good idea to locate the server in a room that can be secured from casual access.

Sometimes LANs are connected to other LANs, to a WAN, or to a stand-alone host system. In such instances it is important to design the layout so that such connections are simple to make. For example, locating modem servers in close proximity to telephone lines is important for telephone-line connections. Locating servers in computer rooms provides for easy connection to a WAN or stand-alone host computer.

The primary maxim you should observe when doing the site planning is "Proper prior planning prevents poor performance." Anticipate everything. Be mindful of wiring lengths and interconnection points. Allow for extra cable lengths needed to keep wiring out of the way. Make sure all devices can be located where they are needed; that is, be sure that maximum wire lengths between connecting points are not exceeded. It is important to identify all current and future equipment locations. Usually it is easier to install extra wiring during the initial wiring stages than to come back and add it later. Other site planning considerations include providing proper power supplies, cooling, and other ambient conditions such as proper humidity levels, distances from electrical and magnetic interference, and protection from direct sunlight. If you are working with a vendor, you should work closely with the vendor's staff to ensure that your plans are valid.

Medium Installation

After site planning you ought to be ready to install the medium. If you are working with a wireless LAN, installation is considerably easier than installing a wire-based LAN. With a wire-based LAN, you must find a way to string wires or cable through the areas housing servers, workstations, and printers. Often wires are strung through ceilings, walls, over the floor, along walls, through floors, through wiring closets, and so on. As mentioned earlier, when installing wiring you must be sure to comply with building codes.

With a wire-based LAN, you have four basic medium choices: unshielded twisted-pair wires, shielded twisted-pair wires, coaxial cable, and fiber optic cable. These options were described in Chapter 3. In some cases you also have other options. If your building is wired correctly for telephone service, you may be able to use the existing telephone wires as the medium. Some lower-speed LANs use a **digital private branch exchange (DPBX or digital PBX)** for data delivery as well as voice telephone communications.

Sometimes it is impossible or impractical for a company to install LAN wiring. This might be the case when wires must pass through concrete walls or between buildings. One company was prevented from installing wires between two buildings because the wires would have had to cross a public street. The company could not legally install wires over or under the street. The company had two options: contract with a common carrier for a line, or use a wireless medium like microwave or infrared light. The company chose a wireless medium to connect LAN segments in the two buildings, as illustrated in Figure 7-2.

In some areas the telephone companies offer a service called **integrated services digital network (ISDN).** ISDN has the potential for serving as a LAN medium. We will discuss this possibility in Chapter 14.

You may need to pull wires through conduit. One method of pulling wires is to insert a pulling wire through the conduit or area (for example, a ceiling) through which the wires are to be pulled. The new wires are attached to the pulling wire, which is pulled through the wiring area towing the new wires along with it. Inserting the pulling wire can be time consuming; therefore, before disconnecting the pulling wire, it is best to ensure that all wires have been pulled through and that there are no wiring breaks.

After the wire or cable has been installed, it should be tested to ensure it was not damaged during the installation process. For example, a wire may have been crimped when bending it around a corner. A wire crimp can cause transmission problems, so you should test the wires for continuity. You test cables with test equipment designed specifically for that purpose. Some cable test equipment manufacturers claim that over 50 percent of all LAN problems are cable related. For example, a cable tester can tell you the following information:

if cable breaks exist

the distance from the test unit to the cable break

where faulty connections exist

if twisted-pair wires can support the high speeds needed by Ethernet or token rings

components that are borderline

Do your testing while you still can make corrections easily. For example, if you are pulling wires through conduit, check the cables immediately. If errors are found, you can usually correct them more easily when the wires are exposed and the pulling wire is still in place than after the wires are connected or the pulling wire has been removed.

Hardware Installation

As illustrated in the PERT chart in Figure 7-1, hardware installation can begin before wiring the premises. Completion of hardware installation, however, requires that both computer and medium hardware be installed. You must carry out several tasks during hardware installation. The primary task

Figure 7-2   Wireless Medium Connecting LANs in Two Buildings

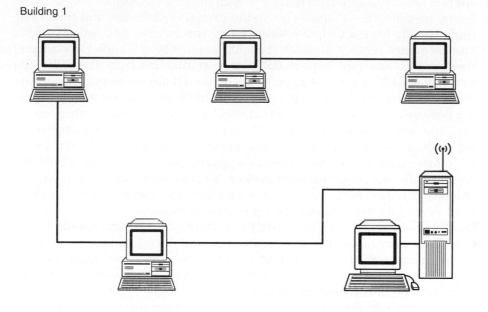

Building 1

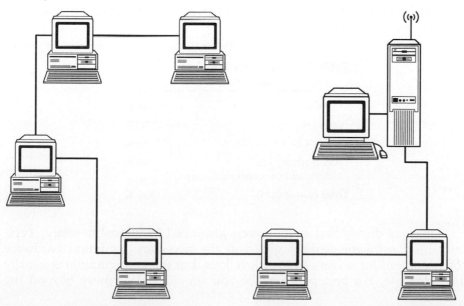

Building 2

is installing the LAN adapters in the workstations and servers. Each work-station and server must have an available expansion slot to house the LAN adapter. Many LAN adapters have switch or jumper settings you must set before installing the adapter card in the computer. Ethernet and token-ring cards usually have a unique address set by the factory. ARCnet cards have an 8-bit switch register in which the address must be set. Each LAN adapter must use an **interrupt request (IRQ)** to gain attention from the CPU. You must set the IRQ for each computer to a value not already being used by an-other device connected to that computer. Therefore, you must know about the devices already installed on the computer and the interrupts they are us-ing. You must also indicate which I/O port the LAN adapter is going to use for reading and writing data and the memory address in RAM that is used to transfer data to and from the LAN. Again, these addresses should not conflict with those used by other devices. To keep these details straight, you should document each workstation's and server's configuration. A sample form you might use for doing this is shown in Figure 7-3.

Some of your workstations may need additional memory. Recall that the overall memory requirement of each workstation increases as a result of the LAN system software. You'll find it easiest to install additional memory when the workstations are opened for LAN adapter installation. The mini-mum amount of real memory required depends on the application and LAN software you use. For example, suppose that you are using Novell NetWare 386 LAN software, DOS 4 operating system software, and WordPerfect word processing software. The memory required on a workstation for each of these software modules is given in Table 7-2. Note that a minimum of 534 K of memory is required. This means you need a minimum configuration of 640 K, since the next lower standard memory configuration is 512 K. Some LAN software requires almost 160 K on each workstation. When the LAN consumes this much workstation memory, you must install extra memory to run applications that are also memory intensive, for example, some database management systems.

Table 7-2 Software Memory Requirements

WordPerfect 5.1	384 K
NetWare	70 K
DOS 4 OS	30 K
DOS buffers, etc. (depends on configuration)	50 K
Total (minimum)	534 K

You may decide that some servers also need additional memory. Typi-cally LAN software vendors give you the necessary minimum hardware configurations for servers and workstations, but this configuration is usually just adequate. For best performance you should add memory beyond the

Figure 7-3 Hardware Configuration Form

- -

LAN Workstation Configuration

Manufacturer _____

Vendor _____

Location _____

CPU: Type _____   Speed _____   Math-Coprocessor _____

Memory _____

Memory Management Software/Hardware _____

Monitor: Manufacturer _____   Graphics Adapter _____

            Screen Size _____   Color? _____

Disks: Drive   Type   Capacity   Comments

          _____   _____   _____   _____

          _____   _____   _____   _____

          _____   _____   _____   _____

          _____   _____   _____   _____

Network Interface Card _____   Manufacturer _____

Node Address _____   IRQ _____   I/O Base Address _____

Operating System _____   Type _____   Version _____

LAN Interface Software _____

Printer: Type   Manufacturer   Network Address

            _____   _____   _____

            _____   _____   _____

185

minimum requirements. Recall that memory is often used to improve performance by caching disk records and increasing buffer sizes. The amount of memory required on servers is almost always greater than that required for workstations. Many of the large LAN systems require 4 MB or more of server memory; for example, Novell's NetWare 386 (4 MB), Banyan's Vines (4 MB), Microsoft's LAN Manager (5 MB), Ungerman-Bass's Net/One LAN (5 MB) and IBM's LAN Server (6 MB). Several systems recommend even more memory than the minimum requirement.

You should check the amount of available disk space when loading the LAN software on workstations and servers. A few LANs need considerable disk space on the workstation for storing network files. The disk space required on the file servers for LAN software alone can be great. For example, one LAN system requires 4 MB of disk storage space for its workstation network files. On your disk you must store not only the LAN software but also memory swap space for executing software, spooler files, and mail message files, and space for new applications like groupware. The disk space required can easily exceed 20 MB, and this does not include the storage required for application programs and databases. Moreover, if your workstations have a variety of operating systems, you may need to load operating system utilities from each version on the server disks. This allows workstations to access utilities from the network rather than from local disk drives. Each diskless workstation requires the presence of these operating system utilities.

Other hardware installation tasks include installing printers, backup units, modems, facsimile devices, and so on. Your site-planning documentation should indicate where these devices are located. Each can create special planning and installation problems. For example, consider data backup. Most networks allow you to back up the system to any workstation or server media. However, there may be some restrictions regarding how the backup is done. Some networks, such as Novell NetWare ELS-1, require that the backup utility be run from a workstation, and that workstation is dedicated to that task until the backup is completed. A file server running under the UNIX operating system and using a UNIX backup utility requires that the backup be done on a server. If several servers exist, all servers may be able to be backed up to a drive on one of the servers. You should investigate the limitations and options available in your system before installing the backup hardware and software.

After the premises are wired and you have installed the LAN adapters and other hardware, you can begin connecting the hardware to the wiring. When this is done, you have the physical network in place.

Software Installation

The software installation process consists of three phases: LAN operating system software installation, application software, installation, and utility software installation. Another task involved in software installation is setting up application and user environments. In this section we are only concerned about software that is stored on the server. Applications used by only one or two users can be installed only on those users' workstations.

Installing LAN operating system software has two subphases: installing the workstation software and installing the server software. On workstations you must install the network system software discussed in Chapter 5. This is usually a rather simple process. The workstation software modules are generated for individual workstations or for groups of workstations. Earlier in this chapter you read about LAN adapter settings. These settings must also be defined for the software. The variations you must typically accommodate between workstations are

operating system version

interrupt requests

memory addresses

I/O port address

After generating the workstation's LAN system software, it must be loaded onto the workstation. For DOS systems the **AUTOEXEC.BAT** and **CONFIG.SYS files** also are updated to set the environment and the startup parameters. An AUTOEXEC.BAT file contains commands that are automatically executed by DOS when the system is booted. Table 7-3 shows a sample AUTOEXEC.BAT file for a Novell NetWare workstation. Lines that begin with REM are remarks and are ignored by DOS. The lines containing the commands IPX, NET5, and F: are network commands. The IPX command starts the process that formats packets for the LAN; NET5 starts a redirector process that interfaces to the DOS operating system (the 5 represents the version of DOS being used); and the F: command changes the default drive to the server drive. The AUTOEXEC.BAT file also contains some settings for **environment variables,** which are stored by the operating system and typically represent hardware, software, and user parameters. Some operating systems have standard environment variables, such as date and time settings. DOS also allows user-defined environment variables, such as the DISPLAY and MENU variables in the AUTOEXEC.BAT file. Environment variables can be an important factor in customizing the LAN environment for the user. Novell's NetWare can check these settings and use them to customize a user's session.

The CONFIG.SYS file contains system environment data. For instance, you can specify how many files can be open concurrently, the number of disk buffers allocated in memory, which device drivers are to be installed, and so on. Again, the steps you follow depend on the network you are using. A simple CONFIG.SYS file is shown in Table 7-4. In an OS/2 operating system, the STARTUP.CMD file is similar to DOS's AUTOEXEC.BAT file. With an OS/2 workstation the STARTUP.CMD file may need to be updated to make the network connection automatically.

Novell's 3.*nn* NetWare network operating system (NOS) also has two **startup files** that are used automatically when the NOS is loaded. These files, named AUTOEXEC.NCF and STARTUP.NCF, contain commands the NOS automatically follows upon starting. Examples of an AUTOEXEC.NCF and STARTUP.NCF files are shown in Tables 7-5 and 7-6 respectively. The AUTOEXEC.NCF file shown provides the NOS with the name of the file server and the internal network number, loads the driver for the LAN adapter card, and binds the driver to the protocol being used for that port.

Table 7-3   Simple Workstation AUTOEXEC.BAT File

```
rem -----------------------------------------------------------
rem    start the Microsoft Window's disk cache program
C:\APPS\WINDOWS\SMARTDRV.EXE
set temp = c:\apps\windows\temp
rem -----------------------------------------------------------
rem      start DOS 5's command recall utility
doskey
rem -----------------------------------------------------------
rem      start the mouse driver
\system\mouse\mouse
rem -----------------------------------------------------------
rem      set the user's prompt
prompt    $p$g
rem -----------------------------------------------------------
rem      start the network communications and redirector programs
IPX
NET5
rem -----------------------------------------------------------
rem      set the default drive to the network drive
F:
rem -----------------------------------------------------------
rem      set user\workstation environment variables
set DISPLAY = VGA
set MENU = LANADMIN
```

Table 7-4   Simple Workstation CONFIG.SYS File

```
BREAK = ON
BUFFERS = 20
FILES = 40
LASTDRIVE = Z
SHELL = C:\DOS5\COMMAND.COM /P /E:256
DEVICE = C:\DOS5\ANSI.SYS
```

The STARTUP.NCF file loads the disk drivers for the server disks. Further details of the startup files are beyond the scope of this chapter.

Table 7-5   Sample AUTOEXEC.NCF File

```
file server name SERVER1
ipx internal net 123
load sys:\system\trxnet port = 2E0 mem = D0000 int = 2
bind ipx to trxnet net = 1
```

Table 7-6   Sample STARTUP.NCF File

```
load ISADISK port = 1F0 int = E
```

In addition to the LAN workstation software that interfaces to the operating system and the network, you must install workstation software to interface to network printers. We cover this topic in Chapter 9.

Usually installing the LAN server software is more complex than installing the LAN workstation software. As mentioned earlier, some LAN server software is self-contained; that is, operating system and LAN software are integrated. Other implementations load the LAN software as a set of tasks run under a general-purpose operating system like UNIX or OS/2.

When installing the LAN software, you must understand the impact of the installation. If the LAN software is integrated with an operating system, it probably changes the format of the server's disk drives. An integrated LAN operating system may have a file and directory format different from a general-purpose operating system. For example, it may change the disk directory structure because the operating system uses different naming conventions and provides more security attributes for files. It may change the file allocation table because it allocates disk space differently from the method used by a general-purpose operating system. If this is the case, before starting the installation, you should back up all files on the server's disks. This is a good idea even when installing LAN software that runs under the server's current operating system. Moreover be sure that the backup is compatible with the eventual state of the system. For example, if you back up the data under the DOS operating system, and a new operating system is installed that does not allow you to run a DOS RESTORE program, be sure a mechanism exists for getting those files back on the server.

LAN software is tailored to an individual server. You may need to generate an operating system version that is compatible with the hardware settings you indicated when installing the LAN adapter. The details of installing the LAN software vary from one LAN to another. In some cases it is a very simple process and requires little time. This does not imply that the LAN software is simple. For example, installing Novell NetWare 386 is quite easy, requiring only that you answer a few questions and insert diskettes when asked to; it takes less than 30 minutes. Despite the ease of doing this,

Novell NetWare 386 is one of the most sophisticated LANs for microcomputers. In contrast, earlier versions of Novell LAN software, such as NetWare 286, are noted for lengthy and complex installations.

A typical LAN also has utility software that provides a variety of functions. Some LAN software comes with utility software bundled in. Frequently users supplement this utility software with other utilities, such as

backup/restore utilities

LAN management/administration utilities

file transfer utilities

statistics and reporting utilities

diagnostics utilities

The type of utilities you need for your LAN varies according to the type and scope of the utilities bundled with your LAN software. Most LAN's come with a backup/restore program, but some LAN administrators purchase another backup/restore system that is more comprehensive than the bundled version.

The final installation phase is to customize the applications to the needs of individual users. You may recall from Chapter 6 that applications vary in their ability to accommodate individual users. How you do this customization is therefore application dependent.

Conversion and Data Preparation

Once all application and system software are installed, you must load the data. Sometimes data is converted from an existing computer system, and sometimes you must manually enter new data. When setting up a LAN, an organization must decide what is public data and what is private data. **Public data** is usually stored on a server. **Private data** may be stored at one or more workstations or in secured files on the server. Public data is that which is shared among two or more users. In this section we are concerned only with public data. Some data starts as private data and when sufficiently prepared becomes public, such as budget data and marketing information for new products.

Creating the Operating Environment

Installing software and user profiles is one aspect of creating the operating environment. Setting up security, user IDs, workgroups, and so on is another important aspect. This topic is discussed in the next chapter.

Testing and Acceptance

After installing the hardware and software and setting up the operating environment, you are ready to conduct system testing. The objective of testing is to demonstrate that the system works according to contractual stipulations. Your purchase contract should detail the terms under which the LAN is acceptable. The testing conducted can be separated into two main parts: functional testing and performance testing.

During **functional testing** you test the system components to ensure that they all work correctly both individually and collectively. Thus you check each application to verify that it works correctly. Recall that an application that works correctly on one network may not work at all on a different network, so you should not assume your applications will all work correctly. Moreover you must check that the applications were installed correctly. One problem often encountered is improper security settings. When you check the applications, be sure you log on under the IDs of all users who will be working with the applications. An application that works correctly for the LAN supervisor ID may not work for a user with lesser privileges. You should also check that user profiles are correctly set up, the license provisions operate correctly, the printer system functions as it should, and the application modules can interoperate correctly. Functional testing can usually be conducted with a few users. These users should exercise each component of the systems they intend to use.

Performance testing, sometimes called stress testing, tests to see if the network can sustain the anticipated workload. Again the acceptance criteria in the purchase contract should indicate levels of required performance. This can be the time required to download an application, the response time to database requests, and the throughput of the system (the work that can be accomplished by the workgroup). Your testing must provide an environment that completely tests your system. You must define the functions that need testing and also the environment necessary for conducting stress testing. Stress testing is ordinarily conducted in two ways: For the first approach a large group of users who are representative of all system users simulate the actual working environment using the system. The second approach uses software that simulates the actual working environment by setting up a given number of users and a work rate. The first approach takes more personnel coordination and can be expensive if numerous employees must be paid overtime to conduct the tests. The second approach is not labor intensive but requires some software preparation. The stress testing software can, however, be used again to tune the system and check the impact of adding new users and applications.

If you understand what must be done with acceptance testing, you must realize that you do not wait until the system is completely installed to prepare the suite of test programs. Proper testing is a well-planned event. The PERT chart for installation and acceptance in Figure 7-1 shows you that you can begin planning for testing immediately after you select the system. Once you have accepted the system (or placed it into production without formally accepting it) you assume the responsibility of making it work and keeping users satisfied with performance and capabilities. This is why you have acceptance testing—to have the vendor provide a system that works to your organization's satisfaction.

Cutover

After the system has been accepted, you must move users from the old system or way of doing things to the new system, a procedure known as **cutover.** Commonly when a new system is installed, it is run parallel to the old system for some time to confirm that the new system works the way it should. This may be difficult for a LAN because the old system of stand-alone workstations is likely to be integrated into the network. Moreover it is a relatively simple matter to revert back to using the individual workstations as stand-alone systems. Thus cutover usually can be accomplished after user training and system acceptance.

Even though cutover may be relatively straightforward, it still must be planned. The cutover plans should include when cutover is to occur and if cutover is to be done all at once or in phases. The phased approach, often the most practical, adds users to the network in groups. Thus the network grows incrementally over time until all users are added to the network. Phased implementation allows you to build the network slowly both from the users' and administrators' perspectives. If problems are encountered along the way, they can be overcome with a minimum disruption to the user community.

TRAINING

Three general classes of LAN users must receive training: administrators, group managers, and users. Before conducting training the roles of the participants must be decided. Some employees are users only, some are group managers, some are LAN operators, and one or more has the responsibilities of LAN administrator. Choosing the category or categories into which an employee falls depends on the employee's technical expertise, job functions, and interest. In an organization a group has a manager; however, this manager is not necessarily the person who should be assigned the task of group manager for LAN administration. A LAN group manager may need to carry out technical tasks, such as attaching users to printers, clearing jobs from the print queue, and so on. Someone in the workgroup with a technical aptitude may fulfill this responsibility better than the group's manager.

User Training

By far the least amount of training is needed for users; however, paradoxically, user training often is the hardest to conduct. The reasons for this are twofold: Users tend to have less computer expertise than the other two groups, so some users have a difficult time learning technical details. Also, user training typically is done in-house by in-house staff, which means the trainees sometimes will have their learning interrupted by work emergencies. Moreover in-house training facilities sometimes lack the necessary equipment, and in-house trainers sometimes are less proficient than professional trainers.

Recall from earlier chapters that using a LAN ought to be transparent. In most cases this is true at the application level. That is, once a user environment has been established, the user works as though all the files needed are on a local disk drive. In a well-planned LAN, the LAN administrator sets up an environment that promotes transparency. One way to provide transparency is through startup files like DOS's CONFIG.SYS and AUTOEXEC.BAT files and through **login scripts.** A login script is a set of system commands that creates a user's environment on the network. A login script can set a user's default drive and directory, a search path for executable files (like those in the AUTOEXEC.BAT), map logical disk drives on the file server, set up a printing environment, display a message of the day, and so on. Taken to the ultimate level, the combination of startup files and login scripts can log the user onto the LAN and automatically start a program for the user or display a familiar menu. But a note of caution: Automatically logging a user onto the LAN in a startup file is a potential security hazard and typically should be avoided.

Even with startup files and login scripts, users may notice some operations are a bit different on a LAN compared to a stand-alone system, including

directing printed output to different printers

changing a password

finding resources on the network or other networks

logging off

setting paths

using groupware

finding the disk drive mappings

running electronic mail

finding differences in application environment settings

setting file security

Naturally the type of training users need depends on the LAN software they will be using. Usually LAN users must know how to log on, use electronic mail, set up their own configuration for specific applications, and network differences in the applications they are using. For example, WordPerfect on a network requires each user to enter up to three characters at the start of the session. These three characters are used to make up file names for each user's work environment. These files store user default profiles, which include foreground and background colors, monitor type, and so on. In some cases users need to know some of the LAN system interface language. For example, users might want to use a "send message to user" LAN utility, change passwords, change file security attributes for files they own, and look at their jobs in the spooler's disk queues.

Initial training may be conducted by your vendor, a software consultant, or your own staff. In the long term it is often best if several members of your organization provide the user training. Most organizations experience personnel turnover, so some people will always need training. Hiring outside consultants for this continual process can be expensive. Moreover, much of the training required can be done through self-paced user manuals.

Group Manager Training

Group managers are users with minor LAN administration responsibilities. A group manager must know everything that users know as well as group management tasks. The primary group management tasks are adding and deleting users from groups. A group manager may also be responsible for setting security for files and directories owned by the group. Other possible group management tasks include managing print queues, changing print job priorities, deleting jobs from the print queue, attaching and detaching a queue from a printer, printing specific portions of a job in a queue, and similar print tasks. The most likely source of this training is the LAN administrator.

Operator Training

An operator's responsibilities include starting the network, keeping it running, making data backups, and shutting the network down. Often these duties are carried out by the LAN administrator. Regardless of who bears the responsibility for these tasks, training is necessary. Starting the system involves powering-up shared components like the file and print servers and loading essential software modules like the spooler. When problems occur, the operator must know how to resolve them so the network continues to operate efficiently. Making data backups is another important responsibility of the operator (see Chapter 10). Finally, the operator must know how to bring the network to an orderly halt, ensuring that all users are able to complete their work and that no data is lost or corrupted in the process. These skills are frequently taught in LAN administration classes, and some sources for this training are given in the next section on LAN administrator training.

LAN Administrator Training

Administration of a small, established LAN may require only a slight amount of work, say several hours per week. However, a small LAN needs at least two qualified LAN administrators, one serving as an alternate or backup administrator. Suppose your organization has only one person that knows how to start, stop, and fix the LAN. If that person goes on vacation or a business trip, retires, quits, becomes ill, or for some other reason cannot be there to solve problems, your organization can have its work capability severely reduced when problems with the network arise.

LAN administration for large LANs can be a full-time job for one or more people. The amount of training required for a LAN administrator depends on the sophistication or complexity of the system. A large LAN may have hundreds of users; tens of servers; connections to other LANs, WANs, and stand-alone hosts; a wide variety of applications installed; and a high rate of personnel turnover. The depth of technical expertise the LAN administrator needs for this system is considerably more than the administrator of a three-user LAN used primarily to share printers and disks needs.

The LAN administrator must know everything that users and group managers know, plus a lot more. The administrator's education is usually more formal than that of users and managers. When a LAN is first implemented, the organization ordinarily hires an experienced LAN administrator or sends one of its employees to a LAN administration course oriented specifically toward the LAN chosen. For example, the LAN administrator will take several one-week LAN administration courses, such as elementary LAN administration, LAN troubleshooting, advanced LAN administration, systems programming, and performance and tuning. Training classes are often conducted by the LAN vendor. Other sources of training include in-house experts, consultants, professional education companies, the LAN manufacturer, and colleges and universities. LAN administrators also must have conceptual training oriented toward understanding the technology in general—topics such as data communications and LAN principals. It is definitely a good investment to train LAN administrators before they assume administrative duties. Learning as you go with self-taught on-the-job training has too much potential for costly and time-consuming errors. LAN administrators also must keep their administrative knowledge current. This is done through formal training classes, on the job training, and periodic additional formal training.

LAN administrators must learn all facets of administration. A partial list of topics they must know is given in Table 7-7.

Table 7-7 LAN Administrator Responsibilities

hardware options	software options
hardware installation	software installation
diagnostics and trouble shooting	user administration
group administration	printer administration
security	application installation
backup and recovery	problem reporting
capacity planning	system tuning
systems programming	

SUMMARY

LAN selection leads naturally to LAN installation. During installation, problems frequently arise. Many times these problems result from misunderstandings between the organization and its LAN vendors. To guard against such misunderstandings, a company should have a detailed written contract with all vendors. The contract should protect the rights of the vendor and the organization alike. It should stipulate what is to be delivered, when and where delivery is to occur, and what constitutes acceptance of the system. An organization should have an attorney review the purchase and installation contracts.

Installation consists of several well-defined stages. Some stages can be done in parallel, and some must be done sequentially. A plan must be created that identifies the tasks, their order, and when they must be completed. A PERT chart is one way of organizing this plan. The main stages of installation are documentation, site preparation, medium installation, hardware installation, software installation, conversion, creating an operating environment, testing, cutover, and training. Hardware installation may require upgrades to existing workstations. An organization should test for both functional completeness and adherence to stated performance goals.

Basic LAN training programs are needed for users, group managers, and LAN administrators. Users must know how the LAN environment differs from a stand-alone workstation and how to use the LAN resources effectively. Group managers need more training than users. Group managers are responsible for adding users, deleting users, setting security attributes for files and directories, and manipulating printer settings. LAN administrators need the most extensive training. Essentially LAN administrators must know about all aspects of the LAN: startup procedures; shutdown procedures; hardware and software installation; user, group, and printer management; troubleshooting, and so on. To ensure that an organization always has a LAN administrator available, at least two people should receive LAN administration training.

KEY TERMS

AUTOEXEC.BAT file

channels

CONFIG.SYS file

cutover

digital private branch exchange (DPBX, or digital PBX)

environment variables

functional testing

integrated services digital network (ISDN)

interrupt request (IRQ)

login script

payment schedule

penalty clause

performance testing

preventive maintenance

private data

progress payments

protection clause

public data

purchase contract

restorative maintenance

site planning

startup file

REVIEW QUESTIONS

1. Why is a purchase contract important?

2. What is acceptance testing, and why is it necessary?

3. Why would you make progress payments? How do the vendor and customer benefit from progress payments?

4. What are penalty clauses? Give an example of a penalty clause.

5. Why are software and hardware maintenance agreements important?

6. What is accomplished during site planning?

7. What medium installation options are usually available?

8. What hardware changes might be required when converting a stand-alone workstation to a LAN workstation?

9. Describe the software installation process. In which computers must you install software? What types of files are created or modified to enable network access?

10. Describe eight differences a user may notice when going from a stand-alone environment to a LAN environment.

11. Compare functional and performance testing.

12. What are the four basic user groups that require training? Describe the training required of the four basic user groups.

PROBLEMS AND EXERCISES

1. Draw up a list of tasks that should be completed as part of the site preparation for a LAN in your school or work place. Examples of things you should consider are new power sources, construction to house a server in a controlled access room, and wiring.

2. Draw up a PERT chart for the installation of a LAN for your school or place of work.

3. Suppose you wanted to install a new LAN in your school or work place. What type of medium would be appropriate? Detail how the wires for a wire-based LAN (twisted-pair wires, coaxial cable, or fiber optic cable) would be installed. How would a wireless LAN be installed?

4. Suppose that you are installing a new application on the LAN. The new application replaces a manual system in which all data are kept on 3 × 5 file cards. Describe how you would convert the data to machine-readable form on the LAN.

5. Examine the literature to find the types of classes being presented by LAN vendors or consulting firms for data communications, LAN installation, LAN management, and LAN problem resolution. What are the costs of the course? Where are they held? What would be the cost of the such training for a LAN administrator in your area? Include the costs of travel, lodging, and meals.

REFERENCES

Frank, Alan. "Networking Without Wires." *LAN Technology*, Volume 8, Number 3, March 1992.

Hayes, Victor, "Standardization Efforts for Wireless LANs." *IEEE Network*, Volume 5, Number 6, November 1991.

Klein, Mike. "Cabling Do's and Don'ts." *LAN Technology*, Volume 6, Number 2, February, 1990.

Klein, Mike. "Weapons for Winning: The Batch File Battle." *LAN Technology*, Volume 6, Number 5, May 1990.

Leeds, Frank and Chorey, Jim. "Round Up Your Cable Woes." *LAN Technology*, Volume 7, Number 10, October 1991.

Leeds, Frank and Chorey, Jim. "Twisted-Pair Wiring Made Simple." *LAN Technology*, Volume 7, Number 4, April 1991.

Love, R. D., and Toher, T. "Do the Right Thing: Choosing Tomorrow's LAN Cabling Today." *Data Communications*, Volume 19, Number 13, October 1990.

Machrone, Bill. "Service, Support, and Reliability: Agenda for the Nineties." *PC Magazine*, Volume 9, Number 16, September 25, 1990.

Mathias, Craig J. "Wireless LANs: The Next Wave." *Data Communications*, Volume 21, Number 5, March 1992.

Morris, William T. and Beam, Tony E. "How to Install Fiber-Optic Cable." *LAN Technology*, Volume 6, Number 12, December 1990.

Sanders, Russel. "Mapping the Wiring Maze." *LAN Technology*, Volume 8, Number 11, October 1992.

Sarto, Dan and Campbell, Greg. "An Inside Look at Premises Wiring." *LAN Technology*, Volume 6, Number 2, February 1990.

Saunders, Stephen. "Premises Wiring Get the Standard Treatment." *Data Communications*, Volume 21, Number 16, November 1992.

LAN ADMINISTRATION: USERS, GROUPS, AND SECURITY

CHAPTER PREVIEW

LAN installation can be a difficult task, but it is a one-time task. LAN administration—keeping the system running properly—is an ongoing activity. How much time you spend on LAN administration depends on the number of users on your system, the variety of applications you have, and to a lesser extent on your LAN software itself. Many tasks of the LAN administrator relate to LAN users. Part of the responsibility of a LAN administrator is to help create a friendly user environment by providing easy access to necessary applications and data and by making it easy for users to print or distribute their results. This chapter gives you some guidelines for creating and securing the user environment.

Specific topics you will read about in this chapter include:

users and groups

systems programming

security

virus protection

USERS AND GROUPS

When you implement a LAN, you are creating a community of users who share LAN resources. As in most communities, the members of a LAN community are not all alike. An individual LAN user does not always have the same rights and privileges as other LAN users. One objective of LAN administration is to make available all the resources a person needs for his or her job while withholding or protecting those resources that are unnecessary. For example, a software engineer needs access to some program source files but not to payroll files. A payroll supervisor needs to access and update payroll files but not program source files. Studies have shown that the major security risk facing companies today is its employees, not outside intruders. Some security breaches are accidental, for example, accidentally erasing a

202

Chapter 8
LAN
Administration:
Users, Groups,
and Security

file; other breaches are intentional, such as disgruntled employees intentionally erasing files or providing sensitive corporate data to a competitor. The LAN administrator must create the environment that promotes both productivity and protection.

A network builds its user community through two entities, users and groups. A group can be a workgroup or a collection of employees drawn along other organizational boundaries. However, before we go into the details of groups, let us first look at users.

Users

A LAN community of users may consist of all the organization's employees. In the typical organization, however, some employees must use the LAN to do their work, some simply use output created on the LAN, and others do not use the system at all. From the LAN administrator's perspective, the term *users* applies only to employees who use the LAN in doing their jobs. Since LAN users usually do not all have the same access privileges, it is important to be able to distinguish one user from another. Without such distinction, the LAN software cannot enforce security.

The two most basic LAN administration tasks involving users are adding users and deleting them. Once a user has been added to the system, additional administrative tasks exist to customize that user's environment and to provide that user with access privileges and restrictions. The user's environment is often a matrix of rights covering printers, files, workstations, and time. That is, a user may have rights to use certain printers, have access privileges to certain files, and be restricted to using certain workstations at certain times. Let us look at these privileges and restrictions in more detail.

Users identify themselves to the system by **user identifiers (IDs)**. The user ID is a user's form of **identification** to the system. If security is in force, the user also must provide **authentication** of himself or herself by entering into the system information known only to that user, such as a **password.** More security-conscious systems use **biological identification and authentication** measures, such as retina scans, palm prints, or voice analysis. Once identified and authenticated a user is granted access to the system. Exactly what access is allowed depends on the user's access rights, which are detailed later in the chapter.

Some systems allow functional user IDs that do not correspond to a person. For example, suppose all users on a LAN need access to the electronic mail system. The LAN administrator can secure the mail system so that any user can access all of its files. Another alternative is to create a functional user, say NETWORK_MAIL, which has access to the mail system's applications and files. When someone wants to run a mail program, the mail program runs with the rights of the NETWORK_MAIL functional user rather than the rights of the person running the mail program.

Many LAN systems automatically establish two types of users at installation time. One type of user has a common user ID, say GUEST, with few or no network privileges. The other type of user is all-powerfull, with all rights and privileges on the system. In a Novell network, this user is called

SUPERVISOR. The major function of the SUPERVISOR is to set up LAN user, file, and printer environments, keep the system running correctly, install software and hardware, and solve network problems.

In most systems, adding users is simple. Some systems have a command language interface that requires you to use syntax such as ADD USER <*user-name*>. Some LANs have a menu interface that prompts you through the process of adding a user. Still other systems have a user ID file that you must edit with a text editor, inserting a new line to create a new user. The technique for adding new users is not as important as well-planned user administration. The LAN administrator should devise a plan for creating consistent user names, matching those user names with the users or functions that use them, and setting up user access rights.

Groups

A group is a collection of users. In some systems each user must belong to exactly one group. In other systems a user can belong to none, one, or several groups. The functions of a group are to combine many users into a single entity and to implement security. Of these two functions, security is the most important.

You can think of a LAN as consisting of individual users, formally defined groups of users, and the entire community of users. Some LAN activities can be done by only one or two people, some things can be done by several people (a group), and some things can be done by everyone. Users of groups can do certain things on a LAN because they've been given **access rights,** or privileges. Examples of access rights for individuals, groups, and everyone are shown in Table 8-1. The LAN administrator must find a way to give proper access rights to all users.

Systems Programming

The meaning of **systems programming** depends on the whether the system is a mainframe or a LAN. In a mainframe environment, systems programmers are responsible for maintaining systems software, such as the operating system, database management system, and data communications system software. On a LAN, systems programming consists of running the network, solving network problems, installing new software, writing network utilities, and personalizing the users' environment.

One systems programming task is creating logon scripts. A **logon script** is a file that contains commands to set the user's environment automatically when he or she logs onto the network. Another systems programming task is creating menus for users. If you are using a graphical user interface (GUI), such as Windows, menus usually are created through the GUI's utilities. Some LAN applications also have utilities for building menus.

SECURITY

Setting up effective network **security** is a critical task of the LAN administrator. The term *security* may conjure up images of protecting against hackers, industrial spies, or external disruption. Although security does guard

204

Chapter 8
LAN
Administration:
Users, Groups,
and Security

against these types of outside intrusions, most commonly security protects an organization from accidental or intentional disruption from its own employees. Accidental disruption includes incidents like accidentally erasing files and deleting or modifying data incorrectly. Intentional disruption includes intentionally deleting files or data, changing sensitive data, such as salary and invoice amounts, adding bogus records, and copying data to sell to competitors. Therefore, a comprehensive security program protects an organization from misuse or abuse from both employees and outsiders.

The administrator must realize several key facts about security. First, too much security makes a system hard to use. Total security means that *no one* can access the system. Too little security can result in the loss of data, money, or opportunity because everyone has access to everything. A good security system provides the necessary safeguards without inhibiting the use of the system. Second, security does not deny access to a system. Anyone who wants to spend the necessary time, energy, and money can probably break any security system eventually. Security is merely a delaying factor. Its objectives are to make breaching security more costly than the expected gain or to deter intruders long enough to identify and apprehend them. Vigilance and flexibility in making changes in a security system are essential to keeping a system secure. Technology changes rapidly, for bad as well as for good. That is, some new technologies can render existing security ineffective. Therefore, the LAN administrator may need to constantly improve the security provisions of the system to overcome security loopholes that may arise.

Table 8-1   User Access Rights

Rights extended to everyone
 logon and logoff
 run word processing and spreadsheet programs
 send and receive electronic mail

Rights extended to all members of a personnel group
 change employee addresses, telephone numbers, and names
 add new employees
 retrieve employee data
 use department printers

Rights extended to only a few members of a personnel group
 change employee ratings
 delete employees
 promote employees
 delete files
 create files

Rights extended to specific members of a software development group
 update source program
 delete source files

Security is not absolute, and it is not free. The costs of security cover the labor that goes into setting up user IDs, passwords, access rights, and other security provisions, and for security hardware and software. Security hardware includes physical devices, such as door locks, security guards, and motion detectors. Security software includes programs that analyze the security settings of a system and, perhaps, software that can be used to catch someone intentionally attempting to break security. It takes time, effort, and money to implement a good security system. If you can visualize a large LAN with hundreds of users, thousands of files, and many variations in access rights, you might begin to understand how much work can go into ensuring that each user gets access to everything he or she needs without giving access to critical data outside the scope of the user's job.

A comprehensive security program provides both physical security and data access security. **Physical security** is the traditional method of securing objects. It denies physical access to the objects being protected. Physical security includes measures such as door locks, security guards, closed-circuit television monitoring, motion detectors, and so on. Although physical security still has a place in most networks, it is usually not a sufficient security measure. By nature, networks are distributed, making adequate physical security coverage difficult. For example, if a LAN has workstations distributed throughout an office complex, it is difficult to physically monitor each workstation to prevent unauthorized use. Furthermore, since an organization's own employees are its greatest source of security risks, monitoring a workstation to ensure it is used only by an authorized employee is inadequate. Therefore, physical security must be augmented by data access security.

Data access security uses software and hardware techniques to help protect data. Data access security gives the proper access to data within the scope of an authorized user's job, denies access to data outside the scope of an authorized user's job, and denies access to unauthorized users altogether. Earlier you read about user identification and authentication. The use of passwords is one means of implementing data access security. Since this type of security is the cornerstone of many data security systems, let us look at passwords in more detail.

Password Administration

A properly secured LAN requires all users to identify themselves and then verify their identifications using passwords. In most LAN systems the LAN administrator has the option of making passwords mandatory or optional for individual users. We encourage the requirement of passwords for all users on all LANs.

Providing a user with an ID and a password grants that person access to the system. Access to the system does not necessarily imply access to all data and devices on the system, but it does usually provide the right to run certain programs and access certain data. The security of your LAN system depends to a great extent on your policy for creating and changing passwords. Table 8-2 lists some possible provisions of such a policy.

206

Chapter 8
LAN
Administration:
Users, Groups,
and Security

Table 8-2 Suggested Password Policy

Change passwords regularly—at least once per month.

Passwords should be at least four characters long.

Do not write password down.

Do not use initials, month abbreviations, birth dates, and so on when making up a password.

Change a password if you suspect someone else knows it.

Make successive passwords unique; that is, do not use sequence numbers or letters—for example, PW1, then PW2 then PW3, and so on.

Report any instances of suspected unauthorized logons.

Do not leave your workstation unattended while you are logged on.

A good password cannot be discovered easily by an unauthorized person. The hardest passwords to discover are long (usually a maximum of eight characters is allowed) and consist of random characters. If a password can have up to eight characters (letters and digits only), the total number of passwords possible exceeds $36^8 = 2.8 \times 10^{12}$. This means the average number of guesses is also large—1.4×10^{12} or half the total number of passwords. To prevent systematic password guessing, a secure system disallows a user or program from attempting an arbitrary number of password guesses.

One way to handle unsuccessful logons is to use a **timeout value,** which causes the system to refuse to accept another logon attempt from a user ID station or both after a designated time interval, say five minutes. Using a five-minute timeout value, it would take approximately 13 million years for an unauthorized user to guess a password. A second approach for dealing with unauthorized logon attempts is to deactivate the user's account after some threshold number of unsuccessful passwords have been attempted. Once the user's account has been deactivated, no one, not even the proper user, can log on until the LAN administrator reactivates the account.

A third method used to detect an intruder is for the system to fake a successful logon after the intruder has several unsuccessful attempts. The **fake logon** establishs a controlled environment for the intruder and issues a security warning on the LAN administrator's control console. The objective of the fake session is to make the intruder think he or she has successfully gained access to the system. The session controls the type of access the intruder is given. While the intruder uses the system thinking a successful security breach has been made, the LAN administrator can determine the workstation from which the intrusion is being made and take steps to apprehend the perpetrator. You may enjoy reading Stoll (1989) for an account of detecting security violations and the use of a fake logon session.

The preceding steps are taken to thwart someone who is attempting to gain access through the trial-and-error method of password guessing. Commonly an intruder gains unauthorized access more directly, using more sophisticated measures than trial and error to finding an authorized user's password. Often users select passwords that are easy for them to remember—their names, initials, birth dates, logon names, names of relatives, and so on. Such passwords are easy for an intruder to discover by trying likely combinations of user-relevant data strings. To be most effective, passwords should be lengthy—at least four or five characters long—and randomly created. Such passwords, however, are hard to remember, so users are more likely to write down their passwords, usually near their workstations. These passwords can then be discovered by an intruder who has physical access to the area.

Users should be required to change their passwords at least once a month as another way to thwart intruders. As part of a good security policy, administrators must specify a maximum time between password changes. If a user fails to change the password in that interval, the user ultimately is denied access to the system. Two main methods are used to force password changes. First, the user can be requested to change his or her password after it has expired and cannot log on until the password is changed. For example, in a UNIX-based system, a user attempting to log on with an aged password is prompted to change it. In a Novell network the administrator can grant a user several **grace logons.** For example, if an administrator allows a user two grace logons, the user can log on, under an expired password twice. At each of the grace logons, the user is notified that the password has expired and is prompted to change the password. If the user does not change the password after two grace logons, the user's account is locked and he or she cannot make subsequent logons. The LAN administrator must then reactivate the password expiration date or number of remaining grace logons before the user can regain access to the system.

A security feature offered by some UNIX systems is a minimum period between changing passwords. On the surface this may appear to present the potential for security problems. The intent of this provision is to disallow a user from changing a password as required when the password expires and then immediately changing the password back to its previous value. An administrator also can instruct the UNIX security system to maintain a history of user passwords, say the 12 previous ones. A user is unable to use any of these 12 previous passwords, thus ensuring that the passwords are not recycled. Moreover, a few systems help guard against common passwords by checking that a user does not embed his or her user ID within the password.

Some installations like to maintain centralized control of the security system. One way of doing this is to prevent users from changing their own passwords. The LAN administrator is responsible for assigning all passwords. This policy ensures that the passwords assigned are changed with the proper frequency and that the passwords are suitably random. However, it also means that the passwords must be written down and sent to users, and the randomness of the passwords increases the probability that users will keep written copies of their passwords until they memorize them.

Logon Restrictions

Security can be further enhanced by controlling user access to the system. This requires the LAN administrator to restrict how and where users log on.

208
- - - - -
Chapter 8
LAN
Administration:
Users, Groups,
and Security

One of the simplest of these controls is to limit the number of **concurrent logons** a user has. For example, suppose the LAN administrator limits each user ID to one concurrent logon. If you are logged onto the LAN, no other person can use your user ID to log on, because only one logon is allowed for that ID. Furthermore, if you attempt to logon and are denied because the logon limit will be exceeded, you know that either you or someone else is already using your ID. This is a good way to control user access, but it also has a disadvantage. Sometimes it is convenient to have a single user logged onto the network more than once. For example, you may have two workstations available and be conducting a simultaneous session on each, or you might be running a program on one workstation and documenting how the program works on the other.

Another security feature is restricting the times at which a user can be logged on. For example, an organization may decide that employee salaries can be changed only during normal working hours. The LAN administrator can therefore restrict the logons for users having those access right to the days and hours of normal operation. Typically this is done by setting up a work calendar. Anyone, including an authorized holder of a user ID, who attempts to use an ID that is so restricted outside those specified hours will be denied access to the system. Thus, if payroll files can be updated only during normal working hours, payroll employees can not be allowed to log onto the system on weekends, holidays, or on workdays outside of defined working hours.

An organization can restrict users to specific workstations. For example, suppose a LAN is used by several departments—personnel, payroll, software development and marketing. A good security policy for this organization might be to limit logons for payroll user IDs to workstations in the payroll department area and for personnel user IDs to be limited to logging on from workstations in the personnel department. Thus a programmer cannot log on as a personnel department clerk or a payroll clerk from his or her workstation in the software development department. This restriction has some disadvantages, however. For example, if a payroll clerk who cannot use a workstation outside his or her area is in a meeting in another area of the building and wants to log on and gather data needed during the meeting, the logon attempt would be unsuccessful. A personnel clerk may report a software problem to a programmer who tries to access the system as a personnel clerk to investigate the problem but is denied access because of the logon restrictions. For user IDs with access to sensitive data, usually the benefit of logon restrictions outweigh such inconveniences or disadvantages.

A major breach of security occurs when a user leaves his or her workstation without logging off. For example, an employee may go to lunch and forget to log off. Without any security safeguards against this, an intruder could use that workstation and disrupt the system or make changes that enable him or her to circumvent security at a later time. Two countermeasures exist for this occurrence. First, a workstation can be automatically logged off in the absence of input. For example, with an automatic logoff interval of five minutes, whenever five minutes elapses without input from the workstation, the workstation is automatically logged off. If the timeout interval is too small, user progress is impeded; if it is too long, security is compromised. The UNIX system offers another technique to overcome the absentee user. Before leaving the workstation, a user can lock the terminal using the TLOCK utility. When run, TLOCK asks the user to enter a password. After entering the correct password twice (the second time for verification), the workstation is locked. It remains locked until the user correctly enters another password to reactivate the workstation.

Encryption

If you cannot always prevent users from gaining unauthorized access to data, you can take another measure, **encryption,** to prevent those users from using that data. Encryption is the process of taking data in its raw form, called plain text, and transforming it into a scrambled form, called cipher text. You have probably heard about "secure" telephone hookups that scramble conversations at the sending end and unscramble them at the receiving end, or perhaps you know about code machines that encode data for transmission and decode them on receipt. The scrambling or encoding is encryption, and the decoding or unscrambling is called **decryption,** or deciphering. Anyone who gains access to encrypted data cannot understand that data simply through physical data access; the data must be deciphered to be useful. They key to good encryption is making the deciphering process time consuming or expensive for unauthorized users. Data can be encrypted using hardware devices, software, or a combination of both. The most common encryption technique is the **data encryption standard (DES),** originally established by the U.S. Bureau of Standards. (For details regarding how DES works, see Stamper [1992].)

You almost always find encryption being used on LAN files that contain user passwords. When a password is created by a user, it must be stored somewhere by the system. When the user provides a user ID and password during a logon, a record corresponding to the user ID is retrieved, and the password in the record is compared to the password provided during logon. If the two agree, it is assumed the person has a legitimate right to use that ID; otherwise, logon security provisions take effect. Since passwords are stored in a file, access to the passwords in that file seriously jeopardizes system security if the passwords are stored in clear text. To overcome this problem, almost all systems encrypt the passwords before storing them on disk.

Novell NetWare 386 Data Access Security

At this writing, Novell has three versions of NetWare in common use: Net-Ware 286, NetWare 386 version 3.*nn*, and NetWare 4.0. In changing from NetWare 286 to NetWare 386, Novell made significant changes in the way user access rights to data are determined. We will describe data access security as it is implemented in NetWare 386 version 3.*nn*. If you are using Net-Ware 286, realize that the description that follows does not apply to your network. Also, in this section when we refer to NetWare security, we mean security as implemented in NetWare version 3.*nn*.

210

Chapter 8
LAN
Administration:
Users, Groups,
and Security

Before we can get into the details of how NetWare data access security is implemented, we must first define some of the terms Novell uses in setting up security. The basic goal of data access security is to give each user access to data essential to performing his or her job. Thus individual users may have different data access levels. For example, one user may be able to read and write data in a file while another user might be limited to reading data. Rights a user can be given at the file and directory levels are shown in Table 8-3. The access privileges a user enjoys are called the user's **effective rights.** Sometimes we enclose these rights in brackets ([ ]) and refer to them by their first letters. Within the brackets, missing rights are denoted by a space or a hypen (-) to hold that right's position. Therefore, when we write [-RW---F-] we mean that the Read, Write, and File Scan rights are given.

Table 8-3   Novell NetWare 386 File and Directory Rights

Supervisory	[S]	Supervisory rights to the directory and all subdirectories
Read	[R]	Read an open file
Write	[W]	Write to an open file
Create	[C]	Create a new file
Erase	[E]	Delete an existing file
File Scan	[F]	List names of files or subdirectories in directory
Modify	[M]	Change file attributes, rename files, and rename directories
Access Control	[A]	Give rights other than supervisory to directory or file

Users and groups can be assigned rights to files and directories. Novell calls these assigned rights **trustee rights,** because the user or group has been entrusted to exercise these rights. A user's effective rights accrue from the granting of individual rights, granting rights to a group to which the user belongs and assigning rights to the directory or file being accessed. To simplify administrative matters, many of a user's rights are assumed through groups to which the member belongs. This makes it easier to assign rights that are enjoyed jointly by several users. Rights that are limited to only a few users are granted on an individual basis. In a Novell system a user may belong to none, one, or several groups. Generally, every user belongs to a Novell defined group called Everyone. This group is created by the Novell system at installation, and every new user defined is automatically inserted into this group; thus to be excluded from the Everyone group, a user must be explicitly deleted from the group. This group is used to assign trustee rights held universally by all users (except those who were explicitly removed from the group).

To complete the picture, rights are assigned to directories and files. Novell calls these rights **inherited rights,** because rights assigned to a directory can be inherited by a file or subdirectory and consequently by a user. The inherited rights associated with a directory or file are called **inherited rights masks.** The rights that can be assigned to a directory file are the same rights assigned to users and groups. It is through the combination of user and group trustee rights and file and directory inherited rights masks that a user's effective rights are determined. Inherited rights masks are established in several ways. Whenever a directory is created, all rights are automatically inserted in the **maximum rights mask.** The supervisor or someone with access control rights in the directory must delete rights that should not be in the maximum rights mask. This is done via a utility called FILER. The LAN administrator can change an inherited rights mask to restrict a user's effective rights. Let us now see how these rights are combined to form a user's effective rights.

Determining File Access Security

Trustee rights can be granted by the super user, Supervisor, or by a user who has the ability to grant those rights. The ability to grant other users rights in a directory is called an **access control right.** Table 8-4 shows the trustee rights assigned to four users and two groups and inherited rights masks for a directory, its subdirectory, and two files. The inherited rights masks for the subdirectory and files differ from the directory's inherited rights mask because they have been set explicitly by the LAN administrator to restrict the effective rights of some users. The tree structure of the directories and the file are given in Figure 8-1. We will use these examples to show how a user's effective rights are determined. All four users belong to the Everyone group. All users with the user ID prefixed by Admin belong to the Admin group. Mktg_Chen does not belong to the Admin group. Chen may belong to other groups, but those groups do not have any rights to the directories and files listed.

A user's trustee rights to a file or directory are determined by combining his or her individual and group trustee rights. We will use the DATABASE directory in Table 8-4 to show how trustee rights are derived. First consider Admin_Sally. She has been explicitly granted all rights to the directory. These are her trustee rights because no additional rights can be given. Ad-

Table 8-4   File and Directory Rights Matrix

Directory or file	Inherited Rights Masks	Users and Groups Trustee Rights					
		Everyone (group)	Admin (group)	Admin_Sally	Admin_Tom	Admin_Mary	Mktg_Chen
DATABASE (directory)	[SRWCEMFA]	[--------]	[-RW---F-]	[SRWCEMFA]	[--------]	[-RWCE----]	[--------]
SUB 1 (subdir of DATABASE)	[SRW---F-]	[--------]	[--------]	[--------]	[--------]	[-RWC----]	[-RWCE-F-]
CUSTOMER (file in DATABASE)	[S-------]	[--------]	[--------]	[--------]	[-RW-MF-]	[--------]	[--------]
NOTES (file in SUB 1)	[SR----F-]	[--------]	[--------]	[--------]	[-RW---F-]	[-R----F-]	[--------]

212
Chapter 8
LAN
Administration:
Users, Groups,
and Security

min_Tom has not been given any rights as an individual, and all his rights to the directory must come through group membership. Admin_Tom has trustee rights of [-RW---F-] because of his membership in the Admin group. Admin_Mary has [-RWCE-F-] trustee rights to the DATABASE directory. She received Read, Write, Create, and Erase through personal trustee rights and received File Scan through membership in Admin. Mktg_Chen has no rights to the DATABASE directory because he has neither individual nor group rights assigned. However, Mktg_Chen has been granted Read, Write, Create, Erase, and File Scan rights to the subdirectory SUB1 in the DATA-BASE directory. Chen can issue a DIR command for the DATABASE directory and will see the SUB1 directory listing; however, he will not see a listing for other files and directories in the DATABASE directory. By default, Chen has RWCEF rights for all files and subdirectories in SUB1. As you may have deduced, a user's trustee rights are derived by adding or consolidating individual rights with all the rights given to all groups in which the user has membership.

A file or directory's inherited rights can be used to limit the rights a user inherits in a directory or to a file. In Table 8-4 the DATABASE directory has an inherited rights mask of SRWCEMFA. By default, a user with proper trustee rights can inherit those rights for all subdirectories and files in that directory. As noted earlier, user Admin_Mary has been granted RWCEF to the DATABASE directory. Unless the LAN administrator explicitly assigned

Figure 8-1   File/Directory Tree Structure

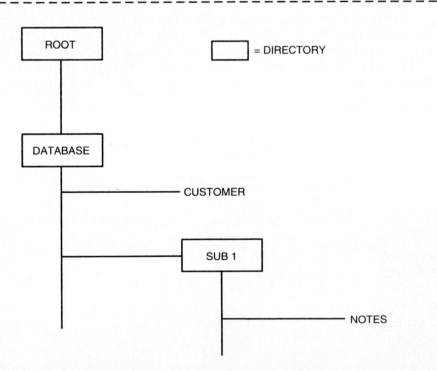

in inherited rights mask for SUB1, the inherited rights mask for SUB1 would include all of the DATABASE rights, and Mary would have her RWCEF DATABASE rights in the SUB1 subdirectory. By setting SUB1's inherited rights mask to SRWF, the administrator limits the rights Mary can inherit from above to those specified in the inherited rights mask; thus Mary is limited to RWF rights in the SUB1 directory. (The supervisory rights, S, cannot be deleted from the inherited rights mask. A user with supervisory rights to a directory has all rights to that directory and to all files, subdirectories and files in subdirectories under that directory. The supervisory right is, therefore, always inherited.)

A user obtains rights beyond those listed in the inherited rights mask by being granted directory trustee rights. To determine a user's effective rights to a directory or a file, you must know

the user's trustee rights to the directory (group rights plus individual rights)

the user's trustee rights to the file (group rights plus individual rights)

the directory's inherited rights mask

the file's inherited rights mask

The following sections describe the rules for determining a user's effective rights for a file.

Explicit Trustee File Rights   A user's explicit trustee rights to a file supersede any inherited rights to the file. In Table 8-4 Admin_Tom has been given RWMF rights to the CUSTOMER file; the inherited rights masks and the directory rights are superseded by these explicit trustee file rights. Admin_Mary has no rights to the CUSTOMER file, even though she has RWCEF rights to the DATABASE directory. Mary has no rights to the CUSTOMER file because the inherited rights mask for the file shows no inherited rights (except the required supervisory right) and Mary has not been given any explicit rights to the CUSTOMER file. Admin_Sally has all rights to the file (and to all files and subdirectories under the DATABASE directory) because she has supervisory rights in the directory. Even explicitly revoking Sally's rights to the CUSTOMER file or explicitly granting her only RWF rights to CUSTOMER would not alter her having all rights to the file; supervisory rights cannot be overcome except by removing the supervisory rights, nor can supervisory rights be filtered out by inherited rights masks. In this case directory trustee and inherited rights are not considered. Sally's supervisory rights are paramount and supersede all other explicit or implicit rights.

Explicit Directory Rights and Inherited File Rights   A user can have explicit trustee rights to a directory but no explicit trustee rights to a file within that directory. The user's effective file rights are determined as a combination of the directory trustee rights and the file's inherited rights mask. The inherited rights mask acts as a filter for the directory trustee rights. In Table

214

Chapter 8
LAN
Administration:
Users, Groups,
and Security

8-4 Mktg_Chen has RWCEF rights to the SUB1 directory, and the NOTES file has an inherited rights mask of SRF. Chen's effective rights to the NOTES file are RF. The inherited rights mask for the file limited the rights that Chen was able to inherit from the directory.

No Explicit Directory or File Rights When a user has not been granted explicit file for directory trustee rights either personally or through group memberships, his or her effective rights are determined by the inherited rights masks for the directory and file and through rights he or she has in a parent directory. The directory inherited rights mask serves as a maximum rights mask filter for the user's effective rights in the parent directory. In Table 8-4 the inherited rights mask for the SUB1 directory is SRWF. Admin_Tom has RWF rights in the DATABASE directory. Tom's effective rights in the SUB1 directory are RWF; he was allowed to inherit those rights in the SUB1 directory. Again, if Tom needs additional rights in SUB1, the rights can be explicitly granted and override the inherited rights.

Generally we can summarize the above rules as follows:

- Supervisory rights are paramount.

- Explicit trustee rights supersede inherited rights.

- Inherited rights masks act as a maximum rights mask to filter directory rights inherited from a parent directory or to filter file rights inherited from the directory containing the file.

Establishing Trustee Rights

Trustee rights are granted and rescinded in a variety of ways. First, there are two utilities, GRANT and REVOKE, that allow a LAN administrator to give and take away trustee rights. The administrator can also assign trustee rights with the FILER and SYSCON utilities and take them away with FILER, REMOVE, and SYSCON. A user can determine his or her rights in a directory with the RIGHTS command. FILER and SYSCON are menu utilities, and REMOVE, REVOKE, and GRANT are command-line utilities. In a menu utility you select the actions you want to take through menu selections. In a command-line utility you must use a command to carry out the desired task. A shortcut to granting security is to grant a user rights equivalent to those of another user. For example, the LAN administrator may want to grant to her personal logon ID the privileges of the Supervisor. This allows the administrator to perform operations usually associated with the user ID SUPERVISOR while logged on under the administrator's personal account. LAN administrators must be careful to use security equivalencing wisely. For example, creating users with security equivalent to the Supervisor increases the potential for security violations.

File and Directory Attributes

In addition to file and directory security, Novell files and directories have **attributes** that control how files and directories are used. Table 8-5 shows file and directory attributes for NetWare 386 versions.

File attributes, which are more extensive than directory attributes, govern how the file may be used. A file can be flagged as Shareable or Non-Shareable to prevent concurrent access. For example, a word processing document usually should not be edited concurrently by two users. Such files should be declared Non-Shareable to prevent the problems of simultaneous updates discussed in Chapters 1 and 5. Some files, such as program files,

Table 8-5 File and Directory Attributes

File Attributes

Read-Only	Can only be read
Read-Write	Can be read from, written to, renamed, or deleted (default if Read-Only is not specified)
Normal	Nonshareable, Read-Write
Shareable	Can be concurrently accessed by more than one user
Non-Shareable	Can be accessed by only one user at a time
Indexed	An index is built to speed access to large files
Execute-Only	File can be executed but not read, erased, modified, renamed, or copied; prevents illegal copying
Archive	File has been modified and archiving is needed on next backup
Copy Inhibit	This attribute is for Macintosh users and prevents a file from being copied
Delete Inhibit	Prevents a file from being deleted, even by users with erase access to that file
Hidden	File does not appear in DIR or NDIR listings and prevents a user from copying or erasing the file
Purge	File is purged when deleted and cannot be reclaimed by the SALVAGE utility
Read Audit	Provides an audit trail of users who have read the file (not implemented in initial versions of NetWare 386)
Write Audit	Provides an audit trail of users who have written to the file (not implemented in initial versions of NetWare 386)
Rename Inhibit	Prevents a user from renaming the file, even if the user has the Modify trustee right to the file
System	Used for DOS files needed for booting (these files are hidden from the user)
Transactional	Used with Novell's Transaction Tracking System (TTS) to ensure that all updates made to the file within a transaction can be backed out if the transaction cannot complete successfully

Directory Attributes

Normal	Cancels other directory attributes
Hidden	Directory does not appear in a directory listing
System	Directory is used for proper functioning of system, directory does not appear in directory search
Delete Inhibit	See Delete Inhibit for files above
Rename Inhibit	See Rename Inhibit for files above
Purge	See Purge for files above

216

Chapter 8
LAN
Administration:
Users, Groups,
and Security

should be protected from accidental or intentional updates. Flagging such files as Read-Only or Execute-Only provides protection from updates.

One of the problems facing the microcomputer software industry is software piracy. When applications are placed on a file server and secured with read access, a user could illegally make a copy of the application. Novell has a file attribute that prevents this. If a file is flagged with the Execute-Only attribute, the file can only be run and deleted, not opened and read, written to, or renamed, even by a user with Supervisor capabilities. File attributes offer companies one means of protecting their software investment.

Security Utilities

To help the LAN administrator implement a secure system, Novell provides two important capabilities, intruder detection and a security-checking program. Intruder detection monitors logon attempts. If someone attempts to log on as a specific user and fails to provide the correct password within a specified number of attempts, the account for that user can de deactivated. Account deactivation is an option. The LAN administrator can specify how many missed passwords constitute an intrusion attempt and how long the system remembers a missed password. For example, the intrusion attempts can be set at five and the memory set for three days. If during any three-day interval five unsuccessful logon attempts are made for that account, the account can be deactivated. The LAN administrator can also set the length of time the account remains deactivated. If an account is deactivated, any logons for that account are denied until the deactivation interval has expired. Once the account has been reactivated, the incorrect logon count is reset to zero. The Supervisor can also explicitly reactivate the account.

The LAN administrator must use care in setting the deactivation reset time. An interval that is too short lowers security, while a lengthy interval may cause problems. For example, one of the accounts an intruder is most likely to attempt to crack is SUPERVISOR. If a two-day reset interval is specified and an intruder uses up the number of logon attempts, no one can log on as SUPERVISOR until two days have elapsed. If such a situation occurs, hopefully there is a station logged on as SUPERVISOR or a logon ID with rights equivalent to SUPERVISOR so the logon restriction can be lifted. Moreover, a lengthy history of unsuccessful logons together with a low logon count can cause another problem: Users occasionally mistype a password. If the history interval is long and the incorrect logon limit is low, it is possible for the account to become locked by accident. Another feature of intrusion detection is the ability to find the station address at which the last unsuccessful logon attempt was made.

The security-checking feature is implemented in a utility named Security. It provides the SUPERVISOR with a listing of possible security weaknesses. The listing gives a breakdown by user and group and checks for security weaknesses, such as those shown in Table 8-6. A sample listing of the data reported by the Security utility is shown in Table 8-7.

Table 8-6 Possible Security Weaknesses

No password assigned
Passwords that are the same as the user name
Short passwords
Passwords that are not required to be changed periodically
User having security equivalent to the SUPERVISOR
User having unlimited grace logons
User having no logon script
Users who have access privileges in the root directory of any volume
Users or groups having excessive rights to the four system directories

Table 8-7 Novell Security Utility Output

File Server SECURITY Evaluation Utility

Checking for network security holes, please wait.

User DUMMY
  Has no logon script
  Has unlimited grace logons
  Is not required to change passwords periodically
  Can have passwords that are too short (less than 5)
  Does not require a password
  Does not have a secure password

User SUPER
  Has no logon script
  Has unlimited grace logons
  Is not required to change passwords periodically
  Can have passwords that are too short (less than 5)
  Does not require a password
  Has no password assigned

User DAVE
  Is security equivalent to user SUPERVISOR
  Has unlimited grace logons
  Is not required to change passwords periodically
  Can have passwords that are too short (less than 5)

User GUEST
  Has no logon script
  Has unlimited grace logons
  Is not required to change passwords periodically
  Can have passwords that are too short (less than 5)
  Does not require a password
  Has no password assigned   (continued)

218

Chapter 8
LAN
Administration:
Users, Groups,
and Security

Table 8-7   Novell Security Utility Output (continued)

Group EVERYONE
  Has [WC M] rights in SYS:MAIL (maximum should be [WC])

User SUPERVISOR
  Has no logon script
  Has no password assigned

VIRUSES

In the past our primary security concern centered around people intentionally or accidentally jeopardizing the system's integrity. Today, we face another threat, computer viruses. A computer virus is so named because it im-
itates the activity of biological viruses. A biological virus uses a nonvirus or
healthy cell to reproduce itself. Sometimes the virus destroys the healthy
host cell. The primary objectives of a computer virus are to reproduce itself
and avoid elimination. A computer virus uses a healthy file, program, memory area, or disk area to reproduce itself. Once the virus has been replicated,
it starts on its second priority, disrupting the system.

A LAN administrator must protect the system from viruses. This is no
easy task. In 1991 over 500 different viruses had been detected, and experts
believe that new viruses are being introduced at the rate of over 50 per
month (some predict that six new viruses will appear daily). Fortunately antivirus technology is also growing at a rapid rate. A list of some of the common viruses is given in Table 8-8.

Viruses disrupt systems in a variety of ways, and some are more destructive than others. The most destructive viruses destroy files by overwrit-
ing or erasing them, corrupt disk directories, reformat disks, cause system
failures, and so on. The more benign viruses are also destructive because

Table 8-8   Some Common Viruses

1575/1591	2560	Anthrax
Azusa	Base *nnn*	BlackJack
Cascade.*nnnn*	Dark Avenger.*n*	Fear
Fellowship/Possessed	Flip	Frodo
Groove	Green Catepillar.n	H-*nnn*
Hydra-*n*	Keypress	Jerusalem
Liberty	Maltese Amoeba	Michelangelo
Peach	Sarah	Sunday-B
Stoned	SVC 6.0	Tequila
Yankee Doodle *nnnn*		

n = version number

they destroy productivity. These viruses do not destroy files, they just disrupt the working environment by displaying annoying messages, erasing the contents of the monitor, or similar activities. Both types hinder normal system operations.

Protecting Against Viruses

LAN administrators must have precautions and policies in place to prevent the introduction of viruses and to detect and eradicate them if they show up. All LANs should be equipped with current virus detection software to carry out these policies and procedures. In this section we discuss some of the precautions, policies, and software for keeping a LAN virus-free. We look first at how a virus enters a system. We then discuss how to keep a LAN free of viruses through virus detection and virus eradication.

Introducing a System Virus   Viruses enter a clean system from a variety of sources. They may be introduced intentionally or unintentionally. A company programmer can purposely create a virus within a program he or she is writing, or a LAN user can enter virus code directly from the keyboard. LAN users may also unintentionally spread a virus through the use of an infected disk, through accessing data from another infected LAN, and from connecting to external computers or networks. A well-intentioned user may use a private, infected disk in his workstation. Immediately the virus attempts to spread itself to other parts of the system. A user may copy a file from a computer or a bulletin board outside the network and receive an infected file. Viruses have even been found in shrink-wrapped software produced by software vendors or by companies that distribute software or data files.

The best way to prevent users from intentionally introducing viruses is to hire trustworthy employees and to immediately deny network access to employees who are leaving the company, particularly employees who are not leaving voluntarily.

One way to prevent unintentional infection is through employee education. Users must know how to scan a diskette for viruses before inserting it into the computer. When users find viruses, they must know how to eradicated them. Employees must also know about the importance of making system backups. Before backing up a file, a user must scan the file to ensure it is not infected. If infected files are placed on a backup tape and then restored at a later time, the virus will be reintroduced to the LAN. A good procedure to follow is to ensure that all files and data entering and leaving the network are virus free. This can be accomplished by checking them as they are being moved or before they are moved.

Virus Detection   Viruses are detected in two ways. The most obvious but least desirable way is to experience the consequences of having a virus. The best way to detect a virus is to find it before it activates itself. A variety of **anti-virus programs** are available for this purpose. Some of these are oriented to single computers and some are designed for both single computers and LANs. Naturally a LAN administrator should select an antivirus program that protects servers and workstations.

220

Chapter 8
LAN
Administration:
Users, Groups,
and Security

Antivirus programs operate in different ways. Some programs are run on demand, while others are constantly running. A program that is run on demand does not continually scan for viruses. On-demand programs must be explicitly run by a user or the LAN administrator. These programs scan for the viruses they know about and either remove or report viruses as they are found. If the detection program simply reports the existence of a virus, another program must be run to remove it. Programs that continually scan for viruses remain memory resident while the computer is running. These programs check new data and programs for viruses as they enter and leave the system. An example of how a continuously running antivirus program works is shown in Figure 8-2. Continually running virus detection programs are constantly using memory and CPU cycles and thus contribute to system overhead. This is one way in which viruses can be disruptive and costly. However, continually running scanners generally provide better protection than on-demand antivirus programs.

LAN antivirus programs vary in capability. Some scan the server only, some primarily scan workstations, and some do both. Choosing a program that scans both the workstations and the servers is the best choice. Alternatively a LAN administrator may choose to use several virus scanners, one that is excellent at detecting workstation viruses and another that is excellent

Figure 8-2   How an Antivirus Program Works

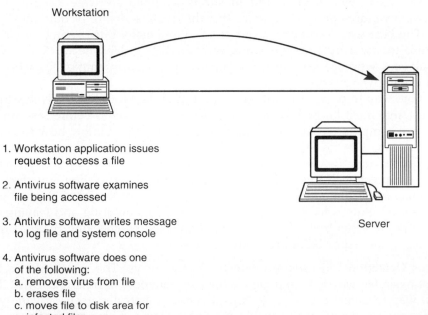

Workstation

1. Workstation application issues request to access a file

2. Antivirus software examines file being accessed

3. Antivirus software writes message to log file and system console

4. Antivirus software does one of the following:
   a. removes virus from file
   b. erases file
   c. moves file to disk area for infected files
   d. renames files
   e. does nothing and allows file to be accessed

Server

at protecting servers. A program that checks both servers and workstations must be more sophisticated because it has to be aware of at least two different operating systems and disk organizations. That is, an antivirus program that can detect viruses on a DOS computer cannot necessarily understand the memory and disk organization of a file server using a Novell, UNIX, or OS/2 operating system. An antivirus program that resides on a server and has the capability of checking workstation nodes typically downloads the antivirus software when the workstation logs onto the server. As an added precaution, a antivirus program could be loaded on the disk of each workstation and automatically started when the workstation is booted. On a DOS computer this can be done by placing the commands to run the antivirus program in the AUTOEXEC.BAT file.

Another way to reduce the risk of virus infection is to use diskless workstations. If individual workstations do not have disk drives, users cannot intentionally or accidentally introduce a new virus; however, a user intent on disrupting the system could still enter a virus via a diskless workstation's keyboard. Furthermore, a diskless system cannot be used when the network is down and must have a boot ROM or PROM that enables it to load the operating system over the network rather than reading if from a boot disk. Sometimes the ROM may need to be changed to enable the use of operating system upgrades. This does not happen frequently but is still a consideration when you are deciding on diskless workstations.

It is best to have a stand-alone computer conveniently available for virus detection. A stand-alone computer is helpful for virus detection because it limits the potential for the virus spreading on the network before it can be found and removed by a LAN antivirus program. Likewise, when transferring data to or from networks or computers external to the LAN, a stand-alone computer can be used. After the data has been received, it and the stand-alone computer can be checked for viruses. After checking for viruses and removing any that are found, the data can then be moved to the LAN. Naturally following these steps takes longer and may be somewhat inconvenient, but they avoid catastrophes that can occur if a virus attacks.

Regardless of how they are detected, a company should have a procedure in place that requires users to report any suspected or confirmed incidence of a virus. A user at a workstation may detect and eradicate a virus found on that workstation. The user may believe that the infection from this virus has been completely eliminated from the LAN when it may have already managed to spread into other nodes. Cooperation of users in this and other aspects of virus control is essential to a comprehensive antivirus plan.

Virus Eradication We destroy biological viruses by being inoculated against them and building an immunity. The immunity is created when our bodies produce virus-killing antibodies that deactivate the virus when it appears. However, we can only be inoculated against known viruses, and new strains appear regularly. The same thing happens with computer viruses. Several companies provide software that searches for known viruses and eradicates them. The antivirus programs scan memory and disk drives look-

222

Chapter 8
LAN
Administration:
Users, Groups,
and Security

ing for traces of the virus. Once found, the virus can be removed, often without destroying the host. However, the virus can be introduced again if an infected floppy disk is used on the system or if infected files are copied from another network or computer. Complete eradication of the virus from a network requires the examination of each disk drive and diskette used in the network.

Viruses are eradicated from a system either by the program that detected the virus or by a separate program designed for that purpose. The more convenient of the two methods is having the virus automatically removed on detection. Moreover, some antivirus programs automatically make repairs to affected memory or disk areas. For example, if a virus is found in the boot sector of a disk, some antivirus programs remove the virus and restore the boot sector to its proper state.

We noted earlier that new viruses are appearing almost daily. As new viruses are introduced, new programs or program updates must be available to detect and remove them. A good LAN antivirus policy is to subscribe to the update service for the virus programs being used. This allows a company to keep pace with changing developments in the war against viruses. Keeping up with changes in viruses is important because new viruses have unique **signatures,** or bit patterns, that must be recognized. Moreover the authors of viruses have begun to create viruses that are harder to detect. These are called **polymorphic viruses,** because these viruses can change their signatures. To further compound the problem, a **mutation engine** has been created that is a virus programmer's toolkit. The mutation engine enables programmers to make existing and future viruses polymorphic. Viruses produced using the mutation engine have already begun to appear.

SUMMARY

One of the most important functions performed by the LAN administrator is to establish a proper user environment. This environment helps provide users transparency, gives them access to the data and applications they need, and protects other resources from inadvertent or intentional disruption. The administrator does this by setting up users, groups, and security provisions. In a large network this combination of needs can be complex.

User access is usually controlled through a process of identification and authentication, normally through entering a user ID and an associated password. To maintain a proper level of security, the LAN administrator must implement a comprehensive security policy. This may include setting up LAN parameters that require minimum password lengths, maximum and minimum intervals between password changes, requirements for unique passwords, and so on. The LAN software can assist the administrator in implementing a security system by detecting intruder attempts, limiting the number of logons per user ID, automatically logging users off, and similar security provisions.

User security is just one dimension of a complete security policy. User and group security is usually coupled with directory and file security. Users are granted certain rights for directories and files. How this is implemented differs from one system to another; however, most of today's LANs give the administrator a way to set up a security matrix that gives users the rights they need while withholding those access rights that are outside their job scopes.

Viruses are an ever-present problem in today's LANs. The LAN administrators must implement a comprehensive plan for detecting and removing viruses and for educating users on proper virus prevention techniques. All viruses are disruptive, and keeping the LAN virus-free is essential to error-free LAN operations.

KEY TERMS

access control right

antivirus program

attributes, file or directory

authentication

biological identification and authentication

concurrent logon

data access security

data encryption standard (DES)

decryption

directory rights

effective rights

encryption

explicit rights

fake logon

file rights

grace logon

identification

inherited rights

inherited rights mask

logon script

224

Chapter 8
LAN
Administration:
Users, Groups,
and Security

maximum rights mask

mutation engine

password

physical security

polymorphic virus

security

signature, virus

systems programming

timeout value

trustee rights

user identifier (ID)

REVIEW QUESTIONS

1. Describe the relationship(s) between users and groups.

2. Why do we define users and groups?

3. What are user access rights?

4. What is systems programming on a LAN? Describe three systems programming tasks.

5. Describe how security protects an organization's data from accidental or intentional misuse by the organization's employees.

6. What are identification and authentication? Describe two methods of identification and authentication.

7. List three biological identification and authentication methods.

8. Describe two ways of responding to unauthorized access attempts.

9. How do fake logons and timeout values help prevent unauthorized logons?

10. Why is it beneficial to limit concurrent logons?

11. What do encryption and decryption do? Where is encryption likely to be found in a LAN?

12. Describe file security in a Novell NetWare 386 system.

13. What are viruses? What problems do they present to a LAN?

14. Describe how viruses are detected and eliminated.

15. What is a polymorphic virus? Why are they more difficult to detect?

PROBLEMS AND EXERCISES

1. Select three different LAN operating systems.

   a. Describe how users and groups are set up in each system. What differences exist between user and group implementations?

   b. Describe the file and directory security attributes supported by each. List the differences between the systems.

   c. Describe the password security features of each. List the differences between the systems.

2. Draw up a comprehensive password security procedure for a business LAN.

3. Table 8-9 shows the inherited rights for several directories and files and the trustee rights for several users and groups. Using the rules for effective rights in NetWare 386, complete the table showing the effective rights for each user for each file and directory.

Table 8-9   NetWare 386 Rights Matrix

Directory or File	Inherited Rights Mask	Everyone (group)	Admin (group)	Admin_Sally	Admin_Tom	Admin_Mary	Mktg_Chen
				Users and Groups Trustee Rights			
DATABASE (directory)	[SRWCEMFA]	[--------]	[-R----F-]	[-RWCEMFA]	[--W-----]	[-RWCE---]	[--------]
SUB 1 (subdir of DATABASE)	[SRWCE-F-]	[--------]	[-RWCE---]	[--------]	[--------]	[-RWC----]	[-RW-EMF-]
CUSTOMER (file in DATABASE)	[S-------]	[--------]	[-RW-----]	[--------]	[-RW-EMF-]	[--------]	[--------]
NOTES (file in SUB 1)	[SR----F-]	[--------]	[--------]	[--------]	[-RW---F-]	[-RW---F-]	[--------]

	DATABASE	SUB 1	CUSTOMER	NOTES
Effective rights for ADMIN_SALLY				
Effective rights for ADMIN_TOM				
Effective rights for ADMIN_MARY				
Effective rights for MKTG_CHEN				

4. You are a LAN administrator and have just been notified that a LAN user has discovered the Stoned virus on her system. Plan a course of action to eradicate this virus from the system. You should realize that the virus may have affected other network nodes, may be on any of the diskettes that have been used on the LAN, and may be on some of your backup tapes.

5. The Michelangelo virus was considered to be widespread in 1992. The virus only spread itself until March 6, at which time it overwrote the boot disk drive. As a LAN administrator what steps (besides using an antivirus program) could you take to avoid the virus activating?

6. Katie Hafner and John Markoff provide profiles of several hackers from three different hacking groups in their book *Cyberpunk*. Describe the methods used by these hackers to penetrate security.

7. Suppose you are a LAN administrator and have implemented what you consider to be effective security measures for your installations. One of the LAN users approaches you and brags about getting around the security. The user proves this claim by showing you a file outside that user's access scope in which the user has placed some extra data to show the file has been accessed. How should you and your company address this issue?

8. Suppose that a small office of 15 people has asked you to help them set up a LAN. Following discussions with the office manager, you outline your plans for setting up security. The office manager responds by saying that she trusts all of the employees and that security is not necessary. Furthermore she tells you that if security were implemented, the workers would feel that they were not trusted, because security was never an issue before. How would you respond to these statements?

REFERENCES

Adney, William M. and Kavanagh, Douglas E. "The Data Bandits." *Byte*, Volume 14, Number 1, January 1989.

Bruno, Charles. "Taking the Work out of Virus Detection." *Network World*, Volume 9, Number 26, June 29, 1992.

Dern, Daniel P. "Make Networks Secure, or Face Trouble." *LAN Times*, Volume 8, Issue 8, April 15, 1991.

Didio, Laura. "Security Breaches." *LAN Times*, Volume 8, Issue 23, December 9, 1991.

Diehl, Stanford, Wszola, Stan, Kliewer, Bradley, and Stevens, Larry. "Rx For Safer Data." *Byte*, Volume 16, Number 8, August 1991.

Hafner, Katie and Markoff, John. *Cyberpunk*. New York: Simon and Schuster, 1991.

Heldenbrand, Dave. "DOD-Grade Security Comes to LANs." *LAN Technology*, Volume 6, Number 5, May 1990.

Powell, Dave. "Safeguarding the Enterprise Network." *Networking Management*, Volume 10, Number 12, November 1992.

Stamper, David A. *Business Data Communications*. Redwood City, CA: Benjamin/Cummings, 1992.

Stephenson, Peter. "Personal and Private." *Byte*, Volume 14, Number 6, June 1989.

Stoll, Clifford. *The Cuckoo's Egg*. New York, NY: Doubleday, 1989.

Sullivan, Kristina B. *Many Users Still Ignore Virus Threat. PC Week*, Volume 9, Number 45, November 9, 1992.

Van Kirk, Doug. "LAN Security." *InfoWorld*, Volume 14, Issue 47, November 23, 1992.

LAN ADMINISTRATION: THE PRINTING ENVIRONMENT

CHAPTER PREVIEW

In Chapter 8 we discussed how the LAN administrator helps create the proper user environment by setting up user IDs and user groups, and combining user and group access needs with directory and file security. These tasks are important to the overall success of the network. Less glamorous but perhaps equally important to user acceptance and network effectiveness is setting up a comprehensive printing environment. LAN administrators must not lose sight of their objective: to provide an environment in which users can be productive both individually and as a group. Creating an environment in which users can produce printed outputs on the right devices and at the right time is one part of this objective. In this chapter we discuss ways in which this can be done.

Specific topics covered in this chapter include:

printing needs

the spooler system

connecting applications and users to printers

print management and administration

printing in a Novell LAN

INTRODUCTION TO PRINTING

A LAN user can get printed output on a LAN in three ways. The first way, using a dedicated local printer, is the same as the method used for stand-alone microcomputer systems: The printer is attached to a port on the microcomputer and the microcomputer's user has exclusive control of the printer. One disadvantage of this technique is that printers are dedicated to a specific computer so they remain idle for much of the time. Also, the cost of having one printer for each microcomputer can be excessive.

The second printing option is for several users to share a printer using a data switch, as illustrated in Figure 1-3. Before LANs this was the primary

230

Chapter 9
LAN
Administration:
The Printing
Environment

way of sharing printers. A variety of data switch capabilities are available. The disadvantage of this alternative is that only one microcomputer can be printing at once; if two microcomputers have jobs to print, one must wait until the other is done.

The third method of printing uses the services of the LAN. This is the method we are concerned with in this chapter. LAN printing avoids the disadvantages of the two other methods. Printers can be shared, and multiple print streams can be active at once. With LAN printing, all users can be logically printing at the same time. A LAN user does not control a printer, as is the case in the first two printing alternatives. Instead, a print server controls the printer and serves as an interface between users and printers. Since all LAN users can be printing at the same time, the print server and its software, collectively known as a spooler, control all LAN print jobs. Shortly we describe how this is done. The important thing to realize at this time is that with LAN-based printing, you have less control over exactly when the printing occurs. Getting your printout immediately can be difficult because other print jobs are ahead of yours in the queue of jobs ready for the printer. On some occasions the wait for a printout might be quite long. For example, the spooler may be printing a 400-page manual, and several other jobs may be queued when your job arrives. Your printout may not be physically printed for several minutes, or even hours. However, from the application's perspective, the printing has been done, and you are free to move on to other computing tasks.

CREATING A PRINTING ENVIRONMENT

Creating a printing environment is not always a simple task. Even in the stand-alone printing environment, illustrated in Figure 9-1, the basic configuration of an application that wants to write data to a printer on one

Figure 9-1   A Stand-alone Printer Configuration

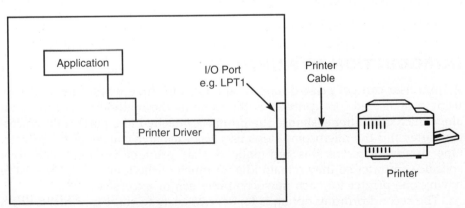

Microcomputer's Memory

side and a printer on the other is complicated by several essential components coming in between.

You have many different types of printers from which to choose, and each printer has a certain set of capabilities, including bolding, underlining, italics, graphics, fonts, color, and so on. These capabilities are enabled in different ways. Some can be set through the printer's control panel, and most can be set through commands transmitted to the printer from a program. Different printers may use different control commands to enable the same capability.

An application usually does not have the logic needed to invoke these capabilities for all types of printers. Instead the application communicates with the printer through another program called the printer driver. Keeping printer-specific knowledge out of applications provides program-printer independence. If a new printer comes on the market, the application does not need to be changed; a new printer driver must be created that interfaces to the application and the printer. An application often comes with a set of printer drivers for the most common printers. The application knows how to interface to the printer driver, and the printer driver knows how to communicate with a specific brand of printer. The application sends a general code like "turn bold on" to the printer driver, and the printer driver translates that code into the proper sequence of control characters for its printer.

The printer is physically connected to the microcomputer through an I/O port, usually a parallel or a serial port. This establishes the physical link between the computer and the printer. The printer driver directs its output to the port to which the printer is connected, thereby completing the connection between the application and the printer.

A GENERIC SPOOLER

In Chapter 5 you were given a brief overview of how a spooler operates. Here we will look at spoolers in more detail. From the preceding paragraphs you probably gained the idea that a spooler serves as a switch between users and devices, and this is correct. However, a spooler does much more than switch data streams. We can separate the spooler's functions into four basic categories: hardware-oriented, application-oriented, administration-oriented, and user-oriented. Table 9-1 lists the various functions under each of these categories.

Hardware-Oriented Functions

High-Speed Buffer   The primary function of a spooler is to serve as a buffer between the high-speed CPU and low-speed output devices like printers. It does this by accepting output destined for the printers and storing it temporarily on disk or, less frequently, on tape. Since disk drives are much faster than most printers, the data can be stored on disk much faster than it can be physically written to the printer. A side effect of temporarily storing print jobs on disk is the ability to logically share a printer. Multiple users can con-

232

Chapter 9
LAN
Administration:
The Printing
Environment

currently be directing their output to the same print device. The print jobs are collected on disk until they are finished and ready to print. Usually the spooler then schedules the completed jobs for printing and prints them according to some priority scheme.

Printer Interface Whenever you use a peripheral device like a printer, you must have a software and hardware interface to the device. The typical **hardware interfaces** for printers are **serial** and **parallel interfaces** and **small computer system interfaces (SCSIs).** The software interface is the printer

Table 9-1   Spooler Functions

Hardware-Oriented Functions
Serve as buffer between high-speed and low-speed devices (CPU and printer)
Provide printer interface
Provide for the introduction of new printers

Application-Oriented Functions
Provide application-level interface
Provide operating system interface
Close print jobs based on timeout interval
Collect printed output
Direct print jobs to designated printers

Administration-Oriented Functions
Provide statistical reports
Add/delete printers
Start/stop printers
Start/stop spooler process
View jobs on hold in print queue
Set print job priorities
Delete jobs from print queue
Attach/detach printers from print queue
Set/change job priorities
Provide user management interface
Provide security
Cancel print jobs

User-Oriented Functions
Print multiple copies
Print banners
Hold jobs in disk queue after printing
Hold jobs in disk queue before printing
View jobs on hold in print queue
Set print job priorities
Delete jobs from print queue
Set/change job priorities
Print selected pages

driver. As we mentioned previously, printing devices provide a variety of different options, such as different colors or shades of gray, different fonts and font sizes, and graphic capabilities. Enabling these different printing capabilities is accomplished through the cooperation of an application, the spooler, and the printer driver. Let us look at how this occurs from the perspective of a word processing program.

To enable a printer's formatting capabilities, you must write a **control sequence** to it. For example, if you want to select the 8-point Roman font on a Hewlett-Packard laser printer, you must send the control sequence ESC(8U to the printer. Each change in characteristic, such as changing margins and bolding, has its unique enabling control sequence. Not all printers support functions like choosing an 8-point Roman font, and different printers may use different control sequences to enable the same capabilities. It is the printer driver that accommodates the individual capabilities of a specific printer.

A word processor user formats his or her document using the commands available within the word processing software. In most of today's word processors, you can specify underline, bold, fonts, font sizes, line drawing, and so on. These characteristics are stored in the text file in the word processor's format, a format independent of any printer. By storing the document in a general format, the document can thus be printed on a variety of printers. When the document is to be printed, the proper printer driver must be selected. It translates the word processor's formatting codes into those that the printer expects.

When you are using a spooler, two printer drivers may come into play: one that converts the word processor codes into printer codes and writes to the spooler, and one that reads the files from a spooler file and physically writes it to the printer. The first typically is provided by the word processing software, and the second usually is provided by the spooler itself.

Provide for New Printers The spooler's printer driver "talks" directly to the printer, so device support is an important consideration in spooler software selection. Widely used LAN spoolers support most commonly used printers. If one of your print devices is not supported by a standard printer driver, or if you get a new printer with a different command set, your spooler can provide a way to generate a new printer driver through a printer definition utility. Using this utility, you define the printer functions and the command sequences needed to carry out those functions. The printer definition utility builds a command table that can be used by a printer driver program to enable print functions.

Application-Oriented Functions

Application-Level Interface The best way for an application to interface with a spooler is to access it directly. You may recall that LANs provide an application program interface (API) for communicating with LAN software. The spooler has a **collector program** that accepts print data streams and writes them to disk. Through an API the application establishes a communi-

234
— — — — — — —
Chapter 9
LAN
Administration:
The Printing
Environment

cations link with the collector program and writes the data to it directly. Some programs that are designed to run on LANs have the ability to do this. Usually these interfaces exist for specific LANs or specific LAN APIs.

Operating System Interface   If you have applications that do not write directly to a spooler collector, you probably can still use them on a LAN using a LAN spooler component known as a **redirector.** The redirector establishes itself between the application and the operating system. The job of the redirector is to intercept output destined for a specific operating system printer port (say LPT1 on a DOS system) and reroute the print stream to the spooler. The application assumes it is writing to a local printer. The redirector filters the operating system calls for printing services and routes the appropriate job streams over the network to the spooler.

Timeout Interval   Many applications are designed to run on stand-alone platforms. When these applications are run on a network, they may have ill-behaved printing characteristics. For example, many spreadsheet programs open a printer and write to it continuously. Once open, the printer is not closed until the application terminates. When run on a stand-alone system, the output is directed to the printer immediately. Thus a user can issue print requests and have them printed without exiting the program. One LAN, however, the spooler by default continues to accept input from an application and prints nothing until it receives a close message for the printer. This difference between printing on a LAN and on a stand-alone system may be a problem for some users.

A spooler can contain a **timeout interval** that helps minimize the differences a user sees between printing on a stand-alone system and on a LAN. If a time-out interval is used, a print job is completed when no additional data is received for the period specified by the timeout interval. For example, suppose you are using the spreadsheet program just described. Without a timeout interval, your print output is scheduled for printing only after you have exited from the spreadsheet program. Suppose instead that a 30-second timeout interval has been specified for your application. When the spooler begins to receive print data, it stores it on the disk file as usual. When data stops arriving, the spooler starts a countdown timer at 30 seconds. If the timer counts down to 0 without receiving more input, the print job is closed and scheduled for printing. If more data is received after the interval has expired, it is treated as a separate print job.

A timeout interval is a compromise solution and is not without its problems. Sometimes in a spreadsheet program you want to specify several print ranges and have them printed at one time. If you are not able to specify the parameters for the second part of the print job before the timer expires, the first part is closed and printed. Furthermore, when printed, other print jobs may be directed to the printer between your first and second job fragments. Thus, it is important to use timeout intervals appropriately and to choose the timeout duration carefully. An interval that is too short makes manual concatenation of several print streams difficult. An interval that is too long delays printing. A graphics program can require considerable compute time to generate output, so a timeout interval of 60 seconds or more may be necessary. The timeout interval for a word processing program can be 15 seconds or lower. Ordinarily the timeout intervals are set for a printer not a job, so the timeout specified should be the longest necessary for any of the applications being used.

Collect Printed Output and Direct Print Jobs to Designated Printers The spooler collects print jobs and stores them on disk. It may do this by storing each job in a separate file, by storing jobs for one printer in the same subdirectory, or by storing all print jobs in one file. Logically all that is necessary is to be able to determine where each print job is located, where it begins, and where it ends. Once an entire print job has been collected, it can be scheduled for printing. Each print job must be directed to the proper printer. This can be accomplished in a variety of ways, as shown in Table 9.2.

Administration-Oriented Functions

Provide Statistical Reports Information supports most management and administrative actions. To manage the printing environment effectively and keep it responsive to user needs, the LAN administrator must have information regarding the status of the printing environment. The spooler provides a wide assortment of statistical reports, as shown in Table 9-3. Let's take a closer look at a few of the user-oriented statistical reports produced by the spooler. A user should be responsible for his or her jobs in the spooler. The

Table 9-2   Spooler Printing Alternatives

Queuing Mechanism
  First in, first out (FIFO)
  Last in, first out (LIFO)
  Smallest job goes to head of queue
  Smallest job goes to head of queue; each job passed over gets page count
    incremented by one, thus ensuring it eventually reaches the head of the queue
    and prints
  Printing priority is the same as the job's priority in the CPU (for multiuser CPU
    print jobs)
  Priority depends on job queue
  Priority set (or changed) by operator or user

Mapping Jobs to Printers
  Job is directed to printer by printer name
  Job is directed to queue and queue is attached to printer
  Job is directed to a queue and queue is attached to multiple printers
  Job is directed to a queue and queue is not attached to printer; queue is later
    attached to one or more printers by a user or operator
  Job is broadcast to multiple printers
  Job is directed to local printer port; local printer port is redirected to a queue that
    is attached to none, one, or several printers

236

Chapter 9
LAN
Administration:
The Printing
Environment

spooler can be used for more than just a staging area for jobs ready to print. For example, a software programmer can direct the output of compiler listings to the spooler with no intent of ever having the job printed. The programmer may be debugging a program and is intent only on eliminating syntax errors. Instead of directing the listing to the printer, the programmer can place it in the spooler in a location not attached to a printer. The job is automatically placed on hold. The programmer can then peruse the listing to find the syntax errors and then simply delete it from the spooler. Usually perusing a file on disk takes less time than waiting for printed output, and no paper is wasted. As another example, consider a technical manual writer who prints a document to the spooler and also places it on hold. Whenever another user needs a copy of the document, it can be printed and the document image kept in the spooler until the next request is received. In the first example the programmer is responsible for removing the document when it is no longer needed, and document stays in the spooler files for a short time. In the second example the document remains in the spooler's files for a long time. Both users are responsible for managing their spooler files. Using the user-oriented data maintained by the spooler, the user can manage his or her jobs by deleting jobs no longer needed or printing and removing jobs that have been placed on hold.

The administrator uses the spooler statistics to tune the spooler and make it adaptable to user needs. The administrator may have to remind

Table 9-3   Spooler Statistics

User-Oriented Statistics
  Number of jobs collected
  Number of lines printed
  Number of jobs on hold
  Number of pages on hold
  Length of time jobs have been held
  Available printers

Administrator-Oriented Statistics
  Number and size of jobs on hold
  How long jobs have been on hold
  Available space for new jobs
  Printer status
  Mapping of jobs or print queues to printers
  User-to-printer mappings
  Queue lengths for jobs ready to print
  Job print priorities
  Number of pages in print jobs
  Users responsible for each job
  Average time for a ready job to begin to print
  Maximum time for a ready job to begin to print

users to delete unnecessary jobs when the spooler files near capacity. By keeping track of the queues of jobs waiting to print and printer statuses, the administrator can detect printing bottlenecks and take steps to eliminate or minimize them.

Printer Control   The LAN administrator occasionally has to add new printers, change printers from one location to another, or delete printers. The spooler must allow for such changes. In some LAN systems the number of printers is limited by the number of file servers. For example, early Novell systems allowed a maximum of five printers, each connected to a file server. Naturally the administrator must be aware of such limitations when planning the expansion of the printing system.

Occasionally the administrator must take a printer out of service temporarily—for example, to change ribbons or toner cartridges and other maintenance tasks—and subsequently bring it back into service. At times the administrator must stop the spooler system altogether—for example, to install new spooler software or to shut down the system over a weekend. The administrator must do each of these functions with as little disruption to users as possible. By checking the various statistical reports of the spooler, the administrator can avoid problems, such as stopping a printer or the spooler during a lengthy job that is nearing completion.

Job Control   Properly controlling jobs in a spooler can be critical in establishing user satisfaction. For example, it is disconcerting to many users to have a one-page job ready to print and have to wait several hours while long jobs are printed. Such problems can be avoided with proper job control. Spoolers have a **priority system** for determining which jobs to print next. The default priority usually is **first in, first out.** The LAN administrator can change the default priority to accommodate different situations. For example, the priority can be based on the number of pages to be printed, placing short jobs ahead of long jobs in the queue. Priorities also can be based on the queue to which the printer is attached. The Novell spooler allows several queues to service one printer, and each queue can be given different priorities. Jobs in a **high-priority queue** have precedence over the jobs in a **low-priority queue.** Another alternative is to give print jobs priority numbers based on user or application priorities: high-priority applications have their jobs printed before lower-priority applications. A LAN administrator can manually change the order of jobs waiting to be printed. Naturally once a job begins printing, it continues until done, and even higher-priority jobs queued after it must wait.

To expedite printing, the LAN administrator sometimes must move jobs from one queue to another, stop jobs that are currently printing, change job priorities, or even delete jobs from the spooler system altogether. Ordinarily this type of action is taken on an exception basis, not as a regular way to manage the spooler. If such manual activity is required on a regular basis, the spooler is probably not set up correctly and should be restructured to provide efficient service on a regular basis.

238

Chapter 9
LAN
Administration:
The Printing
Environment

Security and Management Interface The administrator must be able to monitor and alter the spooler system. This is done through a **spooler interface.** Portions of this interface may be used by system users as well. Users, however, should not have the same privileges as the LAN administrator. Thus the spooler interface must provide for security. For example, users should be able to peruse jobs they have placed in the spooler system themselves but should not be able to peruse other users' jobs. Users should be able to delete their own jobs from the system but not the jobs of other users. A LAN administrator can also decide to allow users to print on certain printers but not on others. The objective of the spooler interface is to provide the necessary balance of management control and security.

User-Oriented Functions

Some of the functions a user can expect to carry out within the spooler system are similar to the administrator's functions, and these have been described earlier. Other functions are more specific to individual users. In some instances, these capabilities are set up by the LAN administrator, and in other cases they are requested by users themselves.

Print Multiple Copies A user may want to print multiple copies of a document. All copies can be printed on one printer, or they can be distributed over several printers. Using several printers speeds the printing process, and using printers in several different locations makes documents more readily available to the recipients. Spoolers make these printing options possible. Sometimes, a user has two options regarding the printing of multiple copies: The application may be capable of printing multiple copies, and the spooler may also have that capability. Usually when the application is responsible for printing multiple copies, what is essentially one print job is sent to the spooler multiple times. This, of course, takes up extra space in the spooler files. If the spooler is responsible for printing multiple copies, one copy of the job is sent to the spooler, and the spooler sends it to the printer(s) multiple times. In general, the second alternative is better. Moreover, if the spooler is responsible for printing multiple copies, it may be better able to print them more efficiently by using multiple printers. Typically a multiple-copy job created by an application appears to the spooler as a single, long print job.

Print Banners When printers are being shared, user jobs are interspersed, and there is a good chance that one user will accidentally take the output of another user. This is particularly ture when one user has two large jobs and another user has a small job sandwiched in between the two large jobs. To help users identify the beginning and ending of their jobs, some spoolers provide an optional **banner page** that contains information in large print identifying the user and the application. Thus banners can be used to identify and separate jobs produced on the same printer. On the negative side, banners can increase the amount of paper required. If most jobs are small, printing an extra one or two pages per document represents a relatively large printing overhead.

Print Selected Pages   Sometimes it is helpful to print a subset of the pages of a particular job. For example, suppose you had a long job to print, and the printer ribbon broke after successfully printing 65 pages. It would be more efficient to print the pages that were not successfully printed than to print the entire document. Most spoolers allow users to print selected pages.

NOVELL SPOOLER CONFIGURATION

We could discuss how to configure a spooler from a generic perspective; however, the way in which spoolers operate differs considerably. Therefore, let's look at one specific example of a spooler system, the Novell spooler. The latest releases of Novell software deemphasize the term *spooler* and simply talk about the printing subsystem. However, we will continue to use the term *spooler* when discussing the printing capabilities of the Novell system. Novell's printing environment is pictured in Figure 9-2. This figure is the basis for much of the discussion that follows. In our discussion we start at the user end of the print job and work toward the server end.

The CAPTURE Program

Some applications running under a Novell LAN are network-printer aware; that is, they can print directly to the network spooler. To effect this capability, the network administrator must properly install the application. With direct printing the user can typically print either to a local printer port or to the network printer. Thus the user can establish several printing paths, for instance, a local printer port using LPT1 and another port writing directly to the network spooler.

Other applications are not network aware; that is, they only know how to print to local printer ports, such as DOS's LPT*n* ports. In this instance a printer redirection program is needed to reroute print streams directed to local ports to the network print spooler. Novell's redirection program is called CAPTURE. The **CAPTURE program** runs as a **terminate-and-stay-resident (TSR)** program on each workstation that needs network printing support. Before print redirection can occur, the CAPTURE program must be run and be memory resident. Often this is done through the AUTOEXEC.BAT file when the workstation is started or on an application-by-application basis through an application batch file that starts CAPTURE, starts the applications, and then removes the CAPTURE program when the application terminates.

CAPTURE has a variety of startup parameters, the most important of which defines which printer port is to be monitored. CAPTURE intercepts printed output destined for that port and redirects it to the spooler. Whenever CAPTURE is redirecting print output for a particular port, that port will not receive any print streams. Therefore, if CAPTURE is intercepting print streams for LPT1, all jobs directed to LPT1 are routed to the spooler, even if there is a printer attached to LPT1.

Some of the parameters that CAPTURE can use are described in Table 9-4. Several of these parameters (including the printer port to be moni-

240

Chapter 9
LAN
Administration:
The Printing
Environment

tored) have default values, which are also shown in Table 9-4. To accept a default setting, the user simply omits the parameter. For example, the default parameter for the local port is $L = 1$, indicating that port LPT1 is to be monitored. If the user wants CAPTURE to monitor LPT1, then this parameter need not be included in CAPTURE's startup string. For self-documentation purposes, it is usually a good idea to explicitly state the parameters you want to use. If the user wants to use a value other than the default value, the parameter setting must be included in the startup string. Be aware that Table 9-4 does not show all of the CAPTURE parameters.

Once started, CAPTURE stays in memory and directs print jobs to queues until terminated with the **ENDCAP** command. You may want to

Figure 9-2 The Novell Printing Environment

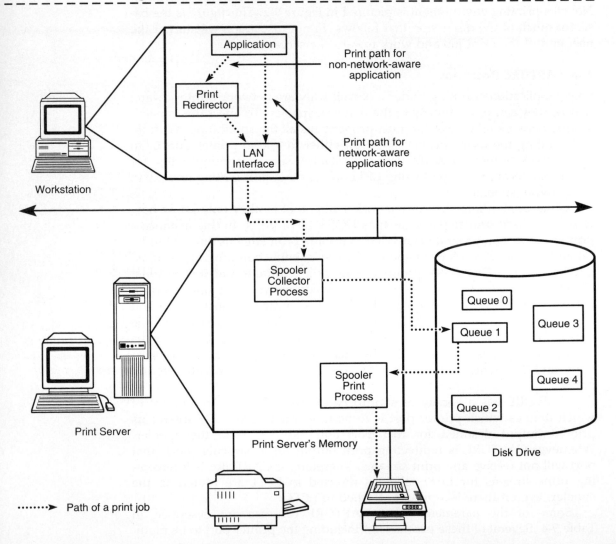

view the CAPTURE parameters that are in effect. If you run CAPTURE with the SHow parameter, it tells you the ports for which Capturing is activated and the parameter settings in effect for each port.

If you run CAPTURE without specifying any parameters and CAPTURE is not currently running, it uses the default settings. On a DOS system this means CAPTURE begins capturing print streams destined for LPT1 with no timeout value and no banners printed. Samples of parameters used in CAPTURE startup strings are shown in Table 9-5, and the output of the CAPTURE SHow parameter is shown in Table 9-6.

Table 9-4   Some CAPTURE Parameters

Local=n	The port being monitored. If $n=1$ then LPT1 is monitored; if $n=2$ then LPT2 is monitored; if $n=3$ then LPT3 is monitored. Default is LPT1.
TImeout=n	The timeout interval. The value ranges from 1 to 1000 and represents seconds. Default is no timeout.
Server=<*name*>	Designates the print server to which CAPTURE is to direct its output. Default is user's default server.
Queue=<*name*>	Designates which print queue to which the output is to be directed.
Job=job	Designates a printer configuration file to use for print job parameters and configuration.
CReate=<*file-name*>	Sends the output to a file rather than to a printer.
Form=<*name*>	Designates a form name or number to be used. For example Form=WZFORM. No default exists.
Copies=n	Directs the number of copies of the job to print. Default is 1 copy.
NAMe=<*name*>	Provides a user name to be printed on upper half of banner pages. Default is user's logon name.
Banner=<*name*>	Provides words that are printed on the lower half of banner pages. Default is LST.
NoBanner	Suppresses printing of banner page. Default is banner is printed.
FormFeed	Issues a form-feed character to the printer after the job has completed. Default is form feed enabled.
NoFormFeed	Suppreses a form-feed character after the job is printed. Default is form feed enabled.
Keep	Keeps all print information in the queue even if the application ends abnormally. If an application writing to the spooler fails, a partial print job will, by default, be automatically removed from the queue. This parameter keeps partially completed jobs in the event the application or its processor hangs or ends abnormally. Default is to discard the job.
SHow	Shows the printer ports for which CAPTURE is in effect and the parameters specified for each port.

Table 9-5   Sample CAPTURE Startup Strings

CAPTURE L=1 TI=15 Q=PRINTQ2 NB NFF K

CAPTURE L=2 TI=15 Q=PRINTQ2 NB NFF K

242

Chapter 9
LAN
Administration:
The Printing
Environment

Table 9-6   Output of CAPTURE SHow Parameter

LPT1: Capturing data to server SERVER queue PRINTQ2 (printer 0).

Capture Defaults : Enabled	Automatic Endcap : Enabled
Banner : (None)	Form Feed : No
Copies : 1	Tabs : Converted to 8 spaces
Form : 0	Timeout Count : 15 seconds

LPT2: Capturing data to server SERVER queue PRINTQ2 (printer 0).

Capture Defaults : Enabled	Automatic Endcap : Enabled
Banner : (None)	Form Feed : No
Copies : 1	Tabs : Converted to 8 spaces
Form : 0	Timeout Count : 15 seconds

LPT3: Capturing Is Not Currently Active.

The Print Server Spooler System

The majority of the work of the spooler is done on the print or file server. It is there that jobs are collected, stored on disk, directed to a printer, and eventually removed from the spooler system. The job is scheduled for printing only after the complete job has been captured in the queue.

A more flexible print-job-routing alternative is to send the output to a queue. The LAN administrator can define a variety of queues to meet varied printing needs. Let us now look at how Novell print queues operate. You may wish to refer back to Figure 9-2 during this discussion.

Novell Print Queues

Print queues can be thought of as containers for print jobs. A job directed to a queue is stored in that queue until it is removed. A job is automatically removed when it finishes printing and the hold flag is not on or when the job owner or print queue operator deletes it. A **print queue operator** is a user who has been given the right to manipulate jobs in that particular queue. For example, a user or a group manager may be given the right to be a queue operator for queues servicing printers in his or her location. The types of things a print queue operator can do are listed in Table 9-7. Some of the print-job parameters that can be changed by the owner of a job or the print queue operator are shown in Table 9-8. Notice in Table 9-8 that a user can make changes to his or her job so long as it does not affect other jobs. The queue operator can do everything a job owner can plus take actions that affect other users, such as changing the order in which jobs are printed and

Table 9-7   Functions of a Print Queue Operator

Edit the job parameters for any job in the queue (see Table 9-8)
Delete any job from the queue
Modify queue status by changing operator flags
Change priority of jobs in the queue

placing a job on operator hold. A job that has been placed on operator hold is scheduled to print only when a queue operator releases the hold. A user cannot release an operator hold for his or her job.

Print queues also offer an element of security. The LAN administrator or queue operator can designate **queue users.** A queue user is a user authorized to direct jobs to that queue. A user cannot direct job streams to a queue unless he or she has been designated as a queue user. Thus, a queue attached to a printer that is used for printing checks can be protected from unauthorized users. If department printers are used, a user in one department can be made a queue user for queues attached to that department's printers but will not be a queue user for queues attached to printers in other departments. Under this arrangement, users in one department cannot tie up printers in other departments.

A printer can be attached to none, one, or several queues. Figure 9-3 illustrates several configurations. A queue that is not connected to a printer will, of course, not be able to print jobs. Jobs directed to that queue are held in the queue and not printed. At a later time the queue may be attached to a

Table 9-8   Print-Job Parameters

Parameter	Meaning	Can be Altered by
Description	Identifies file being printed.	U, QO
User hold	Holds job from printing.	U, QO
Operator hold	Holds job from printing.	QO
Service sequence	Changes priority for printing.	QO
Number of copies	Self-explanatory.	U, QO
File contents	Text or byte stream. With text the spooler interprets formatting like tabs and format codes. With byte stream application handles formatting.	U, QO
Tab size	Self-explanatory.	U, QO
Suppress form feed	Suppresses a form feed after job prints.	U, QO
Defer printing	Yes or no. Choose no if job is to be printed as soon as possible. Choose yes and enter target date and time to print later. A large job, for example, can be scheduled to print overnight.	U, QO
Form	Designates a special print form is required.	U, QO
Print banner	Yes or no.	U, QO
Banner name	Name of banner to print.	U, QO
Banner file	Name of file on banner.	U, QO
Target date	See Defer printing.	U, QO
Target time	See Defer printing.	U, QO

U = user or print job owner
QO = queue operator

244

Chapter 9
LAN
Administration:
The Printing
Environment

printer and the jobs stored there can print. Alternatively the queue may be used for jobs that will never print. For example, a programmer may direct the output of his compiler listing to such a queue. With a print-job perusal program, he can look at the listing and locate all of his compiler errors. When the programmer is done looking at the job, he can delete it from the queue.

Print jobs arrive in a queue and are scheduled to be printed. A queue may be connected to several printers to speed the printing of jobs waiting in the queue. The queue prints jobs to whichever printer is available, so two jobs can be printing from the same queue at once.

Figure 9-3   Queue and Printer Attachment Configurations

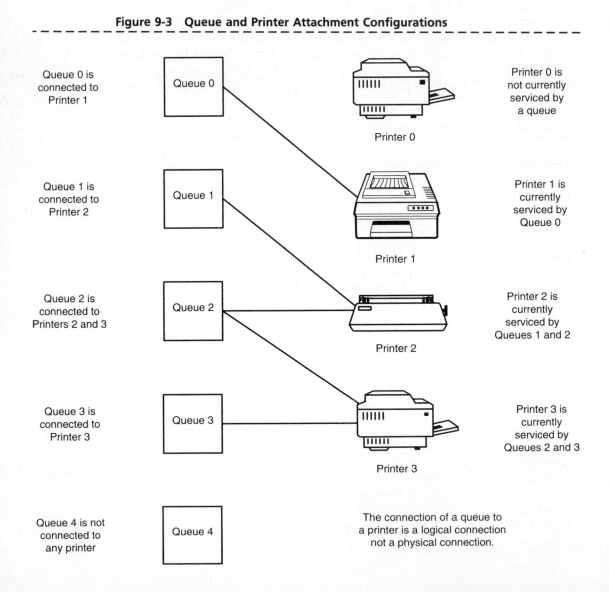

Queue 0 is connected to Printer 1

Queue 0

Printer 0

Printer 0 is not currently serviced by a queue

Queue 1 is connected to Printer 2

Queue 1

Printer 1

Printer 1 is currently serviced by Queue 0

Queue 2 is connected to Printers 2 and 3

Queue 2

Printer 2

Printer 2 is currently serviced by Queues 1 and 2

Queue 3 is connected to Printer 3

Queue 3

Printer 3

Printer 3 is currently serviced by Queues 2 and 3

Queue 4 is not connected to any printer

Queue 4

The connection of a queue to a printer is a logical connection not a physical connection.

A printer can also have several queues servicing it. One reason for this is to establish printing priorities. Each queue can be given a queue priority. Thus, the LAN administrator can create an environment wherein users spooling their output to a high-priority queue get better service than users sending their output to a lower-priority queue. If jobs in the high-priority queue are ready to print, they are printed before any ready jobs in the lower-priority queue.

Queues may be added and deleted as needed. Once created, queues can be attached and detached from a printer. The ability to create, attach, detach, or delete print queues and the ability to direct print streams to a print queue creates a system wherein almost all printing requirements can be accommodated.

Special Printing Needs

Some installations have special printing needs. Suppose your organization has a unique printer that is not completely supported by one of the standard printer drivers supplied by your network software. Some networks help you overcome this with a utility that allows you to define or enhance a printer-definition file. In a Novell network this utility is called **PRINTDEF**. Novell uses a printer-definition file to describe the functions of a printer, such as underline, bold, near-letter-quality, draft mode, and so on. With PRINTDEF you can customize a printer-definition file to take full advantage of unique characteristics of your printer. Moveover, if you purchase a new, state-of-the-art printer that is not fully supported by an existing printer-definition file, you can enhance an existing definition to take advantage of your printer's new capabilities.

Some print jobs must be printed on special **forms,** such as checks, income tax forms, and invoices. To prevent these jobs from printing on standard paper or on the wrong form, the spooler can allow you to define a form by name and paper size, associate a job with a form name, associate a printer with a form name, prohibit a job from printing on a printer that has not been associated with its form name, and provide assistance in aligning the form on the printer. All of these capabilities are provided within Novell's printer system.

Print Servers

Under NetWare an installation can designate a workstation as a print server using a **network-loadable module (NLM)** that comes standard with Net-Ware 386.

A print server can be a dedicated microcomputer or it can be a workstation that provides both user and printing services. Two processes provide these services: **PSERVER,** as NLM or a workstation task for dedicated print servers, and **RPRINTER,** a print process that runs on a nondedicated print server. Both configurations are shown in Figure 9-4.

The PSERVER process can control up to 16 printers, and multiple concurrent PSERVER tasks can be running. The printers can be attached to the

Figure 9-4   Print Server Configurations

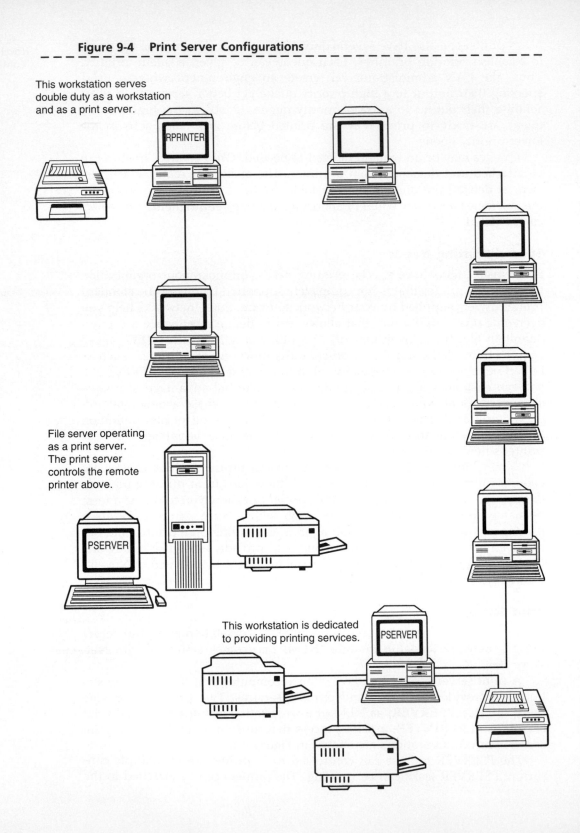

This workstation serves
double duty as a workstation
and as a print server.

File server operating
as a print server.
The print server
controls the remote
printer above.

This workstation is dedicated
to providing printing services.

Figure 9-5   Using A LAN Printer Adapter

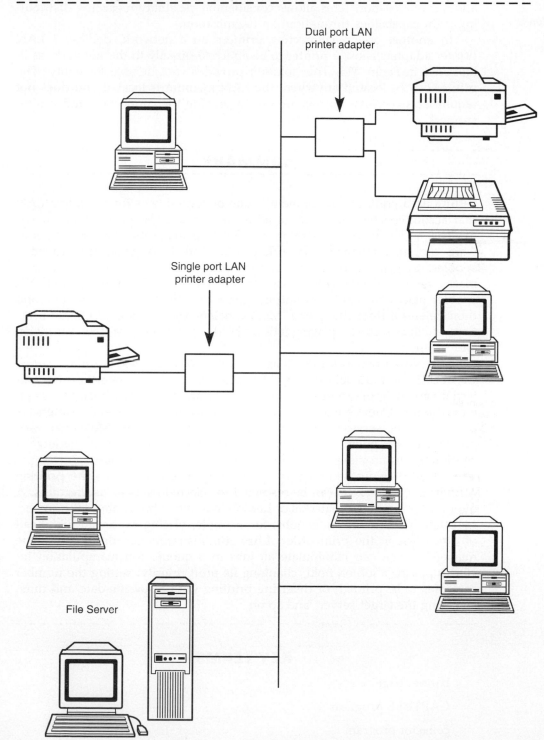

Dual port LAN
printer adapter

Single port LAN
printer adapter

File Server

248

Chapter 9
LAN
Administration:
The Printing
Environment

computer on which PSERVER is running, or the printers may be attached to another workstation. This allows considerable flexibility regarding distributing print capabilities throughout an organization.

In another option connecting printers on a network, dedicated LAN printer adapters allow a printer to be attached directly to the network, as illustrated in Figure 9-5. This solution provides considerable flexibility. The printer can be located anywhere the LAN medium is located and does not require an expensive microcomputer to provide the connection and printer support.

SUMMARY

Setting up a printing environment is one of several keys for creating a LAN that accommodates the needs of all users. On a LAN, printers are shared devices, and software is therefore needed to manage the sharing. The software tool that manages network printing needs is generically called a spooler. In general, a spooler collects print job streams from users and places them temporarily on disk. When a job has been completed, the spooler places the job in an **output queue** for printing, prints the job, and then deletes it from the queue. Most spoolers also provide additional functions, such as security, placing jobs on hold, establishing print job priorities, and so on.

In a Novell network print jobs are collected in queues. A utility named CAPTURE can route jobs destined for local printers to a network printer. Alternatively an application that is network aware can write directly to a network queue. Queues may be attached to zero, one, or several printers. A printer can be serviced by zero, one, or several queues. Moveover each queue can be given a different priority for printing. This variety of configurations provides the flexibility to meet diverse user needs.

Novell provides some degree of security or exclusivity to the printing configuration. A queue can be restricted to selected users or user groups. A queue user can manipulate his or her job in a queue but cannot take any action that affects other queue jobs, for example, placing his or her job ahead of other jobs in the print order. LAN administrators can designate queue managers, who can manipulate all jobs in a queue. Job manipulation includes placing a job on hold, changing its print priority, setting the number of copies to be printed, or deferring printing until a specific date and time, changing the target server, and so on.

KEY TERMS

banner page

CAPTURE program

collector program

control sequence

ENDCAP program

first in, first out

forms

hardware interface

high-priority queue

low-priority queue

network-loadable module (NLM)

output queue

parallel interface

PRINTDEF

print queue operator

priority system

PSERVER

queue user

redirector

RPRINTER

serial interface

small computer system interface (SCSI)

spooler interface

terminate-and-stay-resident (TSR)

timeout interval

REVIEW QUESTIONS

1. List three general functions provided by a spooler and explain how each is accomplished.

2. Describe three application-oriented, administrative-oriented, user-oriented, and hardware-oriented spooler functions.

3. What is the function of the print job redirector? Why and when is it necessary?

4. Why would you have several print queues attached to one printer?

5. Why would you have several printers attached to one print queue?

6. Why would you have a queue that is not attached to a printer?

250

Chapter 9
LAN
Administration:
The Printing
Environment

7. Describe two ways to regulate job printing.

PROBLEMS AND EXERCISES

1. Write the CAPTURE parameter that

   a. directs the print-job stream for LPT1 to a queue named LASER

   b. issues a form feed at the end of the job

   c. suppresses printing of a banner

   d. provides a timeout value of 30 seconds

   Refer to Table 9-4 for a list of some CAPTURE parameters and to Table 9-5 for examples of CAPTURE parameters used in startup strings.

2. The Document Support Group (DSG) in an airplane manufacturing company is responsible for writing and changing airplane manuals and engineering-change notices. Documents range in length from one to several hundred pages. Some documents include graphic images that the application must generate. Generating graphic-images blocks for transmission to the printer can require up to a minute of CPU time. DSG has three printers and wants to share these printers in an optimal manner. Some of their concerns include avoiding short jobs having to wait for long manuals to print and problems of interleaving graphic images because of the time it takes to generate graphic images. Suggest a plan for using the three printers that will satisfy DSG's needs. Your plan should include a description of print queues, printers, job types, and time-out intervals.

3. Investigate a LAN system different from Novell's. Compare this system's spooler capabilities with those of Novell.

4. A variety of printing utilities and hardware is available for LANs. Research the literature and describe three of these.

REFERENCES

Coale, Kristi. "Network Printers: Coming into Focus." *Infoworld*, April 13, 1992.

Coale, Kristi. "Network Printing: Emerging from the Labyrinth." *Infoworld*, March 9, 1992.

Day, Mike. "Network Printing: The Second Generation." *LAN Times*, Volume 9, Issue 15, August 10, 1992.

Lapnig, Arnie. "In Search of the Platonic Print Server." *LAN Times*, Volume 8, Issue 9, February 18, 1991.

Poor, Alfred. "Smart Printer Sharing with the HP LaserJet IIISi." *PC Magazine*, Volume 10, Number 10, May 28, 1991.

"Print Server Reviews." *LAN Times*, Volume 7, Issue 3, March 1990.

Pritchett, Glenn. "Now Printing at a Network Near You." *LAN Technology*, Volume 8, Number 2, February 1992.

LAN ADMINISTRATION: BACKUP AND RECOVERY

CHAPTER PREVIEW

A LAN is not a static entity. Data stored on the LAN changes, new applications are added, old applications are retired, users come and go, workstations are added, moved, removed or replaced, servers are added or upgraded, systems fail, and new threats to security and integrity arise. LAN administration is a process of managing such changes, some of which are planned while others are unplanned. Adding new users, maintaining security, and modifying the printing environment, topics discussed earlier, are examples of planned changes. Managing unplanned changes—those that arise from unanticipated situations, such as hardware and software failures, power failures, disasters like fires and floods, and human errors—are the topic of this chapter.

The key topics in this chapter are:

data backup

data recovery

problem detection

problem resolution

diagnostic hardware and software

disaster planning

At the conclusion of this chapter you should have an understanding of some of the unexpected problems that can arise on a LAN, how to deal with those problems, and how to effect recovery.

DATA BACKUP

Data is a valuable corporate resource. It is the raw material from which information is manufactured, and information is the resource that drives corporate decision making. Corporate data resides in many places—in em-

254

Chapter 10
LAN
Administration:
Backup and
Recovery

ployees' minds, on paper, and in computers. Companies go to great lengths to gather, update, and protect this data.

For years companies have had mechanisms for protecting noncomputer-related data. Employees are encouraged to share what they know with other employees or to write down facts known only to them. Organizations make additional copies of hard-copy data as backups in case the original is lost or destroyed. Companies must do the same with their computerized data; that is, they must provide one or more ways to protect their data from accidental and intentional loss and corruption. One way to do this is to create data backups.

Computer systems process data, and most data is subject to change. One of the most critical functions of system administration—on LANs, stand-alone systems, and WANs alike—is preserving the currency and integrity of data. You may have heard the phrase "garbage in, garbage out." This means that if the data used to produce information is not correct, the information produced from that data is also incorrect. Since information is used as the foundation for management decisions, we go to great lengths to keep it from turning into garbage. Moreover, on computer systems, we have a variety of objects that help us work with data—programs, user profiles, security settings, logon scripts, command files, and so on. If we take steps to protect the data, we also must take steps to protect the objects used to manipulate that data. Garbage programs and improper security settings operating on good data can turn good data into garbage data.

A **data backup** is a snapshot of a database or files at a particular time. Just as a photograph preserves the image of a scene at a particular instant, a backup provides an installation with a historical copy of the data at one point in time. A backup is produced by making a copy of data, programs, and work files stored on disk. The backup is typically written to either another disk(s) or to a tape(s).

The Need for Backups

In computing systems a myriad of things can happen to corrupt or destroy data or the objects used to manipulate it. A partial list of these things is given in Table 10-1. Some of the items on the list are intentional acts, and

Table 10-1   Ways in Which Data Can Be Corrupted

An application program with a logic bug can change data incorrectly.
A user can accidentally erase a file.
A user can accidentally destroy a file by copying a new file over it.
A user can maliciously destroy a file or data in a file.
A system failure can leave the database in a state of partial update.
A disk failure can destroy data or render it unaccessible.
An undetected virus can erase or otherwise destroy data.
A bug in system software, for example, the database management system, can cause data loss, unreliable results, or data corruption.

others are accidental or circumstantial. Regardless of the cause, a good LAN administration policy must provide a method of **data recovery** to correct data problems. The most common way to restore files to a usable state following a damaging incident is to use backups. In addition to data recovery, backups are also used to archive data, to provide low-cost bulk data storage, and to provide data interchange. Following a brief discussion of the uses of backups, we focus on backup procedures for the recovery of lost or damaged data.

Recovery If data in a database becomes corrupted or a text file is accidentally deleted, an organization will want to restore the data to a usable state. Backups are the tool most often used to do this.

Data Archiving Computer users frequently want to maintain historical copies of data, a process known as **archiving.** If you use computer software to calculate your taxes, you probably want to archive your tax software and work files in the event you are audited or to refer back to when preparing next year's return. (You probably do not need to permanently keep the data on your disk drives.)

Low-cost Bulk Data Storage This use of backups is similar to data archiving. The primary difference is that archived data is kept and probably never reused, whereas data kept in low-cost bulk data storage can be used periodically. Rather than keeping the data on-line constantly, a disk is used to hold the data temporarily while it is being used and, when no longer needed, the data is removed and stored. This reduces the hardware costs of the system. For example, a research organization may have large volumes of data that have been collected during testing and experimentation. Using backups, researchers can periodically run programs that analyze certain aspects of the data. Once the results of the analysis have been produced, the researchers take several months to evaluate it and determine additional processing needs. Colleges often use low-cost bulk data storage for classes that are taught once per year. Data for these classes are restored to disks during the term in which they are needed and removed when the class is not being taught.

Data Interchange Before high-speed data communications, one of the primary methods of moving data from one computer to another was to back up the data onto a tape on one system and restore the data to a disk on another system. This is still a viable method for exchanging data today. To do this, of course, the two machines sharing the data must have common hardware and software backup capabilities.

Backups for Static and Dynamic Data

Static data changes infrequently or not at all. An example of static data is a program executable file. The only time a program executable file is changed is when a new release of the product is installed, when patches are made to the code files to fix bugs, or when the code file is infected by a virus.

256

Chapter 10
LAN
Administration:
Backup and
Recovery

Whenever new application files are received or existing ones are updated, the first step a LAN administrator usually takes is to make backup copies. For good measure, two backup copies are made: one copy for on-site storage and another for storage at a different location, called **off-site storage.** Storing a backup copy in another location is a safeguard against a catastrophe, such as a fire or flood, that might ruin the data on the computer's disk as well as the backup copies.

Suppose that something happens to static data; for example, a programmer accidentally deletes a program file, or the disk on which it is stored goes bad. To recover from this problem, the LAN administrator must identify and correct the sources of the problem. After restoring the proper operational environment, say by replacing a failed disk drive, the backup copy of the data is restored to the system. Since the data has not changed since the backup was taken, the program file is available in the same form as before the problem arose, and recovery is complete.

Dynamic data changes frequently. A database is an example of dynamic data. Databases are constantly adding, modifying, or deleting data. A backup is a snapshot of data at a particular time, so if a failure occurs that affects dynamic data, the backup for that data probably will not represent the exact state of the data at the point of failure. A backup can accurately represent the state of a database after a failure only if no database updates have occurred since the backup was taken.

Assuming no recovery mechanism exists other than a backup (later you will see several measures some databases use to protect against failures), recovery for dynamic data begins like the recovery for static data: The sources of the problem are detected and corrected, and the backup copy of the data is restored to the disk. However, to fully recover, the database must be brought forward in time to the last consistent state before the failure occurred. This means that the updates that were made after the backup was made must be done again. This is done by resubmitting transactions posted to the database subsequent to the backup being taken or by using some of the special recovery provisions provided by some database management systems that are briefly described later.

As you can tell, when a failure occurs, having a *current* backup available allows for a fast, comprehensive recovery. In contrast, a backup that is a month old may require that a month's worth of work be redone. Backups are a company's insurance policy against data related disasters and loss. Like insurance, ideally you will never need to use a backup. When needed, they are usually the difference between a timely return to a productive operation and an arduous, time-consuming, system-rebuilding effort.

Backup Hardware, Software, and Procedures

Data backups and restorations require both hardware and software. The hardware provides the medium to which the backup is written or from which data to be restored is read. The software provides the logic to write the correct file to backup medium or to read those files from the backup medium for restoration. Good backup/restore software also provides a variety of options. At this time you may wish to refer back to Chapter 4 for more information regarding backup hardware and to Chapter 5 for more information regarding backup software.

Making Backups

Key questions facing LAN administrators are, How often should backups be made? What should be backed up? How long should backup copies be saved? Where should backup copies be stored? The ideal answers to these questions are backup everything daily, keep the copies forever, and store copies in at least two separate locations. This ideal is not always practical, however. Each installation needs to formulate a backup policy and backup/restore procedures that allow data recovery from any imaginable data disaster. The recovery must be timely and sufficiently comprehensive to allow the organization to resume productive processing. The definitions of *timely*, *sufficiently comprehensive*, and *productive processing* vary among organizations, as illustrated by the following examples.

A university LAN that supports student academic work has a cyclic load. During vacations, the system is hardly utilized. Near the end of a term, the system is often overworked as students rush to meet end-of-term deadlines. During vacation, having the LAN out of service for several days may not have much of an impact. But losing its services for that long at the end of the semester might have serious repercussions for some students' grades. For this university, the term *timely* has different meanings at different periods.

During the busy period students use a wide variety of applications and files. The term *sufficiently comprehensive* in this case means that most of the lost data must be reconstructed so most of the students can complete their work. During a vacation period, *sufficiently comprehensive* may mean simply having the LAN operational so the LAN administrator can create the files and environment for next semester's classes.

The university defines *productive processing* as all students being able to complete their work at the end of the term. Applications and data files must be recovered to a point that allows this to happen.

A lawyer's office uses a LAN to support its activities. One of the main applications the office uses is word processing of legal documents. The file servers have a large number of relatively inactive files. Wills are maintained on-line for three years subsequent to a change, letters are kept on-line for a year, and so on. This means that the number of active documents, the ones currently being worked on, is small in comparison to the bulk of data stored. Moreover, the need to access the older documents is minimum. For the attorney's office, *sufficiently comprehensive* means restoring the active documents and word processing system. Inactive documents can be restored at a more leisurely pace. This is sufficient to allow productive processing for the majority of the staff; that is, the staff can do work of an immediate nature. Timeliness in this case is within a few minutes or hours. Most of the staff

258
- - - - -
Chapter 10
LAN
Administration:
Backup and
Recovery

can temporarily work on other tasks until the system is restored; however, deadlines do exist and some workers must be able to return to their tasks almost immediately.

A LAN being used to control a manufacturing process must be restored quickly to avoid lost production time, costly damage to raw materials, or damage to the processing equipment. In this case getting the system back into operation, even with some data that is not exactly accurate, is probably more cost effective than completely restoring the entire system before resuming processing. That is, time rather than complete accuracy is of the essence. For the manufacturer *sufficiently comprehensive* means just having the system available to resume direction of the work in progress.

What must be recovered and in what time can differ among applications. The LAN administrator must analyze the backup and restoration alternatives—backup frequency, completeness, and retention—and choose the alternatives best suited to the organization's needs. Let us now look at some of these backup procedure considerations.

Backup Procedures

A backup procedure essentially describes what is to be backed up, when, and how backups are taken, the frequency of backups, and the disposition of the backup copies. As described earlier, an application's characteristics are major factors influencing each of these choices. Let us look at each in more detail.

Disposition of Backup Copies A comprehensive backup procedure ensures that several copies of backups are available and that complete copies are stored in at least two separate locations. Separate locations usually does not mean adjoining rooms; it means off-site storage or the equivalent. Some installations store backups in fireproof vaults. This is not always a viable alternative to off-site storage because floods or explosions, for example, could still damage the backup copies. The objective of off-site storage is to allow recovery from catastrophes that might destroy both computer data and backup copies stored on-site.

Several copies of backups may be needed for another reason. The backup medium itself may go bad and render the backup unusable. For example, a magnetic tape backup may get scratched, stretched, broken, or ruined from exposure to a magnetic field. Each of these circumstances can make the tape unusable. Having a backup to the backup provides a recovery alternative.

Having several generations of backups is also important. An axiom of backup procedures is, "Never immediately recycle your backup media." That is, suppose you decide to use one tape and one tape only for backups. Further, suppose that the backup requires the entire tape. What do you suppose happens if a failure occurs while taking the backup? The answer is that the backup being taken is incomplete and the previous backup has been overwritten by the one being taken. Hence, you have no good, complete backup available.

Keeping a history or several generations of backups is called a **retention policy.** Perhaps one of the most difficult backup policy decisions a LAN administrator must make is how long to retain backups. The **grandfather-father-son generations** of backups consists of three generations of backups. When the grandson backup is made, the grandfather backup is recycled and made available for the next backup, the father becomes the grandfather, and so on. This process is illustrated in Figure 10-1. For some installations this may be adequate; however, most companies today have a more comprehensive retention policy. An example of one company's retention policy is outlined in Table 10-2. The tradeoffs you make in formulating a retention policy are based on the volume of data involved, the cost of backup media, the cost of storage, and installation-specific recovery or data-restoration needs.

You can think of backup **comprehensiveness** as the degree of data exactness represented by the backups. A backup with poor comprehensiveness, such as a year-old backup, is not a good approximation to the current state of the data. A backup with good comprehensiveness, such as one that is just minutes old, closely represents the current state of the data. Comprehensiveness is a function of the age of a backup and the amount of change in the data since the last backup was made. The older the backup and the higher the volatility of the data, the poorer the comprehensiveness. A good backup plan provides several levels of comprehensiveness. One reason for levels of comprehensiveness is the need to go back in time to retrieve specific data, like a university's class files used annually. Another reason is that some time may elapse before a data problem is noticed. Several backups may have occurred between the time the data was corrupted and when the corruption was noticed. Recovery may require that several generations of backups be skipped until a backup taken before the corruption occurred is found. When used for recovery, older backups require more work to bring the data up to date. Despite the work required, this approach is used if the alternative of fixing corrupted data is more expensive or time consuming.

Backup Frequency Static data should be backed up at least twice, and the two versions should be stored in separate locations. A file that has been backed up several times and has not changed need not be backed up again unless one of the backup copies is recycled or is defective. Before recycling such a backup, a new backup of the static file should be taken.

Dynamic files must be backed up more frequently. Some installations do daily backups; others find a weekly backup is adequate. You decide the frequency of backups by comparing the time required to do backups with the time required to do recovery. Usually we look at the worst and average recovery scenario when making this decision. For comparison, let us consider two alternatives, daily and weekly backups.

On average failures will occur at about midpoint between one backup being made and the next one taking its place. If you are lucky, a recovery situation occurs immediately after you have made a backup. Unfortunately all too often you find yourself in the worst-case scenario, when a failure occurs just as you are about to start the next backup. This worst-case scenario

Figure 10-1 Backup Generations

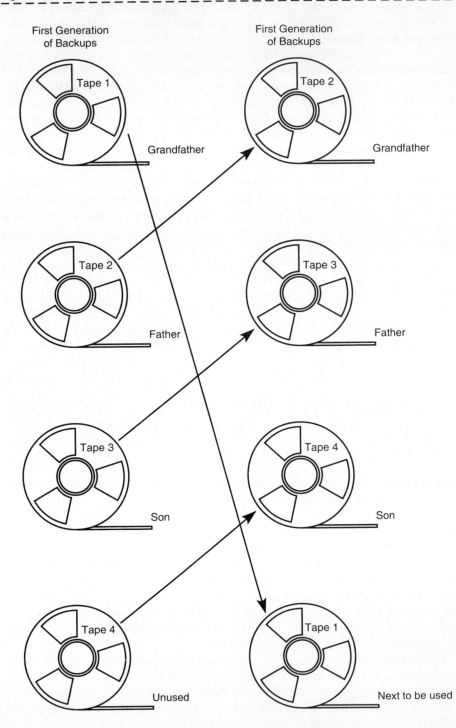

First Generation
of Backups

First Generation
of Backups

Tape 1

Tape 2

Grandfather

Grandfather

Tape 2

Tape 3

Father

Father

Tape 3

Tape 4

Son

Son

Tape 4

Tape 1

Unused

Next to be used

requires you to determine the length and complexity of recovery. If you have made backups weekly, the backups reflect data that is a week old and restoration returns the data to that state. Following the restoration, you must somehow repeat the week's work to bring the data to a current state. If you have made daily backups, the worst-case recovery involves redoing what has changed during the day. Assuming a constant workload, a recovery using weekly backups requires seven times more effort to bring the database to a current status than do daily backups (or five times for a five-day work week). The backup frequency is seven times longer and the average amount of work to be redone is 3.5 days versus 0.5 days.

Two other factors influence the frequency of backups, failure rates and timeliness of recovery. If the frequency of failure is low, less-frequent backups may be acceptable. If the frequency of failures is high, frequent backups are important. If the need to return to operational status immediately is high, then the frequency of backups is greater than if need for an immediate return to operation status is low.

How and When to Make Backups Once you have determined the frequency of making backups, you must next decide when during the workday you want to make backups. On large systems, some backup utilities allow files to be backed up while updates to that file are being made. This is possible because the system coordinates the backup with before-image and after-image audit trails, so data integrity is maintained. Since most of today's LAN backup utilities do not provide data integrity protection for on-line backups, it is usually best to create the backups when data are not being modified. This not only promotes data integrity but also reduces LAN overhead while users are most active. Figure 10-2 illustrates one problem you might experience in making backups while data is being changed. A transaction is moving money from Record A in File 1 to Record X in File 2. Suppose that a backup was started before this transaction began and that File 1 has already been backed up. On the backup tape the contents of Record A has

Table 10-2   A Sample Backup Retention Policy

Backup Policy

Daily	Backup all files changed since the backup of the preceding day. Make two copies; store one copy off-site.
Weekly	Backup all files. Make two copies; store one copy off-site.
End of year	Backup all files as of midnight, December 31. Backup all files as of midnight at the end of the fiscal year. Make two copies; store one copy off-site.

Retention Policy

Retain weekly backups and daily backups for one month.
Retain the first backup of each month for one year.
Retain the end-of-year backups for five years.

Figure 10-2 Instance of Data Inconsistency During File Backup

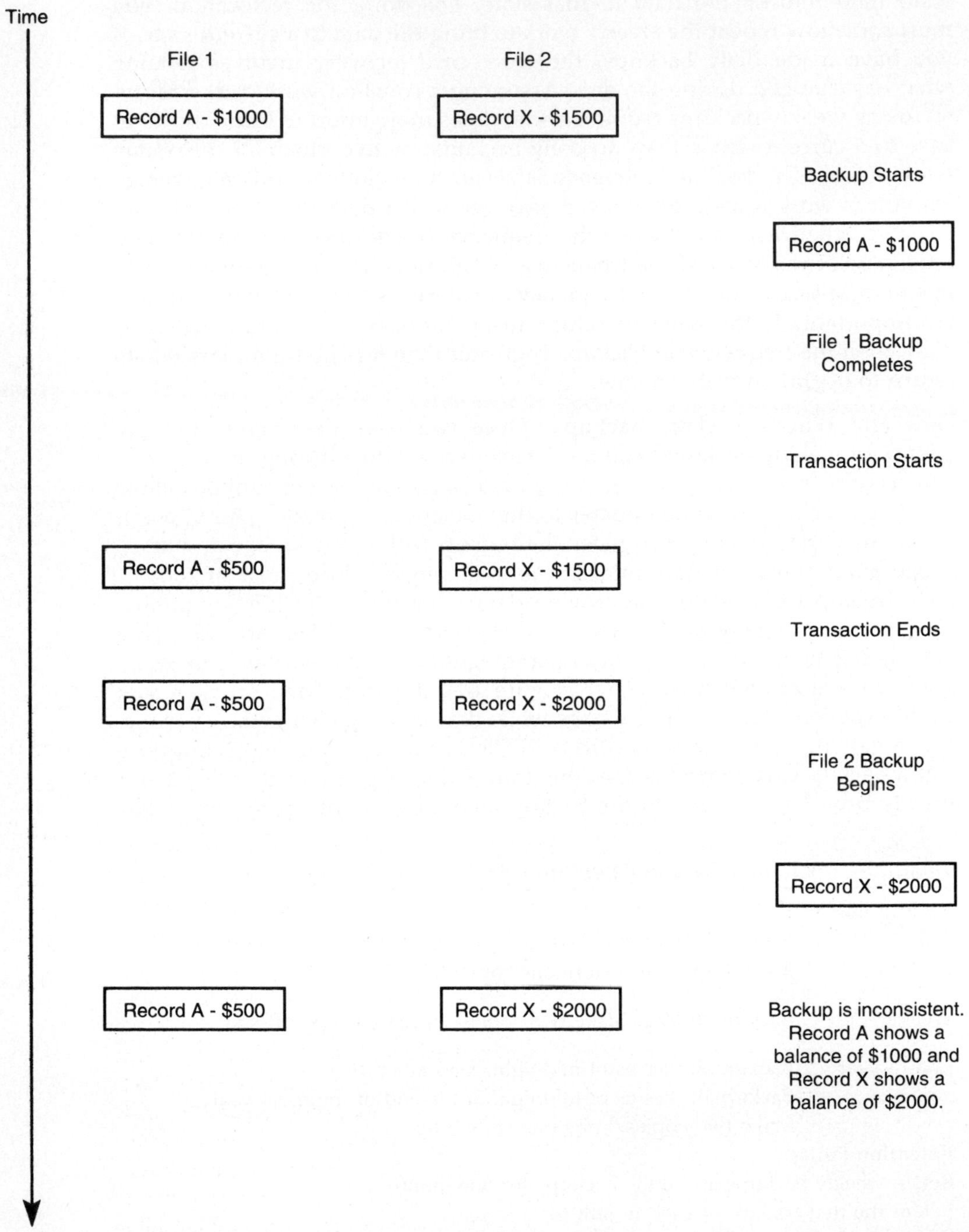

Time

File 1	File 2	
Record A - $1000	Record X - $1500	
		Backup Starts
	Record A - $1000	
		File 1 Backup Completes
		Transaction Starts
Record A - $500	Record X - $1500	
		Transaction Ends
Record A - $500	Record X - $2000	
		File 2 Backup Begins
	Record X - $2000	
Record A - $500	Record X - $2000	Backup is inconsistent. Record A shows a balance of $1000 and Record X shows a balance of $2000.

already been recorded with a balance of $1000. Before the backup gets to Record X in File 2, the transaction begins and ends. When the backup reaches File 2 and records the contents of Record X, the transaction's update has been posted and the balance recorded on the backup is $2000. There is now an inconsistency in the backup. Before the transaction there was $1000 in Record A and $1500 in Record X. After the transaction there is $500 in Record A and $2000 in Record X. However, the backup shows $1000 in Record A and $2000 in Record X, an inconsistency. To ensure backup consistency, backups should not be taken when files are being updated. Sometimes, because of the nature of the application, this cannot be avoided. For example, a police department LAN may be in continuous operation. For these LANs the backup should be scheduled during the time of lowest activity and, if possible, updates should be deferred between the time the backup is started and the time it is completed.

Many LANs have periods when usage is low and when the LAN is not used at all. These are the best times to make backups because users experience fewer disruptions. For example, for many office LANs the best time to make backups is in the early-morning hours, say between 2 and 6 A.M., either during the work week or on weekends. While this time may be the most convenient for LAN users, it may not be convenient for LAN administrators, particularly for LANs that operate during a typical work period of 8 A.M. to 8 P.M. five days a week. The LAN is essentially unused during the remaining time. A LAN administrator has two options for making early-morning backups, go to work during that time or make unattended backups.

Unattended backups are possible through the backup software itself or through separate software utilities. Some of today's backup systems provide unattended backup capabilities. Typically the LAN administrator specifies to the backup program the date and time the backup must start and the files that must be backed up. The LAN administrator schedules the backup before leaving for the day. Naturally the LAN must be up and running when the administrator leaves, the nodes being backed up and the backup server must be running, the backup medium must be on-line, and the backup program must be running or properly scheduled to run. When the administrator arrives at work the next day, he or she must verify that the backup was satisfactorily completed. Reasons that the backup does not successfully complete include a power outage that shuts down the system, unformatted tape in the backup unit, and a tape with insufficient data capacity.

If a company's backup software does not provide unattended backup, the LAN administrator can still conduct them. One way to do this is to start a backup remotely. The administrator might use a home computer and modem connection to access the system at the proper time and initiate the backup. Naturally the preparation steps previously described must have been taken to enable this. A more convenient alternative is to buy or write a utility program that automatically invokes the backup. The utility basically just hooks up to the system clock and at a prescribed time starts a batch

264
- - - - - -
Chapter 10
LAN
Administration:
Backup and
Recovery

command file to begin the backup. This is usually more convenient for the LAN administrator than an early-morning telephone call to start the backup.

Companies with large computer systems connected to their LANs have another backup alternative—initiating the backup from a large system. Often large systems have 24-hour operations. A large computer operator could initiate the LAN backup from the computer's command console; moreover, if the speed of the link between the large computer and the LAN is high enough, it is even possible for the backup to be captured on one of the large system's peripheral devices.

Other Data Reliability Options

Having backups is *always* important. You do, however, have optional procedures available that can protect you from some of the situations that require the use of a backup. None of them either individually or in concert obviate the need for a well-planned and well-implemented backup procedure. But you can lessen the frequency of making backups by using such technologies and procedures as disk mirroring, redundant arrays of independent disks (RAID), DBMS recovery, re-creation and reprocessing, disk editors, and disk utilities.

The first two options improve the reliability and availability of systems and have been discussed in previous chapters. When your system has high reliability, you can elect to reduce the frequency of your backups because the frequency of failures needing data recovery is reduced. Keep in mind, however, that if time is a critical factor in effecting recovery, then time, not reliability, dictates your recovery frequency.

DBMS recovery may allow recovery from some problems without resorting to backups. Other database problems may require the use of backups together with the DBMS's recovery mechanisms. The last options, re-creation and reprocessing, disk editors, and disk utilities, can also be used when backups are not available or if the problems are limited in scope and time is of the essence. Let us take a closer look at each of these alternatives.

DBMS Recovery   Many DBMSs provide a recovery system that gives you two levels of recovery, **minor fault recovery** and **major fault recovery.** Examples of minor faults include inconsistent data resulting from a CPU failure and transaction failures. Minor faults affect a small portion of the database. Major faults result from head crashes, computer room fires, and accidental deletion of files. Major faults typically corrupt large portions of the database.

When the DBMS provides minor fault recovery, the faults are usually corrected automatically by the DBMS and do not require the use of backups. This type of recovery rolls the database back to a consistent point. For example, if a transaction that updates two records fails after one record has been updated but before the corresponding update to the other record, the completed update is reversed. The update reversal rolls the database back to a consistent state. Minor fault recovery is implemented in several ways. A common method involves writing the images of records before they are changed to a disk file. If a failure occurs, these before images are written back to the database, thus reversing the changes the transaction made. Using before images to provide transaction rollback is illustrated in Figure 10-3.

Major fault recovery usually requires the use of a backup together with database update files to roll the database forward to a consistent, current status. A backup version of the database is coordinated with an audit trail of after images collected by the DBMS. An after image is the image of a record after it has been changed by a database transaction and is illustrated in Figure 10-4. Figure 10-5 shows the synchronization of a database backup and the after-image audit trail. The after-image audit trail is a file to which after images are written. If a failure occurs, the database backup is first restored, and then the after images are posted to the database to bring the database forward to a current, consistent state. The use of after images avoids the need to reprocess transactions and is much quicker than reprocessing transactions. Restoration using this technique may still be time consuming because of the volumes of data involved, but the process is mostly automated.

Re-creation and Reprocessing   If a failure occurs and the company does not have a backup, usually the only alternative is to re-create the data and reprocess transactions. Often this must be done manually and is quite time consuming. This is the approach organizations have to use when they have not made backups. After using this method one time, an organization usually realizes the importance of making regular backups. Sometimes another option exists. A few companies specialize in extracting data from damaged media. This might be a faster and more economical solution than manual recovery. A good backup policy obviates the need for either of these kinds of recovery.

Disk Editors   **Disk editors** allow the LAN administrator to edit a disk at a variety of levels. At the lowest level, a disk editor allows the administrator to edit data at the disk sector level. Examples of this type of editor in a DOS environment are the Norton Utilities, Mace Utilities, and PC Tools. Some editors provide editing at higher levels, such as those designed to fix dBASE files and structures. Using a disk editor requires a great deal of expertise by the LAN administrator, because it is easy to further corrupt data using these tools.

Disk Utilities   **Disk utilities** vary widely in scope and capabilities. Generally, compared to a disk editor, a disk utility requires less expertise from the LAN administrator to use effectively. A disk utility performs certain functions that do not require the administrator to do much more than enter commands. For example, Novell provides a utility called BINDFIX that examines the bindery files and fixes errors it finds. The **bindery files** are system files that describe the LAN's characteristics, such as user names, passwords, printing configuration, groups, and so on. To use BINDFIX, the administrator simply enters the BINDFIX command, and the utility automatically does its work. Every LAN administrator should have one or more of these utilities available to diagnose or fix disk-related problems.

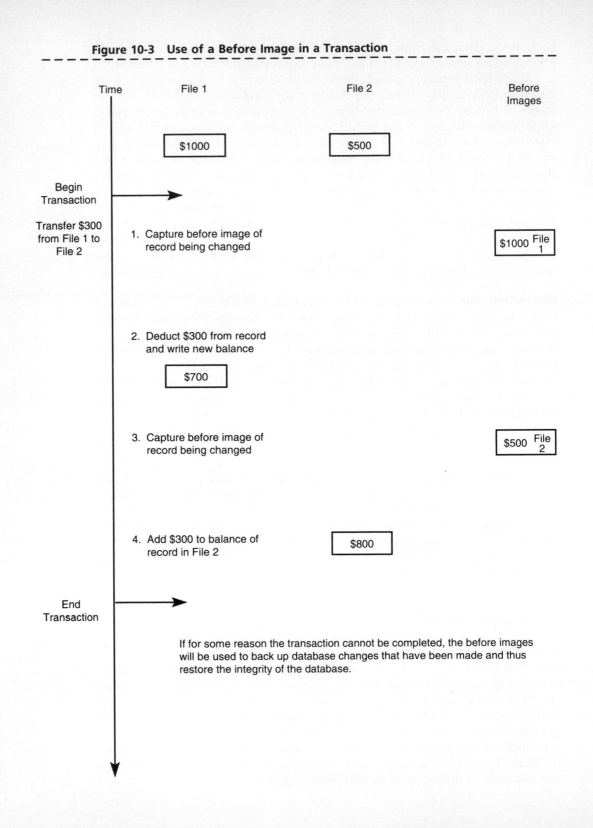

Figure 10-3   Use of a Before Image in a Transaction

Time	File 1	File 2	Before Images

$1000 $500

Begin Transaction

Transfer $300 from File 1 to File 2

1. Capture before image of record being changed

$1000 File 1

2. Deduct $300 from record and write new balance

$700

3. Capture before image of record being changed

$500 File 2

4. Add $300 to balance of record in File 2

$800

End Transaction

If for some reason the transaction cannot be completed, the before images will be used to back up database changes that have been made and thus restore the integrity of the database.

Figure 10-4 Database After Images

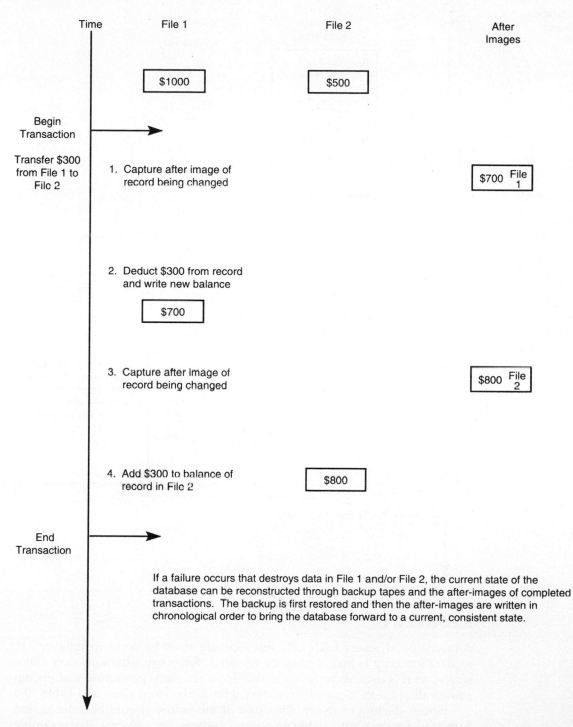

If a failure occurs that destroys data in File 1 and/or File 2, the current state of the database can be reconstructed through backup tapes and the after-images of completed transactions. The backup is first restored and then the after-images are written in chronological order to bring the database forward to a current, consistent state.

268

Chapter 10
LAN
Administration:
Backup and
Recovery

Figure 10-5   Synchronization of Backups and the After-Image Audit Trail

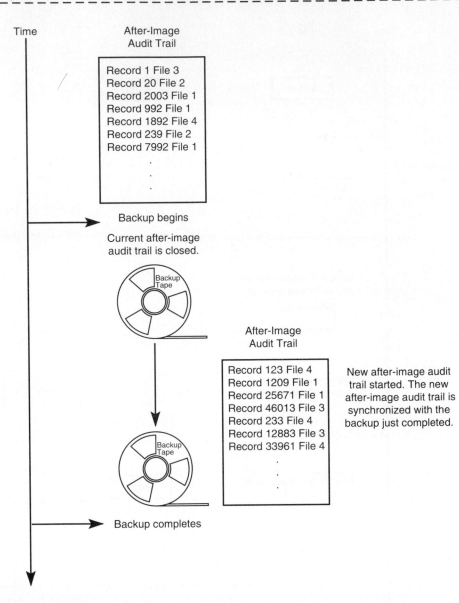

Time

After-Image
Audit Trail

Record 1 File 3
Record 20 File 2
Record 2003 File 1
Record 992 File 1
Record 1892 File 4
Record 239 File 2
Record 7992 File 1
.
.
.

Backup begins

Current after-image
audit trail is closed.

Backup
Tape

After-Image
Audit Trail

Record 123 File 4
Record 1209 File 1
Record 25671 File 1
Record 46013 File 3
Record 233 File 4
Record 12883 File 3
Record 33961 File 4
.
.
.

New after-image audit
trail started. The new
after-image audit trail is
synchronized with the
backup just completed.

Backup
Tape

Backup completes

RECOVERY

At some point, every LAN fails and recovery must be done. Whenever data
or data integrity is lost, it must be restored. Recovery situations vary extensively, so it is unrealistic to try to provide a recovery procedure that encompasses all of them. Generally recovery follows the steps shown in Table 10-3.

Before starting recovery, the cause of the failure should be investigated.
Some events are not readily explained, others are obvious. For example,

suppose a file disappears from the disk. The LAN administrator may never definitively know the cause. Perhaps it was accidentally deleted by an employee, who is not even aware of erasing it. In contrast, a disk head crash is obvious. Whenever the source of the problem can be identified, it should be corrected so it does not happen again.

When backups are used for recovery, the files on the backup tape typically replace those files on disk that have been damaged. Sometimes situations arise that prevent successful restoration; for example, the backup tape may have been damaged midway through the reel, and the data on it past that point cannot be read. Because of this, before starting the restoration process, you should attempt to preserve the corrupted data. This can be done by backing it up, renaming the files, copying the files to another disk, or using a new disk drive. If a problem occurs during restoration, the corrupted files may provide the next best recovery capability.

When you have completed steps 1 and 2 in Table 10-3, you have restored the data on the backup tape. You can restore everything on the backup tape, selectively restore only those files that have been corrupted, or selectively restore only those files needed to put the system back into operation. Less time-critical files can be restored at a more leisurely pace after the system has been restored to operational status. For efficiency, it is best to restore the minimum number of files. Identification of these files should be a part of the recovery procedure. You must care when choosing what files to restore and the version of the backup tape used. Often the most recent backups are used because they are the most current. Sometimes older versions must be used because the problem being corrected has gone undetected for some time and may exist on the most recent backup. In this case restoring data from the most recent backup does not correct the problem.

After restoring the data, you must make sure that the problems have indeed been corrected. As mentioned above, the data errors may be included on the backup and, if so, are reintroduced during restoration. After establishing that the data on the backup is valid, the system can be placed back into operation.

Finally the failure and the recovery events ought to be documented. If possible, new procedures should be drawn up and implemented to reduce the risk of similar problems occurring.

Table 10-3   Recovery Steps

1. Identify and correct the source of the problem.
2. Back up the data that has been corrupted.
3. Restore the most recent, valid backup version of the lost data.
4. Bring the data forward in time until it is both consistent and current.
5. Run diagnostic tests to ensure that the recovery has indeed corrected the problem and that the data is consistent.
6. Document the problem experience, corrective actions, and problems encountered during recovery.
7. Create and implement procedures that avoid similar future occurrences.

270

Chapter 10
LAN
Administration:
Backup and
Recovery

Low-Level Recovery

Once in a while a disk problem occurs that cannot be corrected by simply restoring files: The disk directory or file allocation table may be corrupted, or the problem is localized and can be easily corrected by changing several characters in a file, an index, a disk directory, or the file allocation table. In these instances a well-trained technician with the right tools can carry out recovery without resorting to file restoration. The key to this type of **low-level recovery** is having the right tools and knowing how to use them. A well-intentioned but bad attempt to correct a problem in this way can greatly worsen an existing problem. You may know about tools like the Norton Utilities, Mace Utilities, and Central Point Software's PC Tools for DOS file systems. These tools provide ways to recover lost files and correct data errors on DOS disks. Similar tools exist for most LAN operating systems as well. Be aware that the DOS tools will not work on server disks when the server is running under an operating system other than DOS.

Again, a word of caution when using these low-level recovery tools. Although they can be helpful in some situations, they can also be harmful to your system if not used correctly. They allow the user to make changes to both system and data areas of the disk and can significantly increase the magnitude of the problem. These tools are never a replacement for backup and recovery procedures.

Diagnostic Tools

Two of the recovery steps outlined in Table 10-3 involve finding errors and their causes. Finding some of these problems is made easier with **diagnostic tools.** Diagnostic tools can be hardware or software oriented. We will look at the software diagnostic tools only. Hardware diagnostic tools typically require detailed knowledge of the hardware and are used primarily by hardware engineers. We have already mentioned the low-level disk diagnostic and repair tools, such as Norton Utilities, that contain a variety of checks for the integrity of the operating system portions of the disk; in general, they do not check on the integrity of data stored in files.

Diagnostic tools exist for most common database management system disk areas. DBMS diagnostic tools test the integrity of DBMS portions of the database, such as indexes and block structures. Each DBMS has a strategy for storing data and indexes. Associated with this strategy is overhead data used by the DBMS to carry out its operations. This overhead data is transparent to users of the database; the DBMS uses it on the users' behalf, but the users never see it or manipulate it. Overhead data is not immune to corruption. Database diagnostic tools can analyze the overhead data and determine if it is consistent. If problems are detected, the diagnostic tool reports them and in some cases makes the necessary repairs if the user so directs.

Database administrators often write utility programs to check for the integrity of database data. For example, a retail firm may have customer and order files. Naturally every order must be placed by a customer, and it would not be valid to have an order record that is not related to some customer record. A database utility or query can be used to check for orders that have no associated customer record. A comprehensive DBMS has data integrity rules that automatically prevent the occurrence of an incident like this.

Dealing with Errors

Hardware, software, and human errors are to be expected; however, a network administrator should not put up with repetitive errors. Determining error repetitiveness requires organization and documentation.

Every error encountered on a system should be documented. This includes errors classified as user errors. User errors that recur may be an indication of insufficient training or documentation. The best way to track errors is with a problem-reporting system. The problem-reporting system can be manual or computerized. A computerized problem-reporting system is better able to analyze and track problems and spot trends.

Once a problem has been reported and recorded, resolution begins. The problem must be analyzed and its cause determined. Some errors are caused by users, some by software or procedures created locally, and some by software or hardware furnished by a vendor. The first two cases are resolved locally. Errors caused by vendor supplied hardware or software are usually resolved by the responsible vendor. Problems of this sort are forwarded to the vendor for solution. Responsibility for getting the problem solved, however, remains with the LAN administrator or system support group. Thus, even though the system support person does not solve the problem, he or she is responsible for tracking the progress of the problem, obtaining the solution, and having the corrections installed. A good problem-reporting system assists the support staff in tracking reported problems. We will look at problem diagnosis and correction in more detail in the next chapter.

DISASTER PLANNING

Another component of an organization's recovery procedures and planning ought to be a **disaster plan.** The recovery we discussed earlier addressed issues where single components of a system failed. A disaster plan addresses situations that disable major portions of the system (servers, workstations, cabling, and so on). Disaster planning covers situations arising from fires, earthquakes, floods, and intentional acts of system destruction. In disaster planning the LAN administrator should envision all the scenarios that are likely to occur and make contingency plans that lead to quick and efficient resolution of those scenarios.

It is probably true that most organizations have well-defined backup programs in effect. Those that do not will probably implement one after their first recovery incident (if they are still in business). However, few companies have disaster plans. The prudent LAN administrator has at least the rudiments of such a plan in effect. If the right steps are in place, the LAN administrator can have the network up and running at nearly full capacity

272

Chapter 10
LAN
Administration:
Backup and
Recovery

soon after the disaster has ended. Table 10-4 lists items that should be included in a disaster plan.

A key aspect of a disaster plan is off-site data storage. Hardware and cabling are readily replaced but data, applications, security settings, command files, and so on are not. If the LAN administrator does no more than provide frequent off-site storage of data, he or she has at least set the foundation for disaster recovery.

After planning for software and data recovery, the LAN administrator should also have plans for rebuilding the system. On the hardware side this

Table 10-4 Items Included in a Disaster Plan

Insurance
Amount of insurance coverage for software, hardware, and cabling
Insurance carrier
Steps required to begin replacing/repairing insured components

Software
Location of off-site storage of software
Currency of off-site software backups
Device used to create off-site storage
Sources of replacement software
Companies specializing in recovering data from damaged medium (backup tapes
   and disk drives)

Data
Location of off-site storage of data
Currency of off-site data backups
Device used to create off-site data storage
Methods to bring off-site data forward to a current status
Companies specializing in recovering data from damaged medium (backup tapes
   and disk drives)

Hardware
Workstation configurations
Server configurations
LAN topology/wiring diagrams
Sources of replacement hardware
Sources for repairing broken hardware
Location of spare hardware

Environment
Alternate locations for establishing a new network environment
Minimum requirements for establishing a new network environment

Outside Help
Names of companies specializing in data recovery, setting up a new network, data
   entry, cabling repair, and so on

may include items such as sources of compatible hardware, identification of hardware at other corporate locations that might be commandeered for emergency use, identification of alternate locations for temporarily or permanently installing the new system, and identification of companies specializing in all aspects of LAN hardware, software, cabling, installation, and data recovery. Having these lists of contacts is important for two reasons. First, disasters are unpredictable, and a LAN administrator will not know what LAN components need replacement or repair. Second, having a readily available list of sources for replacement, repair, or assistance saves time during the critical recovery period when time is of the essence.

SUMMARY

All LAN systems fail, even systems configured for fault tolerance. Moreover, even if the hardware and software are not prone to failure, the people using them are. Therefore, it is critical that a LAN administrator have a well-planned set of procedures and policies to recover the system following a failure. One of the major components of a recovery policy is data backups.

Backups are used to restore data and programs to a usable state following a failure that has corrupted the data or software. There are many ways in which data can be corrupted. Regardless of the reason for data corruption, the LAN administrator must have the ability to diagnose the causes, remove the cause of corruption if possible, restore the data to a usable state in a timely way, and restore the network to operational status. Backups are also used for data archiving, temporary storage, and data exchange.

A good backup policy minimizes the work and time needed to recover lost data. It includes details like frequency of backups, off-site storage of backups, backup retention, and disposition of the backup medium after it is no longer needed.

Recovery can sometimes be accomplished without the use of backups. Disk editors and disk utilities are available to fix some problems that may occur. These utilities include capabilities like unerasing files, writing directly to a disk sector, fixing file allocation tables, fixing disk directories, and fixing volume labels. Other utilities are oriented toward patching files in particular formats, such as database index and data files. None of these alternatives are meant as a replacement for taking backups regularly. Improper use of such utilities may compound the problems being experienced.

In addition to backup and recovery plans and procedures, a LAN administrator should also formulate a disaster plan. A disaster plan addresses how to reinstate the network following an event, such as a fire, that disables a major portion of the network. An essential element of a backup policy and disaster plan is off-site backup storage. Off-site storage protects an organization from catastrophes that damage both on-line data and its backups.

274

Chapter 10
LAN
Administration:
Backup and
Recovery

KEY TERMS

archiving

backup

bindery files

comprehensiveness

data recovery

diagnostic tools

disaster plan

disk editor

disk utility

dynamic data

grandfather-father-son generations

low-level recovery

major fault recovery

minor fault recovery

off-site storage

retention policy

static data

REVIEW QUESTIONS

1. What is a data backup?

2. Why do we need data backups?

3. Distinguish between backups of static data and dynamic data.

4. Explain four considerations a LAN administrator must weigh when formulating a backup policy.

5. Why might there be differences between backup policies in different companies?

6. How are disk editors and utilities used in recovery?

7. What are the steps a LAN administrator should take in recovering lost data?

8. What is a disaster plan?

9. How does a disaster plan relate to data recovery?

10. Describe three considerations that should be covered by a disaster plan.

PROBLEMS AND EXERCISES

1. Suppose an organization had never made data backups during its one year in operation. During that time, over 300 MB of data had been accumulated. Suppose further that their server's disk sustained a head crash. How could this organization recover its data? How quickly could the recovery be accomplished?

For questions 2 through 5, consider the following organizational profiles:

A. A medical office has 10 doctors, 14 nurses, and 6 administrative staff. A LAN is used to record patient visits, billing, and insurance claims. The clinic averages 250 patient visits per day. Each visit results in an average of four records being updated. A paper trail exists describing each patient's visit.

B. An office of attorneys has 25 attorneys and 40 support staff. Each attorney and support person has a workstation. All correspondence, trial briefs and notes, legal documents, and so on are stored on mirrored server disks. Both current and noncurrent (aged) documents are stored on the disks. Periodically aged documents must be archived to make room for new work. Much of the current work is time critical; for example, trial notes are needed for trials in session and contracts are needed for scheduled meetings.

C. A university LAN is used to support the academic program only. Students use the LAN to prepare assignments for a variety of classes. The students use programs for static data. The student assignments themselves are, by default, stored on the file server's disks and represent the system's dynamic data. At the beginning of each class, students are warned by their professors that it is the student's responsibility to protect their work files by backing them up to diskette. The university's LAN administrators also have a backup policy.

2. Suppose you were advising each of these organizations regarding a backup policy. Rank them in order of decreasing reliance on frequency of backup (that is, decide which organization would suffer the most from a policy of weekly rather than daily backups.) Justify your answer.

3. Outline a backup policy for each organization you devise. Explain any differences among the policies.

276
- - - - - -
Chapter 10
LAN
Administration:
Backup and
Recovery

4. Suppose each organization experienced a failure that ruined all data on one disk. Explain how each organization would recover from such a problem.

5. Which organization would be most affected by a disaster like a fire? What suggestions regarding disaster planning would you make for that organization?

6. Examine a utility such as Norton Utilities, Mace Utilities, or a disk utility for a specific LAN system. What low-level recovery capabilities does it provide? What is the skill level expected of a user of that utility?

REFERENCES

Carr, Jim. "Making Sense of Backup." *LAN Times*, February 10, 1992.

Cavanagh, Jim. "Smart Backup Within Reach." *LAN Technology*, Volume 8, Number 8, August 1992.

Corrigan, Patrick H. "The Fine Art of Server Backup." *LAN Technology*, Volume 7, Number 8, August 1991.

Crabb, Don. "Backing Up is Hard to Do." *Infoworld*, Volume 12, Issue 7, February 12, 1990.

Dolan, Tom. "Beyond Backup." *LAN*, Volume 7, Number 6, June 1992.

Gentry, Robert M. "Backup for Large Servers: GigaTrend's ServerDAT SL." *LAN Technology*, Volume 7, Number 8, August 1991.

Glass, Brett. "The Backup Safety Net." *Infoworld*, July 23, 1990.

Hurwicz, Michael. "Over Here, Over There." *LAN*, Volume 7, Number 6, June 1992.

"LAN TIMES Tests Data Restore Systems." *LAN Times*, Volume 8, Issue 12, June 17, 1991.

Mathews, Carla. "Network Backup: You Know You Need It." *Infoworld*, May 20, 1991.

Mendelson, Edward. "Premium Insurance: Backup Software Gets Better." *PC Magazine*, Volume 10, Number 11, June 11, 1991.

Seelbach, Geoffre. "Continuous Backup Systems." *Network World*, October 22, 1990.

St. Aubin, Ray and Riser, Joseph. "Anatomy of a Disaster Recovery." *LAN Technology*, Volume 5, Number 11, November 1989.

"Tape Backup Hardware." *LAN*, Volume 7, Number 6, June 1992.

LAN ADMINISTRATION: REACTIVE AND PROACTIVE MANAGEMENT

CHAPTER PREVIEW

In the preceding chapters we covered specific, important LAN administration tasks—installation, security, printing, backup, and recovery. Each of these topics is critical to the overall success of a LAN. However, a LAN administrator must perform additional duties to ensure a successful LAN. These additional duties involve solving unanticipated problems (reactive management) and keeping the LAN running at peak efficiency (proactive management). Although LAN administration efforts cannot completely eliminate unanticipated problems, through good planning, network monitoring, network analysis, and network component tuning, a LAN administrator can reduce the frequency of operating in a reactive mode.

The topics you will read about in this chapter include:

problem identification and correction

system tuning

capacity planning

managing system expansion

network management systems

network management protocols

REACTIVE NETWORK MANAGEMENT

"The network is down!" is a phrase all too familiar to the experienced network manager. Exactly what does this exclamation from a user mean? A LAN administrator could interpret it to mean that the entire network is not functioning, but this is not always the case. What it does mean is the user is unable to redirect requests on his or her workstation over the network in the usual way. The user may have full stand-alone capability, but the services of the network are not currently available. A myriad of reasons, ranging from user error to complete system failure, can cause this to occur. When "the

278

Chapter 11
LAN
Administration:
Reactive and
Proactive
Management

network is down," the network administrator must carry out **reactive network management** to correct the problems experienced by that user.

Consider the LAN illustrated in Figure 11-1. The elements of this system include users, workstations, servers, media, connectors, LAN adapters, and connections to other networks. Each element is subject to failure, which can create network problems. If a problem occurs, the administrator needs the proper tools and the skill to use them to correct it in a timely way. Correcting a problem efficiently can be difficult in a stand-alone LAN because of the variety of equipment and users involved. A LAN problem could be a user, hardware, software, or cabling error. Furthermore, hardware, software, and wiring errors can be at the server or workstation or between the server and workstation. The difficulty in problem resolution lies in the variety of components and possible causes. The ability to find and correct problems be-

Figure 11-1 Connected Local Area Networks

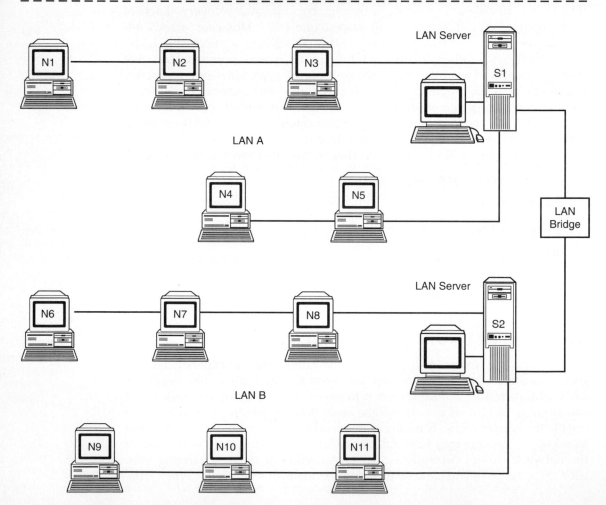

comes even more difficult when administering interconnected LANs. The added difficulty arises from the greater complexity of these networks—the additional interfaces required to make connections between LAN and WAN nodes, the greater variety of data link protocols, media, connectors, and software subsystems that may be responsible for the problem, and the broader knowledge required to diagnose and solve the problem.

Consider one reactive network management problem: Suppose you are a network administrator working at node N1 in Figure 11-1. A user at node N7 reports that he cannot retrieve a file on server S1. Here are a few of the possible causes of this problem:

The user's network software has not been properly started.

The user has forgotten to log onto the network.

The LAN adapter at the user's workstation or server the user is accessing has failed.

There is a wiring problem.

The server is down.

Security is set incorrectly.

Security is set correctly, but the user has no access rights to the file.

The file does not exist.

The bridge connecting the two LANs is not working correctly.

The LAN administrator must define a set of procedures for finding the problem and correcting it, and he or she must have the appropriate tools to locate the problem. This type of analysis is called problem identification and correction.

PROBLEM IDENTIFICATION AND CORRECTION

The following set of procedures is just one of many approaches to solving problems:

1. Information gathering.
2. Diagnosis and analysis.
3. Problem identification.
4. Problem resolution.
5. Documentation.

The sections that follow give you more details on each step.

Information Gathering

Any failure experienced by a user can be the result of user errors, software errors, hardware errors, inappropriate environment settings, or faulty secu-

280
- - - - - -
Chapter 11
LAN
Administration:
Reactive and
Proactive
Management

rity. The first step in problem resolution, **information gathering,** involves the identification of various possible causes of the failure. The LAN administrator must look carefully at the symptoms and identify possible causes. The administrator can then eliminate some of the possibilities because they do not match all of the symptoms. He or she can investigate a possible cause, test it, and prove whether it is causing the problem. When rejecting alternatives, the administrator must be careful, because some problems result from several things being wrong and interacting with each other. Gathering information forms the basis for the diagnostic and analysis phase.

One way of gathering information is by talking to the user. Since many of the errors a LAN administrator encounters are user related or operator errors, the beginning questions should be oriented toward validating or refuting this possibility. The term *operator error* covers a variety of problems that cannot be attributed to malfunctions of the network or its resources. An operator error does not always imply that the user is doing something wrong. Some examples of operator errors were given in the previous section when we described the scenario of the inability to access a network file. Here are some additional examples of incidents usually classified as operator errors:

The user's computer is unplugged.

The user's computer has not been powered up.

The user's keyboard has become unplugged and a screen saver program is in use so touching the keys has no noticeable effect.

The user's AUTOEXEC.BAT file has been modified, and the network interface programs have not been run.

The user is already logged onto another workstation, and the user is limited to only one logon.

Incorrect or incompatible software versions are being used.

Once these sources of errors have been eliminated, the LAN administrator can ask himself or herself, the user, or the user's supervisor any of the following questions:

What are the detailed symptoms of the problem?

What application were you running?

Is running this application within your job scope?

Have you done this task successfully in the past? If so, what is different this time?

What logon ID were you using? Is this the logon ID you should use to do this task?

Have any changes been made to the user's environment recently? If so, what?

What are the implications of not being able to do this?

What is the priority for getting a correction?

The purpose of these questions is to get an understanding of the problem, the user's environment, and the consequences of the user not being able to complete this activity. The consequences are used to set the priority for solving this particular problem.

When preliminary information gathering is complete, the LAN administrator must also learn more about the user's hardware and software environment. Although the administrator probably is familiar with the LAN configuration, it is impossible to remember all the details of each network node; thus, sometimes it is helpful to refresh one's memory regarding details of the hardware and software. The administrator must consult the network documentation to get this information and can use a **configuration management utility,** also called an inventory utility, to get additional current information. A LAN configuration utility maintains hardware and software configurations for all network nodes. Some of the information it collects is given in Table 11-1.

Diagnosis and Analysis

The objective of problem diagnosis and analysis is to isolate the source of the problem. This leads to problem identification and solution. If you have taken a programming class, you may have been exposed to a technique called binary search, which is used to search for an item in an ordered list. You probably use a similar technique to look up names in a telephone book or find words in a dictionary. LAN administrators use this technique to isolate the problem to a specific LAN component—user, workstation, cable segment, server, security, software, environment settings, and so on.

A major LAN failure is sometimes easier to resolve than a failure experienced by a single user or group of users. If many users report the network is down, it is unlikely that the problem is related to a single user or a single workstation. It is then determined to be a problem common to many users. The art of problem determination is somewhat the same in either instance. But the administrator probably begins looking for the problem at different places: For networkwide problems the administrator starts looking at network common resources, such as cabling, LAN adapters, and servers. For user-related problems the investigation usually starts at the user's workstation.

If the preliminary step of data gathering does not lead to a problem solution, the LAN administrator begins the diagnosis and analysis steps. One of the best ways to understand a problem is to observe the user's operating environment. This is easy if the user's office is nearby, but frequently the user's office is some distance away. Even when the user's office is easy to get to, it may be inconvenient to evaluate the problem there. When analyzing most problems, LAN administrators must refer to documentation. This

282

Chapter 11
LAN
Administration:
Reactive and
Proactive
Management

documentation is more apt to be located in the LAN administrator's office than at a user location. By using remote control software, a LAN administrator can experience and analyze problems while maintaining access to documentation in his or her own office.

Table 11-1   LAN Configuration Information

General

Number of servers	Number of workstations
Number of users	Connections to other networks
Backup devices	Hardware serial numbers
Purchase dates	Costs
Support information	Telephone and access numbers

Documentation and procedures

Type
Location
Version

Server and workstations

Network address	NIC configuration
Location	Processor type
Processor speed	Memory
Disk	Device controllers
Controller parameters, e.g., IRQ	BIOS version
Expansion slots	Ports (used and available)
Operating system version	Printers
Directory structures	Startup configuration

Printers

location
type
spooler data

Software

Name	Serial number
Version	License provisions
Server locations	Support information

Users

Access rights—software and hardware	Logon ID
User name	Telephone number
Workstations	Electronic mail address

Network connections

Type	Configuration
Location	Nodes connected

Remote control software allows a user in one location to work with a workstation in another location. Early remote control software had a limited design that allowed two stand-alone workstations to communicate with each other over telephone lines or local lines connected to either a serial or parallel port. Most companies offering these products have enhanced their capabilities so a user can connect to another node using network connections. A list of the capabilities provided by remote control software is given in Table 11-2.

Table 11-2 Features of Remote Control Software

Remote screen display
Remote keyboard entry
Ability for many viewers to be connected to one node
Ability of one viewer to view multiple nodes
Password protection
Audio tone to indicate if someone begins viewing
File transfer
Ability to discover and report the host configuration
Ability to print a memory map of a host
Chat mode, allowing users at both ends to exchange messages over the connection

The principal features of remote control software are the ability to view the monitor of the remote station and the ability to enter commands remotely; basically a remote user can take control of a local workstation. If the administrator can connect to the user's workstation, most problem diagnosis and analysis can be conducted remotely. Moreover, using remote control software can be a good learning experience for users. Users can watch their screen (which is responding to the LAN administrator's remote commands) while the LAN administrator goes through the steps required to solve the problem. This is particularly effective when the problem results from a user error.

If a remote connection is not possible, the LAN administrator usually must go to the user's workstation to further investigate the problem. An inability to make a remote connection can also provide valuable information, such as the cause of a failure of a component along the path to the user or in the user's workstation. If a remote connection can be made to the user's workstation, or to workstations adjacent to the user's, the LAN administrator can conclude that the problem is centered at the local workstation or the workstation-to-medium connection; that is, the problem is local to the workstation itself.

When the administrator has gained access to the user's workstation, he or she can begin to analyze the problem. How the administrator proceeds from this point depends on the types of errors being encountered. The first thing that can be checked is the user's ability to log on to the network, and then the security rights to all necessary files, both program and data, and all

284

Chapter 11
LAN
Administration:
Reactive and
Proactive
Management

directories in which the user is working can be checked. Once security settings are established, they seldom change; however, installing new software, adding or deleting users, or other administration activities can result in changes to security settings. Let us look at two examples that might result in changing users' security settings. When new software is placed on a network server, the network administrator must set up security so that users can access the application. In general, program files are secured so they can be run but not copied or modified, most other files are secured as read-only, and perhaps a few files are secured so users can write to them. Setting up security for new applications means giving new access rights to users and groups. Security settings may also need to be changed when a user's job function changes. A payroll administrator who was not allowed to make salary changes may receive a promotion. The administrator's new responsibilities may include making salary changes. This requires a change in the administrator's security settings.

Checking security takes only a few moments and can save several hours of investigation into other potential sources of a problem. If the LAN administrator can run the application while logged onto the user's workstation with the supervisor's ID, it is likely that the problem is in the security setup; a security or user ID problem is the likely problem in this instance because the supervisor ID allows logon and gives access to all files. If the supervisor ID can successfully avoid the problem experienced by a user ID with lesser security capabilities, it is highly probable that the user has lost access or does not have the proper access to some essential resource.

If security settings prove to not be the problem, the next step in the process of problem diagnosis and analysis begins—determining if a workstation component (hardware or software) is responsible. One of the easiest ways to demonstrate an error in a local workstation component is to attempt the same process from a workstation near the one the user is unable to use correctly. If the problem is not exhibited at the nearby workstation, it is likely that the original workstation or its connection to the medium is at fault.

Another good technique to use at this point is to duplicate the problem using **known good components.** One of the tools in a LAN administrator's arsenal should be a complete, portable, standard-configured workstation that is known to be good. The administrator brings the known good machine to the user's location and connects it to the network. If the problem does not go away using the portable workstation, then it is likely that the problem is outside the local workstation itself.

A simple, easy way to test the reliability of a LAN adapter is to use a **pocket LAN adapter.** A pocket LAN adapter is portable and provides network connection through the parallel or serial port of a workstation. Frequently used to attach portable workstations to a network, a pocket LAN adapter is also a useful diagnostic tool for LAN administrators. It is easy to attach and quickly eliminates or identifies the LAN adapter as the problem source. If the user can access the file using the pocket LAN adapter, the problem is likely a broken LAN adapter.

Another source of workstation problems is application and network software. The LAN administrator must check to see if the user's workstation is running the proper versions of the proper network operating system software. For example, if the user has just upgraded the workstation's operating system but has not made corresponding changes to the workstation's network operating system software, an incompatibility might exist. Therefore, one diagnostic step is to verify the compatibility of all versions of software being used.

If the workstation is eliminated as the problem, the next step is to check the path between the user and the server—including wiring, hardware, and software. Wiring problems are the most frequent source of resource request failures, so the LAN administrator should check the wiring first. Wire continuity can be checked with a **cable tester,** which generates a signal on the medium and monitors the signal. Cable testers can determine if there is a short or break in a cable and pinpoint the problem location within inches. Table 11-3 lists some functions of a cable tester.

It may be that the problem is a hardware malfunction that results in garbled messages. To check for transmission errors, the LAN administrator uses a **protocol analyzer** or a LAN analyzer. The protocol analyzer checks message packets for errors and notifies the user of the type and source of errors it receives. Protocol analyzer capabilities are listed in Table 11-4.

Table 11-3   Cable Tester Functions

Cabling	**Protocols**
Coaxial Cable	Token ring
Twisted-pair wire	Ethernet
Fiber optic cable	ARCnet
	StarLAN

Faults Detected
Cable
Connector
Transceiver
Terminators

Table 11-4   Protocol Analyzer Functions

Utilization statistics	Number of packets sent by a node
Number of packets received by a node	Packet errors
Data logging	Test packet transmission
Packet filtering	Logging of protocol headers
Logging of data portion of packets	Network load statistics
Alarms sounding	Cable testing
Support for multiple protocols	Printed reports

286
- - - - - -
Chapter 11
LAN
Administration:
Reactive and
Proactive
Management

Finally, the problem may be related to the server itself. A user may not be able to log on because of a problem with the user ID file or network system files (perhaps the user's ID has even been deleted). In Novell NetWare LAN systems prior to NetWare Version 4.0, information such as user IDs and passwords are kept in a set of files called **bindery files.** Bindery files are not immune to errors (although they are seldom corrupted). Novell provides a utility, BINDFIX, to examine bindery files and correct any errors it detects.

Identification and Resolution

Once the LAN administrator has correctly identified the problem, it must be corrected. The problem dictates the solution. Since there are so many different types of problems, it is impractical to attempt to discuss here how to solve each one. After the correction is made, the LAN administrator notifies the user that the problem has been corrected and ensures that the user is able to continue with his or her work.

Documentation

Fixing the problem is not the last step in reactive administration. The LAN administrator must also document the problem and its solution. Sometimes one problem occurs several times. Having good documentation of previous problems and their solutions can significantly reduce the time it takes to correct a problem that appears again. Realize that the person who solved the first problem may not be available when a problem reappears. Documentation can assist a new person in solving a problem as well as refresh the memory of the LAN administrator who solved the problem initially.

All the information gathered during the problem-solving process should be documented. You can do this manually, or you can use a **problem reporting and tracking system,** which automates the data-gathering process and provides a fast, efficient mechanism for finding problems of a similar nature, solutions to previous problems, and the status of open problems. A problem reporting and tracking system is a valuable network administration tool. An illustration of a form that might be produced by such a system is shown in Table 11-5.

PROACTIVE NETWORK MANAGEMENT

Ideally the network administrator anticipates problems and corrects them before they occur. This type of administration is called **proactive network management.** This is not always possible because an administrator cannot usually anticipate hardware and software failures. Some problems, however, result from gradual changes. For instance, the time it takes to transfer a file from a server to a workstation takes increasingly longer as the LAN workload increases. The workload consists of the messages that are transferred over the medium, the processing done by LAN servers, and the work done at the workstations themselves. When the number of messages being transmitted increases and the servers become busier processing those messages, the time it takes to complete a single request like a file transfer increases. Sometimes the LAN has enough spare capacity to make the time increase scarcely noticeable. But if the LAN is already near capacity performance, additional work can cause significant degradation in performance. A good LAN administrator notices these changes and takes steps to avoid their becoming major problems for the LAN users. This type of administration is called performance monitoring and **system tuning.**

Another LAN administration task is **capacity planning,** which basically is planning for the future. An administrator must gauge the impact of adding new users, adding new applications, and upgrading existing applications and the network operating software itself. As a LAN evolves, additional hardware and software resources often must be added to sustain adequate performance. The administrator must determine what new components are needed, where they must be placed, and who needs access to them.

In carrying out these duties, the LAN administrator must create and maintain documentation of various types. Included among these are procedures and policies covering topics like backup and restore, recovery, security, adding and deleting users, hardware and software configurations, user profiles, a performance monitoring database, a system log, and a problem reporting, tracking, and resolution system.

SYSTEM TUNING AND CAPACITY PLANNING

System tuning is the art of monitoring a network, analyzing the statistics gathered from monitoring, and using that information to keep the system

Table 11-5 Problem Reporting and Tracking

Problem Identifier: _____ Date: __/__/__

Received by: _____ Time: __:__ AM/PM

Reported by: _____ Telephone: (__)__-_____

Department: _____ Dept. Telephone: (__)__-_____

Other Contacts: _____ Telephone(s): (__)__-_____

Location: _____

Urgency: __ Extremely High   __ High   __ Moderate   __ Low

Key Words: _____   _____   _____   _____   _____

Problem Description:

Software Involved: Hardware Involved:

Problem Consequences: Workarounds:

Assigned to: 1. _____   Telephone: (__)__-_____   Date: __/__/__

2. _____   Telephone: (__)__-_____   Date: __/__/__

3. _____   Telephone: (__)__-_____   Date: __/__/__

Status: Solution:

Solved by: _____   Telephone: (__)__-_____   Date: __/__/__

Installed by: _____   Date: __/__/__

Users Notified by: _____   User(s) Contacted: _____

Telephone: (__)__-_____   Date: __/__/__   Time: __:__ AM/PM

288

Chapter 11
LAN
Administration:
Reactive and
Proactive
Management

running at an acceptable level. Capacity planning is planning for future changes like additional users or applications and ensuring the proper resources are available to provide good service when the changes are implemented. Let us first look at system tuning.

Tuning a System

A variety of tools can be used to assist the LAN administrator in tuning a network. In general, these tools gather and analyze network performance data. One of the primary tools used to do this is a **network management system (NMS).** A good NMS has both data collection and analysis components and creates monitors that raise alarms or alerts if performance degenerates below certain levels. A network administrator uses the NMS to gather and analyze network performance data. Even when there are no obvious problems to correct, the administrator periodically generates and studies reports on the data gathered. The purpose of this analysis is to identify changes in how the network is operating, identify reasons for these changes, and, if necessary, to tune the network to maintain a satisfactory level of service. An NMS plays such an important role in LAN administration that we dedicate an entire section to it later in this chapter.

Another tool used in tuning is a network analyzer. The network analyzer reports on the type and number of packets being sent, the number of transmission errors encountered, and so on. This data can be used to spot system performance problems.

Network use changes over time. It sometimes seems that networks undergo constant change. New nodes are added, new software introduced, users change their work patterns, LANs may be interconnected, and so on. These changes alter the LAN's workload and can change its responsiveness. For example, suppose that a word processing system is upgraded to a new version. Perhaps the new version requires more memory for the software and has new features, such as graphics support or links to spreadsheets. Some users may move immediately to the new software, while others may remain with the older version. This seemingly insignificant change in user resources can have a noticeable affect on the LAN. With users requesting two different word processing programs rather than one, the file server could be less efficient. The server now has to read two sets of execution files instead of one, disk cache is likely to be used more extensively, and there may be fewer cache hits resulting in a decrease in server performance. If there were only one version of word processing software, the file server might satisfy several user needs with one disk access. If the newer version of word processing software has larger execution or operating files, more data must be transferred over the network. If the newer version supports graphics, users may want to transfer large graphic images from their workstation to the server (or vice versa) more often. Even if this one event does not substantially change network performance, a collection of such changes will.

In looking at network performance statistics, the network administrator attempts to find areas where performance is degrading or where other problems seem to be developing. For instance, higher than normal error rates or peak usage bottlenecks are key indicators of potential problems ahead. If any problems are found, the administrator must plan a strategy to resolve them. Sometimes this can be done by **balancing** network components, and sometimes additional hardware components must be added to solve the problem.

Balancing the network involves a juggling act of sorts, requiring the administrator to make use of existing resources but in a slightly different configuration. The administrator may find that one network printer is in constant use while another is relatively idle. Changing the default printer of one or more users to the idle printer may resolve the problem, or moving the low-use printer to another location may make it more convenient and increase its use. Of course, this will not solve the problem if users are overriding the default printer selection and manually directing their output to another printer. If this happens, the administrator should evaluate the printing configuration and attempt to modify it so that default printer selection is the one preferred by each user, keeping in mind the need to balance printing resource requests.

As another example of balancing, suppose two LANs are connected via a bridge, as in Figure 11-1. A **bridge** is a device that connects two similar networks together. If the administrator notices that node N1 on LAN A consistently sends most of its messages to nodes on LAN B, the administrator can transfer node N1 to be part of the configuration of LAN B and reduce the load on the bridge.

A network administrator's first objective is to resolve performance problems by balancing, but if that is not possible or practical, then purchasing or allocating additional hardware may solve the problem. For example, if an administrator notices that the memory swap rate for a file server is too high, he or she can solve the problem in two ways: reduce the memory pressure on the server by off-loading some of its work onto another server or add more memory. Today hardware prices are low enough that it is sometimes cheaper and more expedient to add new hardware than spend a great deal of time attempting to balance the system. However, funding may not always lend itself to this luxury, because most companies do not allow for such expenditures in their budgeting process. Some companies tend to budget for direct resources needed due to an increase in the number of users (for example, new workstations and LAN adapters) and ignore the extra burden of network performance needs.

Sometimes, when tuning a system through balancing or adding hardware, several corrective alternatives are available. The primary rule of system tuning is that you change only one thing at a time. Systems tend to be complicated, and one system component can interact with many other components on the network. When the LAN administrator makes a change in anticipation of improving performance, the change may have a negative effect in another, unanticipated area and actually make the overall system performance worse. If you make several changes at once, it is difficult to determine which change is most responsible for any new problems. The general process of tuning is outlined as follows:

290

Chapter 11
LAN
Administration:
Reactive and
Proactive
Management

1. Measure system performance—collect and analyze data.

2. Identify possible solutions to a problem.

3. Choose one solution that has the highest merit—the best gain, the best gain in efficiency and returned performance per cost of implementation, or the quickest and easiest to implement.

4. Install and test the selected solution.

5. Evaluate the results.

6. If performance is still lacking go back to step 1.

7. Implement and document the solution.

Tuning requires an in-depth knowledge of the network's hardware and software and the interactions between them. Such knowledge is essential for analyzing data and distinguishing between normal and abnormal results, for identifying potential solutions, for understanding the implications of the different alternatives, for selecting the best solution to try, for making the changes, and for evaluating the results. A misguided but well-intentioned attempt to improve the system can cause serious problems.

Capacity Planning

Capacity planning is a key responsibility of the network administrator. We have already stated that a network is a dynamic entity. Performance analysis and tuning keeps the system running correctly under the existing but perhaps changing workload. Capacity planning is the art of anticipating the workload of the network months or years in advance and taking steps to ensure that the network is able to withstand future loads. Capacity planning is an ongoing activity. Sometimes, however, specific events trigger the need to do capacity planning. For example, if a new department is to be added to an existing LAN, the administrator must anticipate the added hardware and software needs and the adjustments that must be made to accommodate the new users while continuing to meet the needs of existing users. If an existing LAN is to be connected to another existing LAN, the administrator must anticipate their change, plan the necessary reconfiguration to accommodate this, order new equipment, plan for the installation of the new equipment, configure and install it, evaluate its performance, and tune the entire network system for optimal performance. In these instances, you definitely do not want to just add the new connections, place the network into operation, and see what happens!

Among the many tools that have been developed for capacity planning on microcomputers, three are particularly effective: performance monitors, simulation models, and workload generators. We will cover performance monitors in the section on network management systems later in this chapter. Let us now look at the other two tools, simulation models and workload generators.

Simulation Models Simulating an object means constructing a model of how the object works and estimating characteristics of the object though working with the model. The **simulation models** can be physical or logical. Automotive and aeronautical engineers often build physical models of cars or airplanes to determine their air flow characteristics. They do this by placing the models in a wind tunnel—a simulated object in a simulated environment. Alternatively, a logical model uses software modules to simulate the performance of objects, thus eliminating the need to build expensive physical models. For example, you can simulate a file server by combining models of the medium, server disks, server CPU, and other server components. You can drive this model by sending it simulated requests and letting the server software simulation modules operate on those requests. By varying the number and type of requests, you can estimate how the server performs in a variety of situations. Naturally these estimates are only as good as the model's ability to accurately represent the server's characteristics. By adding modules representing other LAN components, you can simulate the performance of an entire LAN or even a network of LANs and WANs. Moreover you can conceivably run the simulation on a single microcomputer.

Simulation models allow the user to describe network hardware configurations and application activities. The model analyzes how the system can be expected to perform under the described conditions. This is useful for estimating response times, processor utilization, line congestion, and potential bottlenecks. During operational situations, simulation models help determine what size of transaction load will reach or exceed the network's capacity and the effect of adding new applications and nodes to the existing system. A good simulation model in the capacity planning process can avert performance problems at implementation time.

Simulation models vary significantly with respect to the amount of information they provide and the manner in which the user defines the workload. A simple model for cable segment utilization might interactively prompt the user for the speed of the line, the data link protocol to use, the message size, the average number of messages per transaction, and the number of nodes on the segment. This limited model produces a report indicating the segment performance and the maximum and average response times a user might expect. A comprehensive model, on the other hand, uses a network configuration file and a transaction file as input (both user supplied). The configuration file contains the complete hardware configuration, including disk drives, disk drive performance characteristics, line speeds, data link protocols, node types, and file locations. The transaction file contains a list of transaction types and the activities each transaction performs, such as the number of inputs and outputs to a server's disk and the number of characters transferred between a server and a node.

In addition to the two user-supplied files, the simulation model is driven by software performance characteristics, such as LAN operating system overhead, instruction execution times, and disk access times. Such a model outputs information on expected response times, line utilization, processor

292

Chapter 11
LAN
Administration:
Reactive and
Proactive
Management

utilization, disk utilization, and so forth. Essentially the model enables the user to see how the system performs without ever implementing it. For example, if the model predicts that a particular server will have 200 percent utilization and a response time to 2 minutes, then either a more powerful server or additional servers are needed to support the workload.

The time required to set up a simulation run varies with the amount of detail needed. A detailed, comprehensive model requires a considerable amount of information regarding the application. Usually it is unnecessary to have the correct initial configuration, as the model indicates areas of over and under utilization.

Workload Generators   Whereas the simulation model estimates system utilization and can be run on a single microcomputer, a **workload generator** actually generates transaction loads for execution on the proposed configuration. If the simulation model and the workload generator were perfect, the results would be identical; in actual practice, however, some variation between the two is likely. A workload generator together with a performance monitor can illustrate how the system will actually function in the proposed configuration. It can also be used for stress testing. Unlike the simulation model, which can be used without an actual system in place, the workload generator requires that you build the network to test it out. It is therefore more often used when acquiring a new LAN.

As with any model, the above models are only as good as the input, the people who use and interpret it, and the closeness of the models to real life. Their value decreases with the amount of time required to utilize them and increases with their ability to accurately portray an application. This means that they should be used carefully and the results interpreted sensibly.

Planning System Expansion

If, as a result of capacity planning, the network administrator sees a need to add hardware or software, the changes must be planned carefully. System expansion should begin with documentation, hardware and software acquisition, site planning and site preparation. Configuration of the upgrade (discussed in the next section) includes installation, testing, training, and placing the changes into operation. An upgrade is, after all, a microcosm of a LAN acquisition.

Documentation   As usual, documentation is pervasive. It occurs at each step in the upgrade process. The LAN administrator documents the new hardware and software needs and the justification and costs of the upgrade. Each of the following steps also include documentation.

Hardware and Software Acquisition   The steps a LAN administrator takes in acquiring the upgrade equipment vary from one organization to another and sometimes depend on the cost of the upgrades. Many organizations, particularly government organizations, have a limited amount that can be spent without higher approval or submitting the equipment to a competitive bid. If bids must be invited, the administrator must have a process for evaluating the responses and selecting a choice. Sometimes the acquisition must be done formally via a request for proposal (RFP). The RFP outlines the objectives of the equipment being sought and solicits vendors to provide a solution to the problem. Because the responses may differ significantly, evaluating them and selecting the best one can be a time-consuming process. Remember to assure that capacity planning and costs associated with this are included as well.

Site Planning and Preparation   Once the upgrade equipment has been selected, the LAN administrator must plan for its installation. If new hardware is to be added, he or she may have to prepare the hardware location. For example, power outlets may need to be installed, cables may need to be run to the location, and so on.

CONFIGURATION OF HARDWARE AND SOFTWARE UPGRADES

Installing an upgrade is different from installing a new LAN. Installing hardware and software upgrades affects existing LAN users, whereas initial LAN installation is not impeded by the needs of existing users. LAN administrators must plan upgrades carefully to minimize the disruption to LAN users. Often this means doing the installation and testing when the LAN is being used the least, probably on a weekend, on a holiday, or during early morning hours. Ideally the administrator can first install and test all hardware and software upgrades on an experimental LAN, that is, a small LAN separate from the production LAN. The experimental LAN is used by LAN administrators and programmers to test new hardware and software before installing them on a production. This approach detects most of the flaws in the installation process and the equipment itself and eliminates many of the causes for delays and user disruptions. Many installations do not have the luxury of an experimental LAN and make all changes directly to the operational system.

Upgrade Configuration Steps

The four steps to configuring an upgrade are installation, testing, training, and making the changes operational. Let us briefly describe these steps and then look more closely at software upgrades.

Installation   When the equipment arrives and the site has been prepared, the new hardware and software can be configured and installed. If the new hardware being installed is for a server, the LAN or a portion of the LAN may have to be taken out of service temporarily. Alternatively, if there are several available servers, the LAN may continue operation but at a reduced capacity. If this is the case, the installation should be scheduled so there is a minimal disruption to the users.

Testing   After the upgrade has been installed, the LAN must be tested. Security settings must be checked to ensure that users have access to all the

294

Chapter 11
LAN
Administration:
Reactive and
Proactive
Management

necessary system components and that the new equipment works correctly and interfaces correctly to other parts of the system. Since the upgrade is intended to solve a particular problem, the LAN administrator should also check to see if the expectations of the changes were realized. If problems are encountered, they may take several hours or even days to correct. Thus, in many cases, testing of this type is done on weekends or during the evening to minimize disruption to system users and the conduct of the business.

Training If new capabilities are added to the LAN, users may need new training to learn how to use them. Training should occur before any of the changes are implemented so users will be ready, not confused, when the changes are made operational. Additional training must be available after the changes have been implemented to help users who missed the initial training session. LAN operators and administrators may also need training in the use and maintenance of the equipment. Ideally users and administrators will be able to complete their training when the new capabilities are made available.

Making Changes Operational Once the testing and training are completed, the changes are placed into operation. The LAN administrator should closely monitor the system immediately after making changes. The need for additional tuning of the hardware may surface after the system is used under the normal workload.

Planning Software Upgrades

Planning hardware upgrades and planning software upgrades are equally important tasks. Software upgrades, however, often have a more disruptive effect on users. Many hardware upgrades, such as adding a new disk to a file server, a new workstation to the network, or a new connection to another network, can be made fairly transparent to users because these changes can be accommodated through drive mappings and startup configuration settings. It is usually not so easy to disguise changes in software; therefore, the LAN administrator must carefully plan the migration of users from one version of software to another. There are many variations in the complexity of upgrading software, and we cannot begin to cover all of them. Therefore, to provide you with a general understanding of the issues, let us examine a specific situation, upgrading from one version of a word processor to a new version. The issues we will discuss are similar to those relating to installing a new version of a network operating system, a new workstation operating system, or other application software.

A new software version often has additional functions. To enable the new functions requires a change in the user's interface and may require changes in the format of files created by the application. Suppose, for example, that your current word processor is a DOS application and you have decided to upgrade to a graphical user interface (GUI) version. You have chosen this change because it has a dramatic effect on the way users can interact with the word processor. Some issues you must deal with are user transition, file compatibility, and reliability.

User Transition If the software upgrade is for a network or workstation operating system, a user will make the transition from the old software to the new software when the new version is installed. With application software this is not necessarily the case. As the LAN administrator you should make the old and new versions available for some time, perhaps a year or more. Some users resist change or are slow to learn new interfaces, while others readily adapt to new situations. You must try to minimize the trauma associated with software changes by giving change-resistent users a reasonable time to make the transition from the old system to the new. With the new word processor users click an icon in the GUI to start the application rather than typing a command at a DOS prompt, and they use menus, button bars, scroll bars, and other GUI features to work with the document rather than function keys or control key sequences. Eventually, however, you want to have all users converted to the new system, because running several versions of one application requires extra disk space and duplication in support and documentation. To do this, you must work with the company's management team to plan an orderly transition from the old system to the new one.

File Compatibility Sometimes new software versions require a new file format to accommodate new capabilities. In your word processor change, the windows version may provide new graphics options. A document that makes use of these new capabilities either is unusable in the old version or, if usable, is not able to display the new graphics images correctly. This, of course, can cause problems when documents are worked on by users who are not using the same software version.

Reliability New software systems are more likely to have bugs than older software because widespread software use uncovers bugs not caught during prerelease testing. These bugs are usually corrected by the software vendor and made available to users. For this reason, it is often wise to pilot a new application for several weeks before making a commitment to widespread corporate use. The LAN administrator and corporate management select a group of users who can begin working with the new application. Only those users have access to the product. After several weeks of error-free use, the application can be made available to other users. The pilot group should be selected so that as many of the capabilities of the new system as possible can be exercised. A pilot project not only helps check for reliability but also discloses problems with installation, user configuration, and training.

NETWORK MANAGEMENT SYSTEMS

Earlier in this chapter we described tools a network administrator can use to tune a system. We now take a closer look at one of those tools, a network management system (NMS). An NMS monitors the network operation, gathers network statistics, identifies parameters that are out of tolerance, raises alarms when faults are detected, and, in some systems, suggests ways to correct problems. A network management system therefore allows the

296

Chapter 11
LAN
Administration:
Reactive and
Proactive
Management

LAN administrator to resolve problems that have been reported as well as spot potential problems before they become critical. An NMS is therefore used for both reactive and proactive network management tasks. Table 11-6 lists the functions of a network management system.

Figure 11-2 illustrates the components of a generic network management system. The basic components are devices, device agents or monitors, filters, an alarm or alert, a report generator, a network control center, a network database, network management software, a network management console, a disk drive, and a printer.

Monitors, or **agents,** located throughout the network, can be dedicated hardware or software devices, or they can be intelligent network devices like bridges, hubs, or intelligent microcomputer device controllers. For example, an intelligent bridge can collect information about the number of packets that must be switched from one network to another and the stations responsible for the internetwork transfers. A microchannel or EISA disk controller can report disk access statistics. A monitor continually collects information from components for which it is responsible. Naturally the data monitored varies from device to device. Table 11-7 is a list of representative components and their items that can be monitored. Monitor software passes it's information to network management software components for storage and evaluation.

Network management software collects data from the monitors. The data is usually stored in a database for later analysis. Usually current data is kept in detail form for analysis. After being analyzed, the data should be summarized and stored in a historical database. The historical database is a source of data for spotting network trends that evolve slowly. The network management software also analyzes the data it receives and looks for abnormalities. For example, on a network link a few data transmission errors are likely to occur; however, if the transmission error rate starts to increase, it may indicate the beginning of a problem. When the network management software spots such trends, it forwards out-of-tolerance data to a network control center through a filter. If control is distributed, the system must have several network control centers.

The **filter** receives warning messages, reformats them, forwards the messages to one or more control centers, and suppresses redundant messages. The message may need to be reformatted to make it compatible for

Table 11-6   Network Management System Functions

Event logging	Alerts and alarms
Expert system problem diagnosis	Graphic presentation
Virus protection	User logon statistics
Message traffic statistics	Workstation status monitoring
Server status monitoring	Media monitoring
Automatic log backup	Network topology graphs
Trend analysis	Intruder detection
Meters use of software licenses	

Figure 11-2 Network Management System Components

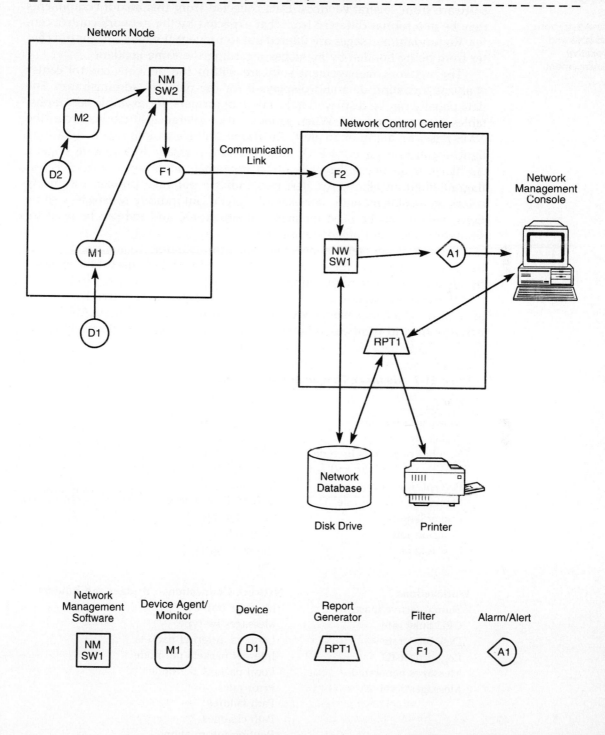

298

Chapter 11
LAN
Administration:
Reactive and
Proactive
Management

the recipient. Realize that today's networks often integrate hardware and software from several vendors. Data collected from this mix of components may be in a format different from that expected by the network control center. Redundant messages are filtered out to prevent the network control center from being flooded by messages regarding the same incident.

The network management software within the network control center analyzes incoming data and displays it for the network administrator. The data usually can be displayed in a variety of formats, for example, as graphs, tables, or formatted text. When serious out-of-tolerance situations occur, the NMS raises an alarm or an alert. An **alarm** can be an audio signal, a flashing light, a call to a pager, a FAX message, or a message to a remote system. An alarm is an event that will attract immediate attention. An **alert** is less flagrant than an alarm. An alert may indicate potential problems by using colors on a color monitor. For example, green can indicate satisfactory situations, yellow can be used for marginal situations, and red can be used for situations needing immediate attention.

The **report generator** allows network administrators to analyze data that has been captured in the network database. This data is useful for spotting trends and for capacity planning.

Network management is a weak spot in many vendor networks, but it is an area in which capabilities are rapidly improving. Sometimes LAN administrators turn to third-party network management tools to effectively moni-

Table 11-7   Network Component Monitoring

Medium	Server
Number of packets	Print queue status
Packets in error	Status—active/inactive
Number of packets by type	CPU busy rate
Packets per node in and out	Memory utilization
Percent utilization	Disk busy rate
Maximum transfer rate	Disk available space
Packet lengths	Cache hit rate
Collision rate	Swap rate
Lost tokens	Queue lengths
	Print activity

Workstations	Network Connections—Bridges and Routers
Status—active/inactive	Message traffic
CPU busy rate	Messages by type
Disk busy rate	Local vs. Internet packets
Logon user ID	Internet packets per node
Messages generated	Local packets per node
Messages received	Error rates
	Path failures
	Path changes
	Routing information

tor their networks. As a network grows, so does the need for effective network management tools. If the network consists of components from multiple vendors, you will need a management system capable of obtaining statistics from them and placing the data into usable formats. Network management systems of this type are called **integrated network management systems**.

NETWORK MANAGEMENT PROTOCOLS

Network management can be complicated, even on homogeneous networks. Network interconnection and a variety of vendor equipment make the management task even more difficult because it is harder to collect and analyze data. Monitoring nodes on one LAN from a node on a different LAN (for example, monitoring a node on a token ring from a network management console attached to a CSMA/CD bus network or from a management console on a WAN) is harder than monitoring nodes on a single homogeneous LAN. To facilitate the exchange of management data among different types of network nodes and devices, a network management standard or protocol is essential. If such standards exist, network designers can build their networks with components that have the ability to capture and exchange management and control data. Two such standards have evolved, the Simple Network Management Protocol (SNMP) and the Common Management Information Protocol (CMIP).

Simple Network Management Protocol (SNMP)

The Simple Network Management Protocol (SNMP) is based on the Transmission Control Protocol/Internet protocol (TCP/IP) file transfer protocol (see Chapter 14). Since the first products appeared in 1988, it has rapidly gained in acceptance and popularity and is endorsed by companies like IBM, Hewlett-Packard, and Sun Microsystems. It has also been approved by the Internet Activities Board (IAB).

SNMP has four key components: the protocol itself, the **structure of management information (SMI)**, the **management information base (MIB)**, and the network management system (NMS). The SNMP protocol is an application layer protocol that outlines the formal structure for communication among network devices. The SMI details how every piece of information regarding managed devices is represented in the MIB. The MIB is a database that defines the hardware and software elements to be monitored. The NMS is the control console to which network monitoring and management information is reported. The SNMP environment is illustrated in Figures 11-3 and 11-4. These figures show a bridge connecting two LANs. We discuss bridges in Chapter 13.

SNMP allows network managers to get the status of devices and set or initialize devices. If problems occur, an event mechanism generates a message that is displayed on the network monitoring console.

Being a simple protocol, SNMP has a few shortcomings. Its command set is limited, it has limited provisions for security, and, lacking a strict stan-

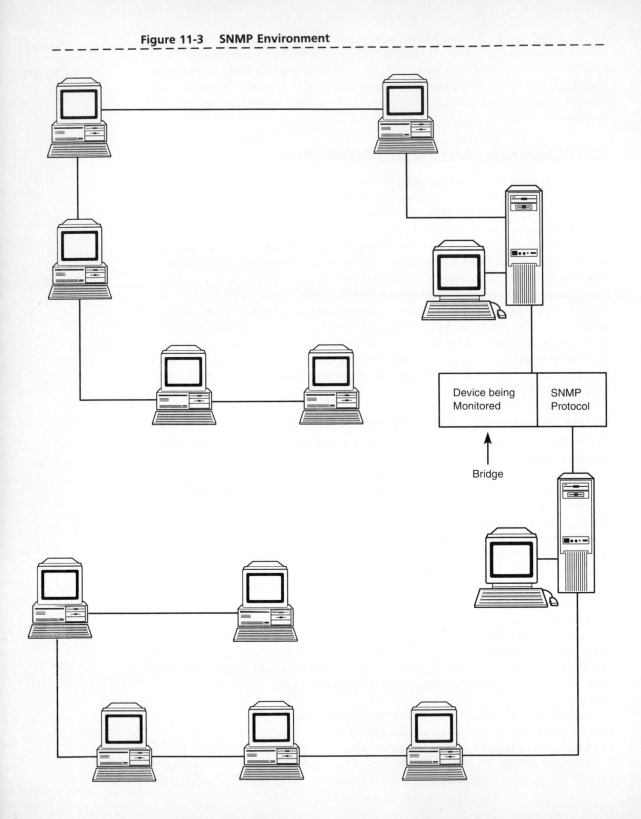

Figure 11-3   SNMP Environment

Device being Monitored

SNMP Protocol

Bridge

Figure 11-4 Details of SNMP Environment

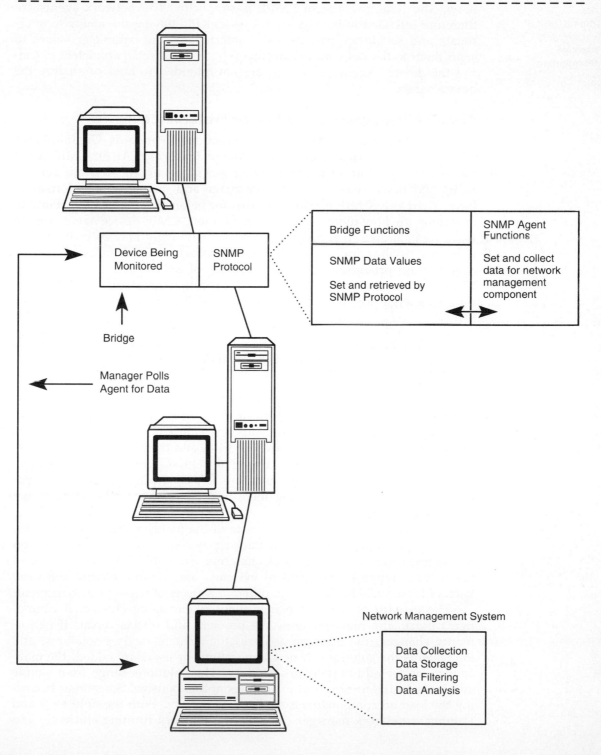

Bridge Functions	SNMP Agent Functions
SNMP Data Values Set and retrieved by SNMP Protocol	Set and collect data for network management component

Device Being Monitored

SNMP Protocol

Bridge

Manager Polls Agent for Data

Network Management System

Data Collection
Data Storage
Data Filtering
Data Analysis

302

Chapter 11
LAN
Administration:
Reactive and
Proactive
Management

dard, there are some inconsistencies among different vendor's implementations. The basic premise of SNMP is simplicity. The network agents are therefore intended to be very simple, essentially having the ability to interrogate and set device parameters. It interrogates the parameter values to send them to the network management system and sets parameters to control the device. Agents, however, are not intended to filter or analyze the device's data.

Common Management Information Protocol (CMIP)

In competition with SNMP is the International Standards Organization's (ISO's) **Common Management Information Protocol (CMIP).** CMIP has a more complex protocol for exchanging messages among network components and has a richer command language and management information base. Therefore, CMIP has the potential for better control and the ability to overcome the limitations of SNMP. In addition, CMIP device agents can be more sophisticated than SNMP agents. A CMIP agent may be given the intelligence to filter and analyze the data it collects. Unfortunately, there are currently no provisions for interoperability of SNMP and CMIP. Because CMIP was developed later than SNMP, operational systems are just beginning to emerge. It will take some time for CMIP to overcome the impetus of SNMP.

SUMMARY

Network management is an important LAN activity. It consists of solving network problems, monitoring performance, tuning LAN components, network capacity planning, and installing new components. Some of these activities are reactive, meaning a problem arises and the LAN administrator reacts to it by analyzing and resolving it. Other activities are proactive, meaning the LAN administrator monitors LAN performance and averts potential problems by anticipating them and taking corrective action before they reach the critical state.

Network management is made easier if the manager has the right tools, including problem reporting and tracking systems, network configuration managers, cable testers, protocol analyzers, simulation models, workload generators, network management systems, and remote control software. Each of these tools has a place in different aspects of network management.

The essence of network management is managing change. If components break, the manager finds the problem and effects repair. If performance changes, the manager analyzes the system, devises solutions, and implements the solutions. If new applications or users are added, the manager plans for adding network capacity. The solutions range from simple and inexpensive to carry out to complex and expensive. Sometimes balancing the load on components is all that is necessary. With the right tools and training, a network manager can keep the network running efficiently and avoid many situations that could develop into critical problems if not acted on early.

Network management can be a complex task, and the task is even more difficult when equipment from different vendors is used. The difficulty arises from creating the interfaces for collecting and formatting performance data. This task is simpler if vendors for network equipment design their components according to a standard. Two network management standards exist, the Simple Network Management Protocol (SNMP) and the Common Management Information Protocol (CMIP). The objective of these standards is to standardize how network management data are reported, stored, and accessed.

KEY TERMS

agent

alarms

alerts

balancing

bindery files

bridge

cable tester

capacity planning

Common Management Information Protocol (CMIP)

configuration management utility

filter

information gathering

integrated network management system

known good components

management information base (MIB)

monitor

network management system (NMS)

pocket LAN adapter

proactive network management

problem reporting and tracking system

protocol analyzer

304

Chapter 11
LAN
Administration:
Reactive and
Proactive
Management

reactive network management

remote control software

report generator

Simple Network Management Protocol (SNMP)

simulation model

structure of management information (SMI)

system tuning

workload generator

REVIEW QUESTIONS

1. What does a network management system do? What are the components of a network management system? Describe the functions of each network management system component.

2. Why are network management systems necessary?

3. List four tools used to help manage a network.

4. Describe the steps taken in solving a network problem.

5. What functions are provided by remote control systems? By a problem reporting and tracking system?

6. What functions are provided by a configuration management system? By a protocol analyzer? By a cable tester?

7. What is system tuning? Why is it necessary? When is it necessary?

8. Why is it prudent to change only one thing at a time when tuning a system?

9. What is capacity planning and why is it necessary? What are the steps to capacity planning?

10. Describe two tools used to assist with capacity planning.

PROBLEMS AND EXERCISES

1. Suppose a user reports an inability to successfully log onto the network. What would you do to help solve this problem? List three likely causes of the problem. What tools would you use to diagnose the problem?

2. Research the literature on a specific network management system. What capabilities does it provide? What networks does it work with?

3. Research the literature on remote control software. What capabilities do they provide? What networks does it work with? Explain how you would use remote control software to diagnose a user's problem.

4. Remote control software allows one to monitor the activities of a workstation anywhere on the network. Thus, remote control software can be used to monitor worker's activities. What problems could arise from the use of this capability? How can LAN administrators and company policies discourage improper use of remote control software? What features does remote control software have to discourage clandestine snooping activities?

5. Suppose you are a LAN administrator. You have just been told that the number of workstations will increase from 25 to 35 because another department will be connected to the LAN. Describe four items that may need to be upgraded to support these new workstations. Explain how the added nodes impact the items you chose.

REFERENCES

Carleton, Mary and Carleton, Russ. "Network Utilities: Building the LAN Toolkit." *Infoworld*, November 4, 1991.

Erwin, Jeff. "Network Control Systems Aid Management." *LAN Times*, Volume 8, Issue 17, September 2, 1991.

Dolan, Tom. "SNMP Streamlines Multi-Vendor Network Management." *LAN Technology*, Volume 7, Number 2, February 1991.

Fisher, Sharon. "Dueling Protocols." *Byte*, Volume 16, Number 3, March 1991.

Hart, Maura. "Control Changes from the Ground Up." *LAN Technology*, Volume 7, Number 11, November 1991.

Hurwicz, Michael. "Taking Inventory of the LAN." *Network World*, October 14, 1991.

Leeds, Frank. "Tips for Troubleshooting Networks." *LAN Technology*, Volume 6, Number 9, September 1990.

Levine, Ron. "Evaluating Three LAN Troubleshooting Devices." *Network World*, September 23, 1991.

Mier, Edwin. "SNMP Management Tools: A Shopper's Bonanza." *Network World*, June 24, 1991.

Pritchett, Glenn. "Establishing a LAN Dossier." *LAN Technology*, Volume 7, Number 11, November 1991.

306
‒ ‒ ‒ ‒ ‒ ‒
Chapter 11
LAN
Administration:
Reactive and
Proactive
Management

Queen, Jim. "Tracking Down Your Troubles." *LAN Technology*, Volume 7, Number 10, October 1991.

Rayl, Eric. "NLM Management Packages Prove Useful Tools." *PC Week*, November 4, 1991.

Sloman, Jeffrey. "Automating Network Management." *LAN Technology*, Volume 7, Number 7, July 1991.

Sloman, Jeffrey. "Control Central." *Byte*, Volume 16, Number 3, March 1991.

Smith, Mark. "Diagnosing Network Disorders." *LAN Technology*, Volume 7, Number 10, October 1991.

Tait, Peter. "Network Diagnostic Utilities: Looking for Trouble." *Infoworld*, May 31, 1991.

Takeuchi, Naomi. "A Day in the Life of a Protocol Analyzer." *LAN Technology*, Volume 7, Number 2, February 1991.

V
CONNECTING TO OTHER
SYSTEMS AND NETWORKS

The computing resources of today's organizations are diverse, ranging from a single microcomputer to multiple LANs to wide area networks (WANs) that establish connections between all the organization's computing platforms. Chapter 12 examines basic WAN principals, network topologies, and terminology. In Chapter 13 you build on this knowledge to explore the ways in which interconnection between LANs and WANs is accomplished. Also you will look forward to the forefront of LAN technology, one of the most dynamic technologies in the computer industry. In Chapter 14 you learn about several important but less commonly used technologies, such as client/server computing and peer-to-peer LANs, that have the potential to become mainstream technologies in the future.

Chapter 12
Wide Area Networks

Chapter 13
Making Network Connections

Chapter 14
Emerging Technologies

WIDE AREA NETWORKS

CHAPTER PREVIEW

In large and small companies alike, LANs have become an integral part of today's data processing environment. A small company's LAN is usually an extension of a stand-alone microcomputer system and represents the company's entire computing system. In contrast, many large companies began their data processing with mainframe or minicomputers and added microcomputers and LANs as extensions of pre-existing computing environments and capabilities. These companies frequently continue to rely on minicomputers, mainframe computers, and possibly wide area networks (WANs) as well as LANs for their computing needs. In such companies it is not uncommon to establish connections between all the computing platforms to form enterprise networks.

Part 5 of this book focuses on interconnecting LANs with other LANs, WANs, or stand-alone computers. To understand this material, you need to know a little about WANs. In this chapter you will read about some basics of WAN implementations.

Topics covered in this chapter include:

WAN terminology and topology

functions of the data link layer

WAN data link protocols

functions of the network layer

network routing

IBM's Systems Network Architecture (SNA)

packet distribution networks

differences between LANs and WANs

At the conclusion of this chapter, you will be familiar with the basic principals of WANs, network topologies, and terminology specific to them. This chapter leads to a discussion in Chapter 13 of network interconnections—LAN-to-LAN, LAN-to-WAN, and LAN-to-host computer.

WAN NETWORK TERMINOLOGY

The world of data communications is rife with terminology, abbreviations, and acronyms. Before we begin our discussion of WAN technology, we will define a few common network terms.

Link The direct connection of two nodes in a network. A link, therefore, connects two computers.

End-to-End Routing Sometimes when one node wants to send a message to another node, the two are not directly connected. The message must then pass through one or more intermediate nodes before arriving at the final destination. Determining how this is done is called end-to-end routing.

Path The links that the message traverses. Figure 12-1 shows two paths available for communication between node A and node C (A → B, B → C and A → D, D → C), with two links on each path.

Hop The number of hops a message takes in going from its source to its destination is the number of links it traverses. Thus a message traveling from node A to node C in Figure 12-1 takes two hops.

Store-and-Forward A technique used by some networks to send data along a path. Each intermediary node along the path stores the message, sends an acknowledgment of message receipt to the sender, and then forwards the message to the next node on the path. When the sender receives an acknowledgment that the message has been received by the next node, it is no longer responsible for retransmitting the message if an error occurs.

Session A communications dialogue between two users of a network. A user can be a terminal operator, an application, or any other originator of messages. In some systems, sessions are quite formal, with well-defined conventions for establishing, continuing, and terminating the dialogue.

Packet Switching The technology of transmitting a message in one or more fixed-length data packets.

Packet Distribution Network (PDN) A packet-switching network, also sometimes referred to as a **public data network** (also PDN), an **X.25 network** (X.25 is a standard designation), or a **value-added network (VAN).** Henceforth we will use the acronym PDN. A PDN generally connects a user and the nearest node in the PDN. The PDN routes the data packets to their final destination by finding the best route for each packet (packet switching). PDNs are available for public use by a service provider called a common carrier. The common carrier provides the transmission media to connect two users. The advantages of a PDN are an initially low cost for transmission services and a service fee based on the amount of use. The user pays a monthly connection fee plus a charge for the number of messages transmitted. Furthermore a PDN allows a user to reach most locations in the industrialized world while accessing the service through a local telephone connection. The disadvantages are higher costs than a leased line if message traffic

Figure 12-1   A Communications Network

311

WAN Network
Topologies

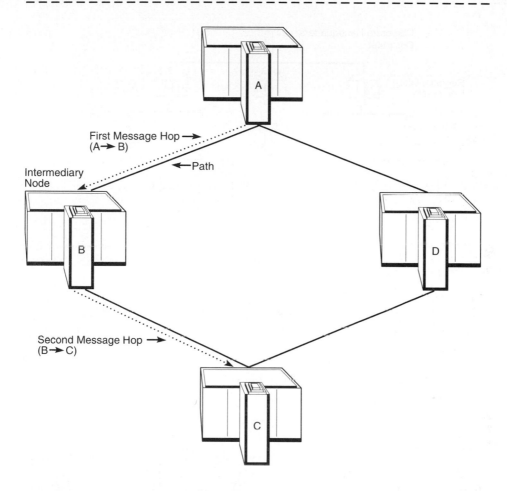

between two points is high and possible congestion and message delays because of message traffic from other companies.

WAN NETWORK TOPOLOGIES

In Chapter 3 we discussed the primary network topologies for LANs: ring, bus, star, and bus with spurs. These topologies can be used by WANs as well. Moreover WANs can be configured in three additional ways: hierarchical, interconnected, and a combination of of these. Most large WANs (those with many nodes) are implemented using these three topologies.

Hierarchical Network

The **hierarchical network** topology, shown in Figure 12-2(a), is also referred to as a tree structure. There is one root node (node A). Several nodes at the

Figure 12-2 Network Topologies

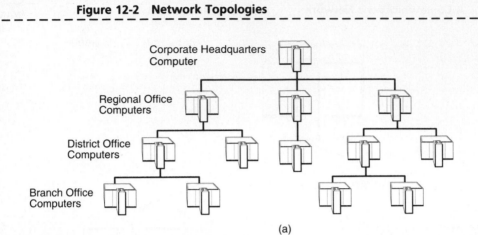

Corporate Headquarters Computer

Regional Office Computers

District Office Computers

Branch Office Computers

(a)

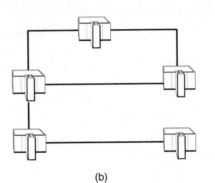

(b)

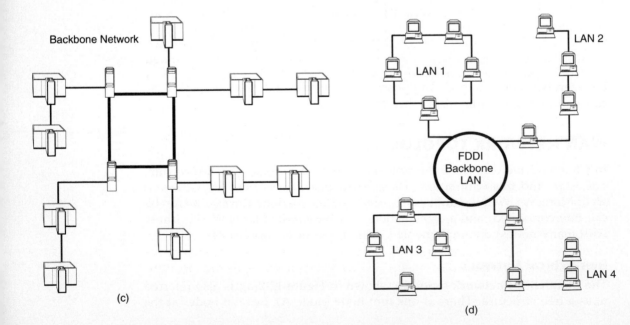

Backbone Network

LAN 1

LAN 2

FDDI Backbone LAN

LAN 3

LAN 4

(c)

(d)

second level are directly connected to node A. Each of these nodes can have a number of cascaded nodes attached. This type of network closely resembles corporate organization charts, and corporate computer centers are one place in which this topology can be found. Figure 12-2(a) illustrates such an organization, with the corporate headquarters computer as root node, regional nodes attached directly to the root, district nodes to regional nodes, and branch nodes to district nodes. Corporate reports from a lower level are easily consolidated at the next higher level, and the network generally mirrors the information flow pattern in the corporation. Information flowing from a district in one division to a district in a different division would need to go through the root or corporate node. As with a star system, this allows for a great deal of network control.

Interconnected (Plex) Network

An **interconnected (plex) network** architecture is shown in Figure 12-2(b). This topology provides a high degree of flexibility because many paths are available between nodes if a link should fail and congestion can be avoided. The performance of an interconnected system is generally quite good because direct links can be established between nodes with high amounts of data to exchange. Costs can also be controlled because interconnected topology is capable of the shortest or least expensive configuration. In fact, any of the other topology types can be mimicked by an interconnected topology, although routing and control mechanisms would probably be different.

Combination Networks

A combination of the two topologies just described is sometimes integrated into one network. One such combination is a **backbone network**—for instance, a ring—with spurs attached. The backbone nodes are dedicated to message transfer and data communications while the other nodes are used for both data processing and data communications. In widely distributed systems with a large number of nodes, this helps reduce the number of hops, the length of the path, and congestion problems. If the backbone is implemented as a ring or with multiple paths available, reliability is also high. A backbone network for a WAN is illustrated in Figure 12-2(c).

Backbone networks are appearing more frequently in LAN technology as well. The Fiber Data Distributed Interface (FDDI) LAN operates at 100 Mbps, can span distances up to 125 miles, and uses a token passing ring architecture. FDDI LANs can be used to interconnect a company's departmental LANs in a metropolitan area. For example, a university might use an FDDI backbone to connect the LANs in different departments, or a government agency might use a FDDI backbone to connect departmental LANs in different buildings, as illustrated in Figure 3-6. A variation of FDDI uses copper wiring, either shielded or unshielded twisted-pair wires, as the medium. This alternative is known as Copper Distributed Data Interface (CDDI).

WAN DATA LINK CONTROL PROTOCOLS

In Chapter 2 we introduced the OSI reference model, and in Chapter 3 we looked at functions and examples of the OSI data link layer. In this chapter we will look more closely at the data link layer and a data link protocol commonly used in today's WANs. Some of the LAN-WAN connections occur at the data link level, so a cursory knowledge of these protocols is beneficial to understanding how the connections are made.

The two primary methods of passing data from node to node in a LAN are token passing and carrier sense with multiple access and collision detection (CSMA/CD). These methods are seldom used in WANs. Like both of these methods, WAN data link protocols accept a transmission packet from the network layer and add data link control data to the packet. Adding this control information is sometimes called enveloping, because the packet is enclosed in the data link control data much like a letter is enclosed in an envelope for transmission. The primary data link control methods used for WANs fall into two general classes, asynchronous and synchronous. In Chapter 3 we briefly discussed asynchronous and binary synchronous protocols. You may want to review those sections at this time. The most common data link protocol used in WANs today is a **bit synchronous protocol.**

Bit Synchronous Protocols

The first bit synchronous data link protocol, **Synchronous Data Link Control (SDLC),** was introduced by IBM in 1972. Since then numerous other bit synchronous data link controls have surfaced, including

SDLC   Synchronous Data Link Control, from IBM

ADCCP Advanced Data Communications Control Procedure, an ANSI standard data link protocol (ADCCP is frequently pronounced "addcap")

HDLC   High-Level Data Link Control, a standard of the International Standards Organization (ISO)

LAPB   Link Access Procedure—Balanced, designated as the data link protocol for the X.25 packet distribution networks

All of these bit synchronous protocols operate similarly. SDLC is used in the following discussion as the model for bit synchronous data link protocols because it is used in many IBM installations and thus represents the majority of bit synchronous implementations.

The SDLC Frame   The basic unit of transmission in SDLC is the frame; its general format is presented in Figure 12-3. The **flag field** is used to indicate the beginning and ending of the frame. The bit pattern for the flag, 01111110, is the only bit pattern in the protocol that is specifically reserved; all other bit patterns are acceptable. The second field within the frame, the **address field,** is eight bits wide. The number of unique combinations that can be made from eight bits is 256, so a maximum of 256 unique addresses are possible. Other data link protocols, such as ADCCP and HDLC, allow the address field to be expanded in multiples of eight bits, significantly increasing the number of addressable stations per link. The **control field,** also eight bits in length, identifies the frame type as either **unnumbered, informational,** or **surpervisory.** Of these three types, only the first two are used to transmit data, with the primary data transport frame being the information frame.

The data field is optional. This field is always omitted for supervisory frames, is optional on unnumbered frames, and is present on information frames. As Figure 12-3 shows, the only restriction on the data field is that the number of bits must be a multiple of eight; each 8-bit group is called an octet. This restriction does not mean that an 8-bit code must be used; in fact, any code is acceptable. But if necessary, the data being transmitted must be padded with additional bits to maintain an integral number of octets. If the data being transmitted consist of five BAUDOT characters, for instance, then, at 5 bits each, only 25 bits would be required for the data and an additional 7 bits would have to be appended to complete the last octet.

Following the optional data field is a **frame check sequence** for error detection, which is 16 bits in length. The final field of the frame is the flag that signals the end of the message. The bit pattern for the ending flag is the same as that for the beginning flag, thus allowing the ending flag for one frame to serve as the beginning flag for the next.

SDLC is a positional protocol; that is, each field except the data field has a specific length and location relative to adjacent fields. Thus, there are no special control characters (except for the flag characters) to delimit the data or headings in the message. For control frames, which are either unnumbered or supervisory, the control funciton is encoded in the control field. Unnumbered frames have 5 bits available to identify the control function, so 32 different function types are available. The supervisory frame has only 2 bits available, and thus a maximum of 4 functions can be defined.

Number Sent (Ns) and Number Received (Nr) Subfields As shown in Figure 12-4, in information frames the control field contains two 3-bit fields known as the **number sent (Ns)** and **number received (Nr)** subfields. The Ns and Nr counts are used to sequence messages. Three bits allow for eight numbers, 0 through 7. When transmitting an information frame, the sender increments the Ns field value. The Ns or Nr number following 7 is 0; thus, the number sequence cycles through those eight values. The Nr field is used for acknowledging receipt of messages. Every time a message is received, the receiver increments the Nr count, which represents the number of the

Figure 12-3   SDLC Frame Format

Flag 01111110	Address	Control Field	Data (Optional Octets)	Frame Check Sequence	Flag 01111110

Figure 12-4 Expansion of Control Field in SDLC Frame

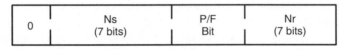

(a) 8-bit Control Field

(b) 16-bit Control Field

frame expected next. Thus an Nr count of 5 means message number 5 should arrive next. The Ns and Nr counts are compared every time a frame is received to make sure that no messages have been lost. This scheme allows seven messages to be sent before an acknowledgment is required.

Although the ability to receive up to seven frames without acknowledgment improves performance, it also places a burden on the sender, which must be ready to retransmit any unacknowledged frames. Since this requires that messages be saved in the sender's buffers until acknowledged, this can create problems for systems with small buffers or memory.

Both ADCCP and HDLC allow the control field to be expanded to provide for larger Ns and Nr counts, as illustrated in Figure 12-4. When expanded to 16 bits, the Ns and Nr fields can both be seven bits in length; this allows 128 sequence numbers, and up to 127 meassages can be transmitted before being acknowledged. This is especially beneficial with satellite links, where because of the propagation delay for response, a small number of unacknowledged frames could create undesirable delays. Consider the effect of the Ns and Nr sizes for satellite transmission. Satellite signals incur a one-way propagation delay of approximately a quarter of a second. If 10,000 bit blocks are being transmitted on a 1 Mbps satellite link, then theoretically 25 blocks could be transmitted every quarter of a second. With 3-bit Ns and Nr fields, only 7 blocks could be sent before waiting for an acknowledgment. In this case transmission time for 18 blocks would be lost, limiting the available capacity.

WAN NETWORK LAYER FUNCTIONS

As discussed in Chapter 2, the OSI network layer performs three major functions: routing, network control, and congestion control. These functions are the same on LANs and WANs. Whereas the data link layer is concerned with getting data between two adjacent nodes, the network layer is concerned with end-to-end routing, or getting the data from the originating node to its ultimate destination. In many networks data may take a variety of paths to go from the originating node to the destination node. The network layer must be aware of alternative paths in the network and choose the best one. Which path is best depends on a variety of factors, some of which are congestion, number of intervening nodes and speed of links.

Network control involves sending and receiving node status information to and from other nodes to determine the best routing for messages. Where priorities are associated with messages, it is the responsibility of the network layer to enforce the priority scheme.

Congestion Control means reducing transmission delays that might result from overuse of some circuits or from a particular node in the network being busy and unable to process messages in a timely fashion. The network layer should adapt to these transient conditions and attempt to route messages around such points of congestion. Not all systems can adapt to the changing characteristics of the communications links, however. In some instances, specifically broadcast-type systems, there is very little that can be done to overcome this problem.

Message Routing in a WAN

Message routing, one of the functions of the network layer on both LAN and WAN systems, is accomplished differently on WANs compared to LANs. The two primary methods of routing a message from node-to-node in a LAN are token passing and CSMA/CD. Token passing sends a message from node to node until it circulates around the ring or bus. In CSMA/CD the message is broadcast to each node simultaneously. The nodes to which the message is addressed accept the message, and the others ignore it. Using such methods in a WAN is often not practical. The speeds of WAN links are usually much slower than that of a LAN, and the time it would take for a message to circulate among all nodes would be prohibitive; moreover some nodes may not be on the path to the destination node, and sending a message to those nodes is not productive. Therefore, WANs typically use different message routing methods from LANs.

Routing is achievable through a number of algorithms used to direct messages from the point of origination to final destination. Because messages in a WAN are not usually broadcast to all nodes as in a LAN, the path a message takes in reaching its destination must be determined by one or more network nodes. Determination of message routing can be either centralized or distributed. Routing itself can be either static, weighted, adaptive, or broadcast and is governed by a network routing table resident at each node. The **network routing table** is a matrix of other nodes together with the link or path to that node. Thus, if a message destined for one node arrives at some node other, the network routing table is consulted for the next node on the path between the two nodes. Network routing tables can also contain more information than just the next link; for example, congestion statistics.

Let's take a look at the varieties of WAN routing techniques starting with how routes are determined.

Centralized Routing Determination In **centralized routing,** one node is designated as the network routing manager to whom all nodes periodically forward such status information as queue lengths on outgoing and incoming lines and the number of messages processed within the most recent time interval. The routing manager is thereby provided with an overview of network functioning, where bottlenecks are occurring, and where facilities are underutilized. The routing manager periodically recalculates the optimal paths between nodes and constructs and distributes new routing tables to all nodes.

This form of network routing determination has many disadvantages. The fact that the routing manager must receive many messages from the other nodes increases the probability of congestion, a problem that can be exacerbated if the routing manager is itself a node used to accept and forward messages. And networks are sometimes subject to transient conditions, such as when the internode transfer of a file saturates a link for a short period of time. By the time this information is relayed to the routing manager and a new routing is calculated, the activity may have already ceased, making the newly calculated paths less than optimal. Moreover some nodes will receive the newly calculated routing tables before others, leading to inconsistencies in how messages are to be routed. For example, suppose that under the old routing mechanism the route was $A \rightarrow B \rightarrow D \rightarrow X$, whereas the new path is $A \rightarrow C \rightarrow D \rightarrow X$, as shown in Figure 12-5. The new path from node B to node X is $B \rightarrow A \rightarrow C \rightarrow D \rightarrow X$. Now if node B receives its new routing chart while node A is still using the old chart, then for a message destined from A to X, A will route it to B and B will route it back to A, continuing until A receives the new routing table. In addition, transmission of the routing tables themselves may bias the statistics being gathered to compute the next routing algorithm.

Figure 12-5 Centralized Routing

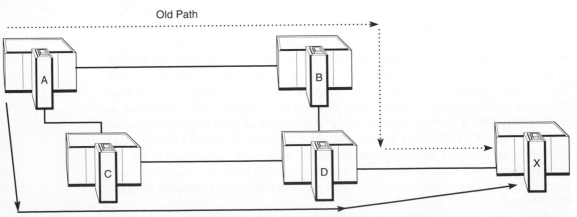

An additional problem with centralized routing calculations is the large amount of processing power needed; a considerable amount of CPU time can be consumed. Reliability of the routing manager is also an important factor. If this node fails, then either the routing remains unchanged until the system is recovered, or an alternate routing manager must be selected. The best situation is to have alternate routing managers available in case the primary routing node fails. The routing manager sends the alternate nodes "I'm alive" messages at predefined intervals. If the backup manager fails to receive this message within the prescribed interval, it assumes the manager has failed and takes over. The backup routing manager's first responsibility is to broadcast the fact that network status messages should now be routed to it.

Distributed Routing Determination   **Distributed routing** determination relies on each node to calculate its own best routing table, which requires each node to periodically transmit its status to its neighbors. As this information ripples through the network, each node updates its tables accordingly. This technique avoids the potential bottleneck at a centralized route manager, although the time required for changes to flow through all of the nodes may be quite long.

In addition to the two approaches to route determination, several message-routing techniques are available. The primary ways we can route messages are static routing, weighted routing, adaptive routing, quickest link, best route, and broadcast routing.

Static Routing   The purest form of **static routing** involves always using one particular path between two nodes; if a link in that path is down, then communication between those nodes is impossible. That is, between any two nodes there is only one path—the link between them; if the link is down, the available network software is incapable of using any of the potentially alternate paths. Fully interconnected networks sometimes use this approach, but fortunately this type of system has largely disappeared. In general, static routing now refers to the situation in which a selected path is used until some drastic condition makes it unavailable, at which time an alternate path is selected and used until the path manually switched, a failure occurs on the alternate path, or the original path is restored.

Weighted Routing   When multiple paths exist, some implementations use **weighted routing,** in which each path is weighted according to perceived utilization. The path is then randomly selected from the weighted alternatives. For example, Figure 12-6 shows three paths from node A to node X via nodes B, C, and D. Suppose the network designers had determined that the path through node B would be best 50 percent of the time, through node C would be best 30 percent of the time, and through node D would be best 20 percent of the time. When a message is to be sent from node A to node X, a random number between 0 and 1 is generated: If the random number is 0.50 or less, the path through node B is used; if the random number is greater than 0.50 and less than or equal to 0.80, the path through node C is selected;

otherwise the path through node D is used. The path may alternate, but each path is used with the same frequency as in the routing tables. This type of routing can only be changed by altering the route weighting in the routing tables.

Adaptive Routing   Adaptive routing, occasionally referred to as **dynamic routing,** attempts to select the quickest or best current route for the message or session.

The simplest adaptive routing technique is to have a node pass along the message as quickly as possible, with the only restriction being not to pass it back to the sending node. Thus the receiving node looks at all potential outbound links, selects the one with the least amount of activity, and sends the message out on that line. There is no attempt to determine if that link will bring the message closer to its destination. This technique is not very efficient and can cause messages to be shuffled to more nodes than necessary, thereby adding to network congestion. The message could conceivably be shifted around the network for hours before arriving at its destination. The advantage of this technique is its simplicity, because routing tables do not need to be maintained. Even though it is the simplest to implement, it is not a viable routing method for most WANs.

The more intelligent adaptive routing techniques attempt to select the best route, as determined by one or more of the following parameters; the number of required hops, the speed of the links, the type of link, and congestion. Routing of this type requires current information on the status of the network. If a node is added to the network or if one is taken off the network, that information must be relayed to the nodes doing route calculation. Knowing the speed of the links as well as the number of hops is important. Traversing two links at 4800 bps is more costly than traversing one link at 2400 bps. The line time for both will be the same, but some time is lost in

Figure 12-6   Weighted Routing

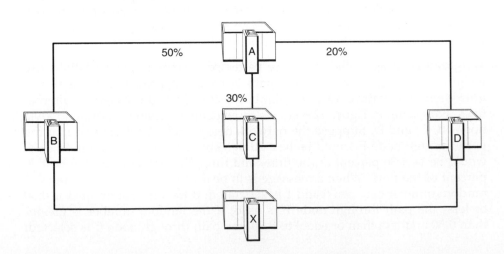

receiving and forwarding the message. Link congestion occurs when message traffic on a link is heavy, similar to freeway congestion during the rush hour. Avoiding congested areas will prevent messages from being stuck on inbound and outbound queues. In the configuration of Figure 12-7, if node B is transmitting a file to adjacent node C, the route from node A to node C through B is the shortest but probably not the quickest at that time. The route through nodes E and D would be more efficient, since the link from B to C is congested.

Broadcast Routing A third type of routing is **broadcast routing,** exemplified by CSMA/CD and token passing. Routing is quite easy: The message is broadcast to all stations, and only the station to whom the message is addressed accepts it.

Figure 12-7 Adaptive Routing

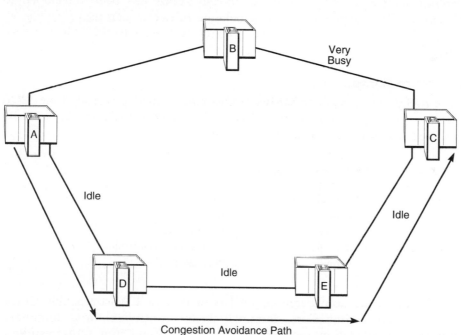

Congestion Avoidance Path

IBM's SYSTEMS NETWORK ARCHITECTURE

Vendor offerings play a major role in network implementation and configuration, and almost every major computer vendor offers a networking capability. Many of today's LANs conform to established industry standards. Often, however, networks are proprietary to the vendor and do not conform to established standards. This, of course, makes attaching equipment from other vendors more difficult, because the other vendors must build their equipment to conform to corporate standards that are more subject to change than industry standards. Vendor networks compete with each other, with packet switching or X.25 networks, and with common carrier networks.

The following section is devoted to one particular network that has become a de facto industry standard, IBM's **System Network Architecture (SNA).** Currently most networks being designed on IBM mainframe systems use SNA. Other vendors' equipment interfacing with an IBM network are likely to do so via an SNA interface. Many computer manufacturers have implemented or are implementing the ability to attach to an SNA network as some type of SNA node.

A network based on SNA consists of a variety hardware and software components in a well-defined configuration. The objective of any network is to enable users to communicate with one another. SNA users are entities with some degree of intelligence, either people working at a terminal or operator's console or applications providing services for other programs or terminal users. A terminal is not a user, though the terms *terminal operator* and *terminal* are frequently used synonymously. SNA has been developed to provide communications paths and dialogue rules between users. This is accomplished via a layered network architecture similar to the OSI reference model.

Hardware Components

SNA defines four distinct hardware groupings called **physical units (PU).** The four physical units are numbered 1, 2, 4, and 5, with no PU currently assigned to number 3. These device types are listed in Table 12-1.

Table 12-1   SNA Physical Units

Physical Unit	Hardware Component
Type 1	Terminal
Type 2	Cluster Controller
Type 4	Communications Controller
Type 5	Host Processor

The hardware configuration consists of IBM or IBM-compatible CPUs, communications controllers, terminal cluster controllers, and terminals, printers, or workstations, connected by any type of medium. Other vendors' equipment may also be included in the network if they conform to the SNA protocols. The preferred data link protocol is the bit synchronous SDLC, but accommodations have been made for asynchronous protocols and character-oriented synchronous protocols as well.

Logical Units and Sessions

Users of SNA are represented in the system by entities known as **logical units (LU).** An LU is usually implemented as a software function in a device with some intelligence, such as a CPU or controller. The dialogue between two system users is known as a session. As agents of the users, the LUs are involved in establishing communications paths between users who want to establish a session.

Session Types   There are many different types of sessions that can be requested, such as program-to-terminal, program-to-program, or terminal-to-terminal. Each of these categories can be further stratified as to terminal type (interactive, batch, or printer) and application type (batch, interactive, word processing, or the like). To further complicate matters, one logical unit can represent several different users, and a user can have multiple sessions in progress concurrently.

Suppose a terminal desires to retrieve a record from a database. The terminal must use the services of an application program to obtain the record. Each user—the terminal and the database application—is represented by a logical unit. The terminal LU issues a request to enter into a session with the database application LU. The application LU can either accept or reject the session request. Rejection typically occurs for security reasons, because the requesting LU lacks authority to establish a session with the application LU, or because of congestion, meaning the application LU has already entered into the maximum number of sessions it can support. If the session request is granted, then a communications path is established between the terminal and the application. The two users continue to communicate until one of them terminates the session. Figure 12-8 shows several sessions between users communicating through their respective logical units.

LU Types   Seven LU types have thus far been defined within SNA. These are numbered from 0 to 7, with the definition for LU type 5 omitted. It is important to note that the LU types refer to session types and not to a specific LU. Thus one specific LU can participate in a type 1 LU session with one LU and a type 4 LU session with another. For two LUs to communicate, they must both support and use the same LU session type.

Of the seven LU types, all but LU types 0 and 6 address sessions with hardware devices such as printers and terminals. LU type 6 is defined for program-to-program communication. It has evolved through two definitions, LU 6.0 and LU 6.1, to its current definition, LU 6.2. LU 6.2 has recently been given considerable attention as a key SNA capability. There are several significant aspects of LU 6.2.

LU 6.2 defines a program-to-program communications interface that is more general and can have wider uses than the interfaces provided by the hardware-oriented LU types. Program-to-program sessions provide a communications path for applications distributed over multiple nodes. The two applications do not have to communicate with each other to be in the same node. This capability supports transaction processing systems with multiple processing nodes. For example, Figure 12-9 shows an application in workstation A in LAN 1 communicating through an SNA LU 6.2 session with an application in workstation X on LAN 2.

Because a program-to-program interface is more generic than a session type involving specific hardware devices, other vendors' equipment can enter into SNA sessions with an application process running in an IBM proces-

Figure 12-8 SNA Sessions and Logical Units

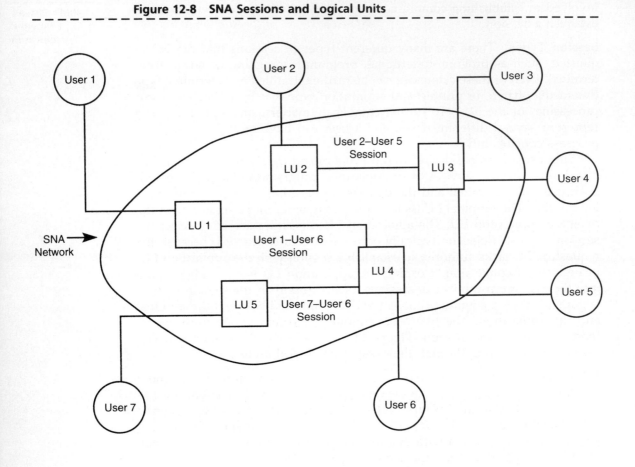

User 1

User 2

User 3

User 2–User 5
Session

LU 2

LU 3

User 4

SNA→
Network

LU 1

User 1–User 6
Session

LU 4

LU 5

User 7–User 6
Session

User 5

User 7

User 6

Figure 12-9 LU 6.2 Interface

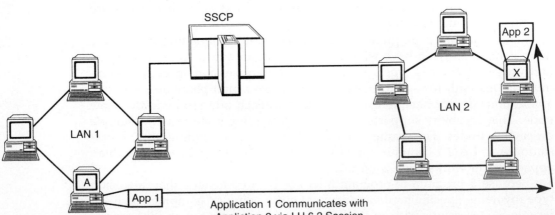

SSCP

App 2

X

LAN 2

LAN 1

A

App 1

Application 1 Communicates with
Appliction 2 via LU 6.2 Session

sor, so long as the communicating program in the vendor's processor adheres to the session rules. For example, an application on a microcomputer could enter into a session with an application running on an IBM node or another microcomputer.

PACKET DISTRIBUTION NETWORKS

The concept of a packet distribution network (PDN) was first introduced in 1964 by Paul Baran of the Rand Corporation. Baran defined a process of segmenting a message into specific-sized packets, routing the packets to their destination, and reassembling them to recreate the message. In 1966 Donald Davies of the National Physics Laboratory in Great Britain published details of a store-and-forward PDN. IN 1967 plans were formulated for what is believed to be the first PDN, ARPANET, which became operational in 1969 with four nodes. The ARPANET has since expanded to more than 125 nodes and was renamed to NSFNET.

PDNs specify several different packet sizes, most commonly 128, 256, 512, and 1024 bytes. All packets transmitted will conform to one of the available packet lengths. Individual users subscribe to a service providing one of the available packet sizes. Eliminating large variations in packet size makes management of message buffers easier and evens out message traffic patterns.

PDN Terminology

A PDN is a packet-switching WAN variously referred to as an X.25 network, a value-added network (VAN), or a public data network. The terms *packet distribution* and *packet switching* both refer to how data are transmitted—that is, as one or more packets with a fixed length. The X.25 designation stems from CCITT's recommendation X.25, which defines the interface between computer equipment and data circuit-terminating equipment (DCE) for devices operating in the packet mode on public data networks. The term *public data network,* which derives from the X.25 recommendation, is somewhat of a misnomer, since packet-switching networks have also been implemented in the private sector. When the network is public, users subscribe to the network services much like they subscribe to telephone services. The term *value-added network* is used because the network proprietor adds not only a communications link but also message routing, packet control, store-and-forward capability, network management, compatibility between devices, and error recovery.

The general configuration of a PDN is given in Figure 12-10. Some CCITT recommendations covering different aspects of PDN access and use are listed in the figure at the points where they apply.

PDN Advantages and Disadvantages

PDNs have several advantages: The user is charged for the amount of data transmitted rather than for connect time. Applications that send low volumes of data over a relatively long period will find the charges for a PDN lower than for either leased lines or switched lines. The PDN also gives access to many different locations without the cost of switched connections, which usually involve a charge for the initial connection plus a per-minute use fee. Access to the PDN is usually via a local telephone call, which also reduces costs (that is, until telephone companies begin using measured billing). Maintenance of the network and error recovery are the responsibilities of the PDN.

Using a PDN also has disadvantages: Because the PDN is usually shared, users must compete with each other for circuits. Thus it is possible for message traffic from other users to impede the delivery of a message. In the extreme case a virtual circuit to the intended destination may even be unobtainable. This is also true for a switched connection from a common carrier. If the number of data packets to be transferred is great, then the cost of using a PDN can exceed that of leased facilities. Because the PDN is controlled by its proprietor, the individual user is unable to make changes that might benefit an individual application, such as longer messages or larger packets, longer message acknowledgment intervals, and higher transmission speeds, all set by the PDN administrators.

Figure 12-10 PDN General Configuration

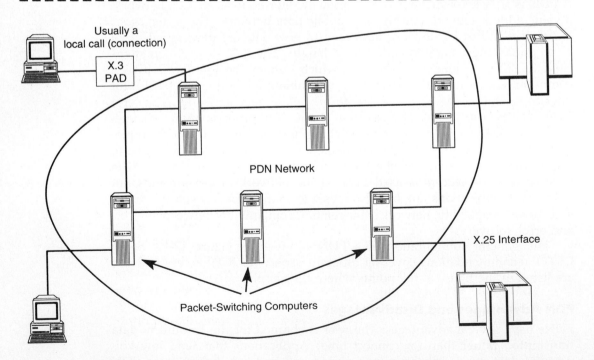

COMPARING WANs WITH LANs

The primary difference between a WAN and a LAN is distance. A LAN serves a limited geographical area, typically within one building or building complex. The maximum allowable distance a LAN can cover varies with the system, but it is generally a few miles, sometimes depending on the type of medium used or by one or more standards. A WAN can cover a large geographical area, or it can be limited to a small area. In the latter case it is distinguished from a conventional LAN in that the network technology can be used without change to set up a geographically distributed network. Distance is not the only feature distinguishing a LAN from a WAN. Other distinguishing factors may include topology, data link protocol, routing algorithm, media, ownership, and transmission speed. Let us briefly look at each of these factors.

Topology, Protocols, and Routing

LAN topologies are usually bus, ring, or star. Sometimes the topology is a combination of these, such as a bus with spurs. WAN topologies are typically hierarchical or interconnected, although rings and stars are also used. Hybrid topologies consisting of combinations of several topologies are also common. For example, a WAN with hundreds of nodes may use a backbone ring network to provide efficient transmission over long distances. The subnetworks attached to the backbone ring may use hierarchical, star, and interconnected topologies. LAN data link protocols are usually CSMA/CD or token passing, while WANs use asynchronous or synchronous protocols. The protocol of choice for most WANs today is a bit synchronous protocol like HDLC. In a LAN, routing is either broadcast with CSMA/CD or always transmit to your neighbor node in token passing. A variety of routing algorithms are used in WANs, and WAN routing is often more complex than LAN routing. WANs often use an adaptive routing technique, meaning that the routing may change based on conditions like congestion, failed links, and failed processors, or a probability function for weighted routing.

Media

LAN media is usually twisted-pair wires, coaxial cable, fiber optic cable, or one of the new wireless media. Although mixed media networks are possible, a single LAN usually uses a single medium type. WAN media are often obtained through a common carrier and may consist of a variety of media, such as telephone wires, fiber optic cable, coaxial cable, microwave radio, and satellite. A company implementing a LAN usually evaluates the media and selects the one that best meets their needs. For WANs a company typically selects a service level based on speed and error characteristics and allows the common carrier to use its variety of media to meet these performance characteristics.

Ownership

A LAN is almost always privately controlled with respect to hardware, software, and media. A WAN, on the other hand, usually consists of computer hardware and software owned or controlled by the user, together with media and its associated data communications equipment provided by a common carrier. It is not always the case that a WAN uses media provided by a common carrier; sometimes WANs have been implemented as totally private networks. Once such company is Commodity News Service (CNS) in Kansas City. CNS provides information on commodities like wheat, gold, silver, and coffee. Some of CNS's subscribers live in rural agricultural areas. In some of these areas CNS has installed its own communications lines to provide its services. In Canada an electric utility uses lines it owns to communicate between geographically distributed centers, and some railroad companies also have private, geographically distributed communications lines. Most often WANs using private media are those having nodes located in a small geographical areas. It is common to have WANs that use both private media and media obtained from a common carrier.

Transmission Speed

LAN nodes are connected via a high-speed communications path. The speed typically is at least 1 Mbps and probably higher. Transmission speeds for WANs vary widely and, like those of LANs, are constantly increasing. However, the usual transmission speeds for long-distance connections are generally less than LAN speeds. Common WAN speeds are 9600 bps, 56 Kbps, and 1.54 Mbps. Speeds of 1.54 Mbps result from a transmission service known as T-1. Higher speeds of 6.3 Mbps (T-2), 45 Mbps (T-3), and 281 Mbps (T-4) are also available but are too expensive for most companies. For example, a 1992 tariff request for a common carrier for T-1 lines was $2500 per month plus $3.50 per mile; for T-3 links the cost was $16,000 per month and $45 per mile. Under this tariff the monthly cost for a 100-mile link would be $2850 for T-1 and $20,500 for T-3.

A variety of different speeds are often found in one WAN. Referring back to Figure 12-5, the speed of the connection between nodes A and B might be 9600 bps, while the speed of the connection between nodes B and C might be 56 Kbps. If the transmission path between nodes A and C is through node B, then the overall speed of transmission is limited by the speed of the lowest communication link, link A-B in this case.

LAN–WAN INTERCONNECTIONS

The differences between LANs and WANs just cited present considerable obstacles to LAN–WAN interconnection. When we connect a LAN to a WAN, many of these differences need to be reconciled. The interconnection must be able to accommodate significant differences in transmission speeds, data link protocols, transmission media, and perhaps internal data codes. LAN speeds can be 10,000 times faster than WAN speeds. The format of a

LAN message can be different from that of the WAN to which it is connected, and the interconnection must translate messages from one protocol format to the other. The type of media and the connectors used to attach stations to the media can differ, and the interconnection must provide for connection to both LAN and WAN media. Although internal data codes are not a part of WAN technology, sometimes mainframe computers attached to a WAN use the EBCDIC code, while LAN computers most commonly use the ASCII code. Thus code translation may be an essential function for LAN–WAN connections.

SUMMARY

LANs do not always exist in isolation. Many companies having LANs also have large stand-alone computing systems and WANs. These various platforms can be interconnected to form an enterprise network of LANs and WANs or LANs and large host systems. Because of the need to interconnect LANs and WANs, many LAN administrators should be aware of the basics of WAN technology.

WANs and LANs often differ in topology. LANs usually use a bus, ring, or star topology. WANs typically use a hierarchical or interconnected topology. Hybrid networks consisting of several subnetworks with differing topologies are also possible in WANs. For example, some WANs with a large number of nodes use a ring backbone network to provide faster service between nodes that are geographically dispersed. Attached to the backbone ring may be subnetworks that use a hierarchical, star, or interconnected topology.

The data link protocols most often used by large systems and hence WANs are asynchronous and synchronous. Asynchronous WANs transmit one character at a time and the sending and receiving station are not synchronized with each other. Synchronous transmissions send a block of data at a time and the sending and receiving stations are synchronized so the data bits can be recognized correctly. In general, synchronous protocols are more efficient than asynchronous protocols. Both are widely implemented and provide means for interfacing to microcomputers and LAN nodes. The data link protocol of choice for most of today's WANs is a bit synchronous protocol. Several variations of bit synchronous protocols exist. Some of these variations are HDLC, SDLC, ADCCP, and LAPB. Bit synchronous protocols are preferred because they are efficient, provide good error detection, and allow any bit sequences to be transmitted as data (transparency).

The network layer is responsible for message routing, and there are a variety of methods for doing so. Routing can be determined by a centralized routing manager, or this function can be distributed among all or several nodes. Common routing algorithms include static, weighted, adaptive, and broadcast.

A variety of WAN implementations exist. In this chapter we looked at two specific implementations, a PDN and IBM's Systems Network Architecture (SNA). Both are significant because of the large number of computers, large and small, that have interfaces to these networks. A PDN is a public network. A service provider provides a customer with an interface to the PDN. The PDN is responsible for services provided by the OSI physical, data link, and network layers, that is, for functions like node-to-node connections, error detection, and message routing. Since many systems interface to PDNs, a PDN can serve as a common connection interface for computers.

SNA is one of the most common WAN architectures, so many different companies have built hardware and software interfaces for SNA networks. These interfaces exist for large and small systems alike. Thus microcomputers equipped with the right hardware and software are able to communicate with nodes on an SNA network. One interface, the LU 6.2 program-to-program interface is particularly attractive because it is designed to allow a program on one computer to communicate directly with a program on another computer. Thus SNA is important not only as a WAN architecture but also for network interfaces.

- -

KEY TERMS

adaptive routing

address field

backbone network

bit synchronous protocol

broadcast routing

centralized routing

control field

distributed routing

dynamic routing

flag field

frame check sequence

hierarchical network

hop

informational frame

interconnected (plex) network

link

logical unit (LU)

LU 6.2

number received (Nr)

number sent (Ns)

packet distribution network (PDN)

packet switching

path

physical unit (PU)

public data network (PDN)

session

static routing

store-and-forward

supervisory frame

Synchronous Data Link Control (SDLC)

Systems Network Architecture (SNA)

unnumbered frame

value-added network (VAN)

weighted routing

X.25 network

REVIEW QUESTIONS

1. Distinguish between a link and a path.
2. What does end-to-end routing mean?
3. Describe two WAN topologies.
4. What are the advantages of an interconnected network?
5. What is a backbone network? What advantages does a backbone network provide?
6. What is the format of an SDLC frame?
7. How are the Ns and Nr counts used in the SDLC protocol?
8. What functions are performed by the OSI network layer?
9. What are the advantages and disadvantages of centralized routing calculations? Of local route determination?

10. Distinguish between static and adaptive routing.

11. What are the advantages and disadvantages of the quickest link routing algorithm? What are the problems inherent in the quickest link routing method?

12. Describe the weighted routing algorithm.

13. Why are there only three layers defined for PDNs? Do the other OSI layers exist? Explain.

14. What are the four types of physical units in SNA? What is the role of each in the network?

15. What is a half-session layer in SNA? What is its purpose? Explain how a session is established in SNA.

16. Compare a LAN and a PDN.

PROBLEMS AND EXERCISES

1. WAN end-to-end transmissions tend to be much slower than LAN transmissions. Suppose that a 1000 byte message needs to go from node A to Node C in Figure 12-5 and that the path is A → D and D → C. How long will it take for the message to arrive at node C? How long would it take in a CSMA/CD LAN operating at 10 Mbps? Assume that the 1000 byte message includes all necessary enveloping data.

2. A hierarchical topology is used by some companies because it mirrors the corporate organizational structure. Would such a topology be effective for a network of university computers? Explain your conclusion.

3. Bit synchronous protocols allow multiple messages to be exchanged before an acknowledgement is received. Suppose Node A must send five 1000 byte messages to Node B over a 9600 bps link. Suppose further that a message acknowledgement requires 8 bytes of data. What is the time difference between sending five messages and getting one acknowledgement and sending five messages and getting five acknowledgements?

4. Suppose that the connection between Node A and Node B in problem 3 was a satellite link in which the time to send a message from Node A to Node B is 1/4 seconds. What is the time difference from sending the 5 messages in this instance?

5. Suppose a company established a ring wide area network with 10 nodes and with all links having a speed of 9600 bps. Suppose the company also decided to use a token passing media access control protocol like that used in LANs. Calculate the average and maximum time a given node must wait to get the token assuming no

other station has a message to send. Assume the token length is 8 bytes. Make the same calculations for a 16 Mbps token ring.

6. Suppose that the quickest link routing method was used for the network in Figure 12-5. Explain how a message from Node A to Node X could loop through the network forever. Would the problem occur for messages from Node X to Node A?

7. A PDN is more cost effective than leasing lines when the number of packets being sent is less than a certain number called the break-even point. Suppose that a leased line between Node A and Node B is $1000 per month and that the charges for a PDN between the same two points is a $400 flat monthly fee plus $2 for every 1000 packets transmitted. What is the break-even point in packets?

8. Suppose that in Problem 7 your company's transmission requirements are right at the break-even point. Would you pick a leased line or a PDN connection? Justify your answer.

REFERENCES

Stamper, David A. *Business Data Communications*. Redwood City, CA: Benjamin/Cummings Publishing Company, Inc., 1991.

CHAPTER 13

MAKING NETWORK CONNECTIONS

CHAPTER PREVIEW

Most organizations have diverse computing resources, ranging from single microcomputers to multiple local and wide area networks that connect hundreds of computers of varying types—microcomputers, minicomputers, mainframes, and super computers. Today a large organization may have several microcomputer LANs, a WAN of large computers, and perhaps connections to public computer networks. When one organization has a variety of computers and networks, those computers must be interconnected. Interconnection provides better use of hardware and software and allows users to communicate easier. Thus a LAN may need to be connected to another LAN, one large host computer, a WAN, remote workstations or terminals, or public networks.

In this chapter we cover the principal ways interconnections are accomplished. Topics you will read about include:

LAN-to-LAN connections

repeaters, bridges, routers, and gateways

TCP/IP protocol suite

LAN-to-host connections

IBM system connections

internetwork connection utilities

THE OSI REFERENCE MODEL REVISITED

In Chapters 2 and 12 we discussed the OSI reference model. You may wish to refer back to those chapters at this time to review the details of the model. When connecting a LAN to another network or computing system, the connection interface may occur at several OSI layers. However, even though the connection interface may be implemented at, say, the network layer, all node-to-node connections must always have a connection at the physical level, and a data link protocol must be involved in sending the data over the medium at the physical level.

What then do we mean when we say the connection interface is made at the network layer, the data link layer, or the physical layer, and so on? An interface that operates at the physical layer must be sensitive to the signals on the medium. It must know and obey all the physical layer connections. A physical layer connection might be used to extend the distance spanned by a LAN. It does this by amplifying the signals transmitted on the medium. A device that provides connections at the physical layer is called a **repeater.** A repeater forwards media signals and is a hardware device. The relationship between a repeater and the OSI model is illustrated in Figure 13-1.

Figure 13-1   A Repeater, Bridge, and Router and the OSI Reference Model

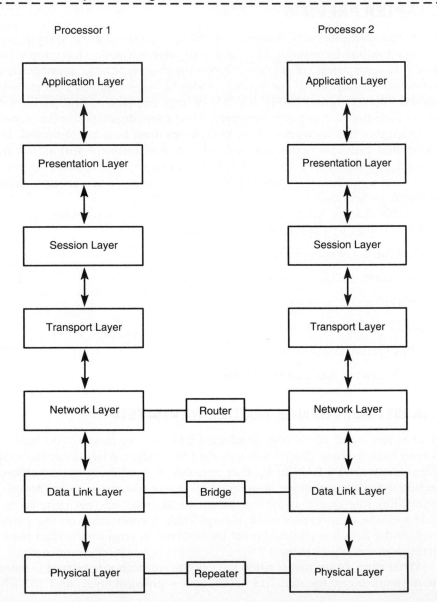

Three major functions of the data link layer of the OSI reference model are delineation of data, transmission-packet-level error detection, and address formatting. A data link protocol is concerned with getting data from the current node to the next node. A message or data packet may pass through several data link protocols on its path from the originating node to the destination node, as illustrated in Figure 13-2. In Figure 13-2 a packet passes from a LAN data link protocol to a WAN data link protocol and back to another (possibly different) LAN data link protocol. On this path the data link protocol at each node is concerned only with moving the data to the next node.

An interface that operates at the data link or media access control (MAC) layer is called a **bridge.** A bridge must know the rules of the data link protocol and be able to interpret the data link portions of the packet. Such a connection can use a variety of physical layer implementations. Thus, if the MAC protocol is the IEEE 802.3 CSMA/CD protocol, the bridge can use twisted-pair wires, coaxial cable, fiber optic cable, or wireless media. Often

Figure 13-2 Message Passing Through Several Different Data Link Protocols

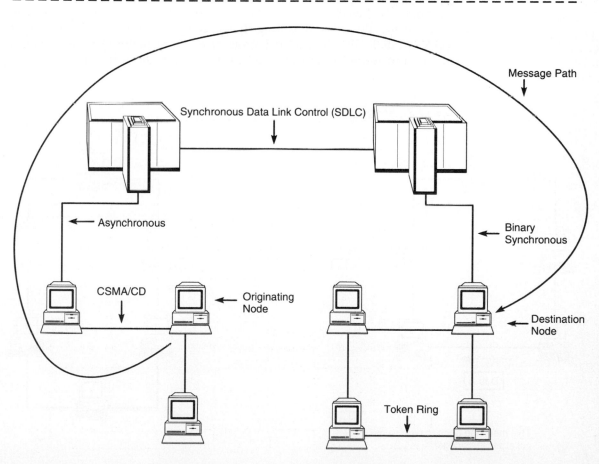

the networks being connected use the same medium; however, in some instances the medium of two LANs being connected by a bridge may differ. For example, two Ethernet LANs, one using coaxial cable and one using twisted-pair wires may need to be connected. Some bridges provide connectors that allow for the connection of different media.

Bridges originally connected LANs of the same type. For example, a bridge might connect two token ring LANs or two IEEE 802.3 LANs. These early bridges blindly forwarded all message traffic from one LAN onto another LAN. Today's bridge technology is more sophisticated and can connect LANs using different data link protocols, such as token ring and CSMA/CD bus LANs. Today a bridge selectively forwards packets of data. Packets sent between two nodes on the same LAN are not acted on by the bridge. Only internetwork packets are forwarded by a bridge, as illustrated in Figure 13-3.

The relationship between a bridge and the OSI model is illustrated in Figure 13-1. Although this figure shows a bridge at the data link layer, the data is still transmitted from the data layer down to the physical layer, over the medium to a physical layer and up to the data link layer.

The network layer of the OSI reference model is responsible for packet routing and for the collection of accounting information. Some networks use a static routing algorithm, meaning that packet routing never changes. In a CSMA/CD bus LAN, a packet is broadcast to every node; in a token ring a packet is transmitted from one node to the next node in the ring. In some

Figure 13-3   Bridge Packet Forwarding

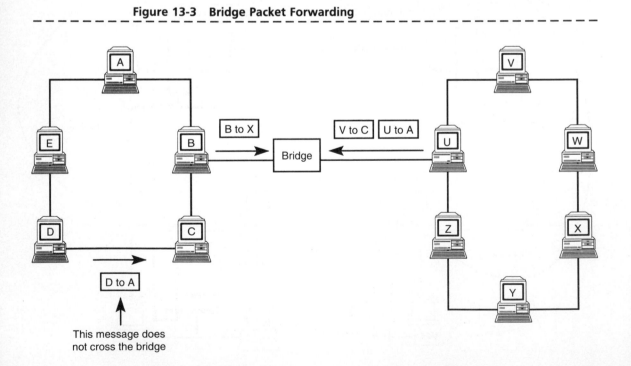

networks several routing paths may be available, as illustrated in Figure 13-4. The network layer is responsible for routing an incoming packet for another node onto an appropriate outbound path. Thus a packet that arrives at a node in a network similar to the one shown in Figure 13-4 arrives at the physical layer and moves up to the network layer through the data link layer. If the packet is not for an application on the receiving node, the network layer determines the outbound path for the packet and sends it down to the data link layer, which formats the packet with the proper data link control data (perhaps a different data link protocol than that of the arriving packet). The data link layer then passes the packet down to the physical layer for transmission to the next node on the path to the final destination.

An interconnection interface that operates at the network layer is called a **router.** A router is not sensitive to the details of the data link and physical layers. Thus it can be used to connect different types of networks, such as a token ring LAN to an IEEE 802.3 LAN or a LAN to a WAN. A router looks at the destination address of a message, determines a route the message should follow to reach that address (possibly passing through two or more networks), and provides the addressing that the network and data link layers along the route require for delivery. For example, a Novell network uses a protocol called **sequenced Packet Exchange/Internetwork Packet Exchange (SPX/IPX)** to transfer packets between nodes. SPX operates at the transport layer and IPX at the network layer. Another protocol used by some networks

Figure 13-4   Alternative Routes in a Network

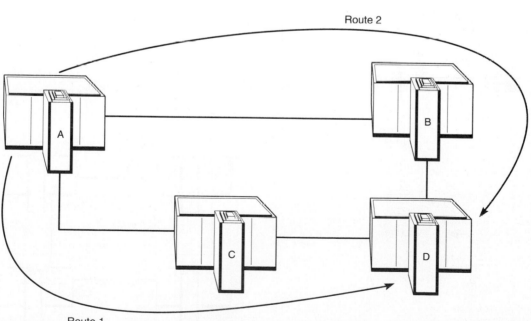

is **Xerox Network System (XNS).** An SPX/IPX router cannot forward XNS packets, and a router that knows only the XNS protocol cannot forward SPX/IPX packets. For two nodes to exchange data using a router, they must both share a common network protocol. Figure 13-1 shows the relationship between a router and the OSI layers.

Network connections that operate at the network layer or above are generically called **gateways.** A gateway connects dissimilar networks or systems and provides conversion from one network protocol to another. For example, a gateway might be used to connect a LAN to a WAN, as illustrated in Figure 13-5. In making this interconnection the gateway must accept packets from the LAN, extract the data from the packets, and format the data in a packet according to the WAN protocol, and vice versa.

LAN-TO-LAN CONNECTIONS

There is a variety of reasons why a company has several LANs and several ways in which they are connected. By definition a LAN serves a limited ge-

Figure 13-5   A Gateway Connecting a LAN and a WAN

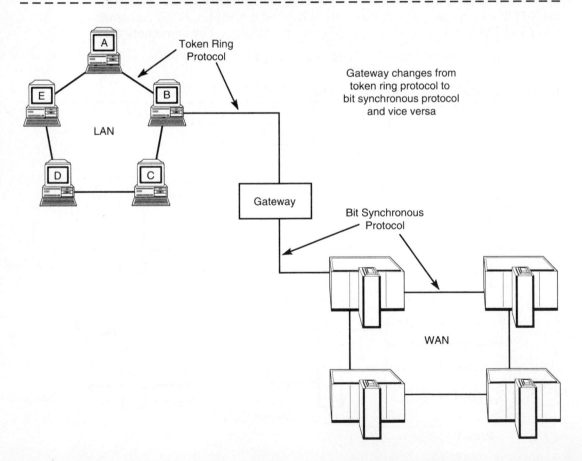

ographical area. Most LAN specifications place a limit on the length of the medium used. Companies that have LANs in separate geographical locations or LANs that cover distances greater than the maximum allowed must be able to make inter-LAN exchanges. Users on one LAN may want to exchange electronic mail message with users on the other LAN, or a user on one LAN may want to use resources located on the other LAN. Thus one reason for having several LANs is distance. But distance or geographical separation is not the only reason for having several interconnected LANs.

LANs sometimes provide department-level computing. A company that is interested in department-level computing might implement a LAN for each department or for groups of departments. For example, consider a computer software manufacturer with departments for personnel, software development, documentation, software support, accounting, and marketing. Most companies like this go to great lengths to protect the integrity of their new products. Often details of new developments must even be protected from some of the company's employees. Having separate LANs allows the company to separate functions and gives an additional level of security. For example, the software company might have one LAN shared by software development and documentation, one for software support, one for accounting, one for personnel, and one for marketing. This separation reduces the likelihood that software the company develops is inadvertently or intentionally made available to customers through the support or marketing LAN. Likewise personnel information can be protected more easily if it is on a separate LAN. Thus another reason for having multiple LANs is departmental computing or separation of functions.

Stephenson (1991) reports that the average LAN has 6.3 nodes, which means many LANs have only a few nodes. These small LANs are found in large and small organizations alike. In many companies microcomputers were introduced as stand-alone systems. Workgroups in some of these companies independently created LANs with several nodes. Later these companies realized there would be advantages to connecting the LANs. Because these LANs began independently, with no corporate direction or standard for LANs, the job of connecting them is very complex. Thus a third reason for LAN connections is to consolidate independent LANs that were formed in an ad hoc manner. Superficially this reason is similar to the preceding one, connecting departmental LANs. The difference is that department-oriented LANs are a planned separation, and workgroup-oriented LANs simply evolved.

A fourth reason for connecting multiple LANs is the number of LAN users. A LAN with hundreds of users might provide poorer performance than the same LAN with tens of users. Even when more users are added, the responsiveness of a LAN must be maintained. Responsiveness can be maintained by adding more resources to an existing LAN—more memory, more disks, another server—or by splitting the LAN into two or more smaller LANs. When a LAN is split, a proper balance must be sought; however, an even balance is not always attainable because of distances and physical location or because of different sizes of workgroups. Because inter-

LAN communications involves more overhead than intra-LAN communications, users and resources should be grouped on the separate LANs in a way that reduces the amount of inter-LAN messages. Often members of a department communicate with each other more than with members of other departments. Thus, splitting a LAN because there are many users being serviced frequently results in a configuration similar to splitting along departmental or workgroup lines.

Let us now look at the specific ways in which LANs or LAN segments can be connected.

Repeaters

Every LAN has a distance restriction. One of the IEEE 802.3 standards specifies a maximum segment length of 500 meters. If you want to span longer distances, you can use a repeater to connect two segments. The standard allows for a maximum of four repeaters, for a total distance of 2500 meters per LAN. Figure 13-6 illustrates two repeaters connecting three segments in an IEEE 802.3 network.

As signals travel along the medium, they lose strength due to attenuation. Weak signals can result in transmission errors. A repeater accepts a signal, regenerates it, and passes it along at full strength. A repeater is a simple hardware device. It does not buffer messages or know about MAC protocols

Figure 13-6   Repeaters Connecting Three LAN Segments

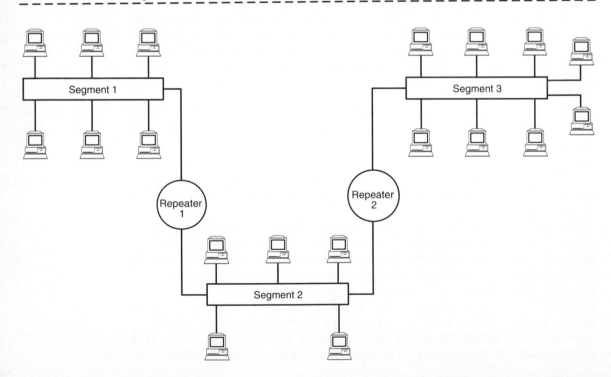

or data packets; it simply gets a signal, renews it, and passes it on. Moreover a repeater does not separate one segment of the network from another. That is, if a station in segment 1 and a station in segment 3 of the network shown in Figure 13-6 try to transmit at the same time, a collision occurs.

A list of repeater capabilities and characteristics is given in Table 13-1. Note that one of the capabilities of some repeaters is media transfer. Thus, you can change media, say from twisted-pair wires to fiber optic cable, at a repeater junction; however, the MAC protocol is the same even though the medium changes. The LAN administrator must also keep in mind that a change in the medium can result in a change in the overall length of the LAN.

Table 13-1   Repeater Characteristics and Capabilities

Media transfer, such as coaxial cable to twisted-pair wires
Multiple ports allowing one repeater to connect three or more segments
Diagnostic and status indicators
Automatic partitioning and reconnection in the event of a segment failure
Manual partitioning
Backup power supply

Bridges

Early bridges were used to connect two different networks, each of which used the same MAC protocol. Today bridges connect LANs having different MAC protocols. These newer bridges must be able to reformat packets from one data link protocol to another. You should be aware that the use of the term *bridge* can vary. Sometimes a bridge is defined in the original sense—a device connecting two identical networks. Others use the broader definition of a device used to connect two networks at the data link layer. For example, you may read about bridges that connect a token ring to an Ethernet LAN. Sometimes a device providing this capability is referred to as a **brouter.** Figure 13-7 illustrates two LANs, LAN A and LAN B, using a token-ring protocol. These two rings may be configured around departments, one ring per department, or around distance, if the distance spanned by the workstations is greater than what can be supported by a single LAN. Regardless of the reason for having two rings, it is likely that a node on LAN A will want to communicate with a server on LAN B or that a user on LAN A will want to send mail to a user on LAN B. A bridge can provide these abilities.

Unlike a repeater, a bridge is selective in what it does. The bridge in Figure 13-7 can be used to move data packets between the two LANs. It accepts packets from both LANs, transfers LAN A packets addressed to nodes on LAN B to LAN B, and transfers LAN B packets addressed to nodes on LAN A to LAN A. These basic bridge functions plus additional functions are listed in Table 13-2.

To do its job, a bridge must know about the addresses on each network. Because the bridge knows the MAC protocol being used, it can find the

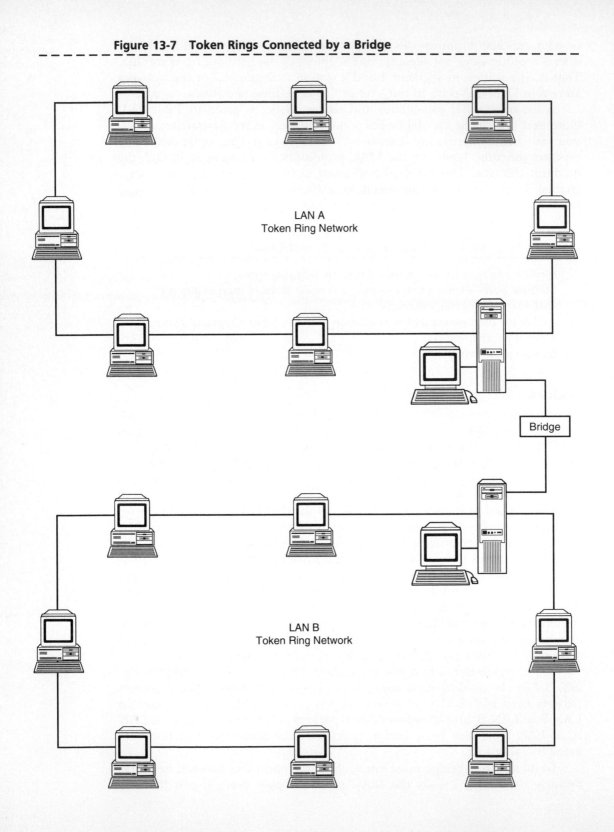

Figure 13-7   Token Rings Connected by a Bridge

LAN A
Token Ring Network

Bridge

LAN B
Token Ring Network

source and destination addresses and use them for routing. (We use the term *routing* here to describe the process of the bridge deciding to which LAN the message must be transferred. In using this term we do not imply that the bridge is performing the functions of a router.) The only additional information the bridge must know is the LAN to which the destination node is connected. This is determined in several ways. Older bridges blindly transferred each message onto both LANs or required network managers to provide a network routing table. The **routing table** contains node addresses and the LAN identifier for the LAN to which the node is connected. Network interconnection can be more complex than a single connection of two networks. Figure 13-8 shows four LANs connected with four bridges. A network routing table for bridge B1 in Figure 13-8 is shown in Table 13-3. These older bridges are static regarding their ability to forward messages. If a new node is added to one of the networks, the routing tables in all bridges must be updated.

Most bridges being sold today are called **learning bridges,** or transparent bridges. A learning bridge builds its routing table from messages it receives and does not need to be loaded with a predefined routing table. Essentially the network administrator just connects the bridge and the bridge is immediately operational.

To understand how bridges of this type work, let's take another look at the bridge configuration in Figure 13-8: four LANs (A, B. C, and D), four bridges (B1, B2, B3 and B4), and five nodes (N1, N2, N3, N4, and N5). Each bridge has two ports labeled P1 and P2. Some bridges may have more than two ports; bridge B2 has a third port, P3. This configuration has at least two paths between each LAN. For example, LAN A can get to LAN D via bridges B1 and B3 or directly via bridge B2; LAN D can get to LAN C directly through either bridge B4 or B2 or indirectly through bridges B3, B1, and B2.

We will start by explaining how a bridge works in a simple, generic sense. Let's assume that each bridge has a fully developed routing table, like

Table 13-2   Basic Bridge Functions

Packet routing function
1. Accept packet from LAN A.
2. Examine address of packet.
3. If packet address is a LAN A address, allow the packet to continue on LAN A.
4. If packet address is a LAN B address, transmit the packet onto the LAN B medium.
5. Do the equivalent for LAN B packets.

Additional Functions

Media conversion	Learning
Remote connection	Signal conversion
Speed conversion	Packet statistics
Token ring to Ethernet conversion	

Figure 13-8 LAN Bridge Routing with Active and Inactive Paths

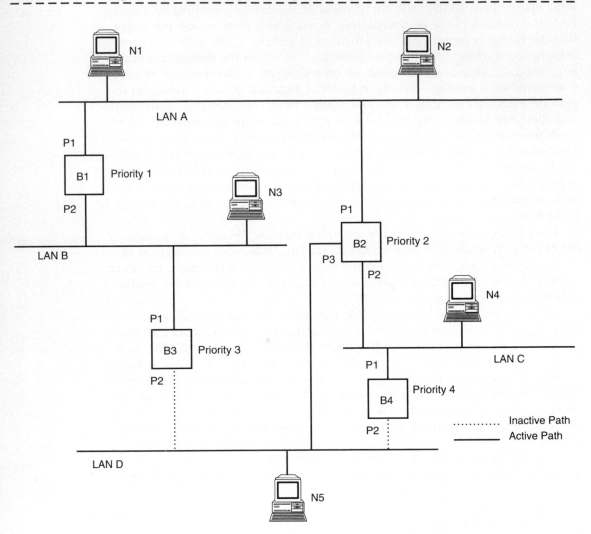

Table 13-3 Bridge B1's Network Routing Table

Node	Port	Comments
N1	P1	
N2	P1	
N3	P2	
N4	P1	Bridge B2 Routes
N5	P1	Bridge B2 Routes

that shown for bridge B1 in Table 13-3. Note also that each node has only one route. If a route changes for some reason, the bridge updates its routing table to show the new route. Some networks use routing algorithms that allow multiple active paths between two nodes, but this is atypical of bridges.

Looking again at Figure 13-8, suppose that bridge B1 receives a packet from N1 destined for N2. Recall that each LAN packet contains the address of the sender and recipient. Since the bridge is aware of the protocol, it finds the source and destination addresses in the packet. The bridge examines its routing table for the destination address. In this case the destination address is local because both the source and destination addresses are on LAN A. Thus the bridge essentially does nothing. In a token-passing LAN the bridge may need to forward the packet to the next node on the LAN on which the message was received. In a CSMA/CD LAN the bridge does nothing because packets are broadcast to all nodes.

Now suppose that bridge B1 receives a packet on port P2 from LAN B with a source address of N3 and a destination address of N2 (on LAN A). The bridge again consults its routing table for the destination address and finds it to be a nonlocal node. The routing table shows the outbound port on which to send the packet P1 in this instance. The bridge simply takes the packet as received and transmits through port P1 onto LAN A (if the LANs have different MAC protocols, the bridge formats the packet to make it compatible with the receiving MAC protocol). Similarly, if bridge B3 receives a packet from node N5 with a destination of N2, it consults its routing table, finds the path to N2 is port P1, and transmits the packet on LAN B. Bridge B1 on LAN B receives this packet, consults its routing table, and forwards the packet to LAN A through port P1. At this point you may be wondering why bridge B4 did not also transmit the packet onto LAN C or why bridge B2 did not also transmit it and cause a duplicate packet. The answer lies in how bridges operate and learn. For details on how bridges learn network addresses, see Soha (1988).

Other Bridge Capabilities

In the preceding discussion the location and media of the interconnected LANs were not described. They might have been geographically separated or confined to a small area. You can also purchase bridges that accommodate media differences. For example, suppose that in Figure 13-9 LAN A uses coaxial cable and LAN B uses twisted-pair wires as the medium. You could select a bridge that has BNC connectors for coaxial cable on one port and RJ-45 connectors for twisted-pair wires on the other port.

You also have bridge options for connecting geographically distributed LANs. A variety of interconnection possibilities exists. The most common of these are listed in Table 13-4. Usually the speed of the connection between remote LANs is much slower than the speed of either LAN. This speed difference can result in the bridge becoming saturated with messages if there are lots of internetwork packets. Bridges have memory that allows some messages to be buffered. The memory buffer helps reconcile the differences

Figure 13-9 LANs Connected With TCP/IP Routers

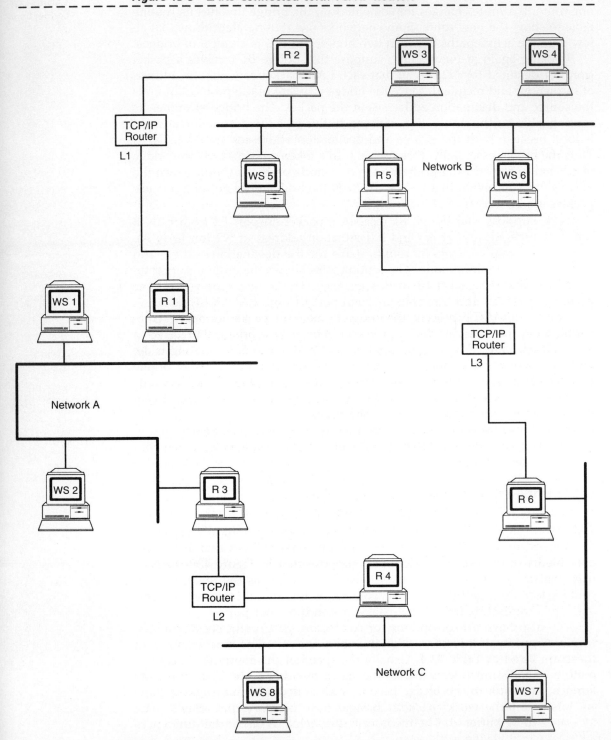

Table 13-4   Remote Bridge Connection Alternatives

RS-232 serial lines	RS-422 serial lines at 19.2 Kbps to 2 Mbps
Synchronous transmission at 56 Kbps or 64 Kbps	T1 Line at 1.5 Mbps
	X.25 packet-switching network
Fractional T1 at 64 Kbps	
Integrated services digital network (ISDN)	

in transmission speed. If too many messages arrive in a short period, the buffer becomes full. Packets that arrive when the buffer is full are lost. Note also that this condition can occur when two local LANs are connected. A bridge must do some processing to determine where a packet must be routed. Except for very slow LANs, the processing time can exceed the arrival rate. Thus bridges connecting LANs experiencing high packet arrival rates can also become saturated.

Routers

Sometimes networks are connected at the network layer. This type of connection is called a router. You will find routers used to connect LANs to LANs and LANs to WANs. As in any form of communication, a common language or protocol is needed. In a bridge the common protocol is the data link protocol. Since the same data link protocol may not be common for all links on networks connected with a router, the common internetwork protocol is formed at the network layer. Although the network interconnection is established at the network layer, you must realize that data link and physical layer services are also involved.

A variety of network protocols are used for network interconnection. For example, Novell's native network protocol is SPX/IPX, which can be used to establish the common basis of communication between a Novell token-ring LAN and a Novell CSMA/CD LAN. However, SPX/IPX cannot be used as a routing protocol in WANs and in LANs provided by other network vendors. The network administrators must find one network layer protocol supported by at least one node on each network. Several internetwork protocols have been developed, but the most common of these is Transmission Control Protocol/Internet Protocol (TCP/IP). As a result, we will use TCP/IP as our router example.

TCP/IP Routing Protocol

Transmission Control Protocol/Internet Protocol (TCP/IP) was developed by the Advanced Research Projects Agency (ARPA) of the United States Department of Defense (DoD). Originally designed as an internetwork protocol, it has evolved over time into a suite of protocols addressing a variety of network communications needs, one of which is that of a router. Note that TCP/IP is not just a microcomputer protocol. On the contrary, it was developed on large systems and was later transported to microcomputers. Since TCP/IP runs on such a wide variety of platforms, it is an ideal choice for a routing protocol. Other functions provided by the TCP/IP protocol suite include file transfer, electronic mail, and logons to remote nodes.

Using TCP/IP's routing capabilities, users can be on the same network or different networks; they can be on networks that are directly connected by a bridge or router; or they can be on networks with one or more intermediate networks. In addition to providing network interconnection, which is the capability that TCP/IP is most commonly known for, TCP/IP also provides services for file transfers and electronic mail, and it makes provisions for a user on one network to log onto another network. While these provisions are important, we will consider only the router functions of the protocol.

Figure 13-9 illustrates how networks might be connected using TCP/IP. In the figure, workstations that function as routing nodes are denoted by Rn and nonrouting nodes by WSn. Internetwork connections are made through specific network nodes, so node R1 on network A has a physical connection to node R2 on network B, and node R3 on network A has a physical connection to node R4 on network C. These networks can be either LANs or WANs, and routing nodes that communicate with each other must share a common data link protocol and a physical link. That is, we speak of routers operating at the network level, but for messages to pass from one node to another, they must pass through the data link and physical layers of each computer. The key is that the information needed to determine how to forward the message is understood by the network layer's logic. For example, in Figure 13-9 let us momentarily assume that network A is a CSMA/CD LAN, network B is a token-ring LAN, and network C is a WAN. Nodes R1 and R2 must share a common data link protocol and medium, and nodes R3 and R4 must share a common data link protocol and medium. A key concept surrounding a router is that any data link protocol can be used.

As the abbreviation implies, TCP/IP consists of two distinct protocols, the transmission control protocol and the internetwork protocol. The TCP operates at the transport layer, and the IP operates at the network layer. Let us look at the functions of each protocol.

The IP provides two basic services, breaking the message up into transmission packets and addressing. In Figure 13-9 there are several network interconnections, and each connection may use a different data link protocol. Many data link protocols have a maximum size for transmission packets. For example, an Ethernet LAN packet contains at most 1500 characters. Some networks have a maximum packet size of 128 characters. An IP must be aware of these data link differences. The IP is also responsible for packet routing. On occasion this requires that the IP break a message into smaller packets of the appropriate size. To do this, it must determine the address of the next node on the path to the message's destination.

The TCP is the protocol responsible for guaranteeing end-to-end message delivery. Thus, if a packet is lost during transmission, the TCP, not the IP, is responsible for resending the message. The TCP also guarantees that individual packets arrive in the correct order. Thus, the primary functions of the TCP are to provide message integrity, provide acknowledgments that a complete message has been received by a destination node, and regulate the

flow of messages between the source and destination nodes. In addition, the
TCP may divide the message up into smaller transmission segments. Usually these segments correspond to an IP transmission packet.

Let us now look at how the TCP and IP cooperate in sending a message
from one node to another. The following example serves as a model for the
functions of a generic router. Suppose that in Figure 13-9 node WS1 on network A needs to send a message to node WS5 on network B. The procedure
followed by the TCP/IP protocol in carrying out this transmission is as follows:

1. The TCP in node WS1 receives a message from an application. The
   TCP attaches a header to the message and passes it down to the IP
   in node WS1. The message header contains the destination address
   and error-detection fields, such as a cyclic redundancy check (CRC)
   and a message sequence number. These are used to ensure that the
   message is received without errors and that messages are received
   in the proper sequence or can be reordered into the proper sequence.

2. Node WS1's IP determines if the destination is an internetwork address. If the address is on the local network, for example, node
   WS2, then the IP passes the message to the local network routing
   facility, which transports the message to the proper node. If the
   destination is a node on another network, the IP finds the best
   path to the destination and forwards the message to the next IP
   node along that path. In this case the IP in node WS1 sends the
   message to node R1.

3. The IP at node R1 receives the message, examines the address, and
   determines the address of the next node, R2 in this example. The
   IP breaks the message up into packets of the appropriate size, adds
   a header to each packet, and passes it down to the data link layer.
   The data link layer appends its transmission information and transmits the packets over the link between R1 and R2.

4. The data link layer at R2 receives a packet, strips off the data link
   layer control data and passes the message to R2's IP. If the destination is local to that IP's network, as it is in this instance, the IP delivers it to the local network routing facility for delivery. If
   the destination is on another network, the IP determines the next
   node along the path and sends the message to it. For example, if
   the node address were WS7, the packet would be routed to node
   R5 and then to R6. Ultimately the message arrives at the destination node.

5. When the message arrives at the final destination node (through
   the services of the IP and local network routing facilities) it is
   passed up to the TCP. The TCP decodes the header attached by
   the sender's TCP. The receiving TCP checks for errors, such as
   message sequence or CRC errors. If no errors are detected, the TCP
   determines the destination program and sends the message to it.

On the path from source to destination, the message passes through several IP nodes and traverses links with several different data link protocols. The router, TCP/IP in this example, is responsible for generating the destination address and intermediate addresses along the way and for ensuring the correct delivery of the message.

From the preceding discussion you should realize that a LAN node that must communicate with a node on another network must run both the TCP and IP software. Most of today's LAN operating system vendors have this available in DOS, OS/2, and UNIX versions. You can also find this software and associated utilities available from independent software vendors. Moreover a variety of TCP/IP utilities can be found in the public domain and are thus available at little or no cost.

Choosing the Right Interface

We have defined three network interconnection capabilities: repeaters, bridges, and routers. How do you choose the right one? In general, you should choose the connection at the lowest OSI level possible. Thus, a repeater is usually preferable to a bridge and a bridge is usually preferable to a router. As you move up the OSI layers, your connection must be more intelligent, do more work, and have a lower packet exchange rate. This is not the only deciding factor, however.

A bridge can replace a repeater, and a router can replace a repeater or a bridge. However, the opposite is not always true; for example, a repeater cannot always substitute for a bridge, and a bridge cannot always substitute for a router. You might choose to use a bridge in place of a repeater, which makes sense if the bridge can handle the message traffic and if you already have the bridge components. Moreover a bridge allows some LAN isolation capability that a repeater does not provide. Many LAN users prefer a bridge over a router because it provides an extra level of network security.

Gateways

The interface between two dissimilar networks is called a **gateway.** A gateway is basically a protocol converter. It reconciles the differences between the networks it connects. With repeaters, bridges, and routers, the communicating nodes share a common protocol at the physical, data link, or network layer, respectively. Suppose that it is necessary to connect two nodes that do not share a common protocol. In this instance a gateway or protocol converter can make the interconnection. Naturally the gateway must be able to understand the protocol of the two nodes being connected and also be able to translate from one protocol to the other. The components of a gateway are the network interfaces and the logic that carries out the conversion necessary when moving messages between networks. The conversion must change the header and trailer of the packet to make it consistent with the protocol of the network or data link to which the message is being transferred. This may include accommodating differences in speed, packet sizes, packet formats, and so on. For example, suppose that both a LAN and a

WAN can interface to an X.25 network. The X.25 network can then serve as an intermediary and allow the stations on the LAN and WAN to communicate. This type of network has two gateways, one from the LAN to the X.25 network and one from the X.25 network to the WAN, as illustrated in Figure 13.10.

LAN-TO-HOST CONNECTIONS

The preceding discussion explored ways of connecting networks together, specifically, ways in which a LAN can be connected to another LAN or to a WAN. For many companies there is another LAN connection need, that of connecting a LAN to a stand-alone computer.

Many companies entered the microcomputer age with a large computer already installed. As these companies grew in their use of microcomputers and then installed one or more LANs, the large computer continued to play an important role in their computing needs. For example, a large computer, which we will call a host, might be used for payroll or large database applications. Even companies that replaced or are replacing the host with LAN technology go through a period when both computing environments exist. Companies that use hosts and LANs usually need to exchange data between the two environments. This can be done via media exchange. For example, data on the host can be copied onto a diskette or tape and transferred to the LAN and vice versa. Often a LAN-host direct connection is a more efficient way to do this. Figure 13-11 illustrates a host computer connected to a LAN.

Before discussing the ways in which the LAN-host connection can be made, let us look at several ways in which a LAN user can interact with a host. In Figure 13-11 a user at node N1 might need to view, update, or evaluate data that is stored in the host's database. This user has two basic options: do the work on the host or do the work on the LAN workstation. A user at node N2 might need to send an electronic mail message to a user at terminal T1. A user at node N3 might need to run an application that exists only on the host. The application may be available only on the host for a variety of reasons: It has not yet been implemented on the LAN, it needs special hardware available only on the host (for example, a typesetting machine), it requires computing power beyond that which is available on the LAN, and so on.

The three preceding examples cover most of the general connection needs of LAN users. These needs can be summarized as follows:

to use host data

to use host applications

to transfer data from the host to the LAN

to transfer data from the LAN to the host

to use host hardware or software resources

to communicate with host users

Figure 13-10   LAN-WAN Interconnection Using an X.25 Network

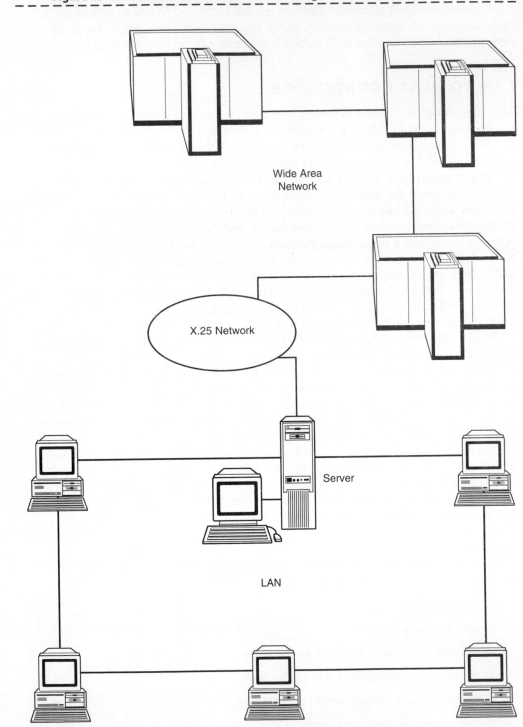

Wide Area
Network

X.25 Network

Server

LAN

Figure 13-11 LAN-to-Host Connection

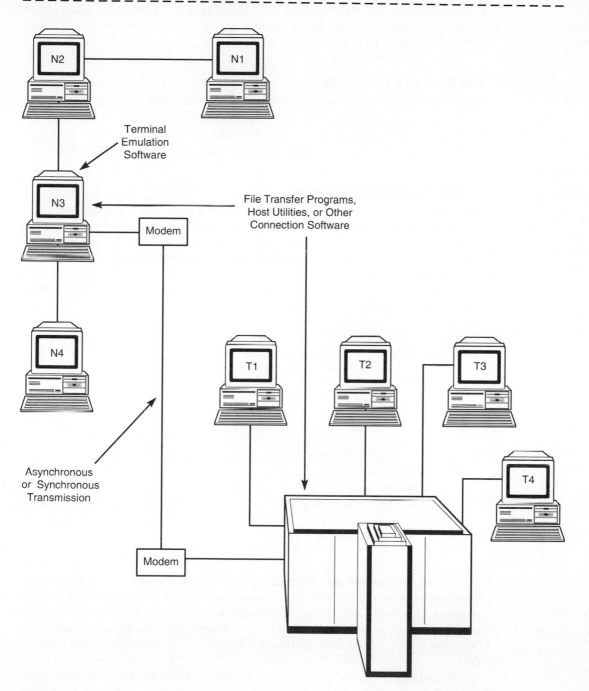

It is just as likely that a host user will have the same basic needs for LAN resources. You have already read about two ways in which a LAN-host connection can be made, using routers and gateways. Let us now look at some other ways to make these connections.

The Host as a LAN Node

Some hosts have the ability to connect to the LAN as a node. This is the most effective way of establishing the connection. The host can thus operate as a server, providing all the needs listed in the previous section. Unfortunately this is not always an option, so we must look at other capabilities.

Asynchronous Connections

Virtually every computer has the ability to send and receive asynchronously. You are probably familiar with the serial port on a microcomputer; it is an asynchronous communications port. Since most computers support the asynchronous data link protocol, it is sometimes used to link a microcomputer to a host. Usually a microcomputer attached to a host asynchronously operates in one of two modes, file transfer or terminal emulation. A listing of **terminal emulation** software capabilities is given in Table 13-5.

Table 13-5   Common Features of Asynchronous Communications Software

Scripts
Mouse support
File transfer—CompuServe, XModem, YModem, Kermit
Terminal emulation—ANSI, DEC VT 220, IBM 3101, TTY
Electronic mail
Phone directory
Capture of data to a disk
Text editor
Password security

Dedicated Connection per Microcomputer   Host computers can usually accommodate many asynchronous connections. Small minicomputers usually support 32 or more, and large mainframes can accommodate hundreds. One way to connect a LAN node to a host is to provide a **dedicated connection** between a port on the host and each microcomputer needing a host connection.

A dedicated connection provides direct host access, and the microcomputer does not use LAN resources for communicating with the host. The typical connection has the microcomputer appear to the host as though the microcomputer were a host terminal. In addition to the serial port, the microcomputer needs terminal emulation software to establish the connection and carry on a host session. Terminal emulation software is available from many sources and has the ability to emulate a wide variety of terminals. With dedicated connections the LAN administrator and data processing department can easily control which LAN nodes have access to the host. Nodes without a direct connection cannot make a host connection.

A dedicated connection has several disadvantages. First, like all asynchronous connections, the speed of the link is slow. Asynchronous speeds can be over 100,000 bits per second (bps) but typically for microcomputer connections it is 19,200 bps or less. If many LAN nodes must communicate with the host, many host ports are required. This not only reduces the number of ports available to the host's terminal users but also is somewhat costly. The cost for host ports can be significant and is burdensome for microcomputers that need only occasional access. Finally, when operating in terminal emulation mode, the microcomputer loses some of its processing capabilities. It can essentially do only what a terminal can do. That is, the microcomputer can send and receive data but usually cannot use this interface to have a local application, such as a database management system, directly access data on the host.

Multiplexing A **multiplexer** is a hardware device that allows several devices to share one communications channel. Multiplexing is typically used to consolidate the message traffic between a computer and several remotely located terminals, as illustrated in Figure 13-12. This technique can also be used to allow several microcomputers to share a communications link to a host processor.

Shared Asynchronous Connections In some applications each LAN node needs occasional access to the host, but the number of concurrent connections is far fewer than the number of LAN nodes. In such situations a dedicated line per node is excessive. A better solution is to share asynchronous

Figure 13-12 A Multiplexer

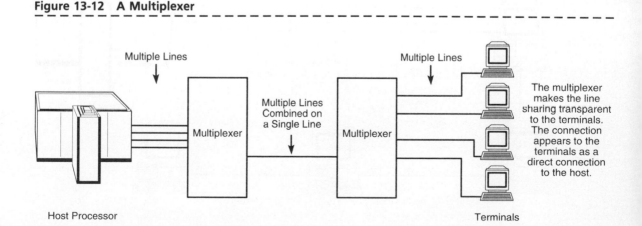

connections. The most common way to share connections is via a **communications server,** as illustrated in Figure 13-13.

In the figure the communications server has four connections to the host. A microcomputer needing host services requests a connection through the communications server. If all four ports are in use, the request is denied. If a host port is free, the request is honored and the microcomputer is connected to a vacant host port. You might note that the communications server functions much like a telephone switch.

Communications servers also provide connections for remote hosts. The usual way a connection is made to a remote host is via a modem connection. The line to the remote host may be dedicated or switched. A dedicated line is continuously available; a switched line connection is established on an as-needed basis. The typical example of a switched line is a dial-up telephone line. The link between two devices is made via a telephone call, remains active during the length of the session, and is broken when the session is completed. Rather than providing each LAN node with a dedicated modem, the communications server can provide **modem sharing.** The technique for doing this is much like the sharing technique described in the previous paragraph.

Figure 13-13 LAN-to Host Connections Using a Communications Server

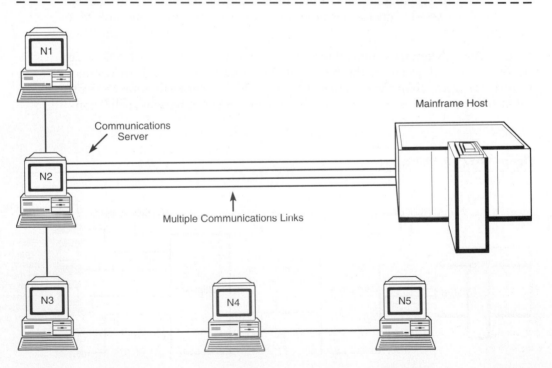

Other Types of Host Connections

Asynchronous connections are common because they are easily implemented and are supported by most host systems. The only host specific characteristic is the type of terminal being emulated or file transfer software. Other vendor-specific connections exist.

IBM System Connections

Because of the dominant role played by IBM systems, many network connections are based on IBM software and hardware technologies. These connections might also work on non-IBM equipment, because many manufacturers of large computers support one or more IBM communications protocols. Two of the most common IBM interfaces are described here.

IBM-3270 Emulation One of the mainstays of IBM's communications networks is the family of 3270 terminals. The family consists of a variety of terminals, printers, and cluster controllers. The communication protocol used for 3270 devices is a synchronous protocol, either the Binary Synchronous (BISYNC) Protocol or the Synchronous Data Link Control (SDLC) protocol (discussed in Chapter 12).

IBM-3270 emulation can be effected through a communications server or through individual LAN nodes. When implemented at individual LAN nodes, a synchronous communications controller must be installed in the microcomputer. The controller provides the necessary line interface. If a communications server is used, the server must have a synchronous communications port. Aside from the protocol interface, the connection works much like the asynchronous connection described earlier.

LU 6.2 Connection For many years IBM networks have been designed around IBM's Systems Network Architecture (SNA), which is discussed in Chapter 12. In SNA users communicate through sessions, and a variety of session types are defined. Logical units (LU's) represent users in establishing, using, and ending a session. One type of session allows programs to communicate with other programs. This type of session is called an LU 6.2 session. Support for LU 6.2 sessions is available for microcomputers and is being increasingly used to establish host connections. The advantage of an LU 6.2 interface is that a microcomputer application can communicate directly with a host application or with an application on another network node (as opposed to the microcomputer simply acting as though it were a terminal).

INTERCONNECTION UTILITIES

Having the ability to establish network connections is one part of communicating among networks. Another part is having utilities that help you exploit those connections. Many such utilities are available. Some are commercial products, while others are available in the public domain for little or no cost. Some utilities you may find useful are briefly described here.

File Transfer Utilities   File transfer utilities allow you to move files between network nodes. File transfer capabilities are an intrinsic part of many routers; part of the TCP/IP protocol suite is a file transfer capability. Kermit is a file transfer utility that runs on a wide variety of computer platforms. It uses asynchronous communications links to transfer ASCII format files. Two common microcomputer file transfer utilities are XMODEM and MODEM. Kermit, XMODEM, and YMODEM are often included in terminal emulation programs.

Remote Logon   Remote logon utilities allow users to log onto a remote system. A remote logon essentially establishes a remote user as a local user on the remote node. Once a user has successfully logged onto the remote node, commands issued by that user are processed and acted on by the remote

Figure 13-14   Two Remote Access Server Technologies

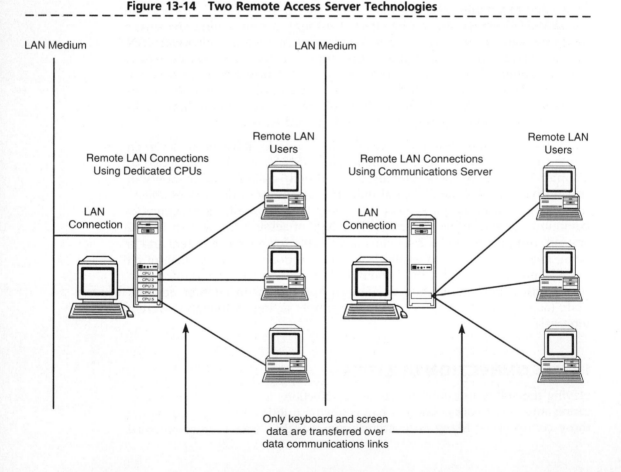

LAN Medium

LAN Medium

Remote LAN Connections
Using Dedicated CPUs

Remote LAN
Users

Remote LAN Connections
Using Communications Server

Remote LAN
Users

LAN
Connection

LAN
Connection

Only keyboard and screen
data are transferred over
data communications links

node rather than by the local node. When the user logs off the remote node, the session is re-established on the local node.

Remote Control   In Chapter 11 we described remote control utilities as a diagnostic tool. We mention it here because some remote control packages also provide connection services, allowing users to transfer data between nodes.

Access Servers   **Access servers** allow remote microcomputers to access LAN resources remotely. For example, suppose you are working at your home microcomputer and must do some work at your office. Specifically, you may have remembered that you had a report due in the morning. Furthermore, suppose that the software, files, and electronic mail essential to creating and distributing the report are available only on the LAN in your office. You have two options: You can drive to the office to complete the work, or you can use the facilities of an access server. The two approaches to access server technology are illustrated in Figure 13-14. To access your LAN remotely, you need a serial port, a modem at your end and on the LAN end, and communications software.

   Access servers provide more than just modem connections. If you try to run a LAN application like word processing remotely, the word processing program must be downloaded into your computer. If your line speed is 2400 bits per second (bps) and the size of the application is 360 KB, it takes at least 25 minutes to download the program (2400 bps is about 20 characters per second). This level of performance is hardly acceptable. An access server is one solution to this problem. The access server runs applications at the LAN end of the connection and passes only the monitor display and keyboard data over the communications link. The remote processing can be accomplished by connections to remote access CPU boards (the user essentially has a dedicated remote CPU at the LAN) or by multiprocessing on a high-capacity microcomputer.

SUMMARY

LANs are not necessarily isolated islands of computing. Often there is a need to connect several LAN segments: homogenous but separate LANs, heteroenous LANs, LANs, to WANs, or LANs to a host. There are many ways in which these connections can be made.

   Repeaters are used to connect segments of a homogenous LAN. The main reason for doing this is to extend the length of the LAN medium. Repeaters operate at the physical level. They simply accept a signal from one segment, amplify or regenerate the signal, and forward it onto the next segment.

   Bridges connect homogenous but distinct LANs. A bridge operates at the data link (MAC) level. A bridge receives a packet, looks at its destination address, and, if the address is a node on a LAN other than the one on which the packet was received, the bridge transmits the packet onto another LAN. Most of today's bridges are **learning bridges.** Learning bridges can adapt to changes in network paths.

Routers operate at the network layer and can connect homogenous or heterogenous networks. A router receives a message, determines the address of the destination, and chooses a route for the message to take. The message may travel through several intermediate networks to reach the destination. Different data link protocols may be used in moving the message from the source to its recipient. Because they operate at the network layer, routers are independent of data link protocols.

A gateway is a name applied to network connections between heterogenous networks. A gateway must perform translation functions like packet formatting, speed conversion, error checking, and so on.

Sometimes LAN nodes must be connected to a host machine. Some hosts can connect directly to the LAN and operate as a LAN node. Asynchronous connections are common and easy to implement but are quite slow. Synchronous connections offer greater speed but usually require additional microcomputer hardware.

Because of the wide variety of connection services available, you should be able to find ready-made solutions to most of your LAN connection needs.

KEY TERMS

access servers

bridge

brouter

communications server

dedicated connection

file transfer utility

gateway

IBM-3270 emulation

learning bridge

modem sharing

multiplexer

remote logon utility

repeater

router

routing table

Sequenced Packet Exchange/Internetwork Exchange (SPX/IPX)

source routing

terminal emulation

Transmission Control Protocol/Internet Protocol (TCP/IP)

Xerox Network System (XNS)

REVIEW QUESTIONS

1. Give two reasons why a company might have two LANs in the same general location.

2. Identify the OSI level at which each of the following operate.

    a. bridge

    b. repeater

    c. router

3. What does a repeater do? Under what conditions can a repeater be used?

4. What does a bridge do? Under what conditions can a bridge be used?

5. What does a router do? Under what conditions can a router be used?

6. Compare the capabilities of repeaters, bridges, and routers.

7. Describe how TCP/IP sends a message from a node on one network to a node on another network.

8. Besides providing network interconnections, list three other functions you might find in TCP/IP.

9. What is a gateway?

10. Describe three distinct LAN-to-host interfaces.

11. What are the advantages and disadvantages of asynchronous LAN-to-host interfaces?

12. Describe two common types of microcomputer interfaces to IBM systems.

PROBLEMS AND EXERCISES

1. Evaluate the following LAN situations. State if the LANs can be consolidated with a repeater, a bridge, or a router. Give all possible

types of connections. State which connection alternative you would choose, and state why you would choose it.

a. A token ring and a token bus.

b. Two IEEE 802.3 LANs. One LAN has a total cable span of 1000 meters and the other has a total cable span of 2500 meters.

c. Two IEEE 802.3 LANs. Each has a total cable span of 1000 meters. Assume that the cable being used meets the IEEE 802.3 standard for maximum segment lengths of 500 meters and a maximum distance of 2500 meters per LAN.

d. Three Novell LANS. One LAN is an ARCnet, one is a token ring, and one is a CSMA/CD bus.

2. Suppose your company has two IEEE 802.3 LANs, one in your eastern office and one in your western office (the distance between them is several hundred miles). The company wants to connect these LANs so users can more easily exchange data. The data being exchanged is primarily small messages, such as electronic mail messages and small data files. Occasionally a file several megabytes in size must be exchanged, but in these situations, the exchange is not time critical (for example, it could occur overnight). Devise a way to connect these LANs. Describe the type and speed of communications channel you would use to make the connection. Explain your decision.

3. Suppose the two LANs described in problem 2 were different, a token ring and a CSMA/CD bus. Would your decision be different? Explain any differences and the reason for your decision.

4. Suppose the situation in problem 2 were different in that the large files (2 MB or less) had to be exchanged within two minutes or less. Would your solution to the connection be different? Explain any differences and the reason for your decision.

5. Suppose a company has two large computers connected by a synchronous communications line having a speed of 56 Kbps. These computers are geographically separated, one in the eastern office and one in the western office. Each of these locations also has a LAN. The company wants to allow all computer users to communicate, those connected to the LANs as well as those connected to the large computers. Can the connection be made using the existing communications link? Explain your answer.

6. Assuming the existing communications link described in problem 5 were used for the long distance connection, answer each of the following.

a. How can the LANs be connected to the large systems?

b. Describe the changes a LAN packet will undergo as it moves from a LAN to a large system to the other large system and then to the other LAN. Assume the LANs are homogeneous.

REFERENCES

Byrnes, Philippe. "Using SNA to link LAN to Host." *LAN Technology*, Volume 6, Number 12, December 1990.

Derfler, Jr., Frank J. "Building Workgroup Solutions: LAN Gateways." *PC Magazine*, Volume 7, Number 20, November 29, 1988.

Derfler, Jr., Frank J. and Rigney, Steve. "Bringing Your Networks Together." *PC Magazine*, Volume 10, Number 15, September 10, 1991.

Dryden, Patrick. "LAN Bridges Get Cheaper, More Powerful." *LAN Times*, Volume 8, Issue 19, October 7, 1991.

Duncan, Thom. "Comparing TCP/IP Gateways." *LAN Times*, Volume 7, Issue 8, August 1990.

Hunter, John. "Bridging the Gap." *Network World*, July 10, 1989.

Nolle, Thomas, "Making the LAN-to-WAN Connection." *LAN Technology*, Volume 5, Number 9, September 1989.

Sheltzer, Alan and Blotter, Ned. "Making the LAN-to-Mini Connection." *LAN Technology*, Volume 7, Number 5, May 1991.

Soha, Michael and Perlman, Radia. "Comparison of Two LAN Bridge Approaches." *IEEE Network*, Volume 2, Number 1, January 1988.

Stephenson, Peter. "Mixing and Matching LANS." *Byte*, Volume 16, Number 3, March 1991.

Zhang, Lixia. "Comparison of Two Bridge Routing Approaches." *IEEE Network*, Volume 2, Number 1, January 1988.

CHAPTER 14

EMERGING TECHNOLOGIES

CHAPTER PREVIEW

In the preceding chapters we concentrated on the LAN technologies that are commonly implemented in today's LANs. But LAN technology, both hardware and software, is one of the most dynamic technologies in the computer industry. Microcomputer LAN technology is approximately 16 years old, and in that time we have already seen many new technologies emerge and others become obsolete. This trend will continue. In this chapter we will look at several technologies that are important but less commonly used. These technologies fill a critical need in a small percentage of today's LANs and have the potential for being mainstream technologies in the future.

Some of the topics covered in this chapter include:

client/server computing

nondedicated servers

peer-to-peer LANs

wireless media

diskless workstations

global naming

ISDN

high-speed LANs

multimedia on LANs

servers—communications, remote access, and FAX

uninterruptable power supplies

pocket LAN adapters

CLIENT/SERVER COMPUTING

You can take several approaches to creating the applications environment of your LAN system. One approach uses the LAN's servers as an extension of a workstation's hardware. The server's disks and printers are shared among users, but the applications run essentially the same as they would on a stand-alone computer. The application on the workstation is responsible for carrying out all the work for the problem being solved. For example, consider a database application running entirely at a network node. A request to compute the average employee salary results in all employee records being transferred to the node for processing. In a large company this creates considerable network traffic.

An alternative approach that is gaining popularity is called **client/server (C/S) computing.** C/S computing technology was not developed for LANs or even for networking; however, networks in general and LANs specifically have created an environment that requires C/S technology. Perhaps looking at the precursors of today's C/S environment will make it easier to understand the extended LAN implementations.

Suppose you have a system with a large computer to which many terminals are connected. Terminal users each have a set of applications and transactions they are allowed to run, and different users may have different sets of capabilities. A person's job determines which applications and transactions can be used. Figure 14-1 shows four classes of software components in the host processor: transaction control process (TCP) software, operating system software, applications software, and database management system software. As an example, consider the needs of a specific terminal user who works in a personnel department and uses the computer to add new employees, update employee records, and delete the records of employees who left the company over three years ago. The add-employee transaction requries the services of three different applications: one each for employee, insurance, and payroll updates.

When the user requests that a certain transaction, say adding a new employee, be run, the request is received by the TCP. The TCP is responsible for routing the transaction to the appropriate applications. In this case three applications must work on the transaction, a capability we call cooperative computing. The TCP requests each application to perform a service. In some systems, the TCP is called a requester, and the applications are called servers. In today's terminology the TCP could be called a client. The client makes requests that are carried out in whole or in part by other processes called servers. In this example the applications in turn make requests of the database management system and the operating system for services they perform. Thus a server can also become a client.

Some companies have extended this type of C/S technology to include WANs by allowing the server processes to be on nodes different from the one in which the client is running. This provides a distributed processing environment in which the hardware, software, and data resources of several computers combine to solve a problem. In essence, with C/S computing the *the network becomes the computer.* A **server class** is represented by one or more applications, all of which can carry out certain tasks. With server classes, a client does not need the services of a particular server process, because any process in the class can perform the requested service.

Figure 14-1 Client/Server Computing in a Mainframe Computer

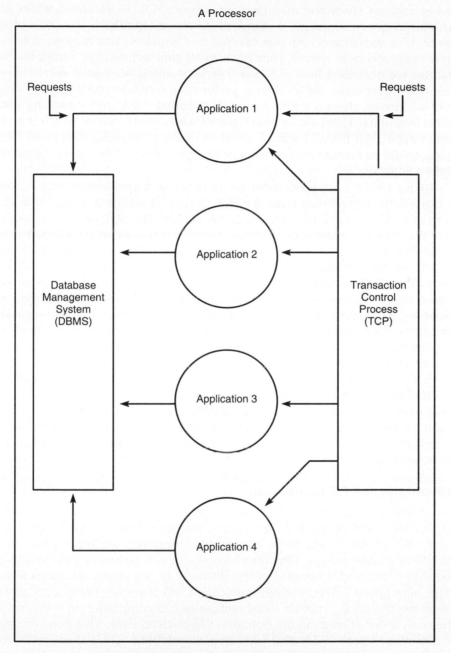

A Processor

Requests

Requests

Application 1

Database
Management
System
(DBMS)

Application 2

Transaction
Control
Process
(TCP)

Application 3

Application 4

TCP has a role as a client with applications as servers

Applications have role as clients with DBMS as a server

C/S Computing Examples

Figure 14-2 illustrates two examples of C/S computing, a database or SQL server and an electronic mail (E-mail) server. SQL is an abbreviation for structured query language, a standard database language. The concept of the SQL or database server was covered in Chapter 4; you may want to review that section to refresh your memory of this technology. Earlier in this chapter we described how a database server works. An E-mail server operates like a post office for its clients, performing functions such as supplying mail addresses given a user's name, distributing mail, and providing mail agent functions. There are several types of mail agents, one of which is a vacation agent. An E-mail vacation agent can collect incoming mail in an electronic folder or reroute mail to another designated user while the original recipient is away.

In Figure 14-3 suppose client C1 is running a spreadsheet application and needs to import data from the SQL server. It makes the request in the form of an SQL query and sends it to the server. The SQL server selects the data meeting the client's request and sends the requested data back to the client. While the SQL server is working on client C1's request, client C2 that is running an accounting application also needs data from the database. C2 formats an SQL command to access its needed data. The SQL server receives this command while working on client C1's request and begins to process C2's request. Thus the server may be working on multiple requests simultaneously. While C1 and C2 are requesting database services, client C3 is using the services of the electronic mail server to find the network address of another user and to send mail to that user.

In LAN C/S technology, clients typically run in workstations and request services from nodes that operate exclusively as servers. Alternatively C/S computing can be implemented in a peer-to-peer LAN, with server and client processes running in the same node. Figure 14-3 shows clients A, B, C, and D running in nodes 1, 3, and 4, while server processes 1, 2, and 3 are running in nodes 1 and 2.

Advantages of C/S Computing

The primary advantages of C/S computing—easy system expansion, better applications, and portability—all relate to the modularity of the C/S environment. Before discussing these advantages, however, we must admit to a couple of disadvantages. One disadvantage of C/S technology on WANs is reduced performance because of the slowness of the communications links. With high-speed LANs, the communication link does not become an obstacle to performance. Another disadvantage of C/S computing on networks is the complexity of creating the optimum C/S environment. This disadvantage is common to both WAN and LAN implementations. Once these problems are overcome, however, you can enjoy the advantages afforded by C/S computing.

Easy System Expansion Growth, a primary objective of many companies, is often accompanied by the need for additional computing power. C/S com-

Figure 14-2   A LAN Client/Server Computing Environment

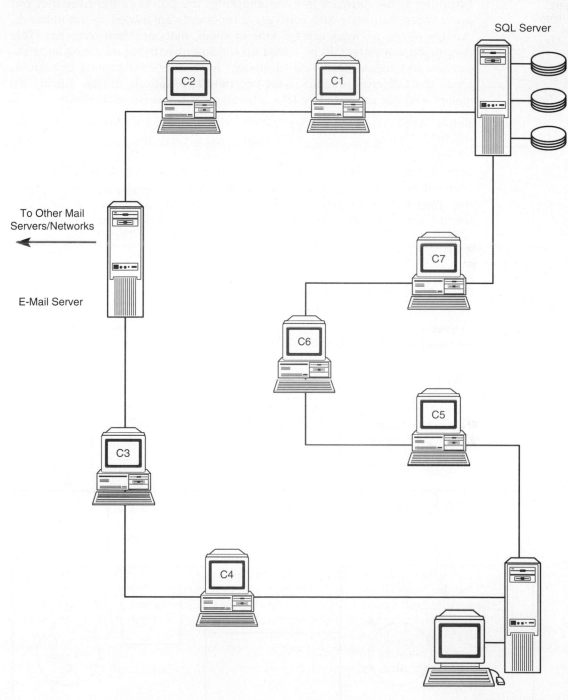

SQL Server

To Other Mail
Servers/Networks

E-Mail Server

File Server

puting distributes the computing power over multiple processors. Since the computer is the network in C/S computing, the power of the computer can grow when hardware and software components are added to the network. Adding to the network can be done in small, manageable increments. This means the computer can be scaled up (or down) without incurring large expenses and major hardware upgrades. Moveover applications can grow. Once the C/S environment is set up, new applications can be quickly installed and can immediately take advantage of the services available.

Better Applications C/S applications should be better because they are modular. Part of the logic is contained in the servers and so does not need to be replicated in the client portion of the code. An analogy may be helpful here. If you are building a house, you probably would not do all the jobs yourself because you would not know all of the necessary carpentry, plumbing, electrical, and landscaping skills. However, if you become a client and use the services of craftsmen who already know how to do those things, you will likely end up with the job done faster and batter. This analogy applies directly to the concept of C/S computing. Server modules are optimized to

Figure 14-3   A Peer-to-Peer Client/Server Environment

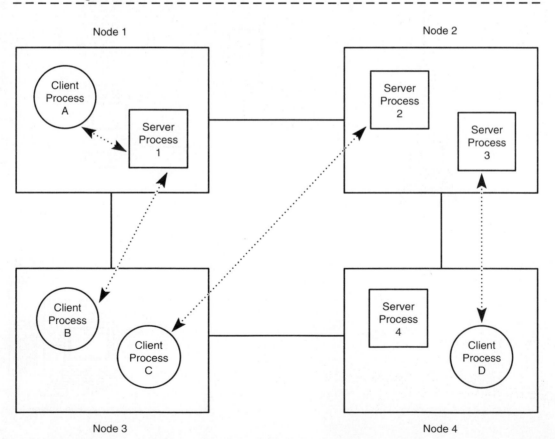

perform their function on behalf of their clientele, and the clients do not need to be burdened with the logic essential to performing those tasks.

Portability   Some computer systems are better able to perform certain jobs than others. For example, some platforms are noted for their ability to do high-resolution graphic applications such as computer-aided design (CAD); other hardware and software combinations are well suited for office automation applications. Moreover the combination of hardware and software on an SQL server make it able to manage data more effectively than a general-purpose computer and operating system. As new technologies emerge, they can easily be integrated into the network with a C/S environment. A company can switch between hardware and software vendors to find its ideal computing system. To again use the house-building analogy, if a new company provides service superior to the one you are using, you can easily switch to that new company for the next project. Ordinarily such changes do not affect the other parts of the project. With C/S computing, using an SQL server as an example, if a new, more powerful server engine becomes available, it should be easy to install it in place of existing SQL servers or to simply add the new server to augment existing servers.

C/S Technology

C/S technology on LANs is in its infancy, but some of its directions have already been established. In this section we will look at some of the technology that underlies C/S computing, the interfaces that exist between clients and servers, and standards that are being developed.

Clients and servers must have a way to communicate with each other. There are two basic ways is which this is done, remote procedure calls and messages. You may be familiar with programming languages that support local procedure calls. With local procedure cells, one segment of a program invokes logic in another program segment called a procedure. The procedure does its work, and then the results and processing control are passed back to the point in the program from which the procedure was called. You can think of the procedure as performing a service for the program. **Remote procedure calls** extend this concept to allow an application on one computer to call on the services of another process. The process being called could be running in the same computer or, as is typical in C/S computing, the process being called could be running in another computer. Moreover, the process being called may not be running at the time of the call. The remote procedure call in this instance initiates the server process on the other computer.

Message exchange is a more flexible method of communication. The client and the server enter into a session (recall the OSI session layer) and exchange information. The client sends a request, and the server responds with the results to the request.

One issue to be resolved with C/S computing is how to find the server or servers that perform the needed functions. Today we are looking primarily at clients and servers that are attached to the same LAN. It is logical to extend this to having servers and clients on different LANs. To maintain the modularity and flexibility of C/S computing, we would like to be able to add new servers, delete existing ones, and perhaps move an existing server from one LAN to another. Moreover changes of this nature should be transparent to the clients. That is, the clients should not have to be reprogrammed to avail themselves of the altered services. These goals can be achieved by having servers "advertise" themselves. For example, they might place an entry into a network directory or send messages to all of the nodes registering their presence.

Clients communicate with servers through an application program interface (API), as illustrated in Figure 14-4. As C/S technology develops, we see new standards beginning to appear that make forming C/S interfaces easier. Again, to provide flexibility, we would like to avoid having lots of different C/S interfaces. Instead, we would like to have one or a few standard interfaces so a company can write clients that will be able to access servers that are written by other companies. These interfaces have come to be called **middleware.** The objective of middleware is to serve as an intermediary between clients and servers; that is, the middleware is responsible for making the connection between clients and servers. This is similar to the function performed by the logical link control layer, which serves as the interface between the network layer and media access control.

One example of middleware and its standardization efforts is the Open Software Foundation's **Distributed Computing Environment (DCE)** specifications. DCE addresses the use of remote procedure calls, security, name services, and messages for C/S computing. Another example is the Object Management Group's **Object Request Broker (ORB).** A client can communicate with a server through the services of the ORB. The ORB receives a client's request, finds a server that is capable of satisfying that request, sends the message to that server, and returns the response to the client. The ORB thus provides client and server independence. Any client that can communicate with the ORB should be able to communicate with any server that can communicate with the ORB. This provides both hardware and software independence. With interface standards available, soft-

Figure 14-4   Client/Server Application Program Interface

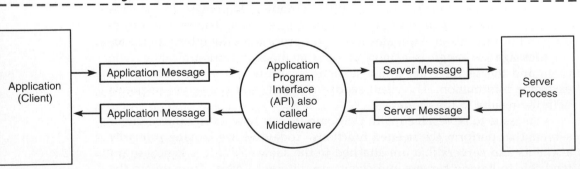

ware and hardware from many vendors can be integrated to create a modular, flexible, extendable computing environment.

NONDEDICATED SERVERS AND PEER-TO-PEER LANS

Many of today's LANs use client/server technology with dedicated server nodes. This is certainly true of most large LANs. However, as we mentioned in Chapter 13, the average number of nodes per microcomputer LAN is 6.3. This implies that there are many LANs with six of fewer nodes. For these small LANs, dedicating an expensive server machine (which will probably be underutilized) reduces the cost effectiveness of the network. Two other technologies, nondedicated servers and peer-to-peer LANs, provide users an alternative to dedicated servers.

Often on a small LAN the most expensive and powerful computer is used as a dedicated server. The server might be idle much of the time. For example, it is hard to imagine four users in a typical office keeping a dedicated server busy most of the time. A few LAN operating systems allow you to have a **nondedicated server,** which works as both a server and a workstation. Usually, a nondedicated server is the workstation with the most resources. Because a nondedicated server also functions as a workstation, it can be used more effectively.

The advantage of nondedicated servers is more effective use of resources, but there are also some disadvantages. Naturally a nondedicated server must divide its workload between its application work and its server work. Sometimes it might be very busy in both roles. In these instances both classes of users, those using the server as a server and those using the server as a workstation, experience some service degradation. If these conflicts occur too often, the LAN administrator should think of making the server dedicated. Another disadvantage of nondedicated servers is the increased likelihood of server failures. Simply running both applications and server software increases the possibility of failures, because the server is doing more and the environment is more complicated. However, the most probable source of nondedicated server failure is the user's application or the user himself. If the application gets locked up, the server may be unable to attend to its server duties. If the user powers the server down or unintentionally formats the server's disk, the server's functions also are disrupted.

Taking nondedicated servers one step further leads us to **peer-to-peer LANs.** In a peer-to-peer LAN, any or all nodes can operate as servers. This type of LAN is quite common when the system has few workstations. Novell's NetWare Lite is one example of a peer-to-peer network.

NetWare Lite runs under the DOS operating system, so it essentially runs as a DOS application and uses the DOS file-management system. This is a benefit because you can quickly install the network software on an existing DOS system without reformatting the disk. The disadvantage is that you are limited to the file attributes and the limited multiprocessing of a DOS system. Because DOS has few file attributes, you cannot store important file and directory information like the owner ID of a file, file-protection attributes like Execute Only, or directory attributes like Create, Open, and so on (see Chapter 8).

NetWare Lite allows you to designate each node as client only, server only, or both. Thus you can tailor the network to the types of computers and users. A server node does more work and uses more system resources, such as memory, than a client node. Capabilities that NetWare Lite provides include logon security, user account restrictions, messages distribution to users, print spooling, disk and directory mapping, and auditing of network activities like user logons, user logoffs, system file backups, and interfaces to other Novell Netware systems.

In general, the main benefit of peer-to-peer networks is the low cost per node, usually under $200 for both hardware and software. Some lower cost, lower performance networks use the microcomputer's serial or parallel ports for communication. This type of connection can reduce the cost per node to $100 or less. NetWare Lite supports only 25 nodes, but several peer-to-peer LANs support many more nodes. For instance, Artisoft, Inc. manufactures one of the leading peer-to-peer LANs that allows 300 users per network.

WIRELESS MEDIA

Wireless media, as mentioned in earlier chapters, is an emerging technology that has considerable potential for expanded use. Installation of wiring can be costly and difficult, particularly in existing buildings. Wireless media can reduce wiring costs and hassles in some of these instances. Several technologies are used to provide wireless LAN connections, and significant speed differences exist between implementations. The four primary transmission technologies for wireless LANs are microwave, spread spectrum radio, infrared light, and laser. At the high-speed end, the Motorola Corporation, one of the leaders in wireless technology, markets a 15-Mbps Ethernet medium using microwave transmission. Motorola has indicated that in the future we may see 100-Mbps wireless LAN speeds.

Wireless LANs are beginning to find niches in LAN implementations in areas other than as a replacement for cables. One use of wireless LANs is in applications requiring mobility such as moving workstations from one location to another. For example, a manufacturing plant LAN user may need to move a node to various inspection stations or to problem areas. Network printers can also be moved to locations as needed. Wireless LANs are a good fit for these applications.

Another use of wireless technology is for mobile remote connections. One of the trends in the communications industry is providing mobile users with communications services such as cellular radio telephones. The bandwidths of today's cellular systems are generally not great enough to drive data-intensive mobile computer applications; however, you should expect changes in this technology as the need for mobile computing increases. Wireless technology will then enable mobile users to access their corporate LANs while moving about or from a fixed remote location.

Some of the obstacles remote wireless connections must overcome are low transmission speeds, high error rates, limited availability, and data security. Because the data delivery capacity of remote wireless connections is small relative to cable-connected or local wireless nodes, the primary use of this technology probably is for the exchange of small amounts of data, such as mail messages. Even though the communications bandwidth will increase over what is currently available, it is unlikely it will exceed 20,000 bps in the near future. This limits the use of mobile remote LAN nodes to applications that exchange small amounts of data between the node and LAN servers. Wireless transmissions are subject to signal interference. Signal disruptions that are commonly encountered may not significantly disrupt voice communication but will likely result in frequent data errors and the need to retransmit the data. Currently, cellular radio is available only in highly populated areas, and thus remote usage is not possible in many rural areas. Soon, however, satellites may be used to provide these services, and mobile wireless computing may be available in all areas of countries providing such services. Because wireless transmissions are broadcast, anyone can receive the signals. Companies that want to maintain the confidentiality of their data must encrypt data before transmission.

DISKLESS WORKSTATIONS

Diskless workstations have been available for quite some time; however, their use is likely to expand. As the name implies, a diskless workstation has no local disk drives. These nodes boot their operating systems from a server, and all disk reads and writes are to server disks. There are many advantages and a few disadvantages to this approach.

The initial advantage of diskless workstations is cost. The computers do not need disks and therefore they may cost as much as $300 less. The only component that needs to be added to the configuration is a LAN boot ROM, which allows the system to be booted from a server disk rather than from a local disk. Cost savings also accrue from lower maintenance costs. Since disks are mechanical devices, they are more likely to fail than most electronic components. Thus a computer without disks should need fewer repairs. Management control is another significant advantage of diskless systems. Because users have no local disks, they cannot introduce viruses, install personal software and files, illegally copy software, and copy sensitive corporate data to a diskette for personal reasons. Moreover data cannot be lost because a user failed to back up work-critical files that resided only on his local disk, and the LAN administrator can control the types and versions of software being used on the network.

Diskless workstations also have a few disadvantages. In the absence of a server, the workstation is nearly useless: it cannot boot an operating system without a server, so network attachment is essential to making the computer operational. Moreover, without disks, programs cannot be started without a server. Because users have no local disks for personal or temporary files, the use of the server's disk is increased and may lead to higher server costs. Furthermore, the number of vendors selling diskless systems is somewhat limited, so purchasers do not have as wide a selection from which to choose. Finally, the node cannot be removed to another corporate location and be used as a stand-alone system without disk drives, and if the server fails,the node cannot be used locally until the server is brought back into service.

GLOBAL NAMING AND DISTRIBUTED SYSTEMS

Frequently LANs are connected to other networks or to a host, as discussed in Chapter 13. Such interconnections make keeping track of nodes and node addresses, users and user addresses, and data or application files more complicated. To accomplish the ultimate goal of connecting all networks worldwide, we will need a way to provide unique identifiers for all users and all nodes worldwide. Keeping track of resources network–wide requires a global network database or dictionary and global naming conventions and procedures.

One of the LAN leaders in providing network interconnections is Banyan Systems. One of Banyan's capabilities is StreetTalk, a network database of resources. StreetTalk provides a way for users to locate resources regardless of where they lie in the network. Users or applications can use the database to find the mail address of other users, the location of a file, a printer address, and so on. In recognition of the international nature of networks, Banyan allows some data in the database, such as error messages and status messages, to be stored in several languages. Novell also introduced a global naming capability with Netware 4.0's Name Service component. Other organizations are also implementing network dictionaries, and the CCITT is addressing this issue with its X.500 standard.

ISDN

Integrated digital services network (ISDN) is a digital communications service offered by several common carriers. It can be found in most major computer-using countries. ISDN provides high-speed data circuits that can carry a variety of communications data, including voice. ISDN service is just beginning to make its presence known. Extensive availability is planned for the future. ISDN will probably have an impact on LAN implementations. It can serve as the medium for small and large LANs alike. Most of today's ISDN services provide lower-speed links, most commonly 56 Kbps and 1.5 Mbps. This is considerably below the speeds of most of our current LANs; however higher-speed links are planned for the future. ISDN may become the medium for some LANs and for others a means for LAN interconnection, as illustrated in Figure 14-5.

HIGH-SPEED LOCAL AREA NETWORKS

High-speed local area networks (HSLANs) are LANs that service wider geographical areas than typical office LANs, for example, 200 kilometers

(125 miles). LANs that service a wider area, say 100 miles or more, are called **metropolitan area networks (MANs).** In addition to serving wider geographic areas, HSLANs also operate at speeds much greater than today's office LANs. The HSLAN speed most talked about today is 100 Mbps, but even greater speeds can be expected in the not-too-distant future. The most commonly referenced HSLAN is the Fiber Distributed Data Interface (FDDI) LAN. FDDI, specified by the American National Standards Institute (ANSI) standard, is a token-ring LAN operating at 100 Mbps on fiber optic cable. Moreover, shielded twisted-pair wires are now being used to provide FDDI-equivalent technology. This variation of FDDI is called the Copper Data Distributed Interface (CDDI) or the Shielded Twisted-pair Wire Distributed Data Interface (SDDI). This technology is also being implemented on unshielded twisted-pair wires.

Figure 14-5   LAN Interconnection Using ISDN

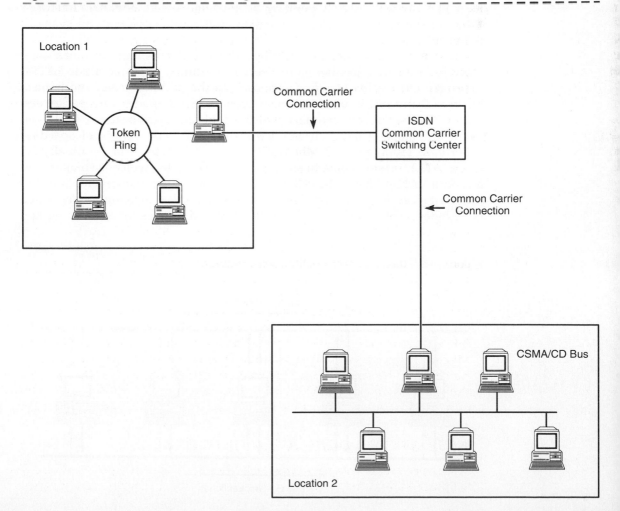

The FDDI family of technologies is not the only HSLAN proposal. The IEEE 802 LAN standards committee has also developed specifications, IEEE 802.6, for a MAN. The IEEE 802.6 standard has also been adopted by ANSI. The standard is also referred to as the Distributed Queue Dual Bus (DQDB) standard.

As the name DQDB indicates, the architecture uses two buses. Each bus is unidirectional, meaning that data is transmitted in one direction on one bus and in the other direction on the second bus, as illustrated in Figure 14-6. Each node must therefore be attached to both buses. The specification also allows for a variation called a looped bus. The loooped bus still uses two one-direction buses; however, each bus forms a closed loop, as illustrated in Figure 14-7. The speeds defined in the standard are dependent on the medium used: The speed is 45 Mbps with coaxial cable and 156 Mbps with fiber optic cable. Distances up to 200 miles are supported.

Another high-speed LAN possibility, the 100-Mbps Ethernet, emerged in 1993 and may become more attractive for LANs in a local geographic area than FDDI-based LANs. Operating at the same speed as FDDI, 100-Mbps Ethernet provides lower implementation costs and a large body of available network software.

Before FDDI, CDDI, or 100-Mbps Ethernet technology becomes commonplace, another technology called **asynchronous transfer mode (ATM)** may take over. ATM was first proposed as the packet-transfer mechanism for broadband ISDN, but it has also been accepted as a private packet service. ATM uses high-speed data switches that can interface to LANs, WAN, and stand-alone systems. It can accommodate a wide variety of speeds— 100 Mbps, 150 Mbps, 155 Mbps, 270 Mbps, 600 Mbps, and eventually 2.5 Gbps. ATM transmits data in small groups called cells (which is smaller than a typical LAN packet). The cell size is fixed for a given implementation, but different sizes are proposed. The most common cell size being implemented is 53 bytes, which consists of 48 data bytes and 5 bytes for addressing and

Figure 14-6   Dual Bus Metropolitan Area Network

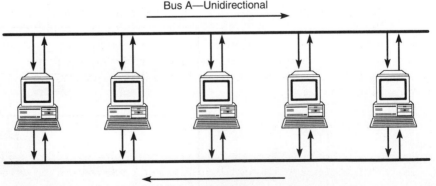

Bus A—Unidirectional

Bus B—Unidirectional

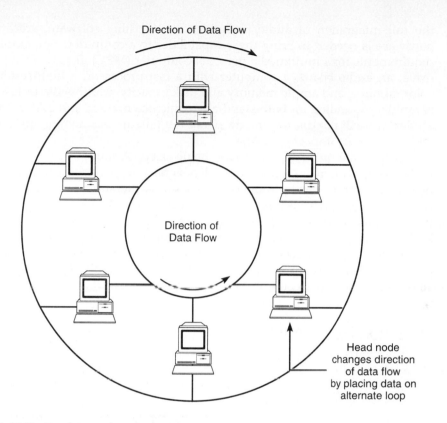

Direction of Data Flow

Direction of
Data Flow

Head node
changes direction
of data flow
by placing data on
alternate loop

Figure 14-7 Dual Bus Loop Metropolitan Area Network

control. Long messages are thus divided into cells for transmission through ATM. The most likely use for ATM in LAN implementations is as a high-speed interconnection of LANs, WANs, and stand-alone devices. In this capacity ATM fulfills the role of a backbone network. Thus we may see high-speed FDDI or SDDI LANs as well as low-speed LANs and WANs interconnected with ATM switches. A possible ATM configuration is shown in Figure 14-8.

It is difficult to accurately predict which of the new technologies will dominate the industry, but one thing is sure; HSLANs will become more common. They will be used to provide faster delivery for large LANs, as backbone networks to connect separate LANs in a building complex or a metropolitan area, and, as you will read in the next section, for LANs providing multimedia services.

MULTIMEDIA ON LANS

Multimedia technology extends a computer's capabilities by adding audio and video. Multimedia is much more than just being able to produce sound, pictures, and animation on a computer. The promise of this technology is the full integration of audio and video into existing software. Additional hardware is needed to bring these capabilities to a computer. The minimum requirements for a multimedia personal computer (MPC) include a CD-ROM drive, an audio board, a computer with a fast processor, a high-resolution color monitor, and ample memory and disk capacity. Multimedia technology is rapidly expanding on both stand-alone microcomputers and LANs. In this section we will not discuss the details of multimedia technology; instead we will examine its impact on LANs.

Multimedia on LANs is already being used. A multimedia server on a LAN delivers digitized audio and video signals to client workstations capable of supporting the technology. The issue is therefore not if multimedia can be done on LANs but how to do it successfully. The main problem with this technology today is the speed of the common LAN. Today's Ethernet LANs operate at 10 Mbps, and token rings operate at 4 or 16 Mbps, both of which are inadequate for extensive use of multimedia. Full motion video to a monitor with a resolution of 640x480 picture elements (pixels) and 24-bit true color at a frame rate of 30 frames per second requires a data rate of 240 Mbps

Figure 14-8   Asynchronous Transfer Mode Configuration

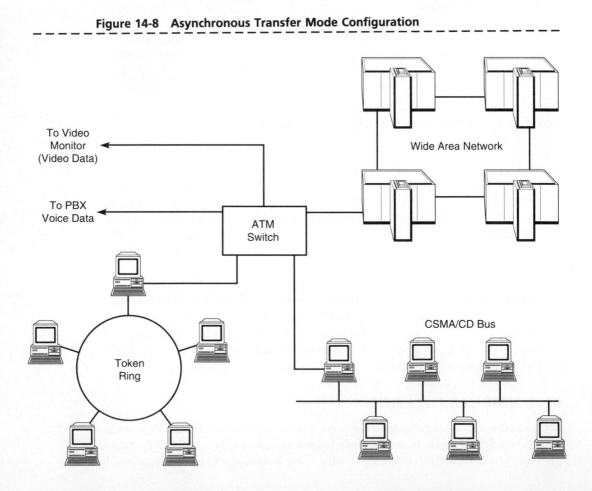

(Lippis, 1993). This is far in excess of common LAN speeds. Still frame video and audio signals do not require such high bit rates, but sustained transfers of between 16 KB and 384 Kbps are needed for the duration of many multimedia video and audio sessions (Davidson, 1992). At the higher rate, 30 users would require more than the entire capacity of a 10-Mbps LAN. Moreover LANs operating at 10 Mbps are not designed to sustain that 10-Mbps data rate because of overheads in the data link protocol, transmission errors, and delays in media access. Obviously changes must be made in LAN technology to support these sustained high data rates.

A combination of several techniques is necessary to realize the full potential of multimedia for large numbers of users. Among these are data compression, higher-speed networks, LAN segmentation, and the asynchronous transfer mode switches described earlier.

Data Compression   Data compression reduces the number of bits that need to be transferred. You may be familiar with this technology through disk compression programs that approximately double the storage capacity of disk drives. Thus an 80-MB disk might be able to store 160 MB of data via compression. If data are compressed prior to transmission and then decompressed at the receiving end, the demand on the transmission media can be significantly lowered. Compression/decompression chips are available that perform these two operations faster than software. Equipping multimedia clients and servers with compression/decompression capability will help by reducing the number of bits being transferred.

Higher-Speed Networks   Even with compression, the capacity of LANs running under 20 Mbps still can be strained by several concurrent users even without multimedia. Several high-speed LAN options are available to accommodate these users, as described in an earlier section.

LAN Segmentation   Even 100-Mbps LANs cannot meet the needs of large numbers of concurrent multimedia users. To allow for greater numbers of concurrent multimedia users, LANs may need to be broken down into small segments, as illustrated in Figure 14-10. Each multimedia segment can be serviced by a dedicated multimedia server or by a multimedia server on a high-speed backbone network. Both of these options are shown in Figure 14-9. Since each segment has few users, the data-carrying capacity of each segment is not exceeded. It is even conceivable that one intensive multimedia user will need his or her own LAN segment.

Asynchronous Transfer Mode (ATM) Switches   Earlier in this chapter we described ATM packet transmission. ATM switches fit naturally into networks needing to quickly transmit high volumes of data. This, of course, will include LANs using multimedia servers.

SERVERS

In earlier chapters we talked about servers primarily in the context of file, printer, and database services. Other types of services are also available.

In Chapter 13 we mentioned communications servers. Communications servers provide several varieties of services, most commonly modem pooling. Modem pooling allows one or more modems to be shared by users, much like a printer is shared among users. Rather than dedicating a modem to each user who is likely to need such services, **modem pooling** allows several modems to be attached to one server. When a user needs to use a modem, the server connects the user to one of the pooled modems if one is

Figure 14-9   Multimedia LAN Configurations

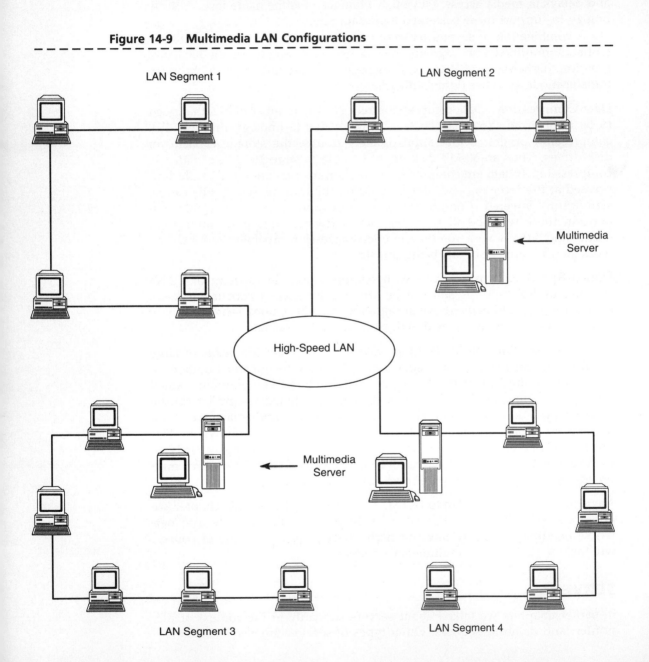

available. The user can then use the modem as though it were locally attached. The advantage of this is the ability for many users to have modems available without purchasing a modem for each user. Moreover, the server can regulate the control of the modems by placing restrictions on who can use them.

Remote access servers, also mentioned in Chapter 13, provide a way for remote users to connect to the LAN and use its services. Remote LAN use via an asynchronous (modem) connection is limited to transfers of small amounts of data. It is impractical to download large program files, because the speed of the connection is too slow. Waiting 20 minutes for a word processing program to be loaded over a slow communication link is not realistic. Access servers allow the full services of the LAN to be used remotely without such extensive time delays. This is effected by having all the processing done at the LAN end of the connection and by passing only keyboard and display data over the communications link. Of course, files can also be transferred to the remote system, but large file transfers tend to be time-consuming. See Chapter 13 for additional details of access servers.

Another method for remote access is remote control software. Using this technique, remote users can connect to idle workstations and operate in much the same way as they would using a remote access server. Remote control software is described in Chapter 11.

The use of facsimile (FAX) transmissions grew rapidly in the latter half of the 1980s. FAX transmissions are not always from one FAX machine to another. FAX images can be stored on a computer's disk and either printed, displayed on a computer screen, or transmitted to another computer or FAX machine. Computer management of FAX images has grown as fast as the use of FAX itself. LAN users can share the use of FAX facilities with a **FAX server.** Capabilities of FAX servers are listed in Table 14-1.

Table 14-1   FAX Server Capabilities

Ability to interface with electronic mail systems
Automatic routing of incoming FAX message to recipients
Detection/correction of line errors
Security via password protection
Automatic redial for busy numbers
Recognition of pages not received and transmission of only missing pages on
   reconnect
Collection of accounting statistics—user information, number called, duration, and
   so on

UNINTERRUPTABLE POWER SUPPLIES

LAN users depend on file and print servers for many of their processing needs, so server availability is critical. In earlier chapters you read about techniques for improving the reliability of a server. These technologies are generally called fault-tolerant capabilities. Fault-tolerant capabilities include mirrored disks, redundant arrays of independent disk drives (RAID) technology, and backup or alternate servers. All of these technologies, however, cannot overcome power failures, one of the most common causes of node failures. An uninterruptable power supply (UPS) fills this void.

Several years ago, the cost of a UPS was quite high, and they were used primarily for large, centralized computer systems. Today, UPS prices start at several hundred dollars.

POCKET LAN ADAPTERS

In Chapter 11 we mentioned the use of a pocket LAN adapter (sometimes called an external adapter) as a diagnostic aid. A pocket LAN adapter provides the interface between the LAN medium and a workstation. On the workstation side of the interface, the pocket LAN adapter plugs into a parallel port or a special interface port, such as a small computer system interface (SCSI) or an external device interface found on some portable workstations. On the medium side, the adapter provides a medium attachment port for twisted-pair wires or coaxial cable. Because the adapter attaches to an existing port on the workstation, the LAN interface does not require a workstation expansion slot.

Pocket LAN adapters are used primarily for portable workstations like laptop computers, for computers that have no available expansion slots, or for workstations that will be connected to the LAN only temporarily, for example, a temporary replacement for a broken workstation.

TECHNOLOGY AND NETWORK MANAGEMENT

As time progresses, network management will become both easier and harder. It will become harder because LANs will be larger, the software, both application and system, will be more complex, and interoperability between a LAN and other devices or networks will increase. Network management will become easier because network management systems will be more sophisticated and will provide the network administrator with more assistance in monitoring, diagnosing, and tuning the network.

The most promising technology in network management systems is expert system technology. An **expert system,** one example of artificial intelligence technology, encapsulates the talents of an expert within a software system. A network management system with an expert system component can diagnose system parameters, suggest corrective measures, and automatically or through manual selection carry out one of the suggested corrective measures.

SUMMARY

The field of data communications is rapidly changing, and nowhere is this change more apparent than in microcomputer LAN technology. Some of our existing technologies will become obsolete and be replaced with newer ones.

In the preceding chapters the focus was on common LAN features. Many specialty capabilities exist, and to cover them all in detail here is impractical. Some of the less common technologies are **high-speed LANs, asynchronous transfer mode, diskless workstations, peer-to-peer LANs,** a variety of server technologies, **wireless technologies, expert systems** in LAN management, **multimedia** on LANs, and other medium alternatives like **ISDN.** Each of these capabilities are available today. Some of them may become leading technologies tomorrow.

KEY TERMS

asynchronous transfer mode (ATM)

client/server (CS) computing

Distributed Computing Environment (DCE)

expert system

FAX server

global naming

high-speed local area network (HSLAN)

message exchange

metropolitan area network (MAN)

microwave transmission

middleware

modem pooling

multimedia

nondedicated server

Object Reqeust Broker (ORB)

peer-to-peer LAN

remote procedure call

REFERENCES

Brambert, David. "It's a Remote Possibility." *LAN*, Volume 8, Number 3, March 1993.

Clegg, Peter. "Communications Servers." *LAN Times*, Volume 8, Issue 6, March 18, 1991.

Davidson, Peter. "Multimedia Finally Appears Within Networks' Reach." *Network World*, Volume 9, Number 14, April 6, 1992.

Derfler, Jr., Frank J. and Thomas, Susan G. "Asynchronous Communications Servers: Dialing in at Large." *PC Magazine*, Volume 11, Number 18, October 27, 1992.

Ewald, Alan and Roy, Mark. "The Evolution of the Client/Server Revolution." *Network World*, Volume 9, Number 46, November 16, 1992.

Ga Cote, Raymond, Apiki, Steve, and Wszola, Stan. "Network FAX on Tap." *Byte*, Volume 18, Number 2, February, 1993.

Goldenberg, Barton and Sonnenfeldt, Walter. "The Sky's the Limit for Wireless LANs." *Data Communications*, Volume 22, Number 3, February 1993.

Koontz, Charles P. "UPS Means Life Insurance for Your LAN." *LAN Times*, Volume 9, Issue 7, April 20, 1992.

Lippis, Nick. "Multimedia Networking." *Data Communications*, Volume 22, Number 3, February 1993.

Mell, Jr., John P. and Wayner, Peter. "Wireless Mobile Communications." *Byte*, Volume 18, Number 2, February 1993.

Nance, Barry. "Peer LANs Offer a Low-Cost Network Alternative." *Byte*, Volume 16, Number 12, November 1991.

Nash, Jim. "Peer Pressure." *LAN*, Volume 7, Number 10, October 1992.

Nitzsche, Kyle. "The Elusive Illusion." *Network World*, Volume 9, Number 48, November 30, 1992.

Ryan, Hugh W. "Issues in Client-Server Development." *Information Systems Management*, Fall 1992.

Schurr, Amy. "Peer-to-Peer Network Operating Systems." *PC Week*, Volume 10, Number 1, January 11, 1993.

Wayner, Peter. "Stretching the Ether." *Byte*, Volume 18, Number 2, February, 1993.

10BASE2 An IEEE 802.3 specification for baseband transmission at 10 Mbps over thin coaxial cable segments of 200 meters.

10BASE5 An IEEE 802.3 specification for baseband transmission at 10 Mbps over thick coaxial cable segments of 500 meters.

10BASE-T An IEEE 802.3 specification for baseband transmission at 10 MBps over twisted-pair wires.

adaptive routing A routing algorithm that evaluates the existing paths and chooses the one that provides the best path for a message. Routes may change due to congestion and path failures.

American National Standards Institute. (ANSI) A U.S. standards-making agency.

American Standard Code for Information Interchange (ASCII) One of two common computer codes that uses seven or eight bits to represent characters. (See also **EBCDIC.**)

application layer One of the layers of the International Standards Organization's Open System Interconnection (ISO/OSI) reference model. The functions of this layer are application dependent.

application program interface (API) The interface between application programs and the network software.

ARCnet Local area network implementation based on Datapoint's attached resource computer network.

asynchronous transfer mode (ATM) A high-speed transmission protocol in which data blocks are broken into small cells that are transmitted individually and possibly via different routes in a manner similar to packet-switching technology.

asynchronous transmission The oldest and one of the most common data link protocols. Each character is transmitted individually with its own error-detection scheme, usually a parity bit. The sender and receiver are not synchronized with each other.

attenuation A weakening of a signal as a result of distance and characteristics of the medium.

bandwidth The difference between the minimum and maximum frequencies allowed. Bandwidth is a measure of the amount of data that can be transmitted per unit of time. The greater the bandwidth, the higher the possible data transmission rate.

baseband transmission Sends the data along the channel by means of voltage fluctuations. The entire bandwidth of the cable is used to carry data.

baud rate A measure of the number of discrete signals that can be observed per unit of time.

binary synchronous communications protocol A transmission protocol introduced by IBM as the data link protocol for remote job entry. It later became a de facto standard for many types of data transmission, particularly between two computers. Data are transmitted a block at a time, and the sender and receiver need to be in time with each other. Specific control characters are used to indicate beginning of text, end of text, start of header, and so on.

bit A binary digit, either 0 or 1.

bit rate One method of measuring data transmission speed—bits per second.

bit synchronous protocol. A data link protocol in which one or more bits are used to control the communications link. Bit synchronous protocols are commonly used on both LANs and WANs.

bits per second (bps) A measure of communications speed.

block A contiguous group of bits or bytes. Often messages are broken into blocks of a specific size for transmission over a data communications line.

bridge An interconnection between like networks, such as Ethernet to Ethernet.

broadband transmission A form of data transmission where data are carried on high-frequency carrier waves. The carrying capacity of the medium is divided into a number of subchannels, such as video, low-speed data, high-speed data, and voice, allowing the medium to satisfy several communication needs.

broadcast A technology that sends signals to multiple stations at once. Satellite is one example of a broadcast technology.

broadcast routing A routing algorithm in which the message is broadcast to all stations. Only the stations to whom the message is addressed accept it.

bus A communications medium for transmitting data or power. A local area network topology.

bus interface unit (BIU) Provides the physical connection to the computer's I/O bus.

carrier sense multiple access with collision detection (CSMA/CD) An access protocol used primarily in local area networks.

centralized routing A routing algorithm in which one node in the network is charged with the responsibility of determining the path between nodes in the network. It determines the routing tables and distributes them to each other node.

central processing unit (CPU) The processing components of a computer. The components of the CPU are control, arithmetic logic unit, and memory.

coaxial cable A transmission medium consisting of one or two central data transmission wires surrounded by an insulating layer, a shielding layer, and an outer jacket. Coaxial cable has a high data-carrying capacity and low error rates.

code independence The ability to successfully transmit data regardless of the data code, such as ASCII or EBCDIC.

collision In a CSMA/CD media access control protocol, a collision occurs when two stations attempt to send a message at the same time. The messages interfere with each other so correct communication is not possible.

common carrier A public utility that provides public transmission media, such as the telephone companies and satellite companies.

common management information protocol (CMIP) A protocol for software to manage a network. (See also **SNMP.**)

communications interface unit (CIU) Provides the physical connection to the transmission medium.

compact disc read-only memory (CD-ROM) An optical disk technology in which data can be read from the compact disc. Often used to distributed software and documentation.

computerized branch exchange (CBX) A private branch exchange (PBX) using a computer as controller.

Consultative Committee on International Telegraph and Telephony (CCITT) An international standards organization.

contention A convention whereby devices obtain control of a communications link. In contention mode, devices compete for control of the line either by transmitting directly on an idle line or by issuing a request for line control.

control signals Signals that are exchanged between a sender and receiver to establish, maintain, and terminate connections, communications, and the flow of data.

copper distributed data interface (CDDI) An ANSI LAN standard for twisted-pair-wire LANs spanning a distance of approximately 200 kilometers and providing speeds of 100 Mbps. An extension of the Fiber Distributed Data Interface LAN.

crosstalk When the signals from one channel distort or interfere with the signals of a different channel.

cyclic redundancy check (CRC) An error detection algorithm that uses a polynomial function to generate the block check characters. A very efficient error detection method.

data communications equipment Refers to modems, media, and media-support facilities such as telephone switching equipment, microwave relay stations, and transponders.

data compression Data compression is used to reduce the number of characters or bits in a message. A common form is repeating character compression where long strings of repeating characters are replaced by the repeating group and the repeat count. Compressing data allows fewer characters to be transmitted and improves line efficiency, increasing the effective aggregate data rate.

data encryption standard (DES) A U.S. National Bureau of Standards encryption standard. Also adopted by the International Standards Organization (ISO).

data link layer One of the layers of the International Standards Organization's Open Systems Interconnection (ISO/OSI) reference model. The data link layer governs the establishment and control of the communications link.

data link protocols Conventions that govern the flow of data between a sending and receiving station.

deadlock A state that exists when two or more processes are unable to proceed. It occurs when two or more transactions have locked a resource and request resources that other involved processes already have locked.

digital branch exchange (DBX) A digital PBX.

digital private branch exchange (DPBX or DBX) A private branch exchange that transmits data in digital format.

digital transmission A transmission mode in which data is represented by binary digits rather than analog signals.

disk mirroring A fault-tolerant disk storage strategy in which data is written to two independent disk drives. If one drive fails, the remaining drive allows processing to continue.

distortion The change of transmitted signals resulting from noise. Distortion can result in transmission errors.

distributed processing Refers to the geographical distribution of hardware, software, processing and data.

distributed routing A routing algorithm in which each node calculates its own routing table based on status information periodically received from other nodes.

downloading The act of transferring programs or data from a host processor to a work station, typically a microcomputer.

electronic bulletin board A software system that allows users to "post" electronic messages. Electronic bulletin boards are frequently accessed by a switched telephone connection and serve as a clearing house for software and hardware exchange and as a medium for information exchange.

E-mail Electronic mail.

encryption equipment Equipment that allows transmitted data to be scrambled at the sending location and reconstructed at the receiving end. Encryption is also used when storing information, for example, before writing data to a database. Encryption equipment encrypts the data before writing and decrypts it after reading.

Enhanced Small Device Interface (ESDI) A disk drive interface for microcomputers. Generally provides good performance and is frequently used as the interface for LAN server drives. (See also **SCSI**.)

environment variable A parameter stored by an operating system or program. The data and time are two environment variables commonly stored by an operating system. In a LAN, environment variables can be used to tailor the user's interface to the LAN.

Ethernet A local area network implementation using the CSMA/CD protocol on a bus. The IEEE 802.3 standard is based on Ethernet. One of the popular local area network implementations.

Extended Binary Coded Decimal Interchange Code (EBCDIC) A data code that uses eight bits to represent a character of information. One of the most common computer codes.

Facsimile (FAX) transmission Electronic transmission of a document image.

fault tolerance A combination of hardware and software techniques that improve the reliability of a system.

Fiber Distributed Data Interface (FDDI) An ANSI LAN standard for fiber optic LANs spanning a distance of approximately 200 kilometers and providing speeds of 100 Mbps.

fiber optic cable A transmission medium that provies high data rates and low errors. One or more glass or plastic fibers are woven together to form the core of the cable. This core is surrounded by a glass or plastic layer called the cladding. The cladding in turn is covered with plastic or other material for protection. The cable requires a light source, most commonly laser and light-emitting diodes.

flow control The pacing of data between a sender and receiver. Three flow control techniques are simplex, half duplex and full duplex.

frame A term used to describe a transmission packet in bit-oriented protocols.

frequency-division multiplexing The bandwidth is divided into several subbands, each of which is assigned to one device.

full duplex A data transmission mode in which data is transmitted over a link in both directions simultaneously.

function keys Additional keys found on some terminals that transmit specific character sequences to the host.

gateway The interface between two different networks.

Gpbs A billion bits per second.

half duplex A data transmission mode in which data travels in both directions over a link but in only one direction at a time.

Hertz (Hz) The term used to denote frequency; one hertz is one cycle per second.

hierarchical network A network topology in which the nodes are arranged hierarchically.

host A processor that provides support and services to terminals or other processors.

infrared light One of the wireless transmission techniques for LANs.

Institute of Electrical and Electronics Engineers (IEEE) A professional society that established and publishes documents and standards for data communications. IEEE has established several standards for local area networks, including the IEEE 802.3 and IEEE 802.5, standards for LAN technology.

Integrated Services Digital Network (ISDN) The integration of voice and data transmission (and other formats such as video and graphics images) over a digital transmission network. A network proposed by numerous common carriers.

International Standards Organization (ISO) An organization that is active in setting communications standards.

Internetwork Packet Exchange/Sequenced Packet Exchange (IPX/SPX) Novell Corporation's protocol for message exchange on a LAN.

Kbps A thousand bits per second.

laser A light source for fiber optic transmission.

light emitting diode (LED) A source of light for fiber optic transmission.

link access procedure—balanced (LAPB) A bit-synchronous data link protocol standard of the CCITT.

Local Distributed Data Interface (LDDI) An ANSI proposal for a high-speed LAN standard.

local area network (LAN) A communications network in which all of the components are located within several kilometers of each other and which uses high transmission speeds—generally one million bits per second or higher.

logical link control (LLC) A sublayer of the OSI reference model data link layer. The logical link control forms the interface between the network layer and the media access control protocols.

logical unit (LU) In IBM's SNA, a unit that represents a system user. Sessions exist between LUs or an LU and the SSCP. Several types of LUs have been defined, including LU 6.2, which represents a program-to-program session.

LPTn A parallel printer port on an IBM-compatible personal computer. There are three available parallel printer ports: LPT1, LPT2, and LPT3.

mark In data transmission, the equivalent of a 1 bit.

Mbps A million bits per second.

media access control (MAC) layer A sublayer of the OSI reference model's data link layer. The media access control protocol defines access station to the media and data transmission. Common MAC protocols are carrier sense with multiple access and collision detection (CSMA/CD) and token passing.

medium In data communications, the carrier of data signals. Twisted-pair wires, coaxial cables, and fiber optic cables are the most common LAN media.

Metropolitan Area Network (MAN) The subject of the IEEE 802.6 standard. Similar in nature to the FDDI LAN specification.

microwave A method of transmitting data using high-frequency radio waves. It requires a line of sight between sending and receiving stations. Capable of high data rates, microwave is used for wide area networks and wireless LANs.

modem Short for modulator-demodulator. A device that changes digital signals to analog signals for transmitting data over telephone circuits. Also used for some fiber optic transmission (digital fiber optics do not require a modem), and any transmission mode requiring a change from one form of signal to another.

multistation access unit (MAU or MSAU) A device used to connect nodes in a token-ring network. The MAU is essentially a wiring hub that provides workstation connection and establishes the ring.

multiplexing A method of data transmission in which several devices are allowed to share a single link.

network Two or more computers connected by a communications medium, together with all communications, hardware, and software components. Alternatively, a host processor together with its attached terminals, workstations, and communications equipment, for example, transmission media, modems, and so on.

network adapter A network interface card.

network control center The organization responsible for monitoring and controlling the network.

network interface card (NIC) An adapter that establishes the link between the LAN medium and the host computer's bus.

network layer One of the layers of the International Standards Organization's Open Systems Interconnection reference model. The network layer is responsible for end-to-end message routing.

network loadable module (NLM) In a Novell NetWare 386 system, NLMs can be linked to the network operating system to provide capabilities like utilities, disk drivers, and file services. Independent software vendors can provide usual network value-added services through NLMs. (See also **VAP**.)

network management Software, hardware, procedures, and human activities for monitoring, controlling, and fixing networks.

nodes Processors in a network, either a LAN or a WAN.

noise Disruptions to data transmission that can result in errors in the data being transmitted. There are several types of noise, such as impulse, white, and echo.

octet A group of eight bits used in bit synchronous protocols. Data, regardless of their code, are treated as octets.

Open System Interconnection (OSI) reference model A seven-layered set of functions for transmitting data from one user to another.

Specified by the International Standards Organization to facilitate interconnection of networks.

OS/2 Operating system for IBM and IBM compatible microcomputers. OS/2 extended version contains LAN management capabilities and data communications interfaces.

packet A unit of transmission. A message may be divided into several packets for transmission. The packets are reassembled into the message at the destination.

parity error An error-detection scheme in which a bit is added to each character when transmitted, to bring the total number of bits in the code representation of each character up to either an even number (even parity) or an odd number (odd parity).

path A group of links that allows a message to move from its point of origin to its destination

physical layer One of the layers of the International Standards Organization's Open Systems Interconnection reference model. The physical layer specifies the electrical connections between the transmission medium and the computing system.

physical unit (PU) In SNA, a hardware unit. Four physical units have been defined: Type 5, host processor; Type 4, communications controller; Type 2, cluster or programmable controller; and Type 1, a terminal or controller that is not programmable.

plain text Unencrypted data.

presentation layer One of the layers of the International Standards Organization's Open Systems Interconnection reference model. The presentation layer addresses message formats.

private branch exchange (PBX) Telephone switching equipment located on corporate premises and owned by the corporation. A PBX allows telephone calls within an office to be connected locally without using the telephone company's end office or transmission circuits.

protocol Convention used for establishing transmission rules. Protocols are used to establish rules for delineation of data, error detection, control sequences, message lengths, media access, and so on.

random access memory (RAM) the primary memory storage of a computer. The control processing unit obtains instructions and data from RAM and updates RAM when data changes.

read-only memory (ROM) Computer memory that may be read but not modified. Used to store programs or data not subject to change.

receiver A device or user that is the destination of a message.

redundant arrays of independent disks (RAID) A fault-tolerant disk storage technique that spreads one file plus the files checksum information over several disk drives. If any one of the disk drives fails, the data stored thereon can be reconstructed from data stored on the remaining drives.

repeater A device used to amplify signals on a network. Repeaters allow the medium distance to be extended.

response time The amount of time required for a user to receive a reply to a request. Usually the time elapsed between the user pressing the ENTER key to send the request (or the equivalent) and the return of the first character of the response.

ring A network configuration commonly used to implement local area networks. The medium forms a loop to which workstations are attached. Data is transmitted from one station to the next around the ring. Generally the access protocol is token passing.

router A network interconnection device and associated software that links two networks. The networks being linked can be different, but they must use a common routing protocol.

routing algorithm An algorithm used to determine how to move a message from its source to its destination. Several algorithms are used: adaptive, broadcast, centralized, distributed, static, virtual, and weighted (See also separate entries for each algorithm.)

security Security is a delaying tactic. Physical security is intended to deny access to a facility. Transmission and data security are intended to restrict access to authorized users. Typical security measures include identification and authorization (passwords), data encryption, user profiles, and so on. Security does not prevent unauthorized access to a system but simply makes it more difficult.

server The routine, process, or node that provides a common service for one or more other entities. In one configuration for on-line transaction processing, application programs act as servers for users' requests. This is called a requester server environment.

session The dialogue between two system users.

session layer One of the layers of the International Standards Organization's Open Systems Interconnection reference model. The session layer is responsible for establishing a dialogue between applications.

shielded twisted-pair wires A common LAN media in which two wires are twisted around each other and are wrapped in a metalic shield to protect against signal interference.

Simple Network Management Protocol (SNMP) SNMP provides a guideline for creating network management software products. SNMP has four key components: the SNMP protocol, structure of management information (SMI), management information base (MIB), and the network management system (NMS).

simplex transmission A mode of data transmission in which data may flow in only one direction. One station is always a sender and another is always a receiver over a simplex link.

small computer system interface (SCSI, pronounced "scuzzy") A microcomputer interface used for disk drives as well as other peripherals. A SCSI disk drive typically provides good performance, and SCSI drives are often used as interfaces to LAN server drives.

space Asynchronous transmission term for a 0 bit.

spooler A software system that collects printer output (typically on disk) and prints the data and schedules the data for printing. Spool is an acronym for simultaneous peripheral operation on-line.

Star A network topology using a central system to which all other nodes are connected. All data are transmitted to or through the central system.

start bit In asynchronous transmission, the line state is changed from one state to another to indicate that a bit is about to arrive. The change in line state represents one bit called the start bit. The start bit is a 0 bit, also known as a space.

static routing A routing algorithm in which one particular path between two nodes is always used.

stop bit In asynchronous transmission, after the start bit, character bits, and optional parity bit are transmitted, a stop bit is sent to end the character. This bit is called a stop bit and is a 1 bit.

store-and-forward When transmitting data between two nodes, the messages are logged at intermediate nodes, which then forward them to the next node.

structured query language (SQL) A relational database language developed by IBM and later standardized by the American National Standards Institute (ANSI). SQL was once called SEQUEL by IBM and is pronounced "sequel."

synchronous A transmission protocol where the sender and receiver are synchronized.

Data is generally transmitted in blocks rather than one character at a time as in asynchronous transmission.

synchronous data link control (SDLC) An IBM positional synchronous protocol that operates in full-duplex or half-duplex modes in both point-to-point and multipoint configurations. Data is transmitted in fixed-format frames consisting of start flag, address, control information, block check character (CRC), and end-of-frame flag.

systems network architecture (SNA) IBM's architecture for building a computer network. Encompasses hardware and software components, establishing sessions between users, and capabilities like office and message/file distribution services.

systems services control point (SSCP) In IBM's SNA, the process that controls a domain. It is responsible for initiating network components, establishing sessions, and maintaining unit status.

telecommunications The transmission of data by electromagnetic systems, including telephone, telegraphy, video, and computer data transmission.

terminal An input and/or output device that may be connected to a local or remote computer called a host computer.

terminator A resistor at a cable end that absorbs the signal and prevents echo or other signal noise.

throughput The amount of work performed by a system per unit of time.

token passing A media access control protocol in which a string of bits called the token is distributed among the network nodes. A computer that receives the token is allowed to transmit data onto the network. Only the stations receiving a token can transmit. Token passing is implemented on ring and bus LANs.

topology A model for the way in which network nodes are connected. Network topologies include bus, ring, and star.

transaction A user-specified group of processing activities that are either entirely completed or, if not completed, leave the database and processing system in a consistent state.

Transmission Control Protocol/Internet Protocol (TCP/IP) A suite of internetwork protocols developed by the U.S. Department of Defense for internetwork file transfers, electronic mail transfer, remote logons, and terminal services.

transceiver A device that receives and sends signals. A transceiver helps form the interface between a network node and the medium.

transparency The ability to send any bit string as data in a message. The data bits are not interpreted as control characters.

transport layer One of the layers of the International Standards Organization's Open Systems Interconnection reference model. The transport layer is responsible for generating the end user's address and for the integrity of the receipt of message blocks.

transport services access point (TSAP) An address used by the transport layer to uniquely identify session entities.

twisted-pair wire A transmission medium, commonly used for telephone wiring and LANs, in which two wires are twisted around each other to reduce signal interference. Twisted-pair wires can be shielded or unshielded.

uninterruptable power supply (UPS) A backup power unit that continues to provide power to a computer system during the failure of the normal power supply. A UPS is frequently used to protect LAN servers from power failures.

unshielded twisted-pair wires One of the common LAN media. A twisted-pair of wires without a protective metal shielding. Signals on unshielded twisted-pair wires are more susceptible to signal distortion than signals on shielded twisted-pair wires.

virtual routing A routing algorithm in which no permanent path is established; instead, each node consults its routing table to determine which node should next receive the message.

value-added process (VAP) In a Novell NetWare 286 system, VAPs become extensions of the network operating system on servers. A VAP is used to provide services like network printing and gateway communications.

weighted routing A routing algorithm used when multiple paths exist. Each path is given a weight according to perceived utilization. A random number is generated to determine which of the available paths to use based upon their weights.

Wide Area Network (WAN) A network that covers a wide geographical area (as contrasted with a local area network).

workstation A term applied to microcomputers or personal productivity devices.

write once, read many (WORM) A type of optical drive that allows the user to write to the medium one time. Data written cannot be erased or changed; it can only be read.

INDEX

(Italicized page number indicates that term is defined on that page.)

Access,
  Control Right, 203, 211
  Servers, 361
  Time, 96
Active Hub, 71
Adaptive Routing, 320, 321
Address Field, 314
Addressing, 75
After Image, 148, 261, 265
Agent *see* Monitor
Alarms, 298
Alerts, 298
American Standard Code for
  Information Exchange
  (ASCI), 29
American National Standards
  Institute (ANSI), 63
ANSI *see* American National
  Standards Institute
Antivirus Program, 220
API *see* Application program
  Interface
Appletalk, 20
Application
  Layer, 34ff.
  Level Interface, 233, 234
  Program Interface (API),
    46, 122, 233, 234, 374
  Settings, 136, 137
Archiving, 255
ARCnet, 71, 75, 107
ASCI *see* American standard
  Code for Information Ex-
  change
Asynchronous
  Connections, 356ff.
  Connections, Shared, 357
  Transfer Mode, 380, 381
  Transfer Mode Switches,
    383
  Transmission, 74
Attributes, File or Directory,
  214ff.
Authentication, 202
AUTOEXEC.BAT File, 187,
  239

Backbone Network, 66, 313
Backup,
  Device, *99*, 100ff.
  Manager, 319
  Software, *135*
Balancing, 289
Balun, *107*
Bandwidth, 61, 62
Banner Page, 238

Baseband Transmission, 60,
  63, 64
Batch
  File, 19, 193, 203
  Processing, 148
Before Image, 148, 261
Binary Synchronous Trans-
  mission, 74
Bindery Files, *265*, 286
Biological Identification and
  Authentication, 202
Bit
  Rate, 74ff.
  Synchronous Protocol,
    314
BIU *see* Bus Interface Unit
Bridge, *287*, 337ff., 343ff.
Broadband Transmission,
  60ff.
Broadcast
  Message, 153, 154
  Routing, 321
Brouter, 343
Bus, 380
  Interface Unit (BIU), 106

Cable Tester, 285
Cache Memory, *97*, 98
Capacity Planning, 287, *288*,
  290ff.
CAPTURE Program, 239ff.
Carrier Sense with Multiple
  Access and Collision
  Avoidance (CSMA/CA), 78
Carrier Sense with Multiple
  Access and Collision Detec-
  tion (CSMA/CD), *77*, 78,
  81ff., 178, 179, 317, 337, 347
Centralized Routing, 318, 319
Certified Mail, 153
Channels, 181
CIU *see* Communications In-
  terface Unit
Client, 373ff., 382
  /Server (CS) Computing,
    367ff.
  /Server Protocol, 121
CMIP *see* Common Manage-
  ment Information Protocol
Coaxial Cable, 21, 29, 45, 46,
  58, 62, 64, 181, 327, 337, 386
Code Independence, 76
Collector Program, 233, 234
Collision, 76, 77
Common Management Infor-
  mation Protocol (CMIP), 302

Communications
  Interface Unit (CIU), 106
  Medium, 21
  Medium Manager, 130,
    131
  Server, 358
Comprehensiveness, 259
Computer Virus, 14
Concurrent
  Login, 208
  User, 44
CONFIG.SYS File, 187
Configuration Management
  Utility, 281
Congestion Control, 317
Connectivity, 45, 46
Connectors, 107
Consistent State, 148, 149
Contention, *6*, 10, 76, 137ff.
  Protocol, 69
Control
  Field, 315
  Sequence, 233
Controller *see* Disk Drive In-
  terface
Copper Data Distribution In-
  terface (CDDI), 58, 66, 313,
  379
Copyright Laws, 162
Corporate License, 165
CRC *see* Cyclic Redundancy
  Check
Critical Path, 155, 156, 179
CS Computing *see* Client/
  Server Computing
CSMA/CA *see* Carrier Sense
  with Multiple Access and
  Collision Avoidance
CSMA/CD *see* Carrier Sense
  with Multiple Access and
  Collision Detection
Cutover, 192
Cyclic Redundancy Check
  (CRC), 75, 351

Data
  Access Security, 205
  Archiving, 255
  Backup, 254ff.
  Communications Net-
    work, 12
  Compression, 383
  Encryption Standard
    (DES), 209
  Field, 315
  Gathering, 281, 282

Data (*continued*)
  Interchange, 255
  Link Layer, 36, 38, 40,
    314, 337ff., 351
  Link Protocol, 73ff., 314,
    337, 339, 350
  Recovery, 255
  Switch, 9, 229, 230
Database
  Management System
    (DBMS), *17*, 147ff.
  Management System, Re-
    covery, 264, 265
  Server, 93, 94
DBMS *see* Database Manage-
  ment System
DCE *see* Distributed Comput-
  ing Environment
DDI *see* Distributed Data In-
  terface
Deadlock, 138
Deadly Embrace *see* Deadlock
Decryption, 209
Dedicated
  Connection, 356, 357
  Line, 358
  Server, 375
Delineation of Data, 73
DES *see* Data Encryption
  Standard
Desktop Computer, 6
Diagnostic Tools, 270, 271
Digital Private Branch Ex-
  change (DPBX or Digital
  PBX), 181
Directory Rights, 214ff.
Disaster Plan, 271, 272
Disk
  Caching, 97
  Drive, 95ff.
  Drive Interface, 96, 97
  Editor, 265
  Operating System
    (DOS), 375
  Seek Enhancement, 125
  Server, 92, 93
  Swapping, 99
  Utility, 265
Diskless Workstation, 14,
  103, 377, 378
Distributed
  Computing Environment
    (DCE), 374
  Data Interface (DDI), 181,
    379
  Queue Dual Bus (DQDB),
    380
  Routing, 319
Distribution List, 152
Document
  Coauthoring Software, 157
  Management Software,
    157, 158

Documentation, 179, 180,
  286, 292
DOS *see* Disk Operating Sys-
  tem
Downloaded, 44
Downsizing, 15, 158
DPBX *see* Digital Private
  Branch Exchange
DQDB *see* Distributed Queue
  Dual Bus
Duplexed Servers, 127
Dynamic
  Data, 256
  Files, 259
Dynamic Routing *see* Adap-
  tive Routing

E-Mail *see* Electronic Mail
EBCDIC *see* Extended Binary
  Coded Decimal Interchange
  Code
Effective Rights, 210
Electronic
  Calendaring, 18, 154, 155
  Conferencing, 18, 154,
    155
  Data Exchange, 14
  Mail (E-Mail), *18*, 152ff.,
    370
  Meeting System (EMS),
    18
EMS *see* Electronic Meeting
  System
Encryption, *5*, 209
End to End Routing, *310*
ENDCAP Program, 210, 211
Enveloping, 37, 314
Environment Variables, 187
Error, 271
  Control, 75
  Detection, 29
Ethernet, 20, 58, 63, 69, 74ff.
Exclusive Open Mode, 137,
  138
Expansion, 292, 293
Expert System, 386
Explicit Rights, 213, 214
Extended Binary Coded Dec-
  imal Interchange Code
  (EBCDIC), 29

Facsimile Machine (Fax Ma-
  chine), 9, 10, 105, 385
Failure Rates, 261
Fake Logon, 206
Fault Tolerance, 125ff.
Fax Machine *see* Facsimile
  Machine
FAX Server, 385
FDDI *see* Fiber Distributed
  Data Interface

Fiber Distributed Data Inter-
  face (FDDI), 20, 66, 313,
  379, 380
Fiber Optic Cable, 21, 29, 45,
  46, 58, 59, 64, 66, 67, 181,
  327, 337
File
  Compatibility, 295
  Rights, 214
  Server, 93, 131, 237
  Services, 91, 92
  Transfer Utility, 360
Filter, 297, 298
First In, First Out, 237
Flag Field, 314
Floppy Diskette Drives, 100,
  101
Flow Control, 38
Forms, Printing, 245
Frame Check Sequence, 315
Frequency-Division Multi-
  plexing, 61
Full-duplex Mode, 38
Functional Testing, 191

Gateway, 340, 356
Global Naming, 378
Grace Logon, 207
Grandfather-Father-Son Gen-
  erations, 259
Graphical User Interface
  (GUI), 8
Group Decision-Support
  Software, 158
Groups, 203
Groupware, 15, 18, 19, 151ff.
GUI *see* Graphical User Inter-
  face

Half-Duplex Mode, 38
Hard Disk Drives, 101
Hardware
  Configuration, 136
  Interface, 232
Header, 351
Hierarchical Network, 311ff.
High Speed Buff.er, 230, 231
High-Priority Queue, 237
High-Speed Local Area Net-
  work (HSLAN), 378ff.
Hop, *310*
Host
  Computer, 29, 356ff., 378
  Processor, 368
HSLAN *see* High-Speed Lo-
  cal Area Network

I/O Optimization, 125
I/O *see* Input/Output
IBM-3270 Emulation, 359
ID *see* User Identifier
Identification, 202

IEEE
  802.3 Standard, 63, 69, 74, 75, 82, 83, 178, 179, 342
  802.4 Standard, 63, 69
  802.5 Standard, 63, 67, 69
  802.6 Standard, 380
  see also Institute of Electrical and Electronics Engineers
Immediate Costs, 41ff.
Information Gathering, 279ff.
Informational Frame, 315
Infrared Light, 21, 29, 59
Inherited Rights, 210ff.
  Mask, 210ff.
Input/Output (I/O), 117, 231
Installation, Upgrade, 293
Institute of Electrical and Electronic Engineers (IEEE), 63
Integrated Network Management System, 299
Integrated Services Digital Network (ISDN), 59, 60, 182, 378
Interconnected (Plex) Network, 313
International Standards Organization (ISO), 32
Internetwork Processor, 350
Interoperability, 132
Interrupt, 122
Interrupt Request (IRQ), 184
IRQ see Interrupt Request
ISDN see Integrated Services Digital Network
ISO see International Standards Organization

Job Control, 237

Key Disk, 163
Known Good Components, 284

LAN
  Adapters, 41, 104, 184
  Administrator, 194, 195
  Environment, 42
  Manager, Microsoft, 125
  Media, 58, 59
  Operating System, 189, 190
  Segmentation, 383
  Server, IBM, 125, 130, 131
  Server Software, 189
  Topology, 58, 64, 67, 73
Latency, 96
Learning Bridge, 345
License Agreement, 161ff.
Link, 310

LLC see Logical Link Control
Lock, Record, 138
Logical Unit (LU), 322, 323, 325
Logical Link Control, 76
Logical Security, 5
Logon Restrictions, 207ff.
Logon Script see Batch File
Low-Level Recovery, 270
Low-Priority Queue, 237
LU see Logical Unit
LU 6.2, 323, 325, 359

MAC Protocol see Media Access Control Protocol
Magnetic Tape Drives, 101, 102
Mail
  Administrator, 152
  Agents, 153
  Interface, 154
Mailbox, 152
Major Fault Recovery, 264, 265
MAN see Metropolitan Area Network
Manageability, 48
Management Information Base (MIB), 299
Manufacturing Automation Protocol (MAP), 63
MAP see Manufacturing Automation Protocol
MAU see Multistation Access Unit
Maximum Rights Mask, 211
Media, 327
Media Access Control Protocol (MAC Protocol), 22, 38, 58, 67, 69, 73, 76, 77, 337, 343
Memory, 97ff., 184, 185
Message, 27
  Exchange, 373
  Routing, 317
  Sequence Number, 36
Metropolitan Area Network (MAN), 379, 380
MIB see Management Information Base
Microwave Transmission, 59, 376
Microwave, 59
Middleware, 374
Minor Fault Recovery, 264
Mirrored Disks, 126, 385, 386
Modem
  Pooling, 384, 385
  Server, 105
  Sharing, 358
Monitor, 296

MSAU see Multistation Access Unit
Multimedia, 381ff.
Multiplexer, 357
Multistation Access Unit (MAU or MSAU), 67
Multithreading, 119, 121
Mutation Engine, Virus, 222

NetWare, Novell, 124, 129, 209ff., 214, 215, 239, 245, 265
NetwareLite, Novel, 375, 376
Network
  Analyzer, 288
  Layer, 36, 38, 316, 317, 338ff., 349, 350
  Loadable Module (NLM), 245
  Management System (NMS), 288, 295ff.
  of Computers, 31
  Routing Table, 317
  Server, 6, 10
NLM see Network-Loadable Module
NMS see Network Management System
Node, 20, 31, 32, 356, 357, 360, 370
Nondedicated Server, 375
Novel Operating System, 129
Nr see Number Received
Ns see Number Sent
Number Sent (Ns), 315, 316
Number Received (Nr), 315, 316

Object Request Broker (ORB), 374
Octet, 75, 76
Off-Site Storage, 256, 258, 272
On-Line Transaction Processing, 148
Open Mode, File, 137
Open systems Interconnection Reference Model (OSI), 32, 34, 36, 38, 40, 64, 335ff.
Operating System (OS), 4, 117, 119, 122ff.
  Interface, 234
Operator Errors, 280
Optical Disk Drives, 101
ORB see Object Request Broker
OS see Operating System
OSI Reference Model see Open Systems Interconnection Reference Model
Overlay Module, 44
Ownership, 328

Packet
   Distribution Network
     (PDN), *310, 311, 325, 326*
   Routing, 339
   Switching, *310*
Parallel Interface, 232
Parity Data, 126
Passive Hub, 71
Password, 202, 205ff.
Path, *310*
Payment Schedule, 176
PC *see* Personal Computer
PDN *see* Packet Distribution
   Network
PDN *see* Public Data Net-
   work
Peer-to-Peer
   LAN, 375, 376
   Network, *129*
Penalty Clause, 177
Performance Testing, 191
Personal Productivity Soft-
   ware, 16
Personal Computer (PC), 4, 6
PERT *see* Program Evaluation
   and Review Technique
Physical
   Layer, 36, 40, 64, 336, 338
   Link, 350
   Security, 5, 205
   Unit (PU), *322*
Platform, 41
Plex Network *see* Intercon-
   nected Network
Pocket LAN Adapter, 284, 386
Polymorphic Virus, 222
Portability, 13, 373
Presentation
   Layer, 34, 36, 37
   Services, *17*
Preventive Maintenance, 177
Primary Business Software,
   158
Print Queue Operator, *242*
PRINTDEF, 245
Printer, 45, 104, 105
   Adapters, 248
   Driver, *105*, 231, 233
   Environment, 230, 231
   Interface, 232, 233
   Server, 230, 242ff.
Priority System, 237
Private Data, 190
Privileges *see* Access Control
   Rights
Proactive Network Manage-
   ment, 286, 287
Problem
   Diagnosis and Analysis,
     281ff.
   Reporting and Tracking
     System, 286

Productive Processors, 257
Program Evaluation and Re-
   view Technique (PERT),
   155, 179, 182
Progress Payments, 176
Protected
   Open Mode, 137, 138
   Read-Only Mode, 138
Protection Clause, 177
Protocol, 327
   Analyzer, 285
PSERVER, 245, 248
PU *see* Physical Unit
Public Data Network (PDN)
   see Packet Switching Net-
   work
Public Data, 190
Purchase Contract, 174

Queue
   Manager, 243
   Printer, 243ff.
   User, 243

RAID *see* Redundant Arrays
   of Independent Disks,
Reactive Network Manage-
   ment, 278, 279
Read-After-Write, 126
Receiver, 28
Recovery, 268ff.
   Facilities, Database, 151
Recurring Costs, 41, 43
Redirector, *119*, 234
Redundant Arrays of Inde-
   pendent Disks (RAID), 126
Remote
   Access Servers, 385
   Access Software, 385
   Control Software, 282ff.
   Logon Utility, 360, 361
   Procedure Call, 373
Repeater, 336, 342, 343
Report Generator, 298
Requester/Server Protocol *see*
   Client/Server Protocol
Restorative Maintenance, 177
Restricted Number of Users
   License, 165
Retention Policy, 259
Rightsizing *see* Downsizing
Ring Topology, 64, 66, 69
Router, *338*, 349, 350, 356,
   360
Routing, 222
   Table, 319, 345ff.
RPRINTER, 245

SAX/IPX *see* Sequenced
   Packet Exchange/Inter-
   network Exchange

SCSI *see* Small Computer
   System Interface
SDLC *see* Synchronous
   Data Link Control
Security, *5*, 19, 48, 140,
   203ff., 238, 243, 284, 341
Seek Time, 96
Sender, *28*
Sequenced Packet Ex-
   change/Internetwork Ex-
   change (SAX/IPX), 338,
   340, 349
Serial Interface, 232
Server, 14, 20, 41, 184,
   186, 187, 356, 370,
   372ff., 383ff.
   Class, 368
   Compatibility, 99
   Expansion, 99
   License, 165
   Platforms, 91
   Software, 123, 124
   Speed, 99
Session, 310, 323, 359
   Layer, 34, 36ff.
SFT *see* System Fault Toler-
   ance, Novell
Shared
   Open Mode, 137
   Read-Only Mode, 137
   Update Mode, 137
Shielded Twisted-Pair Wires,
   59, 67
Signature, Virus, 222
Simple Network Manage-
   ment Protocol (SNMP),
   299, 302
Simplex Transmission, 38
Simulation Model, 290ff.
Single User
   Multiple Workstation Li-
     cense, 164, 165
   Single Workstation Li-
     cense, 164
Site
   License, 165
   Planning, 180, 181, 293
Small Computer System In-
   terface (SCSI), 232
SMI *see* Structure of Manage-
   ment Information
SNA *see* Systems Network
   Architecture
Sneakernet, 9
SNMP *see* Simple Network
   Management Protocol
Software Standards, 158ff.
Spooler, 10, 12, 45, 230ff., 245
   Interface, 238
   Print, 132, 133
SQL *see* Structured Query
   Language

SQL Server, 93, 94, 96
StarLAN, 69, 71, 73
Startup File, Novel, 187, 188
Static
 Data, 255, 256, 259
 Routing, 319
Store-and-Forward, *310*
StreetTalk, Banyan, 131, 378
Structure of Management Information (SMI), 299
Structured Query Language (SQL), *93*, 370, 373
Sufficiently Comprehensive, *257, 258*
Supervisory Frame, 315
Switched Line Connection, 358
Synchronous Data Link Control (SDLC), 314ff.
System
 Fault Tolerance (SFT), Novell, 129
 Network Architecture (SNA), 322, 359
 Programming, 203
 Tuning, 287ff.

TCP *see* Transaction Control Process
TCP/IP *see* Transmission Control Protocol/Internet Protocol
Terminal,
 Emulation, 356, 357
 Network, 29
 Server, 105
Terminate-and-Stay-Resident (TSR), 239
Terminator, 69
Testing, Upgrade, 293, 294
Timely, *257, 261*
Timeout Value,
Timeout Interval, 234, 235

Token-Passing, 66ff., 73, 78, 79, 317
 Bus, 80, 84
 Ring, 63, 66, 67, 75, 79, 81, 85, 379
Topology, 327
Training, 192ff.
 Upgrade, 294
Transaction, 148ff.
 Control Process (TCP), 368
 Processing, 148
 Rollback, 150
Transceiver, 106
Transfer Time, 96
Transmission Speed, 328
Transmission Control Protocol/Internet Protocol (TCP/IP), 349ff., 360
Transparency, *76*, 193, 374
Transparent Use, 19
Transport Services Access Point (TSAP), 38
Transport Layer, 36, 38, 350
Trustee Rights, 210ff.
TSAP *see* Transport Services Access Point
TSR *see* Terminate-and-Stay-Resident
Twisted Pair Wire, 21, 45, 46, 58, 59, 62, 64, 67, 313, 327, 337, 386

Uninterruptable Power Supply (UPS), 105, 386
Unnumbered Frame, 315
Unshielded Twisted-Pair Wires, 45, 59, 67, 181, 379
Upgrades, 293ff.
UPS *see* Uninterruptable Power Supply
User, 202, 203, 210ff., 283, 36
 Profile, 6
 Transition, 295

Value-Added Network (VAN), 210, 325
VAN *see* Value-Added Network
Vendor, 47, 175ff., 321
Vines, Banyan, 125, 131
Virtual
 Memory, 99
 Reality, 19
Virus, 218ff.
 Detection, 14, 219ff.

WAN *see* Wide Area Network
Weighted Routing, 319, 320
"What-If" Analysis, *17*
Wide Area Network (WAN), 18, 20, 21, 22, 31, 32, 47
Wireless LANs, 21, 58, 327, 337, 376, 377
Work-Flow Automation Software, 155ff.
Workgroup Productivity Software *see* Groupware
Workload Generator, 290, 292
Workstation, 6, 43, 102, 103, 118, 119, 184ff., 283ff., 368, 370
 Software Interface, 123
 System Software, 123

X
 .25 Network, 310, 325
 .400 Standard, 36, 154
 .500 378
Xerox Network System (XNS), 340
XNS *see* Xerox Network System